Reinterpreting the Legacy of WILLIAM JAMES

Edited by Margaret E. Donnelly

AMERICAN PSYCHOLOGICAL ASSOCIATION
Washington, DC

Published by the
American Psychological Association
750 First Street, NE
Washington, DC 20002

Copies may be ordered from
APA Order Department
P.O. Box 2710
Hyattsville, MD 20784

This book was typeset in Goudy by Harper Graphics, Hollywood, MD

Printer: Braun-Brumfield, Inc., Ann Arbor, MI
Cover designer: Janice Wheeler
Technical editor and production coordinator: Deborah Segal

Cover design is adapted with permission from Michelle Bakay's illustration, "William James."

Harvard University Press has granted permission to use extended quotations from their edition of *The Principles of Psychology* (1981).

Library of Congress Cataloging-in-Publication Data

Reinterpreting the legacy of William James / edited by Margaret E. Donnelly.
    p. cm.
  Includes bibliographical references and index.
  ISBN 1-55798-180-9
  1. James, William, 1842–1910. 2. Psychology and philosophy.
 I. Donnelly, Margaret E.
 BF109.J28R445 1992
 150'.92—dc20
                                           92-32729
                                               CIP

Printed in the United States of America
First Edition

CONTENTS

CONTRIBUTORS

Helmut E. Adler, Department of Psychology, Yeshiva University

Anne Anastasi, Department of Psychology, Fordham University

James R. Averill, Department of Psychology, University of Massachusetts, Amherst

James R. Bailey, Department of Psychology, Washington University

Donald A. Crosby, Department of Philosophy, Colorado State University

E. Virginia Demos, Harvard Graduate School of Education

Florence L. Denmark, Department of Psychology, Pace University

Donald A. Dewsbury, Department of Psychology, University of Florida

Margaret E. Donnelly, Department of Psychology, Pace University

Raymond D. Fowler, American Psychological Association, Washington, DC

Amedeo Giorgi, Department of Psychology, University of Quebec, Montreal

George S. Howard, Department of Psychology, University of Notre Dame

Cheri L. King, Department of Psychology, Colorado State University

D. Brett King, Department of Psychology, University of Colorado

Gerald E. Myers, Department of Philosophy, Graduate School and University Center of the City University of New York

Daniel N. Robinson, Department of Psychology, Georgetown University

Joseph F. Rychlak, Department of Psychology, Loyola University of Chicago

Gertrude R. Schmeidler, Department of Psychology, City College of the City University of New York

Jonathan Schull, Department of Psychology, Haverford College

Charlene Haddock Seigfried, Department of Philosophy, Purdue University

M. Brewster Smith, Department of Psychology, University of California, Santa Cruz

Michael J. Strube, Department of Psychology, Washington University

Eugene Taylor, Harvard Medical School
Damian S. Vallelonga, Hutchings Psychiatric Center, Syracuse, NY
Wayne Viney, Department of Psychology, Colorado State University
William R. Woodward, Department of Psychology, University of New Hampshire
John H. Yost, Department of Psychology, Washington University

FOREWORD

During the year 1990, I had the good fortune to be president of the Division of General Psychology (Division 1) of the American Psychological Association (APA). I invited Margaret E. Donnelly to organize our convention program, and because 1990 was the centenary year of the publication of William James's book, *The Principles of Psychology*, she decided that the major theme of the program would be James's influence on contemporary American psychology. This was very well received, and the chapters in this volume are a selected group of the total presentations on this topic. It is with great pleasure that I agreed to write the foreword for this book, which we have titled *Reinterpreting the Legacy of William James*.

William James has had a tremendous impact on psychology—in his day as well as in the present. His interests were broad and diverse. He was a radical empiricist and a pragmatist. He stressed the application of psychology to everyday problems, opposing the narrow and exclusive perspective of the laboratory approach alone. Although James shared an interest in the study of sensation and perception with Gustav Fechner, his investigation followed a more philosophical stance, in opposition to Fechner's argument that sensations can be analyzed into individual quantifiable elements. At the same time, James praised Fechner for his originality of thought and scientific approach to psychology. Views held today by many psychologists that propose a unification of the discipline were also suggested by James, who advocated an understanding of the diversity as well as of the convergence of widely different points of view. As such, James's approach to psychology was inclusive of a wealth of human experience.

James was a proponent of free will, believing that one's first act of free will is to believe in it. As a young man, he suffered an episode of severe depression and, at different periods of his life, was plagued by recurrences from which he sought relief through sheer belief in the curative influence of the human will. James held a liberal attitude toward parapsychology, maintaining an open mind on psychic phenomena such as clairvoyance and mediumship.

His enthusiasm extended to the classroom, and his *Psychology: Briefer Course*[1] (or "Jimmy," as it is popularly known), which is an abbreviated version of his 1890 *Principles*, appeared as a textbook in 1892. His *Talks to Teachers*[2] (1899) stressed the application of psychology to daily living with particular reference to education.

Although the number of James's doctoral students was small, many went on to achieve prominence in their own right. Among these were James R. Angell, Mary W. Calkins, William Healy, Edward L. Thorndike, and Robert S. Woodworth. He was an early champion of women's rights as an ardent advocate of education for women. For example, he put his conviction into action when he made it possible for Mary Calkins to receive her graduate instruction at Harvard at a time when that university was opposed to admitting women to doctoral degree programs. Under the initial tutelage and continued support of William James, however, Calkins received what amounted to her PhD from Harvard, although the actual degree was never awarded. Calkins later became the first female president of the American Psychological Association.

Following the publication of *The Principles* in 1890, James devoted himself more to philosophy and was granted an honorary doctorate in philosophy in 1903. As a philosopher–psychologist, he often intermingled the two disciplines in his study of the self, perception, association, thought, and experience. He was inspired by many sources, assimilating and combining knowledge from various movements, philosophers, and leaders in research so as to formulate his own unique ideology. He was an independent thinker who demonstrated little hesitation in criticizing and praising the work of others. Among those with whom he disagreed was Wilhelm Wundt, on whose work he commented, "The finished example of how much *mere* education can do for a man."[3] He was free in his assessment of those whom he admired and considered Hermann Ebbinghaus "one of the best men."[4] He spoke highly also of Mary Calkins: "It (Calkins's examination) was much

[1]James, W. (1892). *Psychology: Briefer course.* New York: Holt.

[2]James, W. (1899). *Talks to teachers on psychology: And to students on some of life's ideals.* New York: Holt.

[3]Perry, R. B. (1935). *The thought and character of William James: As revealed in unpublished correspondence and notes, together with his published writings. Vol. 2: Philosophy and psychology.* Boston: Little, Brown, p. 69.

[4]Perry, R. B. (1935). *The thought and character of William James: As revealed in unpublished correspondence and notes, together with his published writings. Vol. 1: Inheritance and vocation.* Boston: Little, Brown, p. 403.

the most brilliant examination for the PhD that we have had at Harvard. It is a pity, in spite of this that she still lacks the degree."[5]

I am grateful to the editor, Margaret E. Donnelly, who made the Division 1 William James centenary program the success it was, and without whose efforts this fine collection of chapters would not have been possible. I am grateful, as well, to the prominent contributors of this book who have provided readers with greater insight and understanding into the character and accomplishments of William James. It is my hope that this will lend itself to an increased and renewed interest in the contribution of a major founder of American psychology.

FLORENCE L. DENMARK

---

[5]Scarborough, E., & Furumoto, L. (1987). *Untold lives: The first generation of American women psychologists.* New York: Columbia University Press, p. 46.

PREFACE

When in 1989, Florence Denmark, president-elect of Division 1 of the American Psychological Association (APA), asked me to organize the 1990 convention division program, my concern was, "What will our theme be?" Then, one night, while ruminating on this matter, it suddenly occurred to me, "Why, in 1990, we shall be celebrating the centenary of the publication of William James's text, *The Principles of Psychology*. That will be our theme!" And so it was

> William James—Relevant Today. 1990: Celebrating the Centenary of William James's *Principles of Psychology*—Its Influence on the Direction and Development of American Psychology.

Division 1 policy in 1990 was that participants be invited to present convention papers. My task, thereby, was simplified, and I approached some outstanding American psychologists to address this theme. Free to choose any topic from James's extensive corpus, the majority of the contributors enthusiastically responded by preparing talks on many different aspects of his work. No structured uniform format was required; consequently, there is a broad range of topics and of writing styles.

Of the 23 selected articles presented in this volume, most are by psychologists, but we had the good fortune to engage the interest of several philosophers as well, and their contributions acknowledge James's later preferred professional identification. The topics are gathered into six sections and an epilogue, and a glance at the table of contents shows how wide-ranging they are. With the exceptions of the first four chapters in Part II and all of the chapters in Part V, which constitute two symposia, the remaining chapters are single presentations.

In 1989, while I was beginning to prepare the 1990 convention program, it came to my attention that, in 1967, for the celebration of the 75th anniversary of the founding of the APA, the program committee put together a lecture–discussion series featuring Donald Krech, Rollo May, Harry Harlow, and Ernest R. Hilgard, entitled "The Unfinished Business of William James." Just as in 1967 those psychologists celebrating the 75th anniversary (1965) of the *Principles* wondered, "How many of the questions posed so provocatively by William James have been answered?" (APA *Convention Program*, 1967, p. 128), so we, in 1992, celebrating the centenary of its publication (1990), find ourselves still mining the rich mother lode of Jamesian psychology and philosophy in *Reinterpreting the Legacy of William James*.

I should like to thank our contributors for their scholarship, patience, and cooperation that have brought this volume into being. I thank, also, William R. Woodward, the 1989 Division 1 convention program chair, whose many helpful suggestions facilitated my preparation of the 1990 program. To the book-program staff of APA, I offer my deep appreciation for their unfailing resourcefulness and cheerful assistance in this book's preparation. And finally, a special note of acknowledgment to Florence L. Denmark, with whom all this began.

MARGARET E. DONNELLY

INTRODUCTION

Wilhelm Wundt remarked that we all are the intellectual heirs of our predecessors: "Wir Sind Alle Epigonen."[1] And was it not Newton, reflecting on his indebtedness to his scientific forebears, who adapted the twelfth-century aphorism and wrote in a letter (5 February 1675/1676) to Robert Hooke, "If I have seen further, it is by standing on ye sholders of Giants."[2] For American psychologists, William James is the giant on whose shoulders we stand.

Reinterpreting the Legacy of William James exemplifies the ideational generativity of this nineteenth-century psychologist–philosopher who, down the years, has challenged, inspired, and delighted his intellectual heirs. The breadth of James's vision encompassed all areas of human functioning: cognition, affect, and volition; and he wrote comprehensively on topics of fundamental human concern: religion, philosophy, psychology, and education. The 23 chapters in this volume reflect the diversity of James's interests and that of the authors celebrating the publication centenary of *The Principles of Psychology*.

All of the chapters are not necessarily in formal essay style because they were talks presented at the 1990 American Psychological Association (APA) convention and editing was minimal so that this flavor would not be lost. The volume's six sections, in some instances, represent an arbitrary allocation of topics, and in others, a natural affinity. A brief review of these chapters reveals a rich variety of subjects and the challenging viewpoints

---

[1]Merz, J. T. (1965). *A history of European thought in the nineteenth century* (Vol. 3), p. 95. (Original work published 1912)

[2]Merton, R. K. (1985). *On the shoulders of giants: A Shandean postscript*, San Diego, CA: Harcourt, Brace, p. 9. (Original work published 1965)

of authors addressing the relevance of William James for modern American psychology.

Part I, "Present Relevance of James's Legacy," consists of three chapters. In the first, "The Case of a Uniquely American Jamesian Tradition in Psychology," Eugene Taylor presents James in the broad context of his status, both positive and negative, among his contemporaries and with succeeding generations of psychologists, philosophers, and scholars in other disciplines. James's influence is pervasive in modern psychology, and "it cuts across all subdisciplinary boundaries" (Taylor, p. 27).

In the second chapter, Anne Anastasi, recalling James's opinion on the benefits of developing broad general theories in psychology, queries "Are There Unifying Trends in the Psychologies of the 1990s?" She responds positively by presenting, as examples, research evidence supporting theory convergence in psychometrics, in the experimental psychology of learning with educational psychology, and among the manifold theories and practices of psychotherapy.

How germane to the schema of cognitive science are some of William James's core concepts? What could be integrated, what excluded, and what altered to conform to current thinking in this research field? Gerald E. Myers explores these questions in the third chapter, "William James and Contemporary Psychology." He opines that James probably would have rejected such positions as the cognitive psychologists' inferred intermediate mental processes (their "third term"), their stance on consciousness, the mind as computer, and the total exclusion of philosophy in the interpretation of human thought and behavior. Myers concludes that James's psychology has greater affinity with phenomenology and with areas of clinical psychology than with the behavioral and cognitive sciences.

Of the five chapters in Part II, "Celebrating *The Principles of Psychology*," the first four constituted the symposium, "How Would James Have Revised the Principles?" organized by Wayne Viney. D. Brett King's introduction, chapter 4, traces the evolution of the *Principles* from Henry Holt's 1878 request for the text, through the vicissitudes of James's struggle to write it, and finally, to its publication in 1890. With the completion of *Psychology, Briefer Course* ("Jimmy"), published in 1892, James vowed never again to write a textbook.

In "The World We Practically Live In" (chapter 5), Charlene Haddock Seigfried first examines the philosophical basis of James's presentation of psychology as a natural science in the *Principles*, where he uses the natural-history method of pure seeing and neutral description to establish his position. Seigfried then traces James's dissatisfaction with this approach to explain the meaning of reality and discusses his reasons for espousing the methodology of radical empiricism.

Wayne Viney, Cheri King, and D. Brett King, in "William James on the Advantages of a Pluralistic Psychology" (chapter 6), focus on three aspects of James's thought: his arguments against monism, his justification of his pluralist position, and his open-mindedness to incorporate other content areas of psychology into the general corpus of psychological knowledge. If James were to revise his *Principles* today, they argue that he would give more attention to applied psychology and to unconscious processes; and he would address a wider range of topics of current psychological interest.

Philosopher Donald Crosby and psychologist Wayne Viney presented the final paper in this symposium: "Toward a Psychology That is Radically Empirical: Recapturing the Vision of William James" (chapter 7). Their thesis is that the radical empiricism of James's later philosophical period is evidenced embryonically throughout the *Principles*. They note first how James's radical empiricism differs from that of the British empiricists. Second, they indicate where they found evidence of his interpretation throughout the *Principles*. Finally, they discuss how James's matured philosophical position might have influenced his revision of this psychological landmark.

Amedeo Giorgi's autonomous contribution, "A Phenomenological Reinterpretation of the Jamesian Schema for Psychology" (chapter 8), concludes the second section of this volume. Giorgi contends that James's presentation of psychology as a natural science and the assumption that its data can be organized into a four-part schema (the psychologist, the thought studied, the thought's object, and the psychologist's reality) is not psychologically defensible. He juxtaposes his phenomenological development with these Jamesian positions and asserts "that all genuine psychological problems could be approached in terms of it." (Giorgi, p. 24).

The enduring question of interest, Darwin's influence on the development of James's thought, is addressed in the two chapters that constitute Part III, "James's Debt to Darwin."

Jonathan Schull states in chapter 9 that James accepted selection in the Darwinian sense of the term as the essential program in mental processes, but he modified and interpreted it to suit his own purposes, holding, for example, the following: rather than being random, variation might simply be unexplained; mind and society both are subject to the process of natural selection; the influence of environment and variants are interactive; and selection is hierarchical throughout all forms of life. Consciousness is the essential factor in selection. Schull notes also that James's introduction of natural selection into psychology has stimulated the application of these concepts to other disciplines.

William R. Woodward's chapter, "James's Evolutionary Epistemology: 'Necessary Truths and the Effects of Experience' " (chapter 10), has its source in the final chapter of the *Principles*. Woodward's goal is to follow and elucidate the evolution of James's theory of knowledge (i.e., the various kinds of knowledge and how they are acquired). He weighs the influence of the philosophers Chauncey Wright, Charles S. Peirce, and Hermann Lotze on James's maturing theory, and he points out the similar interests of philosophers and psychologists in cognitive development in theories of truth, belief, and meaning. The impact of Darwin on the intellectual community at Harvard and the claim that his theory of evolution was central to James's work are evaluated. The conclusion reached is that James found the answer for a comprehensive theory of knowing in his adaptation of the Darwinian theory of natural selection.

Part IV, "Further Thoughts on the Self," consists of two chapters: "William James and the Psychology of Self" by M. Brewster Smith and "William James and Contemporary Research on the Self: The Influence of Pragmatism, Reality, and Truth" by Michael J. Strube, John H. Yost, and James R. Bailey.

M. Brewster Smith (chapter 11) addresses a core concept in James's psychology—the idea of selfhood. His discussion aims to state James's position, note some of the problems that this view presents for later psychologists, and (drawing on the research of more recent sociologists and psychologists as well as his own proposals) offer suggestions for the clarification of these issues.

How James's philosophical understanding of truth, reality, and the principles of pragmatism influenced his psychological interpretation of the self is the subject of Strube, Yost, and Bailey's chapter 12. They analyze *self-seeking*, which, according to James, is inherent in all three levels of the empirical self; address current debate on this topic; and reflect upon how seeming disagreements might be reevaluated.

Part V, Emotion—"Here's What's Happened to Emotion, Mr. James," was a symposium, organized and introduced by Eileen A. Gavin, who also created its intriguing title.

E. Virginia Demos discusses the application of Silvan Tomkins's post-Jamesian theory of emotion to our understanding of infant affect (chapter 13). Rejecting the current research emphasis on emotion as a function of cognition, she supports Tomkins's stance that emotion is independent of cognition, is part of the infant's biological endowment, and is clearly revealed in the study of the infant's facial expression and autonomic responses.

James R. Averill's purpose (chapter 14) is to bury James's theory of emotion explicated in the *Principles* and to offer as a viable replacement James's "second theory" of emotion that he finds in *The Varieties of Religious Experience* (1902). Taking the thread of creativity analyzed by James on the emotional level, Averill points out how James's explanatory vocabulary seems to have anticipated the Wallas (1926)[3] analysis of creativity on the

---

[3]Wallas, G. (1926). *The act of thought*. New York: Harcourt, Brace & World.

intellectual level. Averill notes how emotions and the self are involved and welcomes the current interest in the cross-cultural study of the emotions.

In "A Phenomenological Response to James's View of Emotion" (chapter 15), Damian S. Vallelonga distinguishes the meaning of *affect*, *feeling*, and *emotion*, and he designates the multidimensional term, *affective situation*, as his choice for encompassing all three concepts. He posits and explains five dimensions he attributes to this state, reporting the position of James and others on the first four: appetitive, cognitive, feeling or corporeally based, and the inchoate conative. The fifth, "dialectical dimension," is Vallelonga's unique contribution to the understanding of affective situation. He concludes by stating that only in exploring the interrelations among these five dimensions can the meaning of the state, affective situation, be understood.

To describe and understand the nature of emotion was an ongoing challenge to James. From his earliest publication (1884) to his last (1911), the influence of his philosophical development is reflected in the evolution of his position on this issue. Wayne Viney, discussant of this symposium, traces this progress and observes its effect on the direction of current research, as he comments in his chapter, (chapter 16) "A Study of Emotion in the Context of Radical Empiricism" on the papers given here.

Part VI, "Selected Topics: Mining the Jamesian Lode," is an aggregate of six chapters on diverse Jamesian subjects.

Helmut E. Adler's, "William James and Gustav Fechner: From Rejection to Elective Affinity" (chapter 17), recounts how James's early highly negative criticism of Fechner's psychophysics contrasts with his appreciation for the philosophical work. Adler reports that, as James later in his career again became more the philosopher, his enthusiasm grew to acceptance and support for Fechner's panpsychism and interest in psychic phenomena.

Instincts were a much discussed and controversial topic among James's contemporaries. Donald A. Dewsbury, in "William James and Instinct Theory Revisited" (chapter 18), argues that, for James, his conception of instincts although "not at the center of his vision . . . did form the core of his psychology" (Dewsbury, p. 265). Any analysis of the concept involves the problems of definition and evolution, and Dewsbury presents a brief enlightening account of extant opinions during the latter part of the nineteenth century, pointing out, particularly, James's debt to D. A. Spalding. The remaining section of this chapter recounts James's position on instincts, how this is integrated into his psychological thought, and, finally, the influence of his instinct theory on the development of American psychology.

Who considers William James a clinician? George S. Howard does. And in his imaginative and amusing "dialogue" with James, he justifies his arresting title: "William James: Closet Clinician" (chapter 19). The designation, "founder of American scientific psychology," is often attributed to the author of the *Principles*. Yet, a study of his later philosophical works, such as *The Varieties of Religious Experience* (1902), *The Will to Believe* (1897), and *Pragmatism* (1907), reveals a profound understanding of the human condition—of "life in the world," and Howard sees these later publications as instructive source books for psychologists in applied fields.

One of the "productive paradoxes" of William James (Allport, 1943)[4] is that of the mind–body relationship. This psychophysical problem seems to have had its roots in the philosophy of the early Pythagoreans, who were the first to distinguish between material and nonmaterial substances. Since then, throughout the ages, philosophers have wrestled with this puzzle, and modern neurophysiologists, as well, have sought a solution. Penfield and Roberts, for example, stated: "We have at present no basis for a scientific explanation of the brain–mind relationship."[5] In chapter 20, "William James on the Mind and the Body," Daniel Robinson recalls the attitudes toward the question in Britain and on the continent during the time that James was writing and how his opinion might have been influenced by these various viewpoints. James rejected both reductionism and transcendentalism. He wanted to develop a nonmetaphysical psychology, but the mind–body relationship is a metaphysical problem, and how James sought to resolve it is the subject of Robinson's chapter.

Theologians and philosophers have analyzed the concept of free will for years, and more recently, psychologists, also, have become interested. William James, the philosopher–psychologist, did not evade the challenge to address this idea, concluding that "the question of free will is insoluble on strictly psychological grounds" (Rychlak, p. 329). In his discussion, "William James and the Concept of Free Will" (Chapter 21), Joseph Rychlak explains that James's theory of free will is based on what he (Rychlak) calls the "second event" argument (a mediational model). He points out two major flaws in this conception and proposes his predicational model of behavior (a first event design)—an intimation of which he discerns in James's philosophical thinking as a more satisfactory interpretation of free will.

To beginning psychology students (given the current skeptical attitude toward parapsychology), it is an oxymoron to emphasize James's striving to establish psychology as a science, and at the same time, to present his enthusiastic support and advocacy of the study of paranormal phenomena. But to James, both psychology and psychical research explore mental activity, so he saw no problem in admitting the latter into his investigations. In her chapter, "William James: Pioneering Ancestor of Modern Para-

---

[4]Allport, G. (1943). The productive paradoxes of William James. *Psychological Review*, 50, 95–120.

[5]Penfield, W., & Roberts, L. (1959). *Speech and brain mechanisms*. Princeton, NJ: Princeton University Press, 10–11.

psychology" (chapter 22), Gertrude Schmeidler presents James's careful delineation of the field and his strict guidelines for methods of research. She then reports supportive current research findings in the areas of ESP (extrasensory perception) and PK (psychokinesis). Modern parapsychology also includes the investigation of such topics as survival after death, out-of-body travel, poltergeists and ghosts, and mind–body relations. But the results here are largely unsubstantiated.

With this brief survey, I invite you to enjoy this reinterpretation of the legacy of William James.

MARGARET E. DONNELLY

I

PRESENT RELEVANCE
OF JAMES'S LEGACY

1

THE CASE FOR A UNIQUELY AMERICAN JAMESIAN TRADITION IN PSYCHOLOGY

EUGENE TAYLOR

I have never been very much interested in James
—E. G. Boring to Gordon Allport[1]

William James, whether loved or reviled, looms large in the history of American psychology. He was the first to wrest control of psychology from the abstract philosophers by appropriating its content from physiology. He was the first to take up the scientific study of consciousness within the context of the new evolutionary biology. He was the first to teach the new experimental psychology in the United States in 1875; the first to open a laboratory for student instruction that same year; the first to grant a PhD in the new discipline—to G. Stanley Hall in 1878; and the first American to write a world famous textbook, his *Principles of Psychology* (1890), from the positivist viewpoint. Moreover, a list of his many beloved students reads like a *Who's Who* of the discipline. As a teacher, colleague, and friend, he

---

[1]From the personal communication of E. G. Boring to G. Allport, 1940.

3

touched the lives of James Angell, Gertrude Stein, Robert Yerkes, E. L. Thorndike, Walter Cannon, William Healey, Robert Woodworth, Boris Sidis, Louville Emerson, Mary Calkins, E. B. Holt, and more.

But James fell out with the social Darwinists when he championed the importance of the individual over the survival of the species. He scandalized philosophers and scientists with his theory that emotions do not follow cognitions, but rather *are* the complex of our immediate physiological perceptions. He offended the medical establishment with his eloquent and successful defense of the mental healers, and he appeared to abandon psychology altogether after 1890 when his experimentalist detractors said that professionally he had fled into philosophy and personally he had become lost in the occult.

The truth of the matter was, however, that, far from abandoning psychology, James was paying close attention to the latest advances in experimental psychopathology, a new field, which historians have shown developed out of psychical research and the French experimental psychology of the subconscious (Harrington, 1988). In both of these lines, James was to become a pioneer (Taylor, 1982a). Moreover, experimental evidence for the pathology of the emotions and for the reality of multiple subconscious states caused James to reevaluate the antimetaphysical position that he had taken in the *Principles*. This led him to his metaphysics of radical empiricism and to a sophisticated critique of experimentalism in scientific psychology after 1890 (Taylor, 1992a).

Psychologists first heard of radical empiricism, although at the time unnamed, when James delivered his presidential address to the American Psychological Association (APA) in 1894. In his address, James asserted that any legitimate scientific psychology must contend with the fact that no scientific system can ever be free of metaphysics (James, 1895). In James's case, this meant that laboratory investigation, based on strict materialism and positivist epistemology, could not possibly establish itself as the only legitimate way to acquire psychological knowledge by asserting that it was antimetaphysical. James's analysis showed that positivistic reductionism was, rather, grounded on a metaphysics of physicalism. James was willing to concede that, by confining attention to models of the external world, replicable effects were produced that approximated normal interactions between the organism and the environment. Such modeling, however, could not possibly apply to an understanding of the internal phenomenological life of the person, to beliefs, attitudes, values, or to the phenomena of changing states of consciousness. Experimentalism, radical materialism, or *reductionistic positivism*, as James came to call it, could never lead to an understanding of the whole personality. Instead of ignoring the individuality of the subject by focusing exclusively on normative scientific data, he believed that the core of the discipline should be a scientific study of consciousness.

This meant, among other things, that psychologists should take an in-depth look at the phenomenology of the science-making process. It also meant that if positivism was itself based on an implied metaphysics, then other philosophical systems could also plausibly govern scientific psychology. James envisioned his metaphysics of radical empiricism as serving such a function, and he used this epistemology, in turn, to justify his pioneering work in abnormal psychology, psychical research, and the psychology of religion, particularly between 1890 and 1902.

The experimentalists, however, ignored James as a psychologist after the publication of the *Principles* in 1890. They criticized him in print for his support of the mental healers; they accused him of making a full flight into theology; and they absolutely denied any philosophical bias to their own definition of science. James was eulogized in public for fathering the "new American psychology," but castigated in private by the laboratory types as irrelevant; nevertheless, when he died in 1910, it was generally recognized that a major figure had passed from the scene.

Since then, James's contributions have been considered so broad and eclectic that whatever has subsequently developed within the field of modern psychology can be found in his worldview. He left no narrow and systematic body of teachings, but rather seemed to write about everything. He produced no lineage of graduate students who thought just like he did, but reinforced original thinking that cut across disciplinary boundaries. As a result, behaviorists, phenomenologists, psychoanalysts, cognitive scientists, psychical researchers, and even humanistic psychologists have all claimed various parts of his thought.

Contrary to this prevailing opinion, I will make a different claim: First, James did, in fact, have a specific and identifiable angle on psychology. He did not stand for everything. He stood for certain ways of proceeding and was against certain others. Second, within the history of psychology from James's time to the present, there is ample evidence for a tradition, particularly in American thought and practice, that can be considered uniquely Jamesian.

THE MESSAGE FOR PSYCHOLOGY

William James's career in psychology can be divided into two somewhat arbitrary parts. Prior to 1890, he wrote as a psychologist. After 1890, he became more philosophical while speaking specifically to psychologists. It was during this second phase that James directly addressed his agenda for the discipline. In my view, this agenda bequeathed to us four major ideas that constitute the core of the Jamesian legacy.

First, James advocated a psychology of immediate experience. Psychology, for him, was the study of consciousness in all its manifestations. All thought and feeling goes on in the here and now. All memory is not a re-creation of the past, but some element of the past created anew in the present. Although the rational and empirical approach of normative science demanded a dualism between subject and object and, hence, their separation in chronological time, James maintained that consciousness and its objects do not exist without each other. The mind does not create the world of material objects, nor could objects exist without human consciousness to cognize them; rather, both must exist simultaneously in the same field. Objective perception alone, which leaves out the subjective factors, must be provisional and incomplete, and any claim to the contrary must therefore be wrong. This also meant that any scientific psychology that took James's proposition seriously would look radically different from the one existing today.

Second, James enjoined psychologists to study not only the stream of our immediate experience, but also the fall of the threshold of waking awareness and the descent of consciousness into the body. Consciousness, he maintained, was like a gigantic ocean that inundates the field of immediate awareness. Sometimes, however, certain experiences occur where the level falls drastically, and what rests below the surface emerges into view. A sudden expansion of the horizon reveals the reality of subconscious domains and the possibility that we might be able to gain voluntary control over not only cognitive states, but also of internal physiological processes.

Third, James conceived of knowledge in terms of a noetic pluralism. Consciousness, rather than being a single homogeneous condition, was actually a plurality of states. Personality consists of many different centers of live energy that are constantly interacting at many different levels. In a social context, this is manifested as a concatenated union between personalities, where everyone is not connected to everyone else at the same time, but only to a finite number of others in a network of relationships that keep changing. Philosophically, noetic pluralism is a way to reconcile different epistemological realms of discourse in psychology.

Fourth, James envisioned that his radical empiricism would become an internal method for self-development, self-correction, and self-repair in psychology because it defined the inherent relation of a philosophical metaphysics to a positivistic science. Positivistic thinking was necessary to launch any science, but sooner or later metaphysics would have to be introduced to overhaul it, because metaphysical inquiry is how any science changes.

THE JAMESIAN TRADITION

Considering this legacy, there is a case to be made, depending on the particular era, for a definite Jamesian tradition in psychology. I will identify three subcategories within such a tradition, all of which stand opposed to a fourth. First, there are those who have declared themselves outright Jamesians. Second, there are those who have declared themselves near-Jamesians by intellectual kinship. Third, and perhaps the largest subcategory, are those psychologists who know who James was, perhaps have his *Principles* on their shelf, although have never read it closely, but who, nevertheless, represent James's call for a noetic pluralism. They are Jamesian because they pursue their specific concerns within the framework of an eclectic tolerance for the various, but widely divergent, epistemological frames of reference within the discipline. Opposed to these three subcategories are those psychologists who are patently against the larger agenda that James represented, who either reject his ideas outright, or else, accept bits and pieces of his thought that somehow relate to their own work although they reject his larger framework.

JAMES'S STUDENTS

As I just mentioned, the first group consists of those who have considered themselves Jamesians by lineal descent, a category that contains the largest number of actual students, colleagues, and friends. John Dewey, Josiah Royce, Charles Peirce, and William McDougall all wrote tributes to James at one time or another. Numerous students of James have rendered their account of his influence, among them Dickenson Miller (1910, 1942), E. B. Holt (1942), Horace Kallen (1942), Ralph Barton Perry (1943), Ross Angier (1943), E. B. Delabarre (1943), E. L. Thorndike (1943), Edwin D. Starbuck (1943), and James R. Angell (1943).

Anecdotes of numerous others also abound. L. Eugene Emerson, the first clinical psychologist on the staff at the Massachusetts General Hospital in 1911, who practiced a modified form of Freudian and Jungian analysis, had turned to psychology as a student after meeting James (Taylor, 1982b). W. E. B. Dubois, whose *Souls of Black Folk* (1903) was influenced by James's ideas about the subconscious, once declared "my two best friends in life have been my mother and William James" (Taylor, 1991). Gertrude Stein, who learned the technique of automatic writing in the Harvard Psychological Laboratory, wrote in her autobiography that James was the most important influence of her Radcliffe career (Taylor, 1992b). Helen Keller, who was acquainted with James for over 18 years, partly because of their mutual interest in Swedenborg, desired to write a book patterned after his *Talks to*

Teachers on Psychology: And to Students on Some of Life's Ideals (Taylor, 1981). These accounts alone show a wider definition of psychology than that limited to strict laboratory experimentation, an effect entirely commensurate with James's orientation and intention.

THE BEGINNING OF THE ANTI-JAMESIAN TRADITION

It should also be noted that even while he was still alive, William James had his detractors. The moral philosophers, such as Francis Bowen, stood against him in the early evolutionary dialogues between the creationists and the Darwinians. James Sully had thought the *Principles* too lively to be a good scientific text. James H. Leuba (1912), a youthful investigator in the psychology of religion, called James's efforts to understand religious experience in the *The Varieties of Religious Experience* (1902) a fiasco.

But the greatest opposition to the Jamesian definition of psychology as a person-centered science came from those who James believed had succumbed to scientism—the experimentally oriented followers of laboratory measurement who were fast taking over American psychology by the 1890s. Chief among them were students of Wilhelm Wundt. As Americans who had gone abroad for a German scientific education or as émigrés who had come to the New World, they established a succession of experimental laboratories at American universities after training in Leipzig and were forced to articulate how their definition of scientific psychology differed from what James's version of psychology represented in the minds of the American public, university trustees, and potential private and government donors. Among the first wave were G. Stanley Hall, who, against the wishes of the trustees, founded a laboratory at the Johns Hopkins University; James McKeen Cattell, who opened a laboratory at the University of Pennsylvania; and Frank Angell, who opened laboratories at Cornell and Stanford. There was also a certain Englishman who wished to become the American Wundt, a man who would prove to be one of James's arch rivals, Edward Bradford Titchener.

One cannot hope in the small space provided here to embark on an exhaustive analysis of the anti-Jamesian movement, which is what it became—a concentrated and full-fledged movement in late nineteenth-century American psychology. Titchener, however, is emblematic enough to warrant an additional word for at least two reasons: He purported to interpret Wundt (although historians feel that he was Wundt's most ardent reinterpreter), and his agenda for an American psychology, modeled after German science, was carried forward into the middle of the twentieth century by his student, E. G. Boring, the influential historian of experimental psychology, a one-time APA president, an editor of numerous APA journals, and a professor of psychology at Harvard.

JAMES AND TITCHENER

Edward Bradford Titchener, 25 years younger than James, was trained at Oxford in philosophy and received his PhD in Leipzig after 2 years of study with Wundt (Boring, 1929/1950). True to the German laboratory tradition, he wrote his dissertation in psychophysics on the binocular effects of monocular stimulation. Titchener arrived at Cornell in 1892 where he was to remain for 35 years. Immediately after arriving, he began to expand the laboratory by instituting *drill courses*, as he called them, "to prove that psychology is a science" (Boring, 1950, p. 413), and between 1896 and 1905, he produced a slew of textbooks, primers, and students and instructors' manuals on his brand of experimental psychology. He assembled a cadre of graduate students to work on various aspects of his structural psychology, and they carried his program of reaction times and the controlled introspective analysis of consciousness to the nth degree while he wrote his articles, reviews, and books and worked on launching the new profession. An importer of German science who remained all his life a British citizen, even according to Boring, "Titchener never became a part of American psychology" (Boring, 1950, p. 413). He did not care for the American trend toward the study of human capacities and individual differences, but rather sought to make psychology over to suit himself.

An example was his differences with the APA. Titchener was a charter member when the APA was first launched in 1892, but dropped out a year later because the Association refused to censure a colleague for what Titchener had thought was blatant plagiarism. Although Titchener rejoined the APA as a nominal member in 1910, by 1904, he had formed his own group, The Experimental Psychologists, now called the *Society of Experimental Psychologists*, which has met annually as something of a purist rival to the APA ever since. According to Boring, "The word *experimental* was kept for the meaning that Wundt and his contemporaries had given it; animal, child, abnormal, and applied psychology, no matter how much they used experiment, were not called 'experimental psychology' " (Boring, 1950, p. 414).

Walter Pillsbury, a student at Cornell in the 1890s, left us a note on Titchener's reaction to James: To several of the graduate students, it seemed that Titchener "esteemed James rather less than was his due" (Pillsbury, 1943, p. 71), in all likelihood, because James "was outside the true experimental group and was not sympathetic with the Leipzig tradition" (Pillsbury, 1943, p. 73). Some of the students were surprised, for instance, that, instead of James's *Principles* as a text, Titchener chose Sully's *Human Mind* (1892) for his course in general psychology. Although Titchener never came out in public with an outright statement of dislike or approbation about James, he did give his private opinion of James to his colleagues. To James McKeen Cattell, for instance, Titchener wrote: "James's influence both in philosophy & psychology appears to me to be getting positively unwholesome: his credulity and his appeals to emotion are surely the reverse of scientific . . . even you, as younger, cannot stem the James tide" (Titchener, 1898).

Titchener also criticized James in print on several occasions. In the first instance, he supported his young friend David Irons, a student of philosophy, in an attack on James's theory of emotion (Irons, 1894). Only after James had died did Titchener publish his own direct comments, not so much to the effect that James was wrong, but that he had had predecessors whom he did not acknowledge and, therefore, was not original (Titchener, 1914).

Second, James and Titchener got into an argument in the late 1890s over the issue of telepathy and whether or not psychical research was a legitimate scientific endeavor (Burkhardt, Bowers, & Skrupskelis, 1986). In that exchange, James forcefully defended himself on the grounds that Titchener was not only trying to assert his position using arrogance and dictatorial authority, but was misreading the evidence and inaccurately attributing credit for experiments performed. Titchener, meanwhile, carried on in the name of purity by proclaiming that any investigator who tried to debunk psychical research, whether right or wrong, was striking a blow for good science.

James, in turn, left us his own impressions of Titchener. One in particular, involving internal deliberations to bring another psychologist to Harvard in case Münsterberg returned to Europe, occurred in 1897. Writing to President Eliot and giving his own candid impressions, James thought of Titchener as "very energetic and reputed to be a great success as a teacher, but apparently not original in the way of ideas, and (although from Oxford) quite a barbarian in his scientific & literary manners, and quarrelsome in the extreme" (James, 1897).

Titchener, as we know, was offered a chair in experimental psychology at Harvard following the death of Hugo Münsterberg, but the negotiations broke down when he became too dictatorial. William McDougall, a friend and colleague of William James, was offered the chair instead, which he took in 1921. That was the same year that Titchener's willing instrument, E. G. Boring, arrived at Harvard to begin his own career, which was to last almost half a century.

JAMES'S INTELLECTUAL DESCENDANTS

Among other Jamesians are those who came after James had passed from the scene. These include a wide range of philosophers, physicists, psychologists, writers, and religious thinkers, who felt themselves influenced by James's works and expressed this influence by writing about James and incorporating his ideas into their own corpus. Jacques Barzun, Ezra Pound, Nils Bohr, even Percy Bridgman are examples. In psychology this includes such prominent figures of the twentieth century as Carl Jung, A. A. Roback, Rollo May, James Bugental, Nevit Sanford, and Silvan Tomkins. Three in particular, whom I will call the great triumvirate, were Gardner Murphy, Henry Murray, and Gordon Allport.

MURPHY AND PARAPSYCHOLOGY

Gardner Murphy, parapsychologist and pioneer personality–social theorist, received his BA from Yale, his MA from Harvard, and then went on to earn his doctorate under one of James's old students, Robert Sessions Woodworth, at Columbia. Murphy had numerous affinities with James.

Both Murphy and James had deep personal connections to Concord, Massachusetts. James's godfather, Ralph Waldo Emerson, had lived there, and James had become heir to the Swedenborgian and transcendentalist literary legacy of Emerson and Henry James, Sr. Murphy lived in Concord as a young boy at the home of his grandfather, a leading citizen of the town and well-known lawyer, one of whose clients had been Leonora Piper, James's famous medium.

Both men were pioneers in parapsychology. James had helped to found the American Society for Psychical Research in 1884, which he headed up with Richard Hodgson until 1905. Murphy was one of the principal officers who ran the Society after 1944 for almost a quarter of a century. Both investigated mediums, conducted experiments in telepathy, and saw an important connection between psychic phenomena and the unconscious.

Both were interpreters of modern dynamic psychology. Inner experience, as interpreted in both the East and the West, formed the basis for their respective definitions of personality and consciousness. James found resonance in the work of George Miller Beard, F. W. H. Myers, Pierre Janet, Theodore Flournoy, and Swami Vivekananda. Murphy found it in Freud, as well as in Akhilananda and Suzuki. Both believed in personality as something more, "plus ultra," than the mechanistic theories could define.

Murphy's own resonance with James is captured in an autobiographical sketch:

> My devotion to William James began very early, waxed strong in encountering his *Varieties of Religious Experience* in 1916, and became a steady passion as I read through the whole *Principles* in the summer of 1920 when working with Fred Wells at McLean Hospital. I encountered

him in new contexts when working on *The Historical Introduction to Modern Psychology*; put him to use in connection with the theory of the self during the 1930s; read aloud with Lois, his 1920 collection of letters published by his son, and, again with Lois, read through the two-volume *Thought and Character of William James* by Ralph Barton Perry in the 1940s. I used James constantly in connection with psychical research over all these and later years; gladly accepted Robert Ballou's suggestion that we edit together a volume on *William James in Psychical Research* (1960); and found him standing nearby, always ready to be consulted, and often profoundly helpful in connection with studies at the Menninger Foundation on perception, attention, thought processes, the will, and the whole evolutionary approach to the growth of the mind. I had several times attempted brief characterizations of him, as in *The Historical Introduction to Modern Psychology*, especially in the revised edition (1949, pp 207-209), and in *Personality* (1947, pp. 22-27), as well as in the introduction and summary to *William James on Psychical Research* (1960). Several times I have taught courses on the psychology of William James. (Murphy, 1967, p. 276)

The key to Murphy's outlook is expressed by the word *devotion*, which I interpret as lineage. We have ample evidence of such lineal traditions in western psychology. Titchener was devoted to Wundt, as Boring was devoted to Titchener. This is a self-consciously defined lineage that Boring exploited in writing his *History of Experimental Psychology* (1950), when he excluded such fields as tests and measurements and developmental, social, and clinical psychology from a work that became a standard textbook and had to be memorized by graduating PhDs for nearly 40 years. Similarly, as Murphy was influenced by James, so too were Murphy's students. The important point is that Murphy, like James, never produced clones of himself, nor did he simply replicate a single research tradition. Like James, he consciously fostered individuality. Under Murphy, such students as Rensis Lichert developed attitude scales, Gertrude Schmeidler pursued psychical research, and Philip Holzman made his mark on psychoanalytic psychotherapy.

Therefore, it should not be surprising that Murphy's work is saturated with references to James's life and work.

MURRAY AND PERSONOLOGY

Henry A. Murray arrived at Harvard as an undergraduate in 1911, just a year after James had died. After marrying a local Boston girl, Josephine Rantoul, he went on to earn his MA in biology at Columbia University and an MD from the Columbia College of Physicians and Surgeons before returning to Cambridge to do blood chemistry work under L. J. Henderson, a physical chemist who had also been a student of Josiah Royce and a friend of Richard Cabot and Walter Cannon. Murray then went off to the Rockefeller Institute in New York to embark on the study of aging in chick embryos, but was called back to Harvard in 1926 by Henderson to become assistant to Morton Prince in abnormal and dynamic psychology. Prince, a neurologist who specialized in multiple personality, had been a close friend of James and a central figure in the Boston School of Abnormal Psychology around 1900. By the mid-1920s, at the end of his long career, Prince endowed the Harvard Psychological Clinic, which was founded within the school of arts and sciences rather than at the medical school, because Prince wished to foster an academic and intellectual rapprochement between clinical and experimental psychology. Prince also offered his services to the university as a professor. He continued his experiment for 4 years until he died in 1929.

Murray inherited the Harvard Psychological Clinic and, in effect, became the leader in clinical psychology at Harvard. Instead of continuing Prince's studies on hypnosis and multiple personality, Murray immediately established the Clinic as the center of Freudian and Jungian psychology in Boston. He then launched a research enterprise on the scientific study of personality, which he called *personology*, the multilevel analysis of single cases by an interdisciplinary team of specialists. This led to the development, with the help of Christiana Morgan, of the Thematic Apperception Test, which is one of the best-selling items on the Harvard University Press book list, and it also led to the publication of *Explorations in Personality* (Murray et al., 1938), which quickly became a standard text in personality theory in American psychology for decades.

Murray was also a Melville scholar, a decorated war veteran for his work on psychological assessment for the Office of Strategic Services (OSS), and, for the last 40 years of his life, an indefatigable researcher on the scientific study of personality through dyadic interaction. He combined these interests to form a total picture of personality. His Melville project, he once said, was a lifelong case study of his personological system, whereas his scientific study of personality was continually tempered by the exigencies of writing a real life history, particularly because he had to struggle constantly to understand the enigmatic core of a person's spiritual aspirations. This conundrum between knowledge and experience is the best example of what James called *functionalism* in American psychology.

Murray often remarked how his own career, beginning in physiology and ending in religion and philosophy, paralleled that of James. The Jamesian ethos was, in fact, everywhere in Murray's endeavors. One episode, in particular, showed the extent to which Murray was associated with this Jamesian tradition at Harvard.

In 1934, when Murray's reappointment first came up for review and the fate of the Harvard Psychological Clinic hung in the balance, President Conant convened a committee to assess Murray's performance. The committee was made up of two deans; E. G. Boring, by then the preeminent historian of experimental laboratory psychology; Karl Lashley, the physiological psychologist; Gordon Allport, still in his first decade as a member of the psychology department; and Stanley Cobb, Bullard Professor of Psychiatry at Harvard Medical School and the chief of psychiatric services at the Massachusetts General Hospital.

At the first meeting in Conant's office, after some discussion, Conant asked what everyone thought about Murray in general. Gordon Allport said that certainly he should be reappointed because he was more like William James than any other psychologist who had come to the university. Lashley broke in at that point and vociferously proclaimed that William James was the biggest mistake that had ever befallen scientific psychology, especially psychology at Harvard. His caustic remark caused some excited confusion in the room, and the meeting went out of control. Conant rose and said "Gentlemen, I have another meeting just now and we will have to reconvene. But I suggest that before we leave, we at least shake hands" (personal communication to author).

The outcome is well known. It took them 3 years to finally reach a decision. Boring, Lashley, and one of the deans voted against Murray. Allport, Cobb, and the other dean voted in his favor. Conant broke the tie with a favorable vote, ostensibly because Cobb had gotten Murray's old classmate, Alan Gregg, to pledge money to the Clinic from the Rockefeller Foundation. Murray remained at Harvard (except for his military service during the war) and virtually founded a field of modern personality research (Triplet, 1983). In the period immediately after the fateful decision, Lashley's career was shadowed by a dark cloud in Cambridge, as if just punishment for defaming William James, a widely beloved figure in the general academic community, even though rejected by the experimentalists in psychology.

ALLPORT AND PERSONALITY–SOCIAL PSYCHOLOGY

Arriving in Cambridge, Massachusetts, just a few years after William James's death, Gordon Allport, another pioneer in personality–social psychology, received his BA from Harvard in 1919 and his PhD in 1923. He entered psychology largely because of his brother, Floyd, who was Münsterberg's assistant, but he was at first personally attracted to the ministry and to social service due to the influence of Richard Clarke Cabot, the noted physician and ethicist, who had been a close friend of William James. Through Cabot, Allport began teaching in the Social Ethics Department at Harvard, and there, in 1925, he taught the first course to be named *Psychology of Personality* at an American university.

After a 4-year teaching stint at Dartmouth, Allport returned to Harvard in 1930 as a junior faculty member in psychology, where he remained for the rest of his career. His research interests in the field of personality focused on prejudice, rumor, and morale, and he also became a leading figure in the psychology of religion. He incorporated James's work into his theories on many occasions, delivered the dedication speech of the James portrait at Harvard, and wrote an introduction to the 1942 edition of James's *Psychology: Briefer Course* (1892).

ALLPORT VERSUS BORING ON JAMES

One incident in particular reveals the extent of Allport's commitment to the Jamesian tradition and illustrates Boring's attitude toward James. This incident occurred in 1940, 2 years before the official celebration of James's 100th birthday in 1942, a year in which the 50th anniversary of the APA was also to be celebrated with a meeting at Harvard. Allport wrote to Boring suggesting that an intellectual celebration of James's life and work might take place quite apart from the APA meeting and other formal celebrations. Allport proposed a one-semester course entitled "The Psychology of William James." He then launched a slew of questions for Boring to consider. Should it be in the academic year 1941–1942 or 1942–1943? "Could we not devise some novel teaching strategy that would allow for combining straight-forward lecture format with small group discussions?" (Allport, 1940). And who would teach such a course?

Allport, of course, offered himself. He said it was something he would love to do, having already succeeded in getting the work of John Dewey and William Stern into manageable course proportions. Allport, knowing the possibilities that could be developed, hinted that a James course could be cotaught. He himself might take "the more speculative half of the *Principles*, *Talks to Teachers*, and the *Varieties* and the implications of *Pragmatism*, while perhaps someone else could bring the students up to date on what James had to say about sensation, memory, psychophysics, and brain localization" (Allport, 1940). This other colleague, Allport suggested, might be Boring.

Allport asked Boring to focus on a variety of questions: Was Boring even interested? How should the subject be divided? When should it happen? At what level should the course be taught? Should it be for graduates? Should it be open to Radcliffe students? What other course should be dropped in order to make room for this one? Should anyone else be brought in, such as James's biographer, the philosopher Ralph Barton Perry?

Allport then closed his letter with an allusion to the fact that his proposal was meant to get the larger APA celebration going, even with World War II raging.

Boring responded the following day with one of his characteristically long letters (Boring, 1940). "A good seminar on William James would be better than nothing," he opened. His big concern, however, was deciding what should be dropped. Would Allport give up his current seminar? Should Boring give up his? Should the graduate students defer their PhDs? Should they slow down their new research programs? Boring pointed out that Allport had really answered his own question. Allport was interested in knowing more about William James, but Boring flatly stated that he was not:

> I have never been much interested in James and have passed through
> a period of thinking psychological systems are important (the 1920s)
> and have been thinking that I now could afford to stick to the more
> directly empirical for the rest of my life, having tried the other and
> found it wanting (Boring, 1940).

Although Boring was sure that he could find better things to do than this, he did believe in the power of *collective intellectualism*, a situation in which good minds work on the same problem, with the possibility of all kinds of unforeseen results. Boring was, thus, in conflict about Allport's proposal and admitted it.

Boring did suggest that, at that time, perhaps only James would appeal to a sufficient number of people to give the desired cross-fertilization. The idea of offering a course, however, did not strike Boring as being particularly fitting, because it suggested that this was the best that Harvard could do. One would not want to do something that would be perceived as a second-rate undertaking, which Boring thought an academic course might be, unless many minds got together on a mutual project that also just happened to involve having a course along with it.

Boring was willing to consider an alternative. To make the under-taking first-rate, he told Allport that it would have to involve an audience much larger than that of just Harvard students. This necessitated publication and competent participators, which Boring did not seem to find among the graduate students whose perspectives he felt were not only often wrong, but also either condescending or too self-confident. Boring did see competency in the staff, however. His alternate proposal was a yearlong staff seminar with numerous papers, where students could be invited to participate, even if not for credit, "if they do not talk nonsense" (Boring, 1940). Even persons from outside Cambridge could be invited, as long as the paper writers were regular attenders. He thought it might also produce some first-class papers for the APA meeting that September.

As it turned out, a Harvard symposium on William James was actually planned, but then canceled because of the war, as was the entire APA meeting for 1942. Boring had even prepared a paper for it, which he delivered instead before the Harvard Psychological Colloquium and published in *The American Journal of Psychology*. His title was "Human Nature vs. Sensation: William James and the Psychology of the Present" (Boring, 1942). In this paper, he interpreted James's opposition to German psychophysics and by so doing clearly delineated those who he thought made up a modern coterie of Jamesians.

Boring began his paper by asking why James embraced the new experimental psychology and then abandoned it. Boring gave two reasons: First, James was a follower of no school. According to Boring, James had "escaped into psychology so he could dabble in physiology and philosophy without really taking them seriously" (Boring, 1940, p. 11). James also grew away from psychology to become a philosopher. The promising adolescence of psychology in the 1870s had grown up by 1890 into a dull bigot in James's eyes. According to Boring, experimental psychology was not a discovery, but a movement that originated in Germany with Helmholtz, Wundt, and Fechner. True, it contained much hypocrisy in the beginning, but it had since grown into a real science. But its accuracy and attention to detail repulsed James, who wanted a functional psychology that governed moral and religious life.

As influential Jamesians, Boring cited Brentano for his influence on Stumpf, Ward for his emphasis on conation, McDougall for purpose, Hocking for the rejection of causality as applied to the mind, Murray for needs, and Kohler for values. As opposed to this kind of phenomenology, Boring put forward the more precise tenets of positivism, operationism, and reductionism. These, he implied echoing Titchener, were the only legitimate foundations on which to develop a scientific psychology.

Allport also produced a paper commemorating James. It, too, was subsequently not delivered, but did appear in *Psychological Review* (Allport, 1943). It was important for two reasons: first, because we have Boring's comments in an unpublished draft, and second, because it revealed the extent to which Allport was a true Jamesian. The piece was entitled "The Productive Paradoxes of William James."

Allport's main point was that modern readers encountered difficulty in reading James because of his many apparent contradictions—lucid inspiration followed by vague allusions and discreet, brilliant observations followed by contradictory propositions. One who reads James finally feels like Bertrand Russell did, as if one were taking a bath in water that heated up so imperceptibly that one didn't know when to scream.

Nevertheless, James's *Principles* has remained an enduring classic. The reason for this, Allport felt, was that James's so-called *contradictions* may, in fact, reflect some of the most vital and persistent riddles of psychology, which most psychologists still ignore, but which James met head on. Allport named six: The riddle of psychophysics, or the relation of mind and body; the riddle of positivism, meaning the goodness of fit between our objective methods and subjective fact; the riddle of the self; the riddle of free will; the riddle of association, meaning the sometime efficacy of the Aristotelian laws of mental connection; and the riddle of individuality, especially why the individual is more than simply the sum total of a psychologist's analysis.

As for the explanation of such paradoxes in James's thinking, Allport turned to James's family influences, agreeing with Henry James, the novelist, who wrote "Of our upbringing, we wholesomely breathed inconsistency and ate and drank contradictions" (Allport, 1943). Brilliant paradox and lawless metaphor, Allport noted, probably drove William James to a near-suicidal depression in his late twenties. As a result, James was quite familiar with the personal struggle over good and evil and the paradox of life and death. Paradox, Allport concluded, somehow rightly characterized James's mature style of work. James, himself, even acknowledged his own inconsistencies, yet knew that contradictions would always occur if you examined the same facts from a different point of view. It often takes two opposing views to cut into any subject, he said, so why not let the science of mind be just as vague and contradictory as its subject? After all, James said, "so far as a man stands for anything, and is productive . . . , his entire vital function may be said to deal with maybes. . . . It is only by risking our persons from one hour to another than [sic] we live at all" (Allport, 1943, p. 115). Consistency could not be bought at the expense of integrity. Instead, the very subject matter of psychology demanded open-mindedness.

Allport then used James to point out the significance of these paradoxes for psychology in the 1940s. By 1942, academic psychology had narrowed its professional focus, not widened it as James had originally suggested. Nevertheless, Allport noted, the majority of psychologists as persons seemed somehow to have remained many sided, internationally minded, distinctively liberal, and genuinely devoted to the interests of humanity, as James himself was. Above all, Allport wanted psychologists to recognize James's moral imperative—that psychological theories may reflect more about the psychologist's attitudes than about reality itself and that, as a profession, psychologists can infect a downward spiral with their pessimism, just as they can urge upward growth with their optimism. In the end, James's open-minded wisdom was the most difficult kind.

Boring responded at length with comments and suggestions (Boring, 1940). Some of his corrections were merely editorial, whereas others revealed the quite different theoretical perspectives between Allport and Boring, especially on James.

For instance, when Allport suggested that James's enigmatic contradictions really dealt with the larger unaddressed questions of psychology, Boring replied

> I do not like apologetic paragraphs. Your conclusion, moreover, shows that you do not really regard these contradictions as defects, but rather as virtues. Why not then say . . . that you present these inconsistencies—paradoxes—as the virtues of a psychology that was too vital to be stable? At this point you quote Ralph Waldo Emerson on consistency as the hobgoblin of little minds. (Allport, 1940)

One cannot help but get the impression from this that Allport was referring to the tendencies of Boring himself and the so-called *biotropes*, meaning the experimentalists within Allport's own department at Harvard. Boring acknowledged the vitality of James's thought, yet damned James with faint praise by highlighting his instability. Once Boring had pronounced the final word on Allport's main thesis, the Emerson quote may have seemed to Boring a contradiction. Did Boring see consistency as a trait that was opposed to James's vitality? Or did he really get Allport's point that only small minds relegate vitality to the level of consistency in one's theories?

Boring also raised a question regarding Allport's six persistent riddles of psychology. Boring's preference, he told Allport, was to substitute *some* for *the* in the phrasing of the problem. He said that Allport had no way of knowing that these six points were really ultimate questions. That is to say, Boring and Allport may have differed radically on which questions they considered of ultimate importance for psychology. For Boring, the questions of science and the questions of psychology were one. Boring, therefore, also objected to Allport's use of the term *psychological science*, as if to say that there were different sciences for each discipline. Allport certainly may have been referring to such a state of affairs. Boring's only comment was "I do not know what psychological science means" (Boring, 1940).

Allport had further claimed in his paper that attempts to posit such riddles in psychology were often attacked as being merely an argument over semantics. Boring's reply was that it seemed a contradiction to refer to important questions as merely semantic, for how can something important be merely anything. The drift of Allport's phrasing suggested that hard-nosed psychologists often dismiss philosophical questions raised by their softer scientific colleagues. Boring, in turn, appeared to have similarly reduced Allport's point to a "nothing but" proposition of semantics.

Boring also queried Allport on his discussion of James's positivism, saying that simply giving quotes on James from Dewey and others was just not convincing. Allport had succeeded in making his point on James, the phenomenologist, and James, the radical empiricist, but he had only lightly touched on James's more rigorous and exactly defined attitudes toward science. As was so characteristic of Allport, however, he drew most heavily from James on the importance of human values and personal experience, using James as a support against the reductionistic and mechanistic position of the positivists. James did espouse a form of positivism, as Boring had rightly pointed out. But James opposed what in Allport's time had come to be known as operationism in psychology, a position that formed the core of the biotropes of Boring's camp at Harvard, with which Allport had so constantly to contend.

In Allport's article, Boring also objected to the use of the historical present in referring to James:

> To say that James thinks, argues, says—instead of thought, argued, said—is to lose perspective, to put James definitely out of the past. Perhaps I have a special dislike of this tense, because it seems historically unreal. You tend to make James timeless by it while you are showing that he changed in time. (Boring, 1940)

Boring then took up several anomalies in Allport's use of tense. For Allport, however, James did not just live in the past. James was alive and ever present. For Boring, on the other hand, James was important only for certain reasons—mainly those that supported psychology as a laboratory science. Other than that acknowledged fact, for Boring, James was effectively dead. He did not see how Allport could maintain that some vague, constantly changing formulations were James's most timeless contribution.

Finally, Allport suggested that a redefinition of functionalism had taken place since 1910, which would not have suited James. By 1942, Allport asserted, functionalism had become allied more with structuralism and laboratory science. Boring took exception with Allport on the point, claiming that James was indeed allied with the functional tradition of Dewey and Angell at Chicago, although Allport had not contested this point in his paper. Boring said,

> In 1907, the year of James Angell's presidential address on functional psychology, William James could say that he did not understand all the bother about structuralism and functionalism. But that is not to say that the Chicago School did not find part of the direct source of motivation in James, nor part of their direct source in James via Dewey. When function got its *ism*, of course James was not for it; but you cannot, I should say, cast doubt on the accepted ancestral position of James in American functionalism unless you go specifically into the matter. (Boring, 1940)

Boring, however, evaded Allport's original point that functionalism, as it was understood in the psychology of the 1940s, was essentially anti-

Jamesian because it stressed nomothetic rather than ideographic methods, was confined largely to laboratory studies of the white rat, and presumed that anything that could not be measured was not a legitimate area of study.

Boring, in sum, carried on the Titchnerian strategy of diminishing the Jamesian tradition, largely through disinterest. He was always willing to consider James as a historical figure, but consistently Boring's penchant was to reinterpret James to fit his own agenda, which was the glorification of the laboratory experimentalists in psychology.

THE CONTEMPORARY SCENE

The more we focus on the present, the more difficult it is to assess the Jamesian influence, partly because living personalities are still around to affirm or deny their private beliefs, and these may or may not be at variance with their public statements. Climate control at least dictates that nothing too disparaging be put into print during the High Holidays that mark the founding of institutions and the passing of cultural heroes. This is to say that, although his modern detractors have kept largely silent, among his adherents, the topic of William James is fast becoming a veritable industry in psychology.

A recent spate of symposia, books, and reviews commemorating the 100th anniversary of James's *Principles*, the present volume included, attest to this phenomenon. At the 1990 convention in Boston, lectures were organized throughout the divisions of the APA; Harvard undergraduates in psychology, through their William James Society, dedicated the annual *Harvard Psychological Review* to James's *Principles* (Tischler, 1990); Henley and Johnson produced a commemorative volume of scholarly chapters (Henley & Johnson, 1990); symposia were held in England and America, papers from which appeared in the *British Journal of Psychology* (Still, 1991) and in *Psychological Science* (Estes, 1990). Individual articles looking at James's contemporary influence were also commissioned by the editors of *The Personality and Social Psychology Bulletin* (Arkin, 1990).

Although one psychologist looked into the *Principles* and claimed he found not one principle there, and another claimed that James has had little impact on psychology today except by hindsight, it is generally agreed that James's influence extends into numerous streams of cognitive science, into self-theory, and into the study of affects. As well, his philosophy is continually evoked when various theorists have taken up a metaphysical inquiry into the basis for psychology as a science.

Curiously enough, it should also come as no surprise to find that the psychology James envisioned actually does exist, but it has persistently appeared throughout modern culture in places other than university-based psychological laboratories. It appears in existential and phenomenological psychology, in the profusion of depth psychologies, in parapsychology, in the self-help movement (particularly throughout the history of groups such as Alcoholics Anonymous), and it pervades the counterculture psychotherapies and the pastoral counseling movement. Within academic psychology, it appears in various phases of personality, abnormal, social, and clinical psychology, largely because James actually did have an influence on the early evolution of these so-called *soft sciences* in ways that are not yet fully acknowledged. As a general attitude of tolerance, eclecticism, and open-mindedness, the Jamesian ethic pervades American psychology in a way that cuts across all subdisciplinary boundaries. Hence, James seems to be everywhere, but in no one concentrated place.

KOCH AND COGNITIVE PATHOLOGISTICS

I cannot forbear at this point to mention one man who seems to me to represent the prototypic contemporary Jamesian, namely, Sigmund Koch. I put his name forward, not because he has written about James, but because, after James, he was the first internationally known scientific psychologist to launch a wide-ranging epistemological critique of modern experimentalism in the twentieth century. His critique, moreover, is remarkably similar to James's metaphysics of radical empiricism.

As James was first attracted to painting before concentrating on science, Koch embarked on his intellectual career as an aspiring young poet. In graduate school, however, he turned his attention to problems of logic and science and received his MA in the philosophy of science under Herbert Feigl at the University of Iowa in 1939. Leaving Iowa, he went on to receive his PhD from Duke in experimental psychology and, for the following 10 years, investigated problems of learning and motivation in the rat. At the same time, he became one of the most important voices for clarifying the relationship between logical positivism, theory construction, and experimentation in psychology as a scientific discipline.

In the mid-1950s, the APA commissioned Koch to lead a massive assessment of scientific psychology at midcentury. In collaboration with 87 authors, comprising the foremost psychologists in their respective subdisciplines, Koch produced a six-volume analysis, *Psychology: A Study of a Science* (Koch, 1959–1963). The essential complex of questions to be addressed required each author to assess the theoretical empirical methods and the achieved (as well as prospective) empirical fertility of their respective endeavors in psychology. The study had two major parts. The first involved an intensive analysis of systematic formulations that had shaped the discipline as a science, and the second attempted to explore the interrelations of major subject-matter areas and situate psychology within the matrix of scientific activity pursued by other disciplines (Koch, 1959).

The results of this investigation had important implications in five subject areas: the use of intervening variables, the problem of generalization, the observation base of psychology, mathematical quantification, and the establishment of formal theories (Koch, Vol. 3, 1959). The following were the results: (a) The widespread adoption of the research paradigm relying on the identification of intervening variables as constructs mediating observation and theory was found to be seriously flawed. (b) The generalization of findings to other spheres of human experience outside specific experimental situations was found to be both severely limited and grossly overstated. (c) The observation base of psychology had been so severely standardized as to define large areas of inquiry lying outside the norm as illegitimate, a trend nevertheless strongly resisted by most of the researchers. (d) Although the ideal demanded mathematical quantification of systematic relationships between variables, the majority of theorists remained largely qualitative in their activities. (e) It was generally concluded that the attempt to formalize the hypothetico-deductive model as a prescriptive means of establishing psychology as a science is both misleading and infeasible.

Over the subsequent decades, the overall effect of this study was developed by Koch into a wider indictment of modern scientific psychology. His analyses have since become well known (Koch & Leary, 1985). If there is no empirical justification for the claim that the industrious application of any specified set of predefined mechanical laboratory procedures is the only method for arriving at truth, for demolishing alternative methodologies, or for defining what could or could not be the legitimate data or domain of the discipline; and if the attempt to construct a single cohesive, internally consistent, and logically sound theoretical framework that would unify all aspects of scientific research in psychology has been a massive failure, then psychology is not, and in all likelihood will never become, a unified science. At the same time, the attempt to force psychologists to compress their research interests into the narrow confines of such misplaced rule-bound behavior has disenfranchised psychology from a potentially fruitful dialogue with the humanities, thus contributing to the wider culture of "ameaningful" thinking presently afflicting modern society. Hence, somewhat tongue-in-cheek, Koch coined the term "cognitive pathologistics" to describe his in-depth analysis of psychologists' past and continuing errors.

At the same time that he has been delineating the culture of "a-meaning" in psychology, Koch has also embarked on a Herculean search for legitimate alternatives to the pathological and quasi-religious urge toward reductionism and quantification, not only in psychology, but also in science more generally. His path has led him into aesthetics and to the study of creativity in the arts and humanities. His example of a new research paradigm is the Aesthetics Research Project, a 10-year study supported by Boston University and the Ford Foundation (Koch, 1991).

Essentially the only research endeavor of its kind that has attempted such an in-depth look at creativity from the standpoint of artists, themselves, the Aesthetics Research Project embarked on a detailed investigation of selected novelists, poets, playwrights, architects, dancers, and painters who were outstanding in their respective fields. Eight-hour individual interviews were conducted with all participants, designed to elicit information about their personal biographies, their major struggles within their respective genre, and matters of process and craft pertaining to the corpus of their lifework. Several hours of discussions within this framework were also devoted to the detailed elaboration of some specific work produced by the artist from its original inspiration to its completion.

Koch's initial conclusions have important implications for qualitative research, especially where certain life experiences simply cannot be comprehended by empirical measurement and synthetic analysis, but must be confronted experientially. Within his research framework, the person, in the form of the unique investigator and the specific artist, is reinstated at the center of a psychology that presumes the individual psyche to be an essence extractor far superior to any artificial method of churning out data devised by man or machine, insofar as the processes of creativity and consciousness are concerned. In its own small way, this single research paradigm represents a major shift in research methodology by its very de-emphasis on method. It is the embodiment of Allport's call for a person-centered science and the reincarnation of James's emphasis on the primacy of immediate experience.

At the same time, Koch's larger analysis of meaning and a-meaning in modern culture allows one to make some important generalizations about the Jamesian tradition in psychology. First of all, James was a man ahead of his time. He not only pioneered the launching of the new science, but he also became its most prescient and sophisticated critic. The alternative he proposed was beyond the understanding of the average psychologist, however, because it involved more than the addition of yet another category of information within the rational pantheon of discriminations. It called for an epistemological leap into a totally new realm of discursive knowledge. For this, James has not only been considered irrelevant, but recently, he has also been wrongly labeled an anarchist (Coon, 1988). He was, rather, a psychologist with a better grasp of problems inherent in the scientific study of consciousness than most modern theoreticians and a philosopher of immediate experience beyond the analytic categories of most contemporary social critics and intellectual historians.

Also, Koch's analysis implies that the derision heaped on the research programs of Murray, Allport, and Murphy by the experimentalists was perhaps undeserved. Rather than being soft, misguided, or unscientific, they now appear to have been some of the few truly visionary psychologists who were able to hold out, theoretically and methodologically, against the inherently flawed agenda of the reductionistic laboratory enterprise.

Finally, Koch's analysis reinforces the idea that psychology is really a pluralistic science (Koch, 1976). Pockets of isolated empirical investigation go on with little generalizable results across what he has called other *search cells*. It is, therefore, appropriate, in his opinion, to speak not of scientific psychology, but of "the psychological studies." By this, he meant to make room for a variety of methods as well as seemingly incompatible epistemic frames of reference that span both the sciences and the humanities, all of which can legitimately be called psychology. James once asked how we should regard these different metaphysical frames of reference, for they seem so discontinuous with the rational ideal of normative science. Yet in their own way, they each have their field of application and adaptation.

Addressing this problem in his presidential address to the Canadian Psychological Association, John Conway presented evidence suggesting that these differences in metaphysical frameworks within the discipline might be accounted for in terms of personality types (Conway, 1992). He reviewed the history of empirical research by psychologists into the origins and present trends of their own interpretative preferences and concluded his address with an analysis of some of the factors in William James's own biography that may have contributed to characteristically Jamesian theories.

Among Conway's several points, Kimble (1984) reported that 96% of a sample of experimental psychologists taken from the APA Division of Experimental Psychology and from the Psychonomic Society endorsed elementarism, determinism, objectivism, and the search for nomothetic laws by laboratory methods. Meanwhile, about 75% in samples of psychotherapists from the APA Division of Psychotherapy and social activists from the Society for the Psychological Study of Social Issues held values such as holism, indeterminism, and intuitionism. Methodologically, these psychologists were also more focused on individual uniqueness and contextual interpretation.

A more comprehensive survey of psychologists across subdisciplines would be desirable. My hypothesis is that, although almost everyone at some level of their training has had to master analysis of variance designs and perform experiments to become credentialed as a professional in psychology, only a minority of psychologists hold radical materialism as a personal worldview. The majority are humanistically oriented Jamesians who think in experimentalist terms when necessary, but spend the majority of their time in their own more expansive epistemological frameworks.

The historical question, then, is what will a psychology of the future look like once it has grown out of its long childhood phase where it naively claims to be positivistic and antimetaphysical. One acknowledges the necessity of this mind-set in order to launch a science. But what does the mature science of psychology look like that finally takes its own implied metaphysics into account?

If there is something inherently Darwinian in the supremacy of one theoretical framework over another, then, given some of the humanistic implications of the modern revolution in the neurosciences, the sociotropes, in the tradition of James, Murphy, Murray, Allport, and Koch, may yet have their day. History, philosophy, and experience may take precedence over laboratory methodology, not to do away with it, but to situate it in its proper contemporary place with regard to the problem of consciousness. Experimentalism as the dominant ethic of research may have to be pushed aside. Perhaps only then will a noetic pluralism finally emerge as the orienting idea of the discipline. After all, as James said, "No one person is given to know the totality of truth. Rather, each person being a syllable in human nature's total message, it takes the whole of us to spell the meaning out completely" (Allport, 1943, p. 95).

REFERENCES

Allport, G. W. (1940). To E. G. Boring, June 19, 1940, File 12, GWA/EGB on William James. Box 1, File 12, HUG.4118.60. Allport papers. Pusey Library, Harvard University Archives, Cambridge, MA.

Allport, G. W. (1943). The productive paradoxes of William James. *Psychological Review, 50,* 95–120.

Angell, J. R. (1943). Toastmaster's speech. *Psychological Review, 50,* 83.

Angier, R. P. (1943). Another student's impressions of James at the turn of the century. *Psychological Review, 50,* 132.

Arkin, R. M. (1990). On celebrating William James's *Principles of Psychology. Personality and Social Psychology Bulletin, 16,* 597–600.

Boring, E. G. (1940). To Gordon Allport, June 20, 1940, File 12, GWA/EGB on William James. Box 1, File 12, HUG.4118.60. Allport papers. Pusey Library, Harvard University Archives, Cambridge, MA.

Boring, E. G. (1942). Human nature vs. sensation: William James and the psychology of the present. *American Journal of Psychology, 55,* 310–327.

Boring, E. G. (1950). A *history of experimental psychology* (2nd ed.). New York: Appleton, Century, Crofts. (Original work published 1929)

Burkhardt, F., Bowers, F., & Skrupskelis, I. (Eds.). (1986). *The works of Williams James: Essays in psychical research.* Cambridge, MA: Harvard University Press.

Conway, J. B. (1992). A world of differences among psychologists. *Canadian Psychology, 33,* 1–24.

Coon, D. J. (1988). *Courtship with anarchy: The socio-political foundation of William James's pragmatism.* Unpublished doctoral dissertation, Harvard University.

Delabarre, E. B. (1943). A student's impressions of James at the turn of the century. *Psychological Review, 50,* 125.

DuBois, W. E. B. (1903). *The souls of black folk.* Chicago: McClurg.

Estes, W. (Ed.). (1990). James symposium. *Psychological Science, 3.*

Harrington, A. (1988). Metals and magnets in medicine: Hysteria, hypnosis and medical culture in fin-de-siècle Paris, *Psychological medicine, 18,* 21–38.

Henley, T., & Johnson, M. (Eds.). (1990). *Reflections on the principles of psychology: William James after a century.* New York: Earlbaum.

Holt, E. B. (1942). William James as psychologist. In M. C. Otto (Ed.)., *In commemoration of William James.* Madison, WI: University of Wisconsin Press.

Irons, D. (1894). Prof. James's theory of emotion. *Mind, 3,* 77–97.

James, W. (1890). *The principles of psychology* (2 vols.). New York: Holt.

James, W. (1892). *Psychology: Briefer course.* New York: Henry Holt.

James, W. (1895). The knowing of things together. *Psychological Review, 2,* 105–124.

James, W. (1897). To Charles William Eliot, February 21, 1897. Eliot Papers, Pusey Library, Harvard University.

James, W. (1902). *The varieties of religious experience.* New York: Longmans.

Kallen, H. M. (1942). Remembering William James. In B. Blanshard & H. W. Schneider (Eds.), *In commemoration of William James: 1842–1942.* New York: Columbia University Press.

Kimble, G. A. (1984). Psychology's two cultures. *American Psychologist, 39,* 833–839.

Koch, S. (Ed.). (1959–1963). *Psychology: The study of a science* (Vols. 1–6). New York: McGraw Hill.

Koch, S. (1976). Language communities, search cells, and the psychological studies. In W. J. Arnold (Ed.)., *Nebraska Symposium on Motivation, 1975* (Vol. 23). Lincoln, NE: University of Nebraska Press.

Koch, S., & Leary, D. (Eds.). (1985). *A century of psychology as science.* New York: McGraw-Hill.

Koch, S. (1991, August). *An example of 1:1 Qualitative research.* Paper presented at the annual convention of the American Psychological Association, San Francisco, CA.

Leuba, J. H. (1912). *A psychological study of religion: Its origin, function, and future.* New York: MacMillan.

Miller, D. (1910). Some tendencies of Professor James's work. *Journal of Philosophy, 7,* 645–664.

Miller, D. (1942). William James: man and philosopher. In O. Marx. (Ed.), *William James: The man and the thinker.* Madison, WI: University of Wisconsin Press.

Murphy, G. (1949). *Historical introduction to modern psychology* (2nd ed.). New York: Harcourt, Brace.

Murphy, G. (1967). Autobiography. In E. G. Boring & G. Lindsey (Eds.), *History of Psychology in Autobiography*. New York: Appleton-Century-Crofts.

Murphy, G., & Ballou, R. (1960). *William James on psychical research*. New York: Viking.

Murray, H. A. (1938). *Explorations in personality*. New York: Oxford University Press.

Perry, R. B. (1943). James the psychologist—As a philosopher sees him. *Psychological Review, 50*, 122–124.

Pillsbury, W. B. (1943). Titchener and James. *Psychological Review, 50*, 71–73.

Starbuck, E. D. (1943). A student's impression of James in the middle '90s. *Psychological Review, 50*, 128–131.

Still, A. (1991). Introduction to a centenary symposium on William James's *Principles of Psychology*. *British Journal of Psychology, 82*, 191–193.

Sully, J. (1892). *The human mind: A textbook of psychology*. New York: Appleton.

Taylor, E. I. (1981). William James and Helen Keller. *Studia Swedenborgiana, 4*, 7–26.

Taylor, E. I. (1982a). *William James on exceptional mental states: Reconstruction of the 1896 Lowell Lectures*. New York: Scribner's.

Taylor, E. I. (1982b). Louville Eugene Emerson: Psychotherapy, Harvard, and the early Boston scene. *Harvard Medical Alumni Bulletin, 56*, 42–46.

Taylor, E. I. (1991, June). *Transcending the veil: William James, W. E. B. DuBois, and the Afro-American religious experience*. Paper presented at the Wilfred Gould Rice Memorial Lecture on Psychology and Religion, Harvard University, Cambridge, MA.

Taylor, E. I. (1992a). *Psychology as a person-centered-science: William James after 1890*. Unpublished doctoral dissertation, Boston University.

Taylor, E. I. (1992b, Spring). *William James, Gertrude Stein, and Pablo Ruiz Picasso*. Paper presented at the University Professors Seminar, Boston University.

Thorndike, E. L. (1943). James's influence on the psychology of perception and thought. *Psychological Review, 50*, 87–94.

Tischler, K. (Ed.). (1990). One hundred years of William James's *Principles of Psychology*. *Harvard Psychological Review, 6*.

Titchener, E. B. (1898). To J. M. Cattell, Nov. 20, 1898. Cattell Papers. Library of Congress, Washington, DC.

Titchener, E. B. (1914). An historical note on the James-Lange theory of emotion. *American Journal of Psychology, 25*, 427–447.

Triplet, R. G. (1983). *Henry A. Murray and the Harvard Psychological Clinic, 1926–1938: A struggle to expand the disciplinary boundaries of psychology*. Unpublished doctoral dissertation, University of New Hampshire, Durham.

2

ARE THERE UNIFYING TRENDS IN THE PSYCHOLOGIES OF THE 1990s?

ANNE ANASTASI

First, I will clarify the title of this chapter. I am writing not about psychologists, but about psychology. Psychologists are multidimensional beings. The substantive body of psychological knowledge that they use represents only one of these dimensions. Psychologists also differ in what they do with this knowledge—teach it, conduct research on it, or apply it in solving many different kinds of practical problems; they differ in where they work and the settings in which they function; they differ in the type of populations with which they work; and still other dimensions could undoubtedly be identified. Moreover, many psychologists occupy more than one position on a single dimension—one person may serve in diverse roles.

In the title of this chapter, the plural, psycholo*gies*, is used in recognition of the need for specialization of training and expertise within psychology. The complexity and rapid expansion of the entire field require the individual to specialize in order to attain sufficient depth of knowledge to make an effective contribution to either research or practice. Psychologists can retain adjectival specialties, such as developmental psychology or social psychology, while recognizing a common core of methods and concepts and maintaining communication across specialties. I do not see any conflict between the existence of adjectival psychologies and the promotion of the unifying trends I wish to discuss.

APPROACHES TO UNIFICATION IN PSYCHOLOGY

Unifying trends in psychology can occur at different levels of generality. At the broadest level, the unity of all psychology as a scientific discipline has received increasing attention since midcentury. At this level of generality, the search for "grand unifying principles" has provoked some sharp controversy. On the negative side, overall theoretical unification of psychology has been variously characterized as currently unattainable, intrinsically impossible, and probably undesirable (Gardner, 1988; Koch, 1981; Viney, 1989; see also, Rychlak, 1989; Staats & Mos, 1987). It would certainly be hazardous to insist that, for psychology to survive as a distinct discipline, it must provide a single set of theoretical principles to account for all empirical findings. Achieving unity at this level could indeed have some adverse effects. It could encourage distortion of facts to fit the theory, or it could lead to the exclusion of certain areas of investigation as not belonging properly in psychology. It also suggests a static concept of knowledge, which is not conducive to free imaginative exploration of alternatives.

On the positive side, a major, long-term program aimed at unification across all psychology has been in progress for several decades in the work of Arthur Staats (1963, 1970, 1975, 1981, 1983, 1987a, 1987b). Designated *social behaviorism*, Staats's approach takes learning in its broadest sense as a likely basis for unifying psychological knowledge. While striving for overall theoretical integration, Staats now recognizes the various pitfalls in the way of achieving unification at its highest level. Hence, he recommends and has been pursuing integration at intermediate, narrower levels as steps toward his ultimate goal. At such intermediate levels, unification is also likely to encounter less resistance from confirmed adherents of conflicting theoretical orientations. There is now a growing realization within several fields of psychology that unification at intermediate levels of generality is well-worth pursuing for its own sake, regardless of one's views about the likelihood and the desirability of achieving total unification.

Because this volume was particularly conceived as a centennial reinterpretation of the legacy of William James, it is appropriate to note that, in several of his writings, James expressed views about unification that appear timely and useful today (James, 1890, 1907/1978). In line with his pluralistic view of the universe, he did not favor one grand, all-embracing theory of psychology. He did, however, grant that working toward such a goal could be beneficial, provided it was not forcibly imposed on the available empirical data.

At the same time, James clearly advocated and practiced unification at lower levels of generality. In his lecture, "The One and the Many" (James, 1907/1978), he stated that "acquaintance with reality's diversities is as important as understanding their connexion" (p. 65), and again, "There are innumerable kinds of connexion that special things have with other special things; and the *ensemble* of any one of these connexions forms one sort of *system* by which things are conjoined" (p. 67). His attitude toward intermediate-level unification is also illustrated in the *Principles* (James, 1890). Although James himself was not especially interested in gathering experimental data, he was firmly committed to the empirical method. In the *Principles*, he provided a thorough survey of empirical psychological findings available at the time, and he consistently linked the empirical findings through his own theoretical interpretations. James seemed to be constantly looking for convergences of findings from widely different sources and obtained by diverse methods. For example, in the chapter on memory, he incorporated materials that ranged from Ebbinghaus's studies with nonsense syllables to hypnosis, aphasias, and double personality (James, 1890, vol. 1, chap. 16). This approach parallels current efforts to integrate laboratory and naturalistic research on memory by highlighting the adaptive function of memory (see, e.g., Neisser & Winograd, 1988).

UNIFYING TRENDS IN PSYCHOMETRICS

I will now turn to examples of unifying trends currently observable within my own field of specialization, psychometrics. I define this field, methodologically, to include psychological testing and statistical analysis, and, substantively, to cover the nature and sources of individual differences, that is, differential psychology.

Trait Hierarchies

The first example concerns the identification of psychological traits through factor analysis. Beginning with Spearman's (1927) theory, with its emphasis on a single *g* factor, this research soon led to the identification of several broad group factors, some found by Spearman's own students and recognized by him. Most were identified by American investigators, notably Thurstone (1938) and Guilford (1967). Over the years, there was a proliferation of narrower and narrower factors, most of which represented a further breakdown of the earlier broad factors. Concurrently, there developed sharp controversies among the proponents of different trait theories. Even today, there are a few surviving exponents of *g*, on the one hand, and of particular patterns of multiple aptitudes, on the other. In the meantime, there have been methodological developments demonstrating that the different solutions are mathematically equivalent and transposable from one to another (Harman, 1976, chap. 15; Schmid & Leiman, 1957). There have also been theoretical developments in the form of trait hierarchies (see Anastasi, 1985b, pp. 130–133; 1988b, pp. 387–388).

This concept of trait hierarchies represents the convergence of the various conflicting theories. It is now coming to be widely recognized that individual differences in intellectual functioning can be described at different levels of generality, from a single common factor within a whole set of variables through increasingly narrower factors at successively lower levels. For different practical applications, a different level of this hierarchy is most appropriate. No one level and no one set of traits corresponds to *the* basic, universal human abilities. The trait hierarchy thus provides a comprehensive, theoretical model that permits practical flexibility in test development and use for specific purposes. The traits identified through factor analysis are simply an expression of observed (and measured) behavioral consistencies. They are not underlying causal entities, which leads to the next question.

Trait Formation

How are traits formed? What determines the behavioral consistencies from which traits are derived? In contrast to trait development, which refers only to the individual's relative standing in different traits, trait formation refers to the organization of behavior into the very traits in terms of which the individual's performance is described. For example, it has been repeatedly shown that an individual may improve his or her performance in quantitative or verbal aptitude by appropriate learning procedures. But the present question is more fundamental: What brings about the correlational pattern that leads to the emergence of a verbal trait or a quantitative trait in the first place?

Several mechanisms have been proposed to explain trait formation. One type of explanation focuses on the contiguity or co-occurrence of learning experiences (Anastasi, 1936; Carroll, 1966; Vernon, 1961). For example, children are likely to develop a broad verbal–educational factor running through all activities learned in school. A narrower factor of numerical aptitude may result from the fact that all mathematical processes tend to be taught together, by the same teacher in the same classroom. Hence, the child who is discouraged, bored, or antagonized during the math period will tend to lag behind in learning *all* mathematical processes; the one who is stimulated and gratified in the math class will tend to learn well all that is taught in that class period and to develop attitudes that will advance his or her subsequent mathematical learning.

A second type of explanation, which has received considerable attention in research on trait formation, is that of differential transfer of training. Some investigators have concentrated on different aspects of acquired knowledge, such as concepts, cognitive skills, information-processing strategies, or learning sets, whereas others have proposed a comprehensive mechanism applicable to all forms of learning (Carroll, 1966; Ferguson, 1954, 1956; Tryon, 1935; Whiteman, 1964). Moreover, because one's culture influences what will be learned at each age, different cultural environments may lead to the formation of different trait patterns. The breadth of the transfer effect determines whether the resulting trait is broad, like verbal comprehension, or narrow, like a specialized perceptual skill.

Research on trait formation offers opportunities for convergence and unification in several directions. The statistical studies on traits have thereby been linked to the following: (a) experimental learning studies with both humans and animals (Anastasi, 1936, pp. 906–908; 1986, pp. 186–189; Burns, 1980; Staats, 1981, 1983; Staats & Burns, 1981; Staats, Staats, Heard, & Finley, 1962); (b) developmental studies of changing ability patterns with age (Anastasi, 1970, pp. 901–902; 1986, pp. 189–191; Lerner, 1986); and (c) cross-cultural studies on the composition of intelligence, as well as similar comparative studies among other populations (e.g., socioeconomic, occupational, geographic), which differ in experiential histories (see Anastasi, 1986, pp. 191–196).

Traits and Situations

Another angle from which traits have been investigated is by comparing trait variance with situational variance in behavioral differences. A long-standing controversy regarding the generalizability of personal traits versus the situational specificity of behavior reached a peak in the 1960s and 1970s (Mischel, 1968; see also Anastasi, 1983b). In its initial stages, this controversy involved, in part, the rejection of an outdated view of traits as fixed, underlying causal entities, a view that psychometricians themselves had been criticizing for several decades. Commenting on the rarity of this stereotype of a "trait theorist," Jackson and Paunonen (1980) wrote in the *Annual Review of Psychology*, "Like witches of 300 years ago, there is confidence about their existence, and even possibly their sinister properties, although one is hard pressed to find one in the flesh or even meet someone who has" (p. 523). It seems to be a popular sport to fabricate a description of what psychometricians allegedly believe and then to demonstrate the obvious falsity of the belief. This is the familiar technique of setting up a straw person and then demolishing it. The psychometric barn is littered with a superabundance of loose straw.

With regard to situational specificity, it is much more characteristic of affective or so-called *personality traits* than it is of abilities. For example, a person may be quite outgoing and sociable at the office, but shy and reserved at social gatherings. Extensive empirical evidence has been assembled (Mischel 1968; Peterson, 1968) showing that individuals do exhibit considerable situational specificity in several noncognitive dimensions, such as aggression, social conformity, dependency, honesty, and attitudes toward authority. Part of the explanation for the higher cross-situational consistency of cognitive functions over that of noncognitive functions may be found in the greater standardization of the individual's reactional biography in the intellectual than in the affective domain (Anastasi, 1970, 1983a). The formal school curriculum, for example, contributes to the development of broadly applicable cognitive skills in the verbal and numerical areas. Affective development, on the other hand, occurs under far more haphazard conditions. Moreover, in the affective domain, the same response may lead to social consequences that are positively reinforcing in one situation and negatively reinforcing in another. The individual may thus learn to respond in quite different ways in different contexts.

The gradual abandonment of extreme views and eventual rapprochement in the trait–situation controversy led to a more comprehensive and flexible model of individual behavior (Epstein & O'Brien, 1985; Mischel, 1977, 1979; Mischel & Peake, 1982). The intermingling of trait and situational components is illustrated by the finding that individuals differ in the extent to which they alter their behavior to meet the demands of each situation. In this trait of social discriminativeness (Mischel, 1979), moderate inconsistency indicates effective and adaptive flexibility, whereas excessive consistency indicates maladaptive rigidity. Another example of the mingling of trait and situational concepts is provided by test anxiety, a well-established trait that is itself defined in part by situational specifications.

Cognitive and Affective Variables

Another linkage that is rapidly emerging is that between cognitive and affective variables (Anastasi, 1985a). In psychometrics, the artificial separation between abilities and so-called *personality traits* has been perpetuated by the available testing instruments. In interpreting test scores, however, personality traits and aptitudes cannot be kept apart. An individual's performance on an aptitude test, as well as his or her performance in school, on the job, or in any other context, is influenced by his or her achievement drive, persistence, value system, presence or absence of handicapping emotional problems, and other characteristics traditionally classified under the heading of "personality."

There is a considerable body of data indicating the effects of transitional affective states on the individual's current performance (see Anastasi, 1985a; Kanfer, Ackerman, & Cudeck, 1989, Part IV; Snow & Farr, 1987). Even more significant, however, is the cumulative effect of more enduring dispositions, or personality traits, on the development of aptitudes. Relevant data have come from several types of research, including long-term longitudinal studies (Eichorn, Clausen, Haan, Honzik, & Mussen, 1981) and, more recently, the application of structural equation modeling to the analysis of causal relations (Shavelson & Bolus, 1982). The findings suggest that the prediction of a person's subsequent intellectual development can be substantially improved by combining information about motivation, attitudes, and self-concept with scores on aptitude tests.

Of special relevance are recent studies of infant development. Several investigators have found substantial correlations between ratings of infant behavior on personality variables and subsequent cognitive development assessed by such instruments as the Bayley Scales of Infant Development and the Stanford-Binet (Birns & Golden, 1972; Matheny, Dolan, & Wilson, 1974; McCall, 1976; Yarrow & Pedersen, 1976). Infants who exhibit positive affect, active interest, and responsiveness in a test situation are likely to learn more and advance faster in intellectual development. They are also likely to respond favorably in later, academic activities that require interaction with adults in goal-oriented tasks. A further advantage arises from the influence such infant behavior has on the behavior of adult caregivers, which will in turn enhance the child's opportunities for learning (Haviland, 1976).

More specifically, studies of the environmental-mastery motive in infants have revealed some promising relations to subsequent measures of intellectual competence. Environmental-mastery behavior is characterized by the infant's observation, exploration, and manipulation of his or her environment. By its very nature, this motive should be a major contributor to cognitive development, and there is increasing evidence in the experimental literature that it is (Hrncir, Speller, & West, 1985; White, 1978; Yarrow & Messer, 1983). In fact, some of the findings suggest that early indicators of a child's environmental-mastery motive may be a better predictor of later intellectual competence than are early measures of competence. Current research on infancy is leading toward a rapprochement between the study of affective and cognitive development. This may help to bring about a more integrated utilization of affective and cognitive data in the interpretation of test results at any age level.

Heredity and Environment

One of the most durable controversies in psychometrics concerns the role of heredity and environment in individual differences. It was soon recognized that traits could not be classified as being *either* hereditary or acquired, but that it was a question of how much of the variance was attributable to one or the other. Investigators were still labeled with the stereotypes of *hereditarians* or *environmentalists*, depending on where they placed the major emphasis. However, the controversy was commonly considered settled, because both kinds of investigators generally asserted that, of course, heredity and environment are equally important—presumably acknowledging the fact that, if you took away either one, you would not have a living organism. Moreover, they often added that heredity and environment always *interact*—that magic word!

These statements exemplify the kind of superficial eclecticism that fails to be truly integrative; they are meaningless statements for several reasons. First, heredity and environment are not unitary constructs; each covers a vast number of variables, and it is these variables that interact with one another, both within and between the two categories. Second, the large majority of studies still deal with either hereditary or environmental variables; rarely are the two joined in a single study to permit the testing of hypotheses about interaction. Some investigators study the effects of learning on individual performance, either through naturalistic studies or through experimental interventions (e.g., Hunt, Mohandessi, Ghodssi, & Akiyama, 1976). Other investigators analyze familial resemblances by correlational procedures, usually ending with a heritability index (see Anastasi, 1971; 1972; 1988b, pp. 364–367; Lerner, 1986, pp. 122–138). This index gives the proportional contribution of heredity to the total variance of a particular trait in a specified population under existing conditions. The information provided by this index, thus, is quite limited. It applies only under the hereditary and environmental conditions in effect at the time; it refers to populations, not individuals; and it does not indicate the degree of modifiability of the trait.

In my Presidential Address to the Division of General Psychology (Division 1) of the American Psychological Association (APA), I argued that investigators may have been asking the wrong questions about heredity and environment and that a more productive approach might be to ask the question, "How?" (Anastasi, 1958). Rather than asking how much of the variance is attributable to heredity and how much to environment, it would be better to investigate the modus operandi of hereditary and environmental influences in the development of individual differences. What is the chain of events whereby particular hereditary and environmental variables interact to produce the behavioral differences observed at any given stage of individual development?

The approach I proposed had some direct impact on subsequent treatment of the heredity–environment problem, particularly among developmental psychologists (Lerner, 1986, chaps. 3, 4, 5; Lerner & Busch-Rossnagel, 1981; Lipsitt, 1970, pp. 151–152; see also Cravens, 1978, pp. 269–270). Combined studies of the influence of genotypes and learning histories of individuals have been rendered more feasible by certain methodological developments, such as *sequential designs*, which combine features of traditional cross-sectional, longitudinal, and time-lag studies; and by *structural equation modeling*, which permits analyses of causal relations among empirically assessed constructs (Gustafson, 1989; McCardle, 1989).

From another angle, some investigators have proposed that the effect of genes on aptitudes may be mediated by affective and motivational factors (Dreger, 1968; Hayes, 1962; Scarr, 1981). That genes could directly determine individual differences in, for example, verbal or mathematical aptitude seems unlikely in the light of current knowledge about the complexities of behavioral development. What is needed is more information about the many intervening steps in the etiological chain from genes to behavior. The role of motivation may represent one such step. The rationale is that abilities develop through the individual's motivationally determined learning history. Supporting evidence is provided by a growing body of animal studies, as well as recent research with human infants (Hayes, 1962; Scarr, 1981; Scott & Fuller, 1951; Searle, 1949; Whimbey & Denenberg, 1966; Yarrow & Messer, 1983). This research also ties in with the previously mentioned linkage between cognitive and affective variables.

Testing in Context

The next example pertains directly to psychological testing, an area where misconceptions abound—among the lay public as well as among some psychologists. My 1966 Presidential Address to the Division of Evaluation, Measurement, and Statistics (Division 5) of the APA opened with the sentence, "It is the main thesis of this paper that psychological testing is becoming dissociated from the mainstream of psychology" (Anastasi, 1967, p. 297). I went on to explain that this dissociation accounted for many of the criticisms underlying the popular antitest revolt, criticisms that frequently arose from actual misuses of tests and misinterpretations of test scores. Such misuses, in turn, resulted from inadequate knowledge about the behavior domain that any particular test was designed to assess. Many vexing problems and controversies have arisen from this source: the futile search for "culture-free tests," the detection and control of test bias, the misapplication of norms, and the misconstrued rises and falls of population scores over time, to name only some of the most conspicuous issues (Anastasi, 1985b, 1989, 1990).

What such problems have in common is a failure to consider the context in which all behavior occurs; from this it follows that all psychological measurement, too, must consider context. Test scores indicate *how well* individuals perform at the time of testing, not *why* they perform as they do. To find out why, we have to evaluate test scores within the person's *antecedent context*; we need to delve into the individual's experiential background. Usually test scores must also be evaluated within the person's *anticipated context*. What is the setting—educational, occupational, societal—in which this person is expected to function and for which he or she is being assessed?

The need for better informed test users has been widely recognized in recent years (Eyde, Moreland, Robertson, Primoff, & Most, 1988). Some investigators have focused on *measurement literacy*, or the statistical knowledge required for proper quantitative interpretation of test scores (Lambert, 1991). Equally important, although less obvious, is the psychological literacy required for substantive interpretation of test performance.

The contextual approach to test interpretation has been variously discussed and advocated under such titles as the "assessment of personal competence" (Sundberg, Snowden, & Reynolds, 1978) or simply "intelligent testing" (Kaufman, 1979; Wesman, 1968). The increasing attention given to such forms of "testing in context" represents a significant unifying trend that is bringing psychological testing closer to the basic science of psychology.

Cognitive Task Analysis Versus Correlational Analysis

Another example of unification within psychometrics pertains to the contributions of cognitive psychology. The construction of psychological tests has, heretofore, relied largely on correlational methods in item selection and in the assessment of reliability and validity. Such analyses are applied to the *products* of thinking, available in the form of item responses and test scores. A different approach is used in cognitive task analysis, which focuses on the *processes* of thinking, whereby the products are constructed by the test taker.

Task analysis, in one form or another, has been in use for many years. Job analysis is one of its forms, which has itself evolved into some highly systematic and elaborated versions (McCormick, 1983; McCormick,

Jeanneret, & Mechan, 1972; Menne, McCarthy, & Menne, 1976; Primoff & Eyde, 1988). Over the years, there has also been scattered research conducted with more broadly applicable, microlevel task analyses, some using thinking-aloud protocols of individuals engaged in task performance (e.g., Brigham, 1932; French, 1965; see also Anastasi, 1988, August). More recently, cognitive psychologists have been developing sophisticated procedures for microlevel task analysis and have applied these procedures extensively to functions ranging from simple laboratory tasks to complex forms of human thinking by experts in various fields of achievement.

Despite the impressions created by popularized versions of the so-called *cognitive revolution*, some of the leading cognitive psychologists have identified significant linkages of cognitive psychology with psychometrics, as well as with other established areas of psychology (Ericsson, 1987; Estes, 1974; E. Hunt, 1987; Simon, 1990). For instance, the microlevel task analyses developed by cognitive psychologists are especially appropriate in the development of diagnostic tests and instructional programs to fit individual needs. Analyzing an individual's performance by dividing it into component processes should help to pinpoint each person's strengths and weaknesses and, thereby, enhance the diagnostic use of tests. This, in turn, should facilitate the tailoring of training programs to the individual's needs.

On the other hand, for selection and classification purposes, tests of broader traits, identified through correlational and factor-analytic procedures, are proving to be more effective. A possible reason is that, except at the most elementary levels, information-processing skills tend to be domain specific and are acquired as the content domain is mastered. Now, the traits identified through factor analysis cover chiefly content domains. Hence, it is possible that such traits may be indirectly identifying clusters of processing skills appropriate for the given content domain. Thus, high performance in verbal aptitude may indicate that the person has developed good information-processing skills for handling verbal functions; the high performer on quantitative or spatial tasks may be displaying good information-processing skills required in those content domains. This may explain why the trait approach has proved so effective in predicting real-life performance.

At a more theoretical level, I can cite Susan Embretson's comprehensive concept of construct validity, which merges cognitive and correlational approaches. Embretson (1983, 1985) described two principal aspects of test validation. The first, *construct representation*, uses the various procedures of cognitive task analysis to identify information-processing components and knowledge stores required to perform the tasks set by the test items. The second, *nomothetic span*, uses correlation with other measures, including other tests, criterion data, and other real-life information, to provide the network of relations within which the test scores are embedded. For tests to have both a scientific rationale and practical utility, both kinds of validity information are needed.[1]

UNIFYING TRENDS IN OTHER FIELDS OF PSYCHOLOGY

I have cited seven examples of unifying trends within my own specialty, psychometrics. These examples were chosen because they seemed to be especially significant and worth pursuing further. Having found more evidence of convergence within psychometrics than is generally recognized, I looked around to see what was happening in other fields of psychology. Even a casual glance revealed a most encouraging picture, with instances of convergence in virtually every field. Although it is beyond the purpose of this chapter to discuss developments in other fields, two examples quickly caught my attention. Because of their scope, comprehensiveness, and potential impact, they are developments that should interest all psychologists. Fortunately, they have both been so fully covered in recent publications, that I need to do little more than mention them.

The first example pertains to the evolving linkage between the experimental psychology of learning and the educational psychology of instruction. This development has been summarized with admirable clarity and thoroughness by Robert Glaser in recent publications (Glaser, 1990; Glaser & Bassok, 1989). For several decades, what would seem to be a natural linkage between the science of learning and the practice of education was conspicuously absent. A major obstacle, which alienated many educators, was the focus of much learning research on extremely simple performance— by animals, by young children, or by college students—on contrived laboratory tasks. Although essential for investigating basic behavioral principles under carefully controlled conditions, these types of experiments were not enough to cover all that learning involves in the lives of twentieth-century humans. It was one of the major contributions of cognitive psychology that learning research was expanded to cover complex human intellectual functions and to include task analyses of both novice and expert performance in many real-life activities. Glaser and his associates have themselves been major contributors to the evolving links between experimental psychology and education, and their own continuing activity augurs well for the viability of this particular convergence.

The second example comes from clinical psychology, or more precisely, from psychotherapy. During the last 50 years, the number of psychotherapy "schools," differing in theoretical orientation and in therapeutic procedures,

---

[1]For other suggested uses of task analysis, in combination with factor analysis, in research on the nature of intelligence, see Anastasi, 1986, pp. 196–197;1988a).

has been growing at an astounding rate. Estimates of the current number range from 250 to over 400 (Beitman, Goldfried, & Norcross, 1989; Norcross, 1986). As early as 1930, some psychologists advocated the search for common principles of psychotherapy (see Goldfried, 1982; Goldfried & Newman, 1986), and basic integrative research dates back to the 1950s (e.g., Dollard & Miller, 1950). However, the current comprehensive rapprochement did not begin until the mid-1970s (e.g., Wachtel, 1977). Some of the momentum for convergence arose from the realization that client treatment would benefit and the training of clinical students would improve with the identification of essential common elements and the utilization of the most effective components from different psychotherapies. Further momentum is provided by professional concerns about the confused image of clinical psychology presented to the public, including potential clients, government agencies, the courts, and third-party insurance payers.

The present integrative movement is pressing forward at such an astounding rate as to constitute a significant event in the history of psychology. It envelops such diverse orientations as the behavioral, the psychodynamic, and the humanistic. A clear picture of what is happening can be found in two well-integrated recent books, one edited by Marvin Goldfried (1982) and the other edited by John Norcross (1986). The movement itself is spreading through many channels. There is an avalanche of articles, books, symposia, conferences, and workshops; new journals have been established and national and international societies formed specifically to explore and facilitate psychotherapy integration. According to one account, "The Zeitgeist is more receptive to integrative efforts than it has ever been before" (Goldfried & Newman, 1986, p. 55).

As a byproduct, the integrative movement is stimulating the systematic exploration and classification of diagnostic categories, of therapeutic processes, and of types of therapy outcome. The identification and precise definition of specific variables within each of the three domains should in turn permit well-designed research on the effectiveness of psychotherapy—research that has, heretofore, proved to be virtually impossible. There is, in fact, a resurgence of research in this area, with extensive participation by the National Institute of Mental Health (e.g., Elkin et al., 1989; Robinson, Berman, & Neimeyer, 1990; Wolfe & Goldfried, 1988).

A FINAL COMMENT

Unifying trends are all around us, in all fields of psychology. They are there to be found by anyone who looks for them. They occur at many levels of generality, although convergence can be most readily effected at intermediate levels. The linkages can extend in various directions: across theoretical orientations, across major fields of specialization, across methodologies, across cultures, across age levels, between theory and empirical research, and between basic science and practice.

At the same time, there are some conspicuous instances of the reverse trend, in which new developments are treated as revolutionary. When this occurs, existing ideas, theories, or methods are discarded to make room for the new (see, e.g., Appley, 1990; Deese, 1987; Gardner, 1985, 1988). It is as though science were regarded as a zero-sum game.

Several thoughtful observers of the current scene (e.g., Appley, 1990; Bevan, 1986; Brislin, 1989, 1990; Rotter, 1990; Staats, 1970, 1987b) have noted that present reward systems, especially in academic and research settings, may encourage individuals to emphasize the novelty of their own contributions and to eschew efforts at integrating them with existing knowledge. A new theory, with its freshly coined label, attracts maximum attention, thereby contributing to career advancement. Such a strategy may yield short-term benefits for the individual psychologist, but it tends to retard the progress of psychology as a science, its effectiveness in solving practical problems, and its public acceptance and credibility—and in the long run, what is good for psychology is also likely to be good for psychologists.

REFERENCES

Anastasi, A. (1936). The influence of specific experience upon mental organization. *Genetic Psychology Monographs*, 18, 245–355.

Anastasi, A. (1958). Heredity, environment, and the question "How?" *Psychological Review*, 65, 197–208.

Anastasi, A. (1967). Psychology, psychologists, and psychological testing. *American Psychologist*, 22, 297–306.

Anastasi, A. (1970). On the formation of psychological traits. *American Psychologist*, 25, 899–910.

Anastasi, A. (1971). More on heritability: Addendum to the Hebb and Jensen interchange. *American Psychologist*, 26, 1036–1037.

Anastasi, A. (1972). Interpretation of heritability: A rejoinder. *American Psychologist*, 27, 975.

Anastasi, A. (1983a). Evolving trait concepts. *American Psychologist*, 38, 175–184.

Anastasi, A. (1983b). Traits, states, and situations: A comprehensive view. In H. Wainer & S. Messick (Eds.), *Principals of modern psychological measurement: A Festchrift for Frederic M. Lord* (pp. 345–356). Hillside, NJ: Erlbaum.

Anastasi, A. (1985a). Reciprocal relations between cognitive and affective development—With implications for sex differences. In T. B. Sonderegger (Ed.),

Nebraska Symposium on Motivation (Vol. 32): Psychology and gender. Lincoln, NE: University of Nebraska Press.

Anastasi, A. (1985b). Some emerging trends in psychological measurement: A fifty-year perspective. *Applied Psychological Measurement, 9,* 121–138.

Anastasi, A. (1986). Experiential structuring of psychological traits. *Developmental Review, 6,* 181–202.

Anastasi, A. (1988a). Explorations in human intelligence: Some uncharted routes. *Applied Measurement in Education, 1,* 207–213.

Anastasi, A. (1988b). *Psychological testing* (6th ed.). New York: Macmillan.

Anastasi, A. (1988, August). *Discussant comments to the two approaches to defining proficiency in military jobs.* Paper presented at the annual convention of the American Psychological Association, Atlanta, GA.

Anastasi, A. (1989). Ability testing in the 1980s and beyond: Some major trends. *Public Personnel Management, 18,* 471–484.

Anastasi, A. (1990). What is test misuse? Perspectives of a measurement expert. *Proceedings of the 1989 ETS Invitational Conference* (pp. 15–25). Princeton, NJ: Educational Testing Service.

Appley, M. H. (1990, Winter). Time for reintegration? *Science Agenda* (American Psychological Association), pp. 12–13.

Beitman, B. D., Goldfried, M. R., & Norcross, J. C. (1989). The movement toward integrating the psychotherapies: An overview. *American Journal of Psychiatry, 146,* 138–147.

Bevan, W. (1986). The journey is everything: General-experimental psychology in the United States after a hundred years. In S. H. Hulse & B. F. Green, Jr. (Eds.), *One hundred years of psychological research in America: G. Stanley Hall and the Johns Hopkins tradition* (pp. 365–397). Baltimore: Johns Hopkins University Press.

Birns, B., & Golden, M. (1972). Prediction of intellectual performance at 3 years from infant test and personality measures. *Merrill-Palmer Quarterly, 18,* 53–58.

Brigham, C. C. (1932). *A study of error.* New York: College Entrance Examination Board.

Brislin, R. W. (1989, August). *Cross-cultural influence on theory development: Developmental and social psychology examples.* Paper presented at the annual convention of the American Psychological Association, New Orleans, LA.

Brislin, R. W. (1990). Applied cross-cultural psychology: An introduction. In R. W. Brislin (Ed.), *Applied cross-cultural psychology* (pp. 9–33). Newbury Park, CA: Sage.

Burns, G. L. (1980). Indirect measurement and behavioral assessment: A case for social behaviorism psychometrics. *Behavioral Assessment, 2,* 197–206.

Carroll, J. B. (1966). Factors of verbal achievement. In A. Anastasi (Ed.), *Testing problems in perspective* (pp. 406–413). Washington, DC: American Council on Education.

Cravens, H. (1978). *The triumph of evolution: American scientists and the heredity–environment controversy, 1900–1941*. Philadelphia: University of Pennsylvania Press.

Deese, J. (1987). The age of cognition. [Review of *The mind's new science: A history of the cognitive revolution*]. *Contemporary Psychology, 32*, 597–598.

Dollard, J., & Miller, N. E. (1950). *Personality and psychotherapy: An analysis in terms of learning, thinking, and culture*. New York: McGraw-Hill.

Dreger, R. M. (1968). General temperament and personality factors related to intellectual performance. *Journal of Genetic Psychology, 113*, 275–293.

Eichorn, D. H., Clausen, J. A., Haan, N., Honzik, M. P., & Mussen, P. H. (Eds.). (1981). *Present and past in middle life*. Orlando, FL: Academic Press.

Elkin, I., Shea, M. T., Watkins, J. T., Imber, S. D., Sotsky, S. M., Collins, J. F., Glass, D. R., Pilkonis, P. A., Leber, W. R., Docherty, J. P., Fieser, S. J., & Parloff, M. B. (1989). National Institute of Mental Health Treatment of Depression Collaborative Research Program: General effectiveness of treatments. *Archives of General Psychiatry, 46*, 971–983.

Embretson, S. E. (1983). Construct validity: Construct representation versus nomothetic span. *Psychological Bulletin, 93*, 179–197.

Embretson, S. E. (Ed.). (1985). *Test design: Developments in psychology and psychometrics*. Orlando, FL: Academic Press.

Epstein, S., & O'Brien, E. J. (1985). The person–situation debate in historical and current perspective. *Psychological Bulletin, 98*, 513–537.

Ericsson, K. A. (1987). Theoretical implications from protocol analysis on testing and measurement. In R. R. Ronning (Ed.), *The influence of cognitive psychology on testing* (pp. 191–226). Hillsdale, NJ: Erlbaum.

Estes, W. K. (1974). Learning theory and intelligence. *American Psychologist, 29*, 740–749.

Eyde, L. D., Moreland, K. L., Robertson, G. J., Primoff, E. S., & Most, R. B. (1988). Test user qualifications: A data-based approach to promoting good test use (Report of the Test User Qualifications Working Group of the Joint Committee on Testing Practices). *Issues in Scientific Psychology*. Washington, DC: American Psychological Association.

Ferguson, G. A. (1954). On learning and human ability. *Canadian Journal of Psychology, 8*, 95–112.

Ferguson, G. A. (1956). On transfer and the abilities of man. *Canadian Journal of Psychology, 10*, 121–131.

French, J. W. (1965). The relationship of problem solving styles to the factor composition of tests. *Educational and Psychological Measurement, 25*, 9–28.

Gardner, H. E. (1985). *The mind's new science: A history of the cognitive revolution*. New York: Basic Books.

Gardner, H. E. (1988, August). *Scientific psychology: Should we bury it or praise it?*

Paper presented at the annual convention of the American Psychological Association, Atlanta, GA.

Glaser, R. (1990). The reemergence of learning theory within instructional research. *American Psychologist, 45*, 29–39.

Glaser, R., & Bassok, M. (1989). Learning theory and the study of instruction. *Annual Review of Psychology, 40*, 631–666.

Goldfried, M. R. (Ed.). (1982). *Converging themes in psychotherapy: Trends in psychodynamic, humanistic, and behavioral practice.* New York: Springer.

Goldfried, M. R., & Newman, C. (1986). Psychotherapy integration: An historical perspective. In J. C. Norcross (Ed.), *Handbook of eclectic psychotherapy* (pp. 25–61). New York: Brunner/Mazel.

Guilford, J. P. (1967). *The nature of intelligence.* New York: McGraw-Hill.

Gustafson, J.-E. (1989). Broad and narrow abilities in research in learning and instruction. In R. Kanfer, P. L. Ackerman, & R. Cudeck (Eds.), *Abilities, motivation, and methodology* (pp. 203–237). Hillsdale, NJ: Erlbaum.

Harman, H. H. (1976). *Modern factor analysis* (3rd ed.). Chicago: University of Chicago Press.

Haviland, J. (1976). Looking smart: The relationship between affect and intelligence in infancy. In M. Lewis (Ed.), *Origins of intelligence: Infancy and early childhood* (pp. 353–377). New York: Plenum.

Hayes, K. J. (1962). Genes, drives, and intellect. *Psychological Reports, 10*, 299–342.

Hrncir, E. J., Speller, G. M., & West, M. (1985). What are we testing? *Developmental Psychology, 21*, 226–232.

Hunt, E. (1987). Science, technology, and intelligence. In R. R. Ronning (Ed.), *The influence of cognitive psychology on testing* (pp. 11–40). Hillsdale, NJ: Erlbaum.

Hunt, J. McV., Mohandessi, K., Ghodssi, M., & Akiyama, M. (1976). The psychological development of orphanage-reared infants: Interventions with outcomes (Tehran). *Genetic Psychology Monographs, 94*, 177–226.

Jackson, D. N., & Paunonen, S. V. (1980). Personality structure and assessment. *Annual Review of Psychology, 31*, 503–551.

James, W. (1890). *The principles of psychology* (2 vols.). New York: Holt.

James, W. (1978). *Pragmatism.* Cambridge, MA: Harvard University Press. (Original work published 1907)

Kanfer, R., Ackerman, P. L., & Cudeck, R. (Eds.). (1989). *Abilities, motivation, and methodology.* Hillsdale, NJ: Erlbaum.

Kaufman, A. S. (1979). *Intelligent testing with the WISC-R.* New York: Wiley.

Koch, S. (1981). The nature and limits of psychological knowledge: Lessons of a century qua "science." *American Psychologist, 36*, 257–269.

Lambert, N. M. (1991). The crisis in measurement literacy in psychology and education. *Educational Psychologist, 26*, 23–35.

Lerner, R. M. (1986). *Concepts and theories of human development* (2nd ed.). New York: Random House.

Lerner, R. M., & Busch-Rossnagel, N. A. (Eds.). (1981). *Individuals as producers of their development: A life-span perspective*. New York: Academic Press.

Lipsitt, L. P. (1970). Developmental psychology. In A. R. Gilgen (Ed.), *Contemporary scientific psychology* (pp. 147–182). New York: Academic Press.

Matheny, A. P., Dolan, A. B., & Wilson, R. S. (1974). Bayley's Infant Behavior Record: Relations between behaviors and mental test scores. *Developmental Psychology, 10,* 696–702.

McCall, R. B. (1976). Toward an epigenetic conception of mental development in the first three years of life. In M. Lewis (Ed.), *Origins of intelligence: Infancy and early childhood* (pp. 97–121). New York: Plenum.

McCardle, J. J. (1989). A structural modeling experiment with multiple growth functions. In R. Kanfer, P. L. Ackerman, & R. Cudeck (Eds.), *Abilities, motivation, and methodology* (pp. 71–118). Hillsdale, NJ: Erlbaum.

McCormick, E. J. (1983). Job and task analysis. In M. D. Dunnette (Ed.), *Handbook of industrial and organizational psychology* (pp. 651–696). New York: Wiley.

McCormick, E. J., Jeanneret, P. R., & Mechan, R. C. (1972). A study of job characteristics and job dimensions as based on the Position Analysis Questionnaire (PAQ). *Journal of Applied Psychology, 56,* 347–368.

Menne, J. W., McCarthy, W., & Menne, J. (1976). A systems approach to the content validation of employee selection procedures. *Public Personnel Management, 5,* 387–396.

Mischel, W. (1968). *Personality and assessment*. New York: Wiley.

Mischel, W. (1977). On the future of personality measurement. *American Psychologist, 32,* 246–254.

Mischel, W. (1979). On the interface of cognition and personality: Beyond the person-situation debate. *American Psychologist, 34,* 740–754.

Mischel, W., & Peake, P. K. (1982). Beyond déjà vu in the search for cross-situational consistency. *Psychological Review, 89,* 730–755.

Neisser, U., & Winograd, E. (Eds.). (1988). *Remembering reconsidered: Ecological and traditional approaches to the study of memory*. New York: Cambridge University Press.

Norcross, J. C. (Ed.). (1986). *Handbook of eclectic psychotherapy*. New York: Brunner/Mazel.

Peterson, D. (1968). *The clinical study of social behavior*. New York: Appleton-Century-Crofts.

Primoff, E. S., & Eyde, L. D. (1988). Job element analysis. In S. Gael (Ed.), *The job analysis handbook for business, industry, and government* (Vol. 2, pp. 807–824). New York: Wiley.

Robinson, L. A., Berman, J. S., & Neimeyer, R. A. (1990). Psychotherapy for the treatment of depression: A comprehensive review of controlled outcome research. *Psychological Bulletin, 108,* 30–49.

Rotter, J. B. (1990). Internal versus external control of reinforcement. A case history of a variable. *American Psychologist, 45,* 489–493.

Rychlak, J. F. (1989). Unification in psychology: My way! our way! no way! [Review of *Annals of theoretical psychology, Vol. 5*]. *Contemporary Psychology, 34,* 999–1001.

Scarr, S. (1981). Testing *for* children: Assessment and the many determinants of intellectual competence. *American Psychologist, 36,* 1159–1166.

Schmid, J., & Leiman, J. (1957). The development of hierarchical factor solutions. *Psychometrika, 22,* 53–61.

Scott, J. P., & Fuller, J. L. (1951). Research on genetics and social behavior at the Roscoe B. Jackson Memorial Laboratory, 1946–1951—A program report. *Journal of Heredity, 42,* 191–197.

Searle, L. V. (1949). The organization of hereditary maze-brightness and maze-dullness. *Genetic Psychology Monographs, 39,* 279–325.

Shavelson, R. J., & Bolus, R. (1982). Self-concept: The interplay of theory and methods. *Journal of Educational Psychology, 74,* 3–17.

Simon, H. A. (1990). Invariants of human behavior. *Annual Review of Psychology, 41,* 1–19.

Snow, R. E., & Farr, M. J. (Eds.). (1987). *Aptitude, learning, and instruction, Vol. 3: Conative and affective processes and analyses.* Hillsdale, NJ: Erlbaum.

Spearman, C. (1927). *The abilities of man.* New York: Macmillan.

Staats, A. W. (1963). *Complex human behavior.* New York: Holt, Rinehart & Winston.

Staats, A. W. (1970). A learning-behavior theory: A basis for unity in behavioral–social science. In A. R. Gilgen (Ed.), *Contemporary scientific psychology* (pp. 183–239). New York: Academic Press.

Staats, A. W. (1975). *Social-behaviorism.* Homewood, IL: Dorsey Press.

Staats, A. W. (1981). Paradigmatic behaviorism, unified theory, unified theory construction methods, and the Zeitgeist of separatism. *American Psychologist, 36,* 239–256.

Staats, A. W. (1983). *Psychology's crisis of disunity: Philosophy and method for a unified science.* New York: Praeger.

Staats, A. W. (1987a). Humanistic volition versus behavioristic determinism: Disunified psychology's schism problem and its solution. *American Psychologist, 42,* 1030–1032.

Staats, A. W. (1987b). Unified positivism: Philosophy for the revolution to unity. In A. W. Staats & L. P. Mos (Eds.), *Annals of theoretical psychology* (Vol. 5, pp. 11–54). New York: Plenum.

Staats, A. W., & Burns, G. L. (1981). Intelligence and child development: What intelligence is and how it is learned and functions. *Genetic Psychology Monographs, 104,* 237–301.

Staats, A. W., & Mos, L. P. (Eds.). (1987). *Annals of theoretical psychology, Vol. 5.* New York: Plenum.

Staats, A. W., Staats, C. K., Heard, W. G., & Finley, J. R. (1962). Operant conditioning of factor analytic personality traits. *Journal of General Psychology, 66,* 101–114.

Sundberg, N. D., Snowden, L. R., & Reynolds, W. M. (1978). Toward assessment of personal competence and incompetence in life situations. *Annual Review of Psychology, 29,* 179–221.

Thurstone, L. L. (1938). Primary mental abilities. *Psychometric Monographs,* No. 1.

Tryon, R. C. (1935). A theory of psychological components—An alternative to "mathematical factors." *Psychological Review, 42,* 425–454.

Vernon, P. E. (1961). *The structure of human abilities* (rev. ed.). London: Methuen.

Viney, W. (1989). The cyclops and the twelve-eyed toad: William James and the unity–disunity problem in psychology. *American Psychologist, 44,* 1261–1265.

Wachtel, P. L. (1977). *Psychoanalysis and behavior therapy: Toward an integration.* New York: Basic Books.

Wesman, A. G. (1968). Intelligent testing. *American Psychologist, 23,* 267–274.

Whimbey, A. E., & Denenberg, V. H. (1966). Programming life histories: Creating individual differences by the experimental control of early experiences. *Multivariate Behavioral Research, 1,* 279–286.

White, B. L. (1978). *Experience and environment: Major influences on the development of the young child* (Vol. 2.). Englewood Cliffs, NJ: Prentice-Hall.

Whiteman, M. (1964). Intelligence and learning. *Merrill-Palmer Quarterly, 10,* 297–309.

Wolfe, B. E., & Goldfried, M. R. (1988). Research on psychotherapy integration: Recommendations and conclusions from an NIMH workshop. *Journal of Consulting and Clinical Psychology, 56,* 448–451.

Yarrow, L. J., & Messer, P. J. (1983). Motivation and cognition in infancy. In M. Lewis (Ed.), *Origins of intelligence: Infancy and early childhood* (2nd ed., pp. 451–477). New York: Plenum.

Yarrow, L. J., & Pedersen, F. A. (1976). The interplay between cognition and motivation in infancy. In M. Lewis (Ed.), *Origins of intelligence: Infancy and early childhood* (pp. 379–399). New York: Plenum.

3

WILLIAM JAMES AND
CONTEMPORARY PSYCHOLOGY

GERALD E. MYERS

When listing the reasons for continuing to honor *The Principles of Psychology* 100 years after its publication, let us not neglect its style. Reviving the hoary saying that its author wrote like a novelist is not my intention. I refer, instead, to its unabashed display of the special personality of William James, for example, in the *Principles*'s final chapter (1890/1981):

> The obstinate insisting that tweedledum is *not* tweedledee is the bone and marrow of life . . . A thing is important if anyone *think* it important . . . The Shah of Persia refused to be taken to the Derby Day, saying "It is already known to me that one horse can run faster than another." He made the question "*which* horse?" immaterial. Any question can be made immaterial by subsuming all its answers under a common head. Imagine what college ball-games and races would be if the teams were to forget the absolute distinctness of Harvard from Yale and think of both as One in the higher genus College. The sovereign road to indifference, whether to evils or goods, lies in the thought of the higher genus. (p. 1267)

This idea carried over to James's conception of the audience for whom he wrote. Although it was designed to be a textbook, the *Principles* was composed not for a faceless profession, but for inquiring individuals with different interests and persuasions. The *Principles* contained something for everyone, and the effect of this was to produce an ongoing readership of solitary prospectors mining the *Principles* where their own lights fall.

Consequently, individuals rather than schools of psychology have reported successful prospecting in the *Principles*. R. B. MacLeod (1964) found phenomenological veins in the Jamesian stream of consciousness; Karl H. Pribram (1976) discovered neurophysiological nuggets in the chapter on emotion; Carl Hovland (1948) located historical lodes in the chapter on memory; and successive researchers continue to uncover Freudian ore as David Shakow and David Rapaport (1964) did previously. Because a scattering of individuals associated with the profession's different divisions confess to Jamesian explorations, the entire field of psychology manifests the enduring significance of the *Principles*. Curiously, however, if O. M. Marx (1968) is right, American psychiatry, which understandably could regard James as a native son, seems underrepresented in paying its respects.

In my book on James (Myers, 1986) that placed the *Principles* center stage, I tried to explain what from that work continues to be of interest. But Philip N. Johnson-Laird (1987), although he reviewed the book generously, regretted that it did not connect James with current cognitive science. This is regrettable because

> the current science of the mind is addressing exactly those problems that James raised. Cognitive scientists are busy reinstalling the machinery of the Kantian workshop [which, as my book emphasized, James had denied]. They accept the reality of both mental and physiological phenomena, but embrace a new and more potent monism: the doctrine that brain and mind are bound together as computer and program. (Johnson-Laird, 1987, p. 13)

Although I still believe that it was beyond my book's scope to connect James's psychology with present-day cognitive science, I want to move in that direction in this chapter.

The story of the cognitive revolution in psychology during the past 2 or 3 decades is also a story of behaviorism's decline. Johnson-Laird (1985) began his review of a recent defense of behaviorism with a joke about two behaviorists who have sex together, after which, one says to the other, "That was fine for you. How was it for me?" When B. F. Skinner (1987a) heard this, he protested that the joke perpetuates the erroneous but too-common assumption that behaviorists are not supposed to have feelings. The question is not whether one is depressed, but what one is feeling when one is depressed. Skinner wrote, "William James anticipated the behaviorist's answer: What we feel is a condition of our body. We do not cry because we are sad, said James, we are sad because we cry" (p. 49).

What James said about emotion and other topics in the *Principles* has led many, besides Skinner, to view the book as a turning point in psychology, away from nineteenth-century rationalistic psychology and toward contemporary behaviorism. But James, who subsequently renounced those slapdash remarks on emotion as cited by Skinner while he also advocated an introspective psychology that was attacked by early behaviorists such as J. B. Watson, relished Johnson-Laird's joke; he would have applauded the revival by cognitive psychologists of his own questions about attention, memory, imagery, and cognition, which were shelved during behaviorism's heyday. Nothing, after all, is more alien to Jamesian psychology than the disappearance of subjectivity in the formulations of operant conditioning.

The practical side of behaviorism would naturally have appealed to James. Impatient with both the dense theorizing and the experimental minutiae of German psychology, he would have preferred Skinner's results at Harvard, for instance, to Clark Hull's quest at Yale for a general theory of behavior. Pragmatism was not officially announced by James until almost a decade after the *Principles* was published; however, it appears unofficially throughout the work. Like Skinner, James demanded theories with cash values, and there is no doubting the payoff of Skinner's principles of animal training. Yet James would surely have balked at the almost total triumph of technology over theory in operant conditioning, or, when theory triumphs, it is a philosophy of behaviorism that is obviously inimical to such chapters in the *Principles* as "The Stream of Thought," "The Consciousness of Self," and "Will."

Today, psychologists studying cognitive processes justifiably see themselves revitalizing tradition. W. K. Estes (1989), in introducing a recent proceeding on cognitive processes, made the following point:

> Its appearance bracketed by the widely celebrated centennial of Ebbinghaus' monograph on memory, and the forthcoming centennial of the publication of William James' *The Principles of Psychology*, this volume combines the experimental and theoretical motifs that have flowed from those two epoch-making works. (p. 11)

In a similar vein, Johnson-Laird (1977) applauded cognitive psychology for its balance of theory and experiment. It rectifies modern psychology's obsession with experiments and the resulting sacrifice of theory, recognizing that the "explanation of experimental results has often been taken as the actual goal of psychology. It is a poor substitute for understanding human behavior and mentality" (p. 2). Recalling the extraordinary mix of experiment reporting and theory constructing in the *Principles*, would James have agreed with this? No, because all evidence points to James's preference for cognitive psychology's look, prolific in theoretical thickets, over behaviorism's desert-like appearance.

But beyond cognitive psychology's look, how would James have felt about its substance? He would have found it bewildering, I believe, and for understandable reasons. *Cognitive science* (Garnham, 1985) attempts to be nothing less than a synthesis of cognitive psychology, artificial intelligence (AI), linguistics, and the logic and philosophy of science. Cognitive scientists are, themselves, the best witnesses to the complexities and difficulties of their enterprise, to the resistances both to syntheses between these disciplines and to consensus within them. The controversies are so quick to change, technical, and philosophically ramified that trying to track James's probable moves would be a fruitless assignment. But relating one feature of cognitive science, the reinstatement of the Kantian mental workshop in the form of inferred cognitive processes, to Jamesian psychology is, as Johnson-Laird suggested, a task worth doing.

This question then arises: If cognitive scientists successfully hunt down cognitive processes, would this not force revisions in the *Principles*? Consider James's claim against Helmholtz that object perception does not involve unconscious sensation interpretation. James (1981) wrote, "Now there seem no good grounds for supposing this additional wheelwork in the mind" (p. 756). Also recall his claim that the Kantian theory, espoused by nineteenth-century psychologists who held that the perception of space (time and causality also) is a mental process and is "mythological, because I am conscious of no such Kantian machine-shop in my mind . . . I have no introspective experience of mentally producing or creating space" (p. 905). Add similar contentions in the *Principles* such as the objections to Wundt's feelings of innervation and to psychologists' analyses of emotion—the objections urged on behalf of allegedly more accurate introspective reports and more elegant models of underlying physiology—and James's concept of a two-term psychology becomes apparent. One term is conscious experience, the second is corresponding physiology, and psychology's job is to correlate the two. A putative third term such as an intermediary collection of unconscious, inferred mental processes, of the kind that are nowadays the bread and butter of cognitive science, is evidently rejected by Jamesian psychology.

Whether James was always consistent on this issue is problematic, given his apparent acceptance of unconscious inferences in the chapters in the *Principles* on discrimination and comparison, reasoning, and necessary truths. Johnson-Laird's interest was aroused by what I (1986) wrote on this, because he (1977) had once associated himself with James in asserting the role of abstract mental operations in reasoning. Consider an instance of those inferences called *three-term series problems* or *linear syllogisms* that are used in intelligence tests: If John is shorter than Fred, and John is taller than Charles, then Charles is shorter than Fred. Johnson-Laird adopted I. M. L. Hunter's analysis that two discrete mental operations are involved in the inference. The second premise must be converted to *Charles is shorter than John*, and the two premises must be mentally rearranged as (a) *Charles is shorter than John*, and (b) *John is shorter than Fred*. "Like William James, he [Hunter] took the view that once a canonical set of premises had been constructed, the transitive deduction could easily be made: . . . Charles is shorter than Fred" (Johnson-Laird & Wason, 1977, p. 77).

Serial reasoning, James (1890/1981) emphasized, involves mental operations or cognitive processes:

> In passing from term to term in any such series we are conscious not only of each step of difference being equal to (or greater or less than) the last, but we are conscious of proceeding in a *uniform direction*, different from other possible directions." (p. 464)

The ability to reason serially and independently of the order that our experiences occur is a native mental capacity rather than the result of habit or association. It was this line of thought that led me (1986) to suggest that James's view on this bears some resemblance to Noam Chomsky's as shown in his famous (Chomsky, 1959) critical review of Skinner's *Verbal Behavior in Language* (1957).

Where does this leave the relation of James and cognitive science? In admitting mental opeations as a kind of reasoning that results, not from experience, but from the mind's own innate structure, did James not, in effect, acknowledge a set of cognitive processes intervening between conscious mental events and their corresponding cerebral–physiological conditions? I continue to think that James, despite seeming vacillations, intended to preserve the simpler two-term scheme; accordingly, mental operations hunted down by cognitive psychologists would either be introspectively discoverable and, thus, among the class of conscious mental events, or they would not be introspectively discoverable and, thus, among the class of nonconscious cerebral–physiological events. But this position is hardly defensible if cognitive psychology successfully infers a vast range of cognitive processes that are neither introspectively discoverable nor evidentially assignable to the brain.

Neither James nor anyone else, I suppose, can offer sound a priori reasons for rejecting nonintrospectively discoverable mental processes that otherwise resemble introspectively discoverable ones. And whether the processes are inferred by Johnson-Laird (1976), Nisbett and Wilson (1977), or Kosslyn (1983), they are inferred for plausible, if not conclusive, reasons—

maybe James would have been convinced by the evidence that these psychologists have presented. His own penchant for speculating about internal mental workings left him unsympathetic to Skinner's (1977) claim that "cognitive psychology is an appeal to ignorance. It is putting explanatory entities of one kind or another inside the organism" (p. 279). I conclude that apart from preferring a simpler two-term system, which he himself had trouble respecting fully, James had no overriding objections to the reinstatement of the Kantian mental machine-shop by current cognitive science. Accordingly, some revisions in the *Principles* on this issue would have seemed appropriate to James where the evidence warrants.

Unlike the Shah of Persia, however, James would certainly have asked *which* alleged mental processes should be acknowledged. To be convincing, the evidence must meet several standards, and, not surprisingly, some candidates proposed as cognitive operations look more promising than others. What proves that inferred events actually occur rather than just appearing as if they do? Returning to Johnson-Laird's example of linear syllogistic reasoning, what guarantees that the deductive step—*Therefore, Charles is shorter than Fred*—is preceded by two actual, rather than appearing-as-if, mental operations? When the reasoning is explicitly reconstructed as a methodical three-step argument, it will be clear how the conclusion can be deduced from the premises, but of course, it does not prove that this is how it must be accomplished. Perhaps the actual process, whether psychological or neurological, is a one-step process, an intuitive sprint from grasping the premises to making the conclusion.

The reference to intuition raises other concerns. Are concepts, such as insight and intuition, treated fairly in the specialized inquiries of individual cognitive psychologists? T. Bastick (1982), alluding to experimental work by Johnson-Laird and others, observed, "There is also a series of logic experiments using the term insight. They have little to do with the concept of insight as generally used except they use the term insight as a synonym of understanding of a logical relationship" (p. 20). So it may prove troublesome to check out specific claims about *which* concepts are instantiated by the inferred processes. This points to another problem: How informative are descriptions, customarily applied to conscious experiences, when they get transferred to cognitive processes? It is not always evident whether "I considered p, then q, and deduced r" is meant to describe an inferred process or a conscious one that the inferred process is meant to explain. If the hunted functions are conceived on either AI or neurological models, what is or is not achieved in applying everyday psychological descriptions to them is far from clear.

Kosslyn (1983) helped to clarify the issue. Experiments have shown that, when asked to rotate objects in images, we mentally respond in ways not revealed by simple introspection, for example, rotation time increases linearly and our minds function at a constant speed while we attempt to accelerate the rotation. These are consequences of mental activity, not of conscious or introspectively discoverable experience, but of underlying neural activities or representations. Kosslyn (1983) asserted, "We haven't the faintest idea of how to theorize about the nature of conscious experience per se. In fact, the experience itself may well be entirely epiphenomenal with regard to mental activity" (p. 208). But if this is so, if the kind of conscious experience to which "using imagery in certain ways" is ordinarily applied is theoretically irrelevant to the cognitive scientist's inquiry, and if the relevant processes are matters of conjecture, to *what* is "using imagery in certain ways" now being applied with any remaining confidence at all?

Kosslyn (1983) stated that experiments "validate the introspection that objects in images seem to rotate by passing through intermediate positions along a trajectory" (p. 39), and this would definitely have intrigued James whose psychology aimed at centering in consciousness via introspection what was previously overlooked or was only dimly apprehended at the margins of consciousness. A new psychology, unveiling mental operations for conscious inspection via careful introspection combined with ingenious laboratory testing, would have excited James. But a psychology that theoretically bypasses conscious experience in pursuit of conjectured processes would have disappointed him because of its perpetuating behaviorism's prejudice that conscious experience can be skirted in developing a science of behavior. The durability of cognitive science, I presume, will be tested by public perception of how practically significant its yield is. An ever-accumulating mass of unmanageable processes, unavailable for the pleasures of introspective discovery, with only theory in its favor, is unlikely to sustain interest. Curiously, the literature of cognitive science may someday resemble James's *Principles* in being a prospector's quarry—considerable dull rock for some, yet, for others, some real gold in the form of cognitive processes that are either revealed to introspection or, if not that, are agreed on as being essential for certain kinds of psychological explanations and predictions.

The *Principles* provides a marvelous historical backdrop. It gives contemporary theorizing a temporal texture and a linkage with the traditions that it surveys. It has assisted psychologists intent on developing their field's scientific potential, which is consistent with James's announced goal of presenting psychology as a natural science. For many, however, its charm resides elsewhere. It resides in those pages where the limitations of psychology as a science are strongly intimated, where psychology is conceived as inherently fragmentary and requiring philosophical supplements. Examples of this can be found in the *Principles* in the discussions of the self, will, emotion, perception, and the mind–body relation.

One's attitudes toward science and psychology largely determine one's attitudes toward the *Principles* and the intellectual career of James. Its natural affinities are less with cognitive or behavioral science than with phenomenological disciplines and clinical areas of psychology where the art rather than its science receives notice. James's spirit in the *Principles*, I surmise, is shared by M. Merleau-Ponty, P. McKellar, A. Gurwitsch, J. Adelson, R. May, J. J. Gibson, E. Minkowski, E. Strauss, D. Shakow, D. Rapaport, R. B. Macleod, K. Pribram, J. Singer, G. Allport, G. Murphy, A. Maslow, S. Rosenweig, T. Natsoulas, and C. Rogers.

Differences in points of view are often better disclosed in journalistic exchanges than in more ponderous publications. Consider Rosenweig's reaction to Skinner's (1987a) declaration in "Outlining A Science of Feeling." Skinner wrote, "All words for feelings seem to have begun as metaphors, and it is significant that the transfer has always been from public to private. No word seems to have originated as the name of a feeling" (pp. 490, 501). Rosenweig (1987) objected to this on the grounds that chance verbal behavior (contingencies of reinforcement) cannot explain the impressive variety of feelings revealed to the introspections of poets, patients, and phenomenological psychologists. Skinner (1987b) replied that, instead of denying the great variety of introspectively discoverable feelings,

> I was simply saying that no one has ever consistently described them introspectively, certainly not poets or patients, or, at least so far, phenomenologists . . . by looking at the contingencies of reinforcement under which what is felt occurs a much better account may be reached. (p. 579)

If one were actually to engage in the systematic fussiness demanded by Skinner's program, no time would be left for facing one's experiences poetically or phenomenologically, a contingency that would have depressed James intensely. Understandably, the personal cost involved has inhibited Jamesian temperaments from making a science of feeling their top priority.

In the *Principles*, one comes across a special reason, albeit mostly unnoticed, for further skepticism about a science of feeling. This reason lies in James's habit of giving meaning to expressions that are initially vague, sometimes to the extent that whether they are considered literal or metaphorical is beside the point. James's language is often idiosyncratic, even when he formulated a major question or topic for investigation. For example, he asked his readers to join him in identifying "the central part of the self" (p. 371), as if readers would know immediately what this means and how to proceed in making the identification. But, of course, his audience, unaccustomed to conversing about "the central part of the self," would wait in suspense until he further indicated what this meant. And, depending on the reader, the suspense is or is not terminated as James teased his audience with definitions, the following being perhaps the clearest:

It is the source of effort and attention, and the place from which appear to emanate the fiats of the will. A physiologist who should reflect upon it in his own person could hardly help, I should think, connecting it more or less vaguely with the process by which ideas or incoming sensations are "reflected" or pass over into outward acts. (p. 285)

Feelings are being described in this quote (how one feels in trying to connect certain words with one's introspectively discoverable experiences), but expressions like "the central part of the self" and "pass over into outward acts" that describe are given meanings in the process; contrary to Skinner's claim, their meanings largely originate in James's way of tagging feelings or states of consciousness. Whether one believes he or she has grasped those meanings depends on whether one finds his or her experiences aptly indicated by Jamesian language. It is a kind of language in which phrases and sometimes paragraphs (not single words) are given meanings in the very process of being applied to conscious experience.

If introspective language is of this kind, defined in use, and often redefined on the next occasion, then Skinner's hope for a codified, consistent terminology worthy of a science of feeling is doomed. Introspective language need not imitate James's language; pedestrian versions exist and are used as data by behaviorists and cognitive scientists. It is only introspective language of the personal kind, conveyed through applications to personal experience for which standard descriptions are unavailable, that defies translation into ready-made public editions. For those whose aim is science, such language is frustrating. For others, however, in the Jamesian language lies his psychology's appeal. These people enjoy the process of connecting that language with their own consciousness, because making those connections produces new experiences that, compared with former ones, expand introspective awareness in various ways. The *Principles* demonstrates that introspective language is not always meant to lay bare what is already present to consciousness; it is used to induce novel, laminated-like experiences through spontaneous welding of words with feelings.

Cognitive psychology seeks a science of the mind, while admitting, as Johnson-Laird observed, the reality of mental as well as physiological phenomena. It proposes, he said, to integrate both into a potent new monism that links brain and mind as computer and program. Would James have had reasons, beyond those already mentioned, for resisting this new monism? Yes, although the explanation is complex.

The *Principles* vehemently rejects mechanistic accounts of mental processes, so, if identifying the mind as the brain's software is to mechanize it, then James would have indeed objected to the computer analogy. Johnson-Laird's cognitive psychology, however, seems to limit the analogy, stop short of mechanism, and resemble James's concept of mind more than one would expect. He ended his *Mental Models* (Johnson-Laird, 1983) on a rather enigmatic note, conceding that there may be "aspects of spirituality, morality, and imagination" (p. 477) incapable of being modeled in computer programs and, thus, are forever inexplicable. In any scientific theory, however, the mind is an automaton; but this, he added (without elaboration), is merely a consequence of the computability of scientific theories and is neither dehumanizing nor inconsistent with our being responsible agents.

> It *is* a proposition, however, that may lead us in time to revise our concept of computation. At the moment that I am writing this sentence, I know that I am thinking, and that the topic of my thoughts is precisely the ability to think about how the mind makes possible this self-reflective knowledge. Such thoughts begin to make the recursive structure of consciousness almost manifest, like the reflections of a mirror within a mirror, until the recursive loop can no longer be sustained. (Johnson-Laird, 1983, p. 477)

New interpretations stemming from this might well have intrigued James, especially when they are joined with other suggestions by Johnson-Laird in *Mental Models*. Johnson-Laird, like Kosslyn, was cautious about consciousness. "No one really knows what consciousness is, what it does, or what function it serves" (p. 448). But if it is not wholly mysterious, it is partially open to scientific explanation so that some mental processes are conceivable as being the cerebral computer's programming. Johnson-Laird's hypothesis that consciousness is a property of a special class of algorithms rather than of the functions they compute—"it's not what you do, it's the way that you do it" (p. 475)—also indicates why an organism's consciousness might not be decisively testable.

> Consciousness might have no obvious hallmarks in behavior if behavior depends on the functions that are computed and not on how they are computed. They can always be computed by a serial device, such as a Turing machine, which cannot be conscious. (p. 475)

James would have found these ideas ingenious and stimulating, some of them resembling his own in certain respects, but, despite the psycho–physical dualism officially adopted in the *Principles*, he would surely have questioned Johnson-Laird's confidence in asserting the existence of consciousness as a distinct type of occurrence to be fitted to a scientific explanation. His doubts that *consciousness* names something special occur throughout the *Principles*, usually in asides or footnotes, and were later elevated to philosophical doctrine in "Does 'Consciousness' Exist?" (1904) and the other papers in *Essays in Radical Empiricism* (1912). He was, of course, not denying the obvious, that we are conscious beings, but only that something called consciousness sticks out for discrete identification within our experiences. The challenge of locating a monistic replacement for psycho–physical dualism, for James, focused on how to unite experience (not consciousness) with the brain and body.

James's monism that later replaced the psycho–physical dualism of the *Principles*, called *neutral monism* by Bertrand Russell and others, purportedly showed that experiences, on the one hand, and physiological–physical processes, on the other, are not only more alike than is ordinarily realized, they are in fact dual variations of what James called *pure experiences*. His idea was that the distinction between mental (experiences) and physical (brain) is a distinction within something more basic, pure experiences, which in themselves are neither mental nor physical. James's monism, compared with Johnson-Laird's or that of cognitive science, is more extreme; whereas the latter leaves the hardware–software distinction unquestioned, this dichotomy was precisely the sort of thing that James's monism tried to dissolve. Picturing the mind (experiences) as the brain's program would, therefore, hardly have satisfied James, because that would leave a dualism or irreducible difference between the brain's hardware and its programmed experiences.

Putting aside his metaphysical monism, how would James have regarded the computer model of the mind? He could accept that some mental processes are computational and can be simulated by computers, but that all or most are, he could not. (Artificial intelligence, he would likely have asserted, is well named, thus, behooving us always to remember that however helpful it may be to compare human intelligence with artificial intelligence, they are two different things, which is why they can be compared.) James could not accept the monism of cognitive science, given his concept of *intentionality* as formulated, for instance, in the chapter in the *Principles*, "The Stream of Thought." States of mind or mental processes are intentional in being about or referring to things. This question then arises: Can this feature of intentionality be modeled in computer programs?

No, James, in effect, said in the *Principles*, because intentionality is inseparable from introspective experience, and if computers have no experiences to introspect, then they cannot be programmed to intend things as we do. Subsequently, in developing pragmatism, James seemingly abandoned intentionality as an introspectively discoverable, yet mysterious, self-transcendent feature of mental processes by trying to analyze it behavioristically. A move of this sort, however, does not transfer intentionality into the computer model nor does it transfer the mind into the brain, as behaviorists like Skinner would insist.

James would probably have agreed with recent philosophical dissents to the computer model of the mind. Hilary Putnam, who years ago pioneered the software concept of the mind, now disavows it, because he sees no way of construing intentionality in terms of algorithms. Putnam argued that, semantically, intentional reference on our part is historically conditioned, and this is sufficient for disqualifying states of mind from being computational states of the brain–computer.

The meanings of our words used to express our beliefs and desires, Putnam (1988) held, are determined by the conditions under which they were learned; therefore, the meanings of our words cannot be literally in our heads. Two beliefs, one held by Jones and one held by Smith, might be qualitatively the same and, thus, take the same software descriptions; however, due to their being situated in two different historical chains of events or careers, which define the differences between Jones and Smith, they may differ in what they are about or refer to. Whether or not the descriptions of two distinct mental states that are qualitatively identical mean the same thing cannot be ascertained merely by examining them in isolation, outside their historical and environmental contexts; this also cannot be ascertained merely by inspecting isolated computational states. Thus, our mental states, with their special feature of intentionality, cannot be equated with a computer's computational functioning.

Johnson-Laird considered Putnam's earlier arguments in the 1970s for concluding that mental states cannot be modeled in computer programs, because meanings or concepts cannot be envisaged as cerebral entities that are scientifically describable. (How he would respond to Putnam's latest writing on the issue remains uncertain.) As I understand him, Johnson-Laird (1983) reacted to Putnam's contentions by denying that language reflects a particular metaphysics; consequently, some meanings are correctly assigned to the world and others to the mind. Psychology has the last word here, because "whatever the semantics of a term, its relation to the world depends on human cognitive capacity" (p. 204). Because Putnam's point is that no account of human cognitive capacities can reduce them to computational functions (parallel or otherwise), it seems that in continuing to offer a computational account, Johnson-Laird has not actually joined Putnam on the crucial issue.

Had James lived some 20 years longer, to digest the significance of Kurt Gödel's contributions to mathematical logic in the 1930s, he would have delighted, if only out of his own impatience with formal logic, in Gödel's famous proof that formal mathematical systems have built-in limitations. Such systems, Gödel demonstrated, contain propositions that can be neither proved nor disproved within those systems; no algorithm can be used for establishing them as theorems within the systems. The most recent of a long line of thinkers to draw the implications of this for theories of the mind and consciousness is Roger Penrose. The implications, he believed, are still not understood by our computer culture.

What struck Penrose—and would surely have struck James—is that mathematicians can recognize the truth of a proposition even though that proposition is not formally provable. The truth of some mathematical propositions can and must be seen independently of computations that are fully formalized. Besides computations, consciousness seems necessary for comprehending mathematical truths. Penrose (1989) wrote

> We must "see" the truth of a mathematical argument to be convinced of its validity. This "seeing" is the very essence of consciousness. It must be present *whenever* we directly perceive mathematical truth. When we convince ourselves of the validity of Gödel's theorem we not only "see" it, but by so doing we reveal the very non-algorithmic nature of the "seeing" process itself. (p. 418)

This would have delighted James because it vindicates his contention throughout the *Principles* that a state of mind that is understanding or knowing is not reducible to something else allegedly more basic. States of mind or consciousness are experiences, and the introspective descriptions of experiences that are understandings or knowings, as Penrose reminded us, typically refer to seeing (with the mind's eye). It may well be that computational cognitive processes are prerequisites for certain kinds of problem solving, but as such, they condition rather than constitute the experience itself of seeing the solution. Experiences or consciousness of this sort may or may not assist in the computations that precede, but they are quite certainly an essential part of the computations' results that are not themselves still further computations. Arriving at a conclusion is not the same as basking in it.

Although Penrose did not refer to James, his anecdotal, introspective reports of what it is like to experience moments of insight and realization, if appropriately inserted in the *Principles*, would admirably serve Jamesian intentions. Especially interesting are his remarks about the role of aesthetic criteria in forming our judgments. Citing Dirac's claim, for instance, that it was his strong sense of beauty that led to his finding the equation for the electron, Penrose (1989) wrote, "My impression is that the strong conviction of the *validity* of a flash of inspiration . . . is very closely bound up with its aesthetic qualities. A beautiful idea has a much greater chance of being a correct idea than an ugly one" (p. 421). James concluded the *Principles* on almost the same note, suggesting that our sense of rationality consists, in part, of aesthetic criteria that are native to our mental structure rather than acquired through experience. In declaring that "many of the so-called metaphysical principles are at bottom only expressions of aesthetic feeling" (p. 1265), he meant that the full story of how natural science develops must include the presence of both aesthetic and moral criteria. The value-free characterization of physics and chemistry, much less of psychology, is sheer myth. James never really did justice to his respect for the role of the aesthetic in cognition, and no one has done justice to the lifelong role of the aesthetic in James's thought. I (Myers, 1986) made a small effort, but only that, in this direction. In any event, when Johnson-Laird acknowledged the possible elusiveness of aesthetic and moral dimensions of mind for cognitive science, it is clear that James would have heartily concurred.

Axiological principles, including aesthetic ones, assume renewed importance when, as it is in cognitive science, theory is granted equal status with experimentation. The history of science shows how theoretical considerations inevitably embrace evaluations, weighing and comparing strengths and weaknesses of components within a theory as well as those of rival theories. The scientist's requirement to step back from the theory in order to assess it from time to time proves the point that theory building is inherently a normative activity, and it points to a fresh way of appreciating a concept in the *Principles* that some psychologists still remember, what James called the *psychologist's fallacy*.

James (1890/1981) wrote, "The *great* snare of the psychologist is the *confusion of his own standpoint with that of the mental fact* about which he is making his report. I shall hereafter call this the 'psychologist's fallacy' *par excellence*" (p. 195). Confusing an act of thinking with its object is a glaring instance of this fallacy, often leading to the erroneous conclusion that if the object of one's thinking is complex, so must be the thinking itself. To avoid this fallacy, psychologists need to recognize the differences between thinking and what the thinking is about; whereas thinking is intentional or referential, the objects of thinking are not, and whereas objects of thought may be the same for diverse acts of thinking, no two acts of thinking are ever identical.

Adapting James's concept for distinguishing the psychologist's standpoint from the objectives of that standpoint may be useful today. The psychologist's fallacy occurs when the distinction is forgotten, when the standpoint itself is supposed to be another research product. The fallacy resembles the Cretan's fallacy, "All Cretans are liars;" it occurs in permitting the standpoint from which the assertion is made to be absorbed into the assertion's own domain of reference.

Certain criticisms of behaviorism, such as Johnson-Laird's joke at the beginning of this chapter, in effect, charge it with committing this fallacy. To his critics, Skinner's behaviorism suffers from the fact that Skinner's standpoint is, itself, explained behavioristically. Cognitive psychology risks the same if it allows its own distinctive viewpoint to be explained computationally. It is perhaps Johnson-Laird's appreciation of this that led him to conclude his *Mental Models* on the somewhat enigmatic note referred to previously.

A memorable feature of the *Principles* is the way that James retained his own identity amid all the psychologizing that took place. As a theorizer, avoiding the psychologist's fallacy, he was never eclipsed by the theorized. This is what is referred to when talking of the personal flavor of Jamesian psychology. James, the psychologist, was always on top of his data, ever sorting, speculating, and evaluating.

What is sensed in the *Principles* is the limit that the psychologist's standpoint imposes on psychology itself. Physicists do not run the risk of losing themselves to their own theories, but psychologists do; professionally, there is no physicist's fallacy. James's psychology is as impressive for what it does not claim as for what it does. The concluding words of the *Principles*, "Even in the clearest parts of Psychology our insight is insignificant enough" (p. 1280), illustrate this point. James is remembered no less for his perspective on psychology than for the psychology itself. He removed all danger, therefore, of our confusing some tweedledee in psychology with the Jamesian tweedledum.

REFERENCES

Bastick, T. (1982). *Intuition*. New York: Wiley.

Chomsky, N. (1959). [Review of *Verbal behavior in language*]. *Language, 35*, 26–58.

Estes, W. K. (1989). Early and late memory processing in models for category learning. In C. Izawa (Ed.), *Current issues in cognitive processes* (pp. 11–24). Hillsdale, NJ: Erlbaum.

Garnham, A. (1985). *Psycholinguistics*. London: Methuen.

Hovland, C. (1948). Retention and transfer of learning. In E. G. Boring et al. (Eds.), *The foundations of psychology* (pp. 164–180). New York: Wiley.

James, W. (1904). Does "consciousness" exist? *Journal of Philosophy, Psychology, and Scientific Methods, 1*, 477–491.

James, W. (1912). *Essays in radical empiricism*. New York: Longmans, Green, and Company.

James, W. (1981). *The Principles of Psychology* (3 vols.). Cambridge, MA: Harvard University Press. (Original work published 1890)

Johnson-Laird, P. N., & Miller, G. (1976). *Language and perception*. Cambridge, MA: Harvard University Press.

Johnson-Laird, P. N., & Wason, P. C. (Eds.). (1977). *Thinking: Readings in cognitive science*. Cambridge, England. Cambridge University Press.

Johnson-Laird, P. N. (1983). *Mental Models*. Cambridge: Harvard University Press.

Johnson-Laird, P. N. (1985, July 19). You exist, do I? Critical review of G. E. Zwiff's *Behaviorism*. *Times Literary Supplement*, pp. 787–788.

Johnson-Laird, P. N. (1987, March 3). Introspection and the body. Critical review of G. E. Myers' *William James*. *London Review of Books*, pp. 13–14.

Kosslyn, S. M. (1983). *Ghosts in the mind's machine*. New York: Norton.

MacLeod, R. B. (1964). Phenomenology: A challenge to experimental psychology. In T. W. Wann (Ed.), *Behaviorism and phenomenology* (pp. 47–48). Chicago and London: University of Chicago Press.

Marx, O. M. (1968). American psychiatry without William James. *Bulletin of the History of Medicine, XLII*, 52–61.

Myers, G. E. (1986). *William James: His life and thought*. New Haven, CT: Yale University Press.

Nisbett, R. E., & Wilson, T. (1977). Telling more than we can know: Verbal reports on mental processes. *Psychological Review, 84*, 231–259.

Penrose, R. (1989). *The emperor's new mind: Concerning computers, minds, and the laws of physics*. New York: Oxford University Press.

Pribram, K. (1976). Self-Consciousness and intentionality: A model based on an experimental analysis of the brain mechanisms involved in the Jamesian theory of motivation and emotion. In G. Schwartz & D. Shapiro (Eds.), *Consciousness and self-regulation: Advances in research* (pp. 51–100). New York: Plenum.

Putnam, H. (1988). *Representation and reality*. Cambridge, MA: MIT Press.

Rosenweig, S. (1987, May 29). Towards a science of feeling. Letter to editor. *Times Literary Supplement*, p. 579.

Shakow, D., & Rapaport, D. (1964). The influence of Freud on American psychology [monograph]. *Psychological Issues, iv*, Abstract No. 1. New York: International Universities Press.

Skinner, B. F. (1957). *Verbal behavior in language*. New York: Appleton-Century-Crofts.

Skinner, B. F. (1977). Burrhus Skinner. In D. Cohen (Ed.), *Psychologists on psychology* (pp. 262–290). New York: Taplinger.

Skinner, B. F. (1987a, May 8). Outlining a science of feeling. *Times Literary Supplement*, pp. 490, 501.

Skinner, B. F. (1987b, June 19). A science of feeling. Letter to editor. *Times Literary Supplement*, p. 661.

II

CELEBRATING *THE PRINCIPLES OF PSYCHOLOGY*

4

EVOLUTION AND REVISION OF THE *PRINCIPLES*

D. BRETT KING

Few, if any, twentieth-century psychologists would deny the landmark contribution of William James's monumental classic *The Principles of Psychology* (1890/1981). James's genius for molding ideas into riveting prose has stimulated and inspired numerous generations of psychologists. A cursory reading of the first seven volumes of the *History of Psychology in Autobiography* (Boring, Langfeld, Werner, & Yerkes, 1952/1968; Boring & Lindzey, 1967; Lindzey, 1974, 1980; Murchison, 1930/1961, 1932/1961, 1936/1961) reveals the pervasive influence of James's writing; psychologists such as James Rowland Angell, Mary Whiton Calkins, Harvey Carr, John F. Dashiell, John Dewey, Donald O. Hebb, Harry Helson, Walter Hunter, William McDougall, Gardner Murphy, Lewis M. Termin, and Edward L. Thorndike cite the commanding relevance of *The Principles of Psychology* to their intellectual quests.

The Principles of Psychology remains as more than a historical artifact. Perry (1935) noted that James's *Principles* "was a tolerant, curious book; and because its author saw so wide a range of possibilities, and was so promiscuously hospitable to them, almost any recent development in psychology

67

can trace a line of ancestry there" (p. 91). Perry's observation is still remarkably true. According to the annual *Social Sciences Citation Index* (Institute for Scientific Information, 1990, 1991), in 1989 and 1990, scholars cited *The Principles of Psychology* in more than 240 articles in journals as diverse as *Memory and Cognition, Journal of Conflict Resolution, Journal of Economic Issues, Journal of Nonverbal Behavior, Canadian Journal of Aging,* and *Journal of Mathematical Psychology*. In this individual celebration, I will briefly trace the evolution of *The Principles of Psychology* and discuss James's interest in a revision of his great book.[1]

THE EVOLUTION OF THE PRINCIPLES

In 1872, Henry Holt supervised the publication of the American Science Series, a succession of volumes by leading scholars who presented American science from an evolutionary perspective. Initially, Holt asked John Fiske, a prominent Spencerian scholar, to write a psychology textbook for the series (Madison, 1966). When Fiske became too burdened to accept the offer, he recommended William James as a suitable candidate for the project. In 1878, Holt petitioned James to write the psychology textbook. James accepted the challenge with the condition that the book have a fall 1880 deadline. Holt confessed in a June 8, 1878, letter

> I am a little staggered by the length of time which you think it would take to write the Psychology and hope that your health will improve and your engagements admit of modifications so that the work can be done sooner. . . . It would be important to have the book done by early Summer so that it could be printed & circulated before studies begin in the Fall, so we'd better say two (?) years from *now* rather than from Fall. (James, 1890/1981, pp. 1532–1533)

James signed the contract on June 12, 1878, and began the project without hesitation while on his honeymoon. James intended to call the book *Psychology, as a Natural Science* and began developing outlines for the text (Perry, 1935). Despite such a vigorous start, he did not complete his brilliant textbook until 12 years after signing the contract.

The fact that James, who began this project at the age of 36, less than a decade after earning his medical degree, was able to produce this work in 12 years is extraordinary. All the more remarkable is that James wrote his

---

[1]For an extensive archival account of the history of *The principles of psychology*, see James (1890/1981, pp. 1532–1579) and Evans (1981). In addition, Sokal (1984) provided an insightful and scholarly treatment of the history of *Psychology: Briefer course*. The Sokal (1984) work deals more with the history of *Briefer Coures* than with its content.

two-volume masterpiece, arguably the greatest book in the history of psychology, under considerable personal adversity; indeed, the period spanning from 1878 to 1890 was perhaps the most turbulent period of James's life. Aside from the arduous task of assimilating the world's literature on psychology, James faced a number of personal and professional demands. A brief reflection on his life during this period reminds us that, although he had taught at Harvard University as an instructor in anatomy and physiology since 1872, James was still struggling to establish his academic career when he agreed to write the *Principles*. His academic duties, spread over the disciplines of physiology, psychology, and philosophy, consumed a significant amount of James's time. By the fall of 1879, he was teaching a graduate seminar on physiological psychology, undergraduate classes on the philosophies of Charles Renouvier and Herbert Spencer, and a weekly lecture on physiology (Lewis, 1991). Additionally, the routine tasks of teaching were laborious for James. The eminent philosopher George Santayana (Lyon, 1968) drew from his memories as a student at Harvard during the 1880s when he wrote that

> Perhaps in the first years of his teaching [James] felt a little in the professor's chair as a military man might feel when obliged to read the prayers at a funeral. He probably conceived what he said more deeply than a more scholastic mind might have conceived it; yet he would have been more comfortable if someone else had said it for him. . . . I think he was glad when the bell rang, and he could be himself again until the next day. (p. 88)

In addition to his classroom responsibilities, James conducted informal investigations on hypnosis, automatic writing, and the sense of dizziness in deaf mutes (Lewis, 1991), and he published more than 75 articles, reviews, reports, and notes from 1878 to 1890. In 1885, he founded the American branch of the Society for Psychic Research, spearheaded a drive to raise money for the psychology laboratory at Harvard, and, in 1882, edited a commemorative volume of his father's writings, titled *The Literary Remains of the Late Henry James*.

On July 10, 1878, James married Alice Howe Gibbens, a union that would produce five children, all during the years that the *Principles* was being written: Henry (born 1879), William (born 1882), Herman (born 1884), Margaret Mary (born 1887), and Alexander (born 1890). James's personal life and work schedule were radically altered by his new family, and his grief must have been profound when his third child, Herman, died from bronchopneumonia in 1884. In 1882, both James's mother, Mary, and his father, Henry, Sr., died. Shortly thereafter, his younger brother, Garth Wilkinson ("Wilky"), died in November of 1883. Another brother, Robert, had repeated bouts with alcoholism and was temporarily hospitalized in a Hartford, Connecticut, asylum in 1888. James's brilliant but frail sister, Alice, suffered from nervous and physical disorders during the majority of her life. Around this same time, James purchased a farm on the shore of Lake Chocorua in New Hampshire and built a new house in Cambridge, Massachusetts.

In addition to the turbulent events of his personal life, James also suffered from significant physiological ailments that impeded progress on his book. James's symptoms, including visual fatigue, insomnia, and "acute brain-fag" (James, 1890/1981, p. 1535), were not unlike those described in 1881 by the American neurologist George Bard as *neurasthenia*, a broad diagnostic term given to a wide range of psychosomatic disorders during the Victorian period (Schlereth, 1991). Whatever the genesis of his maladies, James could be productive when such distractions were minimal. In a letter to his brother Henry, James (H. James, 1920) wrote,

> I am running along quite smoothly, and my eyes,—you never knew such an improvement! It has continued gradually so that practically I can use them all I will. It saves my life. *Why* it should come now, when, bully them as I would it wouldn't come in the past few years is one of the secrets of the nervous system. (pp. 242–243)

Like a vast number of privileged Americans and Europeans in the Victorian era, James sought relief from his afflictions through popular miracle treatments. In February 1887, he wrote to his cousin, Katherine James Prince, "I have made 10 visits to a mind-cure-doctress. . . . I cannot see that the mind cure has done me any positive good, though I shall go twice more, having resolved to give the good woman at least a dozen settings, for fair trial's sake" (Scott, 1986, pp. 42–43).[2]

During the same year as his mind cure treatment, James had completed two thirds of the book. By April of 1890, he signed a new contract. Holt was quick to admonish James: "If you don't have your manuscript ready May 1st, let that day be a day of fasting over your sins" (James, 1880/1981, p. 1559). As with previous episodes, James failed to meet Holt's imposing deadline. James was not the only author to test Holt's tolerance. After prodding S. W. Johnson of Yale to complete a volume on chemistry, Holt remarked in exasperation, "Lord, what a job it is to get you wise men to work and to keep you at it" (Madison, 1966, p. 20).

---

[2]James's letter about such therapeutic treatment doubtlessly had particular relevance to his cousin. About the time of this letter, Katherine Barber James was admitted to a Boston asylum after the death of her husband, William Henry Prince, first superintendent of the Northampton State Hospital (Lewis, 1991).

After completing his book in May 1890, James (Scott, 1986) wrote an enthusiastic letter to Christine Ladd-Franklin:

> Congratulate me! I have this day finished the manuscript of a 'Principles of Psychology' which ought to be out in September; and which has been sticking to me like an old man of the sea for the last 8 or 9 years. I feel like a barrel with its hoops gone! and shall grow young again. (p. 65)

Holt authorized the publication of about 1,800 copies of the 1890 edition of the *Principles*. On September 25, 1890, Holt began distribution of James's book at $6 for the two-volume set or less than $5 after a dealer discount (Madison, 1966).

Despite disparaging reviews from G. Stanley Hall, James Sully, and Charles S. Peirce, James's book was largely a critical triumph. This success may have been due to the eager anticipation for *the Principles* by its intellectual audience. Holt had begun advertising the book as early as 1881, and James had published selected chapters in *Mind, Journal of Speculative Philosophy, Popular Science Monthly*, and *Scribner's Magazine*. His early articles in *Popular Science Monthly* and *Scribner's Magazine*, among other cultural magazines, also cultivated enthusiasm about James's psychology among the general public. Perry (1935) wrote that "James's *Principles of Psychology* was successful in a sense that is unusual for a book of science—it was widely read, not only by other psychologists, or by students of psychology, but by people who were under no obligation to read it" (p. 91). During James's lifetime, an additional nine editions of the *Principles* were printed, including an Italian translation by Guilio Cesare Ferrari (James, 1900).

Although *Principles of Psychology* became one of psychology's monumental publications, James indicated his dissatisfaction with the book. After mailing a section of the *Principles* to Holt in May 1890, James wrote to his wife Alice "if it burns up at the printing-office, I shan't much care, for I shan't ever write it again" (H. James, 1920, p. 295). James's dissatisfaction is further reflected in his descriptions of the *Principles* as "the enormous rat" (H. James, 1920, p. 293); "the big *étape* of my life . . . that infernal book" (H. James, 1920, p. 295); "my tedious book" (H. James, 1920, p. 296); and, perhaps his most famous statement, "a loathsome, distended, tumefied, bloated, dropsical mass" (H. James, 1920, p. 294). Despite such colorful appellations, James was actively revising the *Principles* into a briefer version by the spring of 1891. By his count, "[a]bout two fifths of the volume is either new or rewritten, the rest is 'scissors and paste' " (James, 1892/1984, p. 1). Published in 1892, *Psychology: Briefer Course* proved even more successful than its illustrious predecessor; James's abridgment sold 47,531 copies in its first decade, whereas the *Principles* sold only 8,115 copies after its first 12 years in print (Madison, 1966).

Despite the success of his psychology texts, James's intellectual pursuits were shifting toward philosophy. Indeed, Boring (1950) noted that James "never ceased to be a psychologist, but he grew away from psychology" (p. 511). This notion is evident in several items in James's correspondence, including an 1894 letter to Théodore Flournoy:

> My intellect is somewhat stagnant. I enjoyed last year reading a good deal of stuff which might connect itself with lectures on 'Cosmology' . . . and, as for psychology, it has passed away from me altogether since the publication of my book. (LeClair, p. 35)

Despite the sentiment in his letter to Flournoy, James remained active in select areas of psychology following the publication of his *Briefer Course* in 1892. He taught graduate seminars on mental pathology from 1892 to 1898 at Harvard and, under the sponsorship of the Lowell Institute, he delivered a series of eight public lectures in 1896 on such topics as dreams, hypnosis, hysteria, multiple personality, and genius (see Taylor, 1983). James remained fascinated by psychic research (an interest shared with Holt) throughout his professional career, and he continued to publish on this topic until the last year of his life (James, 1910). Aside from such diversions, however, James clearly committed the majority of his later intellectual work to the pursuit of philosophy.

Despite his adherence to philosophy, several publishers petitioned James to author a revision of his celebrated psychology textbook. His aversion to this task is clear in a letter to publisher W. T. Harris:

> I am very sorry to have to say no to you again—but it is quite impossible that I should do what you want, under any title. It would take me two years to do the work and kill me in the end. I have no facility for writing, as some people have; and I registered a solemn vow last summer, after abridging my Psychology, that I should never, never, never, write a text book again! (Nethery, 1968, p. 504)

THE HINT OF A REVISION

Contrary to the tone of such letters, James did not abandon plans for a revision of his psychological treatise. After noting the neglect of chapters on aesthetics, pleasure and pain, and the moral sense in his revised edition, James (1892/1984) added that "possibly the defect may be made up on a later edition, if such a thing should ever be demanded" (p. 1). In part, his reconsideration was stimulated by the persistent urging of a former student, Edward L. Thorndike. In 1902, Thorndike wrote James with a plea for a revision of *Psychology: Briefer Course* and suggestions for potential changes in the manuscript (Jonçich, 1968). James neither replied nor dismissed this offer. Ten months after Thorndike's letter, James (1892/1984) mentioned in a postcard to Édouard Claparède the possibility of revising "my smaller psychology" (p. 475).

James did consent to write a preface for Thorndike's 1905 text, *The Elements of Psychology* (Jonçich, 1968). Despite the successful publication of his own book, Thorndike again wrote James in 1905 with an invitation to jointly revise *Psychology: Briefer Course*:

> Let me do the hack work of revising your Briefer Course this spring and summer. You could get someone to do it better, but no one who would do it more promptly. You can plan what you want done to it. I will free myself for the time from crudities of style and pedagogical eccentricities and make a cast which you can chisel into shape without much waste of time. The "Principles of Psychology" ought never to be revised but to stay as a landmark of Psychology of its day; but in the Briefer Course the renovation of brain physiology and the addition of the functional point of view and (if you thought wise) a diminution of the criticisms of philosophical dogmas about psychology would make the Briefer Course a bit more useful to classes and probably more certain to continue its sale. Please take a day and jot down notes in a copy of the Briefer Course of what you would do to it in a new edition and send them to me to let me try my hand. (Jonçich, 1968, pp. 235–236)

James responded the next day with a gracious refusal:

> Your offer is a most extraordinarily generous one to me and disinterested one from the point of view of your own book. I've no doubt that you could give to mine a new lease on life much better than I could myself for, you see it objectively, and have had experience of its way of being taken by students which I have not. Nevertheless I must decline your offer for a reason that I am sure you sympathize with. A book is a man's own flesh and blood, as it were, and when I revise that one, and partly rewrite it, as I soon must, I want it still to be, for better or worse, my own. I have preserved those notes you sent me a couple of years ago, suggesting certain emendations, and I shall probably apply for more. (Jonçich, 1968, p. 236)

Although it is tempting to wonder what sagacity might have arisen from such a collaboration, Thorndike never persevered beyond this point and plans for a revision were subsequently abandoned, but perhaps not forgotten. James mentioned his interest in a revision during the course of a 1906 letter to his daughter, Margaret Mary (James, 1892/1984), and, little more than a year before his death in 1910, three diary entries reveal that James had written Holt about the possibility of a revision (see James, 1892/1984, p. 477). Whatever his intent, James never produced a revision of *The Principles of Psychology* beyond his *Briefer Course*.

We can only speculate about what James would have included in a revision of the *Principles* or, more likely, the *Briefer Course*, had he survived another few years. Evans (1981) remarked that "No one who reads James's *Principles* from cover to cover can call him unsystematic" (p. xli); Evans's statement is equally true with regard to James's mature philosophical writings. In this spirit, the chapters in this section explore the degree to which James might have integrated the principal themes of his philosophical system, specifically pluralism, pragmatism, and radical empiricism, into an early twentieth-century revision of *The Principles of Psychology*.

REFERENCES

Boring, E. G. (1950). *A history of experimental psychology.* New York: Appleton-Century-Crofts.

Boring, E. G., Langfeld, H. S., Werner, H., & Yerkes, R. M. (Eds.). (1968). *A history of psychology in autobiography* (Vol. 4). New York: Russell & Russell. (Original work published 1952)

Boring, E. G. & Lindzey, G. (Eds.) (1967). *A history of psychology in autobiography* (Vol. 5). New York: Appleton-Century-Crofts.

Evans, R. B. (1981). Introduction: The historical context. In W. James, *Principles of psychology* (Vol. 1, pp. xli–lxviii). Cambridge, MA: Harvard University Press.

Institute for Scientific Information. (1990). *Social sciences citation index: 1989 annual.* Philadelphia: Author.

Institute for Scientific Information. (1991). *Social sciences citation index: 1990 annual.* Philadelphia: Author.

James, H., Jr. (Ed.). (1920). *The letters of William James* (Vol. 1). Boston: Atlantic Monthly Press.

James, W. (1900). *Principii di psicologia.* (G. C. Ferrari, Trans.). Milan: Società editrice libraria.

James, W. (1910). A suggestion about mysticism. *Journal of Philosophy, Psychology, and Scientific Methods, 7,* 85–92.

James, W. (1981). *The principles of psychology* (3 Vols.). Cambridge, MA: Harvard University Press. (Original work published 1890)

James, W. (1984). *Psychology: Briefer course.* Cambridge, MA: Harvard University Press. (Original work published 1892)

Jonçich, G. (1968). *The sane positivist: A biography of Edward L. Thorndike.* Middletown, CT: Wesleyan University Press.

LeClair, R. C. (Ed.). (1966). *The letters of William James and Théodore Flournoy.* Madison, WI: University of Wisconsin Press.

Lewis, R. W. B. (1991). *The Jameses: A family narrative.* New York: Farrar, Straus & Giroux.

Lindzey, G. (Ed.). (1974). *A history of psychology in autobiography* (Vol. 6). Englewood Cliffs, NJ: Prentice-Hall.

Lindzey, G. (Ed.). (1980). *A history of psychology in autobiography* (Vol. 7). San Francisco: W. H. Freeman.

Lyon, R. C. (Ed.). (1968). *Santayana on America: Essays, notes, and letters on American life, literature, and philosophy.* New York: Harcourt, Brace & World.

Madison, C. A. (1966). *The owl among colophons: Henry Holt as publisher and editor.* New York: Holt, Rinehart & Winston.

Murchison, C. (Ed.). (1961). *A history of psychology in autobiography* (Vol. 1). New York: Russell & Russell. (Original work published 1930)

Murchison, C. (Ed.). (1961). *A history of psychology in autobiography* (Vol. 2). New York: Russell & Russell. (Original work published 1932)

Murchison, C. (Ed.). (1961). *A history of psychology in autobiography* (Vol. 3). New York: Russell & Russell. (Original work published 1936)

Nethery, W. (1968). Pragmatist to publisher: Letters of William James to W. T. Harris. *The Personalist, 49,* 500–513.

Perry, R. B. (1935). *The thought and character of William James* (Vol. 2). Boston: Little, Brown.

Schlereth, T. J. (1991). *Victorian America: Transformations in everyday life, 1876–1915.* New York: HarperCollins.

Scott, F. J. D. (Ed.). (1986). *William James: Selected unpublished correspondence, 1885–1910.* Columbus, OH: Ohio State University Press.

Sokal, M. M. (1984). Introduction: The historical context. In W. James, *Psychology: Briefer course* (xi–xli). Cambridge, MA: Harvard University Press.

Taylor, E. (1983). *William James on exceptional mental states: The 1896 Lowell lectures.* New York: Scribner.

5

THE WORLD WE PRACTICALLY LIVE IN

CHARLENE HADDOCK SEIGFRIED

In his last book, *Some Problems of Philosophy*, William James (1911/1979) said that "the world we practically live in is one in which it is impossible (except by theoretic retrospection) to disentangle the contributions of intellect from those of sense. They are wrapt and rolled together as a gunshot in the mountains is wrapt and rolled in fold on fold of echo and reverberative clamor" (pp. 58–59). Like these auditory reverberations, thought and perception mutually resonate: "The more we see, the more we think; while the more we think, the more we see in our immediate experiences" (p. 59). But in his first book, *The Principles of Psychology* (1890/1981), James sought to unwrap the perceptual nucleus as an antidote to ungrounded philosophical speculation.

His solution to the interminable quarrels of competing philosophical schools was to adopt a natural-history methodology to discover the unbiased facts of human experience and to use these facts to put metaphysics on a firm foundation, a foundation that would withstand the assaults of positivist science on the freedom and dignity of the human individual. What is one to make of the phenomenal findings in the *Principles*, however, once it is recognized that it is impossible to begin with a neutral description of facts as the objective basis for further claims? This 100th anniversary of the publication of James's historic work provides a fitting time to begin reconstructing his psychology in light of his philosophical insights.

James's mature philosophical position superficially resembles functionalism, which has been criticized for removing objective grounds for action. Functionally, the legitimacy of any course of action is determined by the end in view. Workers are functionally healthy, for instance, if they can satisfactorily perform the professional tasks expected of them. Whether the job is above-ground nuclear testing in the Pacific, selling crack, or suturing the wounds of emergency room patients is irrelevant to the criterion. If there are no independent criteria outside the narrowly instrumental one of means to ends, then there are not objective natural or moral restraints on actions.

All of his life, James argued against functionalism. Despite his attraction to philosophical humanism, for instance, he could not fully embrace it because of what he took to be its functionalist assumptions (Seigfried, 1990b). He sought independent grounds for action, both in a direct acquaintance with reality and in a belief in an eternal moral order (e.g., see James, 1890/1981, p. 653, 1907/1975, p. 264). But he also recognized—and even provided many reasons to support—the experiential evidence that reality is always mediated through our subjective dispositions and that there is no moral order, except that which we ourselves create. He was intensely aware of the discrepancy between the demands we make of the universe and the shocking scientific evidence for the "aimless drifting to and fro" of phenomena, "without inward rationality" that mocks such demands (James, 1920/1969, p. 23). Like others who were troubled by the increasingly positivist materialism of late-nineteenth-century science, he was one

> of those who feel in their bones that man's religious interests must be able to swallow and digest and grow fat upon all the facts and theories of modern science, but who yet have not the capacity to see with their own eyes how it may be done. (James, 1920/1969, p. 284)

In his philosophy of radical empiricism, James, like the functionalists, argued that there are no independent criteria for action in the nature of reality or eternal moral values. Unlike functionalists, however, he also argued for the validity of interdependent criteria. What we take to be the given facts of any case are actually a synthesis of the expectations, values, and tasks we set for ourselves and the existing conditions. We can distinguish the objective from the subjective contributions only retrospectively, that is, only according to some other project of ours that imposes the criteria we choose on the prereflective situation. James was not advocating nihilism as his analysis seemed to suggest, and therefore, took as his own lifelong project the search for the fundamental facts of the human situation that would provide objective grounds for our subjective choices (e.g., see Seigfried, 1990b).

I believe that it is possible to argue that all reality is subjective, but to still develop methods for distinguishing warranted from unwarranted claims and, thereby, to avoid the nihilism of functionalist relativism. We analyze our experience in order to bring about a situation thought to be more valuable. The determination of what is is always relative to the values we hold. Therefore, the instrumentalist reasoning of means and ends is only part of a more encompassing horizon of our being in the world. James's investigations of concrete, lived experience in his psychology are deepened and extended in his radical empiricism and can be developed into a determination of those legitimate grounds for acting for which he sought in vain in metaphysical thinking. The issue will first be developed as James formulated it, and then hints for a radical reconstruction for understanding the self and reality will be suggested.

ORIGINAL PROJECT OF THE *PRINCIPLES*

James's original project depended on the possibility of pure seeing and neutral description (Seigfried, 1990a). He bracketed metaphysical presuppositions in order to describe the phenomenal conditions of our being in the world. In chapter 7 of the *Principles*, for instance, in which James explained the new science of psychology, he pointed out that psychologists investigate distinct individuals who inhabit real space and real time. Without questioning their presuppositions, psychologists investigate "*objects*, in a world of other objects" (James, 1890/1981, p. 183). They report subjective as well as objective facts, but their experimental methods of investigation are objective because "facts are facts, and if we only get enough of them they are sure to combine" (James, 1890/1981, p. 192–193). Nonetheless, he also noted that in the early stages of the development of various methods of investigation, there will be a wide latitude for interpretation, and the biases of investigators will be largely unchecked. Unlike psychologists, "the total world of which the philosophers must take account is . . . composed of the realities *plus* the fancies and illusions" (James, 1890/1981, p. 920). In other words, subjectivity and objectivity become the issues for philosophically reflective thinking.

In the *Principles*, James assumed an empirically realist position, but this position was already moderated by the recognition of the role of our spontaneity in discriminating the details of our lived world from the experiential totality. He argued, for example, that "as a rule, no sensible qualities are discriminated without a motive" (James, 1890/1981, p. 883). Nonetheless, in examining figures that induce illusions, James thought that we could learn to discount our usual perspectival distortions and "take the optical sensation before us *pure*" (James, 1890/1981, p. 896). He dismissed the Kantian constructivist view presupposed by the English associationist school as inevitably foundering on an unacceptable subjectivism. If space is a "supersensational mental product" (James, 1890/1981, p. 903), then what is to distinguish it from any other mythological construct? He insisted that there is nothing in the final perception that was not originally in sensation. We must be able to identify this sensible core in order to distinguish true from false perspectives.

But James did not always defend such a presuppositionless access to reality that also underlies positivist models of science. Even within the stated limitations of the *Principles*, as a natural science, his appeals to observation were not consistent. He developed two incompatible models of natural-history methodology, which he never clearly distinguished, but which one must (Seigfried, 1990a). Only by distinguishing between an unreconstructed natural-history approach and a reconstructed one, can one avoid misinterpreting James's later appeals to pure experience in his *Essays in Radical Empiricism* (1912/1976) as advocating some direct access to reality as it is in itself.

In the *Principles*, he had already begun reconstructing a natural-history approach into a hermeneutic or concrete analysis of experience. This approach can be found in chapter 21, "The Perception of Reality," where he explained how reality comes to be psychologically distinguished from illusion. It is also evident in the preceding chapter, "The Perception of Space," where he explained that we ourselves select from among our various optical space sensations the ones that we identify as real (James, 1890/1981, p. 869). We substitute a few fixed terms for the manifestly vague original manifold. This is done from a normal perspective, that is, one which is best suited to our visual apparatus. James (1890/1981, p. 871) said, for example, that "in this position our head is upright and our optic axes either parallel or symmetrically convergent; the plane of the object is perpendicular to the visual plane." The normal situation, which includes the position of objects when they are held and in which symmetrical figures appear symmetrical, is a privileged point of view: "Here we believe we see the object as it *is*; elsewhere, only as it seems (James, 1890/1981, p. 871). These physiological constraints limit, but do not uniquely determine, reality. The criteria for distinguishing what something is from what it merely seems to be are taken from our aesthetic and practical rational nature (James, 1890/1981). We translate optical signs into optical realities by our psychic preference for economy and simplification, which are aspects of aesthetic rationality.

The full impact of James's casual reference to rational nature can only be grasped when it is realized that he was referring to his own analysis of concrete rationality, or rationality as it is lived through, not as a theoretical construct handed down in the philosophical tradition. In a series of articles written before the *Principles*, James developed his alternate model of human rationality: Philosophical systems owe their being to "the craving for consistency or unity in thought, and the desire for a solid outside warrant for our thought" (James, 1920/1969, pp. 22–23). This "craving for a consistent completeness" is aesthetically based (p. 28). Any system of philosophy, to be successful, must meet these two great aesthetic needs of our logical nature: unity and clearness (James, 1978). Unity, more often called *simplicity*, is a drive to unify the chaos—to order the multiplicity of the sensible world. Our idea of the universe is not completely rational until each separate phenomenon is conceived as fundamentally identical with every other. Theoretical rationality is often simply identified with this search for principles of unification. "This criterion of identity is that which we all unconsciously use when we discriminate between brute fact and explained fact. There is no other test" (James, 1978, p. 46).

But if this process of simplification is to avoid being merely speculative, it must be joined with the other great aesthetic need—that of clarity. This does not refer to the Cartesian tradition of clear and distinct ideas, but to the empiricist tradition of ideas as vivid sense impressions. Before disparate phenomena can be unified in an ordered system, they must be accurately identified, their essences determined. This means identifying the imbedded character in a single phenomenon and in the maximum number of other phenomena. "The living question" is "to stand before a phenomenon and say *what* it is" (James, 1978, p. 48). This insistence on establishing the data of perception to avoid the sterility of metaphysical entities marked the initial concrete ground or *phenomenal ground* of James's own position (James, 1978). Such determination of essences should not be confused with the Aristotelian account of essences, however. James connected the identification of essences with the characteristics that attract our interest, rather than with the unique, unchanging characteristics abstracted from objects. Thus, essences are a function of our interests, vary with them, and are not discoverable apart from them.

Throughout most of his writings, James used harmony as the criterion for the satisfaction of our concretely rational demands. But as he worked out the details of such a merely aesthetic harmony, he argued more and more for practical rationality guiding aesthetic rationality, rather than the other way around. Practical rationality means acting for ends. James said that the purely aesthetic or "cognitive faculty . . . appears but as one element in an organic mental whole, and as a minister to higher mental powers—the powers of will" (1897/1979, p. 110).

RETRACTION

After publication of the *Principles*, James retracted the strict separation he had uncritically borrowed from the positivist understanding of science as independent of philosophy. In his president's address before the American Psychological Association in 1894, James (1978) said: "I have become convinced since publishing that book that no conventional restrictions *can* keep metaphysical and so-called epistemological inquiries out of the psychology-books" (p. 88). But this realization was no cause for celebration. It meant that the secure grounding that James had pursued in his search for objective facts of the human appropriation of the world was seemingly not possible to achieve. If metaphysics could not be constructed on the basis of facts, then how could the facts be objectively determined retrospectively from the perspective of his not-yet-written metaphysics of radical empiricism?

A decade after publishing the *Principles*, James took the opportunity to review his original intentions in a preface for the Italian translation (James, 1890/1981). He still repudiated the possibility of building a coherent world of experience by identifying the smallest measurable units of conscious activity and then combining them through principles of association and reaffirmed his procedure of bringing the reader into "direct concrete acquaintance" with the "living reality." This reality is "the actual conscious unity which each of us at all times feels himself to be" (p. 1483). In other words, the reality is not investigated as an independent, neutral object that we passively intuit, whether this reality is recognized through sense data or other quantifiable facts. James's reality is the total reality of subject and object, which are inextricably joined. Although they may be functionally separated in various ways for various purposes, they cannot be ontologically distinguished in any absolute sense.

The feeling we have that we organize experiences to fulfill our purposes, which was a finding of the natural-history methodology of *Principles*, is elaborated on in James's radically empiricist philosophy as the "full fact." James (1902/1985) defined this as

> a conscious field *plus* its object as felt or thought of *plus* an attitude towards the object *plus* the sense of self to whom the attitude belongs . . . is a *full* fact, even though it be an insignificant fact; it is of the *kind* to which all realities whatsoever must belong. (p. 499)

Reality cannot be appealed to as an independent check on our experience because reality is only available to us within a horizon made up of our spontaneous ordering of the otherwise inchoate flux of experience.

James's original position was that only the empirically verifiable aspects of this lived sense of unity could be properly investigated in psychology, once psychology had been successfully transformed into a natural science. Psychological investigations are properly limited "to the unity [of] each passing wave or field of consciousness" (James, 1890/1981, p. 1484) and do not assume or use as explanatory principles any metaphysical, that is, transcendent source of unity. In fact, James's goal in writing the *Principles* was to disentangle psychology from a premature alliance with the ultimate questions of metaphysics. As mentioned earlier, James's ambition was to lay the groundwork on which a metaphysics based on the facts of human experience could at last be constructed and to settle the unprofitable disputes that have plagued philosophy for centuries. Even when he confessed that he may not have successfully eliminated all philosophical assumptions from his natural science of psychology, that such a separation may not even be possible, and that a more satisfactory psychology than the one he developed required a more advanced metaphysics of experience, he still defended both his phenomenal findings and his natural-history method.

James's defense is surprising because his aim was to harmonize all legitimate factual findings, undistorted by the metaphysical assumptions of the various schools of philosophy. James (1890/1981) deliberately appealed to those who had not yet been biased by metaphysics: "My hopes lie with the unprejudiced reader, and the newer generation" (p. 1483). His method of bracketing metaphysical assumptions somehow would not apply to his own metaphysics of experience. I do not find this conclusion contradictory because I do not believe that James, in fact, developed a metaphysics, although he called it such, but rather a theoretical defense of his concrete analysis of experience.

This radically empiricist analysis of the human situation replaces foundationalist metaphysics with a concrete analysis of subjectivity as the only defensible basis of objectivity. This is evident in what James (1890/1981) called a *reinterpretation* of the facts; namely, that "the whole concrete course of an individual's thinking life is explicable by the cooperation of his interests and impulses, his sensational experiences, his associations, & his voluntary acts of choice" (p. 1484). He defended a post-Darwinian, nontranscendental version of Kant's synthetic unity of consciousness: "The materials of our thought come from without, but the form which the individual gives to them is almost entirely due to his personal spontaneity" (p. 1484).

In his natural science of psychology, James offered a compromise, one that was neutral as to whether to impute the true cause of unification to brain processes or to objects of thought. His psychology accomplished this by staying on the phenomenal level. Things were taken for what they appeared to be, not for illusions, which after all, are detectable, but they were taken on the basis of experimental hypothesis formation. The determination of fact meant that the experimental results obtained were not questioned as to their ontological status, but only as to their adequacy in meeting the ends in view. It was hoped that the various schools would come together in harmony "on the common basis of fact" (p. 1484). Could this harmony be better achieved once James's radical empiricism was developed and the phenomenal level transcended by a determination of objective reality?

JAMES'S LONG-RANGE PROJECT

I doubt that James was happy with the results of his radically empiricist philosophy and believe that is why he never used it to reconstruct his psychology without presuppositions. To illustrate why he was unhappy, I will sketch out his lifelong project. By the late nineteenth century, the spectacular success of positivist science, with its burgeoning technology, threatened the very foundations of a worldview based on the rationality, freedom, and dignity unique to human beings (e.g., see West, 1990). As Donald A. Crosby (1988) so ably pointed out, this scientific materialism awoke the specter of nihilism among intellectuals in Europe and America. The demand for empirical evidence meant that the traditional appeals to religion and philosophy were no longer convincing, but the threat that cherished beliefs in human freedom and rationality might merely be remnants of a more superstitious age was intensely felt and had to be faced. It was, therefore, a strategic move on James's part to yield the field of psychology to "the men of science . . . of the laboratories" (James, 1983, p. 273), but it was also the first stage of a plan he was working out to overcome the nihilism of a meaningless world and the skepticism bequeathed by a Kantian phenomenalism that forever denied access to things in themselves. If things cannot be objectively known, but only subjectively interpreted insofar as they appear, how could a nihilistic relativism be avoided? James only bracketed metaphysical issues of ultimate human significance in order to set metaphysics on a firmer foundation.

Like Edmund Husserl after him, James wanted to establish the verifiable facts of human experience as a better basis on which to develop a metaphysics than the ones that had been discredited by positivism. The *Principles* is, therefore, a landmark in philosophy only insofar as it is first a landmark in psychology as a strict science. The facts of human experience that were established in the *Principles* were developed further into a pragmatic method and philosophy of radical empiricism and used to rethink traditional issues of ultimate concern.

These facts were warranted by the method of natural science to be objective, that is, free from metaphysical assumptions. James had no quarrel with the positivist program of replacing speculation with pure observation, as long as the restricted scope of such findings was acknowledged. It was outside the scope of psychology, for example, to determine objectivity in the sense of what is true of objects in the real world. This determination would lie in the realm of philosophy. Psychology could only establish the truth of objects as they are perceived, but not as they are. Because James deliberately used the word *experience* as a double-barreled term that could mean either the thought of the object or the object referred to by thought, the strict dichotomy he drew between subjective experience and objective reality is easy to overlook. But as the Miller-Bode (James, 1912/1976, 1988) notebooks attested, James was plagued by the specter of solipsism all his life.

James developed his metaphysics of radical empiricism through an uneasy compromise with humanism (e.g., see James, 1907/1975, pp. 115–129, 1909/1975, pp. 37–60). Humanists such as F. C. S. Schiller and John Dewey had gone too far, according to James (1907/1975), in insisting that all reality is reality for us: "We cannot therefore methodically join the tough minds in their rejection of the whole notion of a world beyond our finite experience" (p. 128). James still hoped to develop a methodology for distinguishing subjective from objective apprehensions of reality. His pragmatic method, like the natural-history method before, was still a way of settling disputes that otherwise might be interminable. Like his psychology, it did so by remaining on the phenomenal level of experience. According to the pragmatic method, it was legitimate to bracket the ultimate truth of disputed positions and to settle them instrumentally. If an actual difference in practice could be determined between positions, and if one practice led to more satisfactory results than the other, then the conclusion was legitimate for the time being. We are temporal and finite beings and, therefore, our knowledge is limited. Because what we take to be true in the present may be disproved by future discoveries, we should avoid claiming dogmatic certainty for any position.

We are also rational beings who crave justification for our actions. Therefore, although, abstractly, it would be better to act only when we are sure of the truth, it is actually better to act when we are less certain. James called this subordinating the demands of our aesthetic rationality to those of our practical rationality. According to his analysis of concrete rationality, we are motivated by both aesthetic and practical rationality, and the pragmatic method is a way of harmonizing the two, sometimes incompatible, demands. Theoretically, both demands should be satisfiable, that is, the aesthetic demand for an absolute coalescence of knowledge and being, which would issue in The Truth, and the practical demand for having a legitimate warrant for acting according to The Good. But we have not yet arrived at such a state. In the meantime, we must still think and act without the benefit of such guarantees, and the pragmatic analysis allows us to do so in a way congruous with our actual condition, namely, that of probable truth and warrantable good.

James could not come up with a harmonious resolution for the demands of our aesthetic and practical rationality, which would move beyond such temporary accommodations that the humanists claimed was all that we could ever hope for. The more James resisted their arguments, the less satisfactory were his rebuttals, which finally came down to his insistence that he would not live in a world without at least the hope that some day his beliefs about reality would coalesce with The Truth and his moral strivings would find their completion in The Good. For an example of this residue of traditional rationalism, which is seldom recognized as still motivating James despite his explicit rejection of it (1897/1979), see the fifth section of "The Moral Philosopher and the Moral Life," where he said that "the chief of all the reasons why concrete ethics cannot be final is that they have to wait on metaphysical and theological beliefs" (p. 159). James argued that the denial of the possibility that the demands of our rational nature would be ultimately satisfied meant aquiescing to nihilism.

Unfortunately for James's position, all the particular arguments of the humanists for our finite and temporal character were convincing, and James even added to those arguments. He only differed with the humanists as to whether this situation was remedial in the long run. In the short run, there was no difference, except for the particular configuration of his concrete analysis of the human condition, which was very rich and very suggestive.

RECONSTRUCTION

Two overlapping hermeneutical circles emerged in the course of James's psychological and philosophical writings. In the first one, he bracketed the relation of experience with nature. He referred to this as the dualism of his natural-science methodology, which took for granted that there is a world to be known and a knower, and it is sufficient for scientific purposes to assume without proof that they are congruent. He also bracketed metaphysical principles and proceeds by way of the natural-history method of pure description. This opened up a space in which scientists can investigate and determine the facts of experience. James accepted some facts, discarded others, and came up with some of his own on the basis of his own investigative procedures and guided by his largely unexamined presuppositions. Positions were rejected by showing that they were derived directly from a specific metaphysical perspective and imposed on the facts, whereas the results of psychological investigations were retained whenever they were said to be derived from, and supported by, facts.

However, the fundamental fact that James always used as a criterion is the fact of human spontaneity. That we actively organize experience to suit our purposes is both assumed in, and proved by, the facts investigated. The first *natural-history* hermeneutical circle begins by using facts of experience to prove that we order the world, but these facts appear only as facts because we assume that we do order the world. Given this assumption, all of the available facts can be marshaled into a coherent and persuasive argument, which demonstrates that we have correctly determined the facts in the first place, but we can only initially determine that the facts are indeed facts on the assumption that . . . ad infinitum.

The second *metaphysical* hermeneutical circle starts by accepting as a concrete fact of experience what the natural-history investigations have proved; namely, that we actively organize experience to suit our purposes. Therefore, the real world exists in just the ways that are disclosed by our organizations because if it does not, then we have deceived ourselves about our nature, which consists precisely in ordering experiences meaningfully. But if the world does not exist according to the order which we have developed, then our organizations of experience are meaningless. But they cannot be meaningless because they derive from our nature as human beings. And we could not be deceived about our nature because we have determined what it is using strictly scientific methods. What natural science proves is that we organize experience . . . ad infinitum.

But descending from these artificial schemas, which James was always trying to avoid, and returning to the details of his concrete investigations, both circles break apart (or perhaps break open) and negate each other. To question the *Principles* based on the insights from his metaphysics of radical empiricism demolishes the neutrality claimed for those simple observational reports and, thus, the truth of the initial findings. But if these concrete facts of experience are called into question, then so is the metaphysics that grew out of them. This conclusion can be avoided by recognizing that undermining the neutral determination of facts only undermines the legitimacy of a metaphysics understood as an arbiter of absolute truth and goodness. An antimetaphysics of the human condition, which develops a concrete rather than an abstract rationality, in fact, enriches and expands on the possibilities for the central insight of the *Principles*, this insight being the spontaneous rather than passive character of our appropriation of reality. Moreover, when it is realized that the central issue of concern is not what the world is like, but what is the value of the world which we are helping to constitute, then the legitimacy of our claims about reality does not depend on proving the facticity of the findings, but on recognizing that facticity itself can only be defined in relation to our expectations and needs. There is no neutral ground, but there are grounds.

The pragmatic method as a mediating strategy then becomes useful, now not as a temporary expedient until the truth about reality as such can be ascertained, but as a methodology congruent with our finite and temporal nature. James's radically empiricist reflections point out that we cannot read off ends from nature, but must supply them ourselves. What things are cannot be determined apart from the interests we have in making the determination. James (1907/1975) suggested that the experience we have of working with conditions to bring about a desired result is "the workshop of being, where we catch fact in the making" (p. 138). Although our particular choices are made according to a subjective configuration of interests, these interests, in turn, are embedded within a more encompassing order of experience, which can be reflectively retrieved. As humans, we act rationally, that is, according to aesthetic and practical interests. My interests can be traced to a concretely determined structure of interests, and what this structure discloses is that we spontaneously order the flux of experience to suit our purposes. We have no choice about whether we want to appeal to an already existent world or to one that we structure. Without this organization, there exists no structure to which we can appeal. Apparently fixed structures are themselves results of decisions, some of which are lost in the dim mists of history, but are preserved in commonsense categories and in language.

My purposes, if they are to be successfully carried out, must harmonize with the tendencies and resistances bequeathed to us through the funded character of experience and encountered anew in everyday life (James, 1907/1975; Seigfried, 1990b). Reflective thinkers can retrieve these structures, articulate them, and develop moral guides for action. But each person is ultimately a unique ordering center who alone can determine for herself or himself the quality of life that will meet all the demands placed on us. The functionalist restriction of discussion to means and ends is thus revealed to be a mere fragment, artificially isolated from a more encompassing living experience. As the dead remains of a once living process, its analyses cannot provide adequate guidance. On the other hand, any dogmatic determination of reality undermines the very conditions that make possible a human form of life with a positive moral dimension. To identify reality tentatively, intersubjectively and interactively with recognized conditions, is both the condition and expression of our nature as finite, spontaneous, moral agents.

Although rationality cannot be grounded rationally, that is, necessarily or irrefutably, there are, nonetheless, sufficient grounds for its pursuit. What is thus warranted is one of the fundamental drives of human beings, that is, a particular sort of striving that is part of our being in the world, and not any given rational system as corresponding to reality. James's reconstruction of rationality was central to his project of changing philosophy from an abstract intellectual pursuit for a perfect theory or logical system to a reflective endeavor to harmonize self and world in pursuit of a better future.

REFERENCES

Crosby, D. A. (1988). *The specter of the absurd: Sources and criticisms of modern nihilism*. Albany, NY: SUNY Press.

James, W. (1969). *Collected essays and reviews*. New York: Russell & Russell. (Original work published 1920)

James, W. (1975). *The meaning of truth*. Cambridge, MA: Harvard University Press. (Original work published 1909)

James, W. (1975). *Pragmatism*. Cambridge, MA: Harvard University Press. (Original work published 1907)

James, W. (1976). *Essays in radical empiricism*. Cambridge, MA: Harvard University Press. (Original work published 1912)

James, W. (1978). *Essays in philosophy*. Cambridge, MA: Harvard University Press.

James, W. (1979). *Some problems of philosophy*. Cambridge, MA: Harvard University Press. (Original work published 1911)

James, W. (1979). *The will to believe*. Cambridge, MA: Harvard University Press. (Original work published 1897)

James, W. (1981). *The principles of psychology* (3 vols.). Cambridge, MA: Harvard University Press. (Original work published 1890).

James, W. (1983). *Essays in psychology*. Cambridge, MA: Harvard University Press.

James, W. (1985). *The varieties of religious experience*. Cambridge, MA: Harvard University Press. (Original work published 1902)

James, W. (1988). *Manuscript essays and notes*. Cambridge, MA: Harvard University Press.

Seigfried, C. H. (1990a). Poetic invention and scientific observation: James's model of 'sympathetic concrete observation.' *Transactions of the Charles S. Peirce Society, 26*, 115–130.

Seigfried, C. H. (1990b). *William James's radical reconstructions of philosophy*. Albany, NY: SUNY Press.

West, D. (1990). *Science, community, and the transformation of American philosophy, 1850~1930*. Chicago: University of Chicago Press.

6

WILLIAM JAMES ON THE ADVANTAGES OF A PLURALISTIC PSYCHOLOGY

WAYNE VINEY, CHERI L. KING, AND D. BRETT KING

Throughout his major philosophical works, William James repeatedly called attention to the importance of the difference between monism and pluralism (e.g., see James, 1897/1979, 1907/1975, 1911/1979). In *Pragmatism*, James (1907/1975) told his readers that after brooding over the monism–pluralism issue for a long time, he had come "to consider it the most central of all philosophical problems, central because so pregnant" (p. 64). James went on to offer the opinion that an individual's position on monism and pluralism provides more clues about that person's other opinions than any other descriptive label "ending in *ist*. To believe in the one or in the many, that is the classification with the maximum number of consequences" (James, 1907/1975, p. 64). James repeatedly discussed the importance of the distinction between believing in the one or in the many for such topics as morality, philosophy, personality, and religion. A deep contemporary awareness of these implications is manifested in the large number of recent papers devoted to various facets of the monism–pluralism issue in psychology (Green & Powell, 1990; Kimble, 1990; Sarason, 1989; Staats, 1989; Viney, 1989).

The purpose of this chapter is threefold: first, to review James's critique of monism; second, to explore his pluralistic vision, including its accommodation of practical unities; and, finally, to consider some of the ways that Jamesian pluralism, a dominant theme in all the philosophical works that followed *The Principles of Psychology* (James, 1890/1981), might have influenced a revision of that work.

JAMES'S CRITIQUE OF MONISM

James left little doubt about where he stood on the monism–pluralism issue. He repeatedly and emphatically referred to himself as a pluralist (James, 1909/1975, 1909/1977, 1912/1976). He maintained that pragmatism forces us "to be friendly to the pluralistic view" (James, 1907/1975, p. 82), and he further asserted that empiricism "inclines to pluralistic views" (James, 1909/1977, p. 9). James's polemical attacks on monism also underscored his temperamental affinities with pluralism. In his *Essays in Radical Empiricism*, James (1912/1976) said "The 'through-and-through' universe seems to suffocate me with its infallible impeccable all-pervasiveness. Its necessity, with no possibilities; its relations, with no subjects, make me feel as if I had entered into a contract with no reserved rights" (p. 142).

One of James's major objections to monism was that he felt it did violence to personal experience. He argued "The world of concrete personal experiences . . . is multitudinous beyond imagination, tangled, muddy, painful and perplexed. The world to which your philosophy professor introduces you is simple, clean and noble. The contradictions of real life are absent from it" (James, 1907/1975, p. 18). According to James, the world we practically live in is a world booming with multiplicities, complexities, confusions, contradictions, and particularities. He might have wondered, for example, how the phenomenal dimensions of a toothache are related to the Pythagorean theorem and how each ties in with Dickinson's poetry, the current state of the stock market, the taste of sweetness, or Kant's theory of moral development. To be sure, the task and the joy of intellectual inquiry is to discover connections, and James was open to the possibility that everything is somehow related to everything else. However, he failed to find any all-pervasive connectedness in experience itself. Moreover, he considered it his duty to defend experience against systematic intellectual strictures that blind us or shield against the robust and diverse character of experience. James believed that the monist, unlike the pluralist, is forced to "rationalize, reinterpret, or even disregard features of the world that do not accord with the monistic vision, but that common sense takes for granted" (Viney, 1989, p. 1262).

A closely related criticism of monism is that it has a constraining effect on the character and expression of reality. James rejected concepts of reality "with the big R, reality that makes the timeless claim, reality to which defeat can't happen" (James, 1907/1975, p. 126). He did not believe that "*reality is ready-made and complete from all eternity* . . . [that] the universe is absolutely secure" (James, 1909/1975, p. 123). He noted that monism gives us "one great all-inclusive fact outside of which is nothing" (James, 1909/1977, p. 21). The result is a belief in only one real edition of the universe, "the infinite folio *edition de luxe,* eternally complete, and then the various finite editions, full of false readings, distorted and mutilated each in its own way" (James, 1907/1975, p. 124). For James, reality was not inert, sterile, static, or complete.

The Jamesian approach to reality is captured by H. S. Thayer (1975) in his introduction to the Harvard edition of *The Meaning of Truth,* where he pointed out that "James argued that growth and novelty are ultimate traits of reality" (p. xxiv). In his lecture notes for a "Metaphysical Seminary—A Pluralistic Description of the World," James (1988) quoted Charles Whitby:

> Reality grows, for we are at once its dark husk and its radiant core, the battlefield of its hard won conquests, and also ourselves the conquerors. And these battles, once gained, are gained for eternity, seeing that the path of the spirit moves not in a blind circle but with upward and widening sweep. (p. 274)

Reality grows, according to James, partly because of its indistinguishable connections with experience itself. As experience grows, reality grows, and it is experience that contributes meaningful additions and alternative ways of seeing reality.

> You can take the number 27 as the cube of 3, or as the product of 3 and 9, or as 26 *plus* 1, or 100 *minus* 73, or in countless other ways, of which one will be just as true as another. You can take a chess board as black squares on a white ground or as white squares on a black ground. (James, 1907/1975, p. 121)

James insisted that "We *add* to the subject and predicate part of reality. The world stands really malleable, waiting to receive the final touches of our hands. Like the Kingdom of Heaven, it suffers human violence willingly. Man *engenders* truth upon it" (James, 1907/1975, p. 123).

James's approach to the world was essentially developmental with an emphasis on process, growth, and an ever shifting frame of reference. In his final publication, an essay on the American author Benjamin Paul Blood, titled "A Pluralistic Mystic," James (1910/1978) said: "Let *my* last word, then, speaking in the name of intellectual philosophy, be [Blood's] word:—

'there is no conclusion. What has concluded, that we might conclude in regard to it?" (p. 190). James saw the world as he saw the field of vision. There is always a fringe, there is an ever shifting horizon, and no static vantage point from which we can make the big claim.

A third criticism of monism, according to James, is that it creates a problem of evil. In his book, *Some Problems of Philosophy*, James (1911/1979) declared that

> Evil, for pluralism, presents only the *practical* problem of how to get rid of it. For monism the puzzle is *theoretical*:—how, if Perfection be the source, should there be Imperfection? If the world as known to the Absolute be perfect, why should it be known otherwise, in myriads of inferior finite editions *also*? The perfect edition surely was enough. How do the breakage and dispersion and ignorance get in? (p. 72)

Still another criticism of monism is that it delivers a philosophy of absolutes, a doctrinaire philosophy confronting us at every turn with words such as *must* and *all*. James was concerned about the "moral holidays" that result when humans focus on the eternal and absolute whole rather than on their personal and immediate perceptions. He was disturbed at the accommodations made possible by absolutistic thinking. He noted that "History shows how easily both quietists and fanatics have drawn inspiration from the absolutistic scheme. It suits sick souls and strenuous ones equally well" (James, 1909/1975, p. 124). Not surprisingly, its saving message and its certitude about theoretical and practical union with the highest reality are deep sources of emotional comfort.

The pluralism James embraced offers no such comfort, and he was convinced that pluralists, unlike monists, cannot take moral holidays unless such holidays are conceived merely as "provisional breathing spells, intended to refresh us for the morrows fight" (James, 1909/1975, p. 124). The reason pluralists cannot take moral holidays is that they cannot base all decisions on indifferent abstractions, but must attend to individual cases with all their genuine complications and ambiguities not covered by absolutistic schemes.

JAMESIAN PLURALISM

In the chapter, "The One and the Many," in *Some Problems of Philosophy*, James (1911/1979) outlined three major advantages of pluralism. First, he saw pluralism as more scientific than monism because it places conjunctions *and* disjunctions on a par with each other. James argued that "To make the conjunctions more vital and primordial than the separations, monism has to abandon verifiable experience and proclaim a unity that is indescribable" (James, 1911/1979, p. 74). In contrast, pluralism permits the scientist to operate naturally in the stream of experience. Pluralism encourages the free exploration of alternatives without the demands and restrictions imposed beforehand by monistic schemes.

James refused to shrink the boundaries of what counts as legitimate science, and he rejected the constraining effects of any all-pervasive political, religious, or philosophical system that forces artificial connectedness. The demand for too much connectedness can be illustrated many ways, but nowhere more vividly than in the reaction of the National Socialist Party to Albert Einstein's theory of relativity. Tolischus (1936) reported that the *Vöelkischer Beobachter*, the official Nazi newspaper, launched an aggressive attack on Einstein's relativity theory as unsound and demanded that a truly German or Aryan physics take the place of the Jewish physics. According to a *New York Times* editorial, the concept of a Nordic science challenged the work of Einstein, Max Planck, Werner Heisenberg, and Max von Laue and further impacted the fields of mathematics and chemistry ("German Science," 1936). The National Socialists' demand for an Aryan physics is one of many possible illustrations of James's point that pluralism is more scientific than monism. The pluralist doesn't have to assume that everything is connected to everything else, but is instead content to let many things stand alone. Thus, pluralism encourages intellectual freedom, whereas monism imposes so many constraints on intellectual processes that it violates the very spirit of science. Monism may also undermine genuine intellectual curiosity because the species of curiosity permitted by monism is always bridled. James would undoubtedly counsel the contemporary scientist against a "politically correct" agenda that produces insensitivity to the anarchy and novelty encountered naturally in experience.

A second advantage of pluralism is that it is more likely to be moderate. Pluralists do not necessarily have to stand for outsized doses of their philosophy. Pluralism is not an extreme philosophy like monism, but instead

> triumphs over monism if the least morsel of disconnectedness is once found undeniably to exist. "Ever not *quite*" is all it says to monism: while monism is obliged to prove that what pluralism asserts can in no amount whatever possibly be true—an infinitely harder task. (James, 1911/1979, p. 74)

It follows that pluralism is open to varieties of unities. Indeed, in *Pragmatism* and in *Some Problems of Philosophy*, James explored many types of unity that are necessary to our general work in the world. Also, as noted by Myers (1981) in his introduction to the Harvard edition of *The Principles of Psychology*, James was deeply committed to a search for continuities between physiological processes and the world of experience. James clearly believed in many continuities and unities: Some are simply given in experience itself, some are merely conventional or practical, and others are discovered in experimentation or in other kinds of intellectual activity. Again, for James, pluralism is a moderate philosophy that accommodates a great deal of connection. Unlike monists, James could view oneness and manyness as coordinate. He argued that "Neither is primordial or more essential or excellent than the other" (James, 1907/1975, p. 68). Wisdom, he told us, is knowing when we need conductors and when we need nonconductors.

Such a condition is illustrated in a great variety of practical situations: the clinician who provides a premature or unacceptable explanation for a trauma; the minister who offers a superficial account of a tragedy; the scientist who advances a premature generalization that is not supported by the data; or the extremist on a social issue who is insensitive to individual cases. As for the first two examples, one may alternatively encounter people who would prefer to believe that a given event has no meaning at all instead of believing in meanings imposed by some larger political or religious system. In other words, for some people, there is more wisdom in real disconnectedness, real dissonance, or real chaos. There is no wisdom in a connectedness that is forced or strained.

A final advantage of pluralism, according to James, is that it "agrees more with the moral and dramatic expressiveness of life" (James, 1911/1979, p. 74). He illustrated this point most extensively in *The Varieties of Religious Experience* (James, 1902/1985) with his graphic descriptions of the ecstasies of the saints, the morbid ruminations of sick souls, and the affinities of the healthy minded for optimism, happiness, and uncomplicated trust in the cosmic order of things. The moral realm, taken empirically, appears to consist of many original principles. In James's treatment of this realm in *The Varieties of Religious Experience*, he rejected the idea that the future is completely determinate and therefore closed. According to James, the moral realm may or may not include a God and, if it does, the relations of God to the world are conceived in every variety of manner from a God that does a retail business with the universe to a more detached or even aloof deity. Evil may be maximized or minimized; it may be treated abstractly or personified. Moral orders, however they are conceived, provoke the most profound commitments and the deepest doubts. There may be greater heterogeneity and plurality of belief in this arena than in any other.

POSSIBLE INFLUENCES OF PLURALISM ON A REVISION OF THE *PRINCIPLES*

Pluralism was a dominant theme developed by James in his later philosophical writings (e.g., *Pragmatism* [1907/1975], *Essays in Radical Em-*

piricism [1912/1976], and *A Pluralistic Universe* [1909/1977]), but it was a theme already nascent in his early psychological work. One may nevertheless raise questions about how a revision of his psychology might have been influenced by his later philosophical work.

One of the more confident assertions that can be made about a revision of the *Principles* is that it would have been guided by a radically pluralistic methodology. There is clearly an evolution of methodology in James's psychological and philosophical works, and the results of this evolution would have become evident in a revision of the *Principles*. In 1890, James declared that *"Introspective observation is what we have to rely on first and foremost and always"* (James, 1890/1981, p. 185). He was quick, however, to call attention to the inaccuracies of introspection. Moreover, he recognized other methods such as those used in comparative psychology and questionnaire techniques. By the time he wrote *Varieties of Religious Experience*, he was using a version of the phenomenological method. His chapter in *Pragmatism*, titled "What Pragmatism Means," clarifies his more mature and flexible vision of methodology. On the subject of methodology, James might have agreed with the former president of the American Chemical Association, Joel Hildebrand (1957), who argued that there is no *one* scientific method. Hildebrand emphasized problem solving and a powerful, practical, goal-directed attitude. To solve a problem, the scientist may have to kick in a door, pick a lock, make a key, cut out a panel, or go around and climb through a window. The zoologist and Nobel Laureate, P. B. Medawar, agreed when he declared there is "no such thing as 'the' scientific method. A scientist uses a great variety of stratagems . . . and no procedure or discovery can be logically scripted" (Medawar, 1984, p. 51). Though James might have been more optimistic about practical methodological unities than Feyerabend (1975), and though he might have disagreed with Feyerabend's unorthodox epistemology, he would nevertheless have argued that diversity, variety, and large-scale doses of anarchy are healthy for epistemology.

A Jamesian revision of the *Principles* would have continued to place strong emphasis on individual experience. The importance of the individual is a theme deeply woven into all of James's writings. His belief in the individual was revealed in the *Principles* in chapters on the stream of thought, the self, attention, and memory. The continuing emphasis on the individual manifested itself in chapters in *The Will to Believe* (James, 1897/1979) such as "Great Men and Their Environments" and "The Importance of Individuals." James's classic book, *Varieties of Religious Experience*, also underscored his focus on the importance of individual experience.

For James, individualism was an integral part of pluralism. Thus, a pluralistic psychology would readily include the study of individual idiosyncrasies. Indeed, to ignore the individual human experience results in a loss of important facts. James (1902/1985) illustrated this point in the following:

So long as we deal with the cosmic and the general, we deal only with the symbols of reality, but *as soon as we deal with private and personal phenomena as such, we deal with realities in the completest sense of the term.* (p. 386)

A pluralistic psychology would focus on the individual as a complement to normative analysis. In a letter to a friend, James expressed his emphasis on the importance of the individual:

As for me, my bed is made: I am against bigness and greatness in all their forms, and with the invisible molecular moral forces that work from individual to individual, stealing in through the crannies of the world like so many soft rootlets, or like the capillary oozing of water, and yet rending the hardest monuments of man's pride, if you give them time. The bigger the unit you deal with, the hollower, the more brutal, the more mendacious is the life displayed. So I am against all big organizations as such, national ones first and foremost; against all big successes and big results; and in favor of the eternal forces of truth which always work in the individual in an immediately unsuccessful way, under-dogs always, till history comes, after they are long dead, and puts them on top. (H. James, 1920, p. 90)

James's mature philosophical works provide another clue about how he might have revised the *Principles*. The clue is found in James's emphasis on contextualism and his growing suspicion of foundationalism. Those who embrace foundationalism or the building block metaphor applied to psychology might be tempted to emphasize one content area as foundational. James's contextualism, or more appropriately, pragmatic contextualism, would have had implications for his treatment of the content areas of psychology. Seigfried (1992) pointed out that, in the *Principles*, James was not always immune to foundationalism. She quoted James's contention that "conceptual systems which neither began nor left off with sensations would be like bridges without piers" (James, 1890/1981, p. 656–657). Seigfried further noted that as James developed his pragmatic method, his emphasis was neither on foundationalism nor antifoundationalism but on alternate ways to organize experience. Such a pragmatic contextualism, applied to the topical content areas of psychology (e.g., learning, memory, sensation, motivation, and cognition) would refute the premise that any area is a foundation for all of psychology.

A revision of the *Principles* might well have applied some metaphors to psychology that the contemporary theoretical physicist, Fritjof Capra, used to characterize modern science. According to Capra (1988), the old paradigm assumed that disciplinary knowledge rested on firm foundations and that there is a scientific hierarchy with physics as most fundamental.

However, Capra argued that the old metaphor of an edifice resting on firm foundations is being replaced by a new paradigm that emphasizes the concept of a network of relationships. He contended that physics can no longer be considered the foundational science because "The phenomena described by physics are not any more fundamental than those described, for example by biology or psychology. They belong to different systems-levels, but none of these levels is any more fundamental than the others" (Capra, 1988, p. 148).

Applying the network concept to psychology, no one topical area that is a genuine part of experience is foundational—there is only a network of relationships. For some problems, the starting point in the network may be learning, for other problems, it may be social influences on behavior, for still other problems, the starting point may be biological influences, motivation, or cognition. No one of these is sufficiently encompassing to serve as an adequate foundation for the entire discipline, nor is any model sufficiently robust to do justice to the complexities of human experience and behavior.

A second edition of the *Principles* would inevitably have been broader in terms of scope and topical coverage than the first edition and would have included more material on unconscious processes as did *Varieties of Religious Experience*. James would also have stressed applications of psychology to education, industry, and the clinic.

Many of James's psychological interests lived on in his work as a philosopher and his mature philosophical vision had important ramifications for a more developed psychology. James did not revise *The Principles of Psychology* and may never have done so even if he had lived a longer life. Nevertheless, it is profitable for us, a century later, to explore the meaning of a pluralistic psychology.

REFERENCES

Capra, F. (1988). The role of physics in the current change of paradigms. In R. F. Kitchener (Ed.), *The world view of contemporary physics* (pp. 144–155). Albany, NY: SUNY Press.

Feyerabend, P. K. (1975). *Against method*. London: NLB.

German science goose-steps. (1936, March 12). *New York Times*, p. 20.

Green, C. D., & Powell, R. (1990). Comment on Kimble's generalism. *American Psychologist, 45*, 556–557.

Hildebrand, J. H. (1957). *Science in the making*. New York: Columbia University Press.

James, H., Jr. (Ed.). (1920). *The letters of William James* (2 Vols.). Boston: Atlantic Monthly Press.

James, W. (1975). *The meaning of truth*. Cambridge, MA: Harvard University Press. (Original work published 1909)

James, W. (1975). *Pragmatism*. Cambridge, MA: Harvard University Press. (Original work published 1907)

James, W. (1976). *Essays in radical empiricism*. Cambridge, MA: Harvard University Press. (Original work published 1912)

James, W. (1977). *A pluralistic universe*. Cambridge, MA: Harvard University Press. (Original work published 1909)

James, W. (1978). Pluralistic mystic. In W. James, *Essays in philosophy* (pp. 172–190). Cambridge, MA: Harvard University Press. (Original work published 1910)

James, W. (1979). *Some problems of philosophy*. Cambridge, MA: Harvard University Press. (Original work published 1911)

James, W. (1979). *The will to believe*. Cambridge, MA: Harvard University Press. (Original work published 1897)

James, W. (1981). *The principles of psychology* (3 Vols.). Cambridge, MA: Harvard University Press. (Original work published 1890)

James, W. (1985). *The varieties of religious experience*. Cambridge, MA: Harvard University Press. (Original work published 1902)

James, W. (1988). Metaphysical seminary—A pluralistic description of the world. In W. James, *Manuscript lectures* (pp. 273–319). Cambridge, MA: Harvard University Press.

Kimble, G. A. (1990). To be or ought to be? That is the question. *American Psychologist, 45*, 558–560.

Medawar, P. B. (1984). *Limits of science*. New York: Harper & Row.

Myers, G. E. (1981). Introduction: The intellectual context. In W. James, *The principles of psychology* (p. xi–xl). Cambridge, MA: Harvard University Press.

Sarason, S. (1989). The lack of an overarching conception in psychology. *Journal of Mind and Behavior, 10*, 263–279.

Seigfried, C. H. (1992). Like bridges without piers: Beyond the foundationalist metaphor. In B. J. Singer & T. Rockmore (Eds.), *Antifoundationalism: Old and new* (pp. 143–164). Philadelphia: Temple University Press.

Staats, A. W. (1989). Unificationism: Philosophy for the modern disunified science of psychology. *Philosophical Psychology, 2*, 143–164.

Thayer, H. S. (1975). Introduction. In W. James, *The meaning of truth* (xi–xlvi). Cambridge, MA: Harvard University Press. (Original work published 1909)

Tolischus, O. D. (1936, March 9). Nazis would junk theoretical physics. *New York Times*, p. 19.

Viney, W. (1989). The cyclops and the twelve-eyed toad: William James and the unity-disunity problem in psychology. *American Psychologist, 44*, 1261–1265.

7

TOWARD A PSYCHOLOGY THAT IS RADICALLY EMPIRICAL: RECAPTURING THE VISION OF WILLIAM JAMES

DONALD A. CROSBY AND WAYNE VINEY

In the introduction to his collection, *The Writings of William James*, John J. McDermott (1977) warned that "to underplay the importance of radical empiricism in any understanding of James, is to risk missing him altogether" (p. xlii). Not only does radical empiricism lie at the heart of James's mature philosophy, as set forth in his *Essays in Radical Empiricism* (James, 1912/1976), but many of its features are also nascent in, and central to, his famous two-volume work in psychology, *The Principles of Psychology* (James, 1890/1981). This chapter will sketch a continuity of ideas in these two writings, showing that radical empiricism was already implicit in the earlier psychological treatise and that it was simply fleshed out and made more comprehensive in the later philosophical work. We contend that the psychology as well as the philosophy of James would be missed if, oblivious

The authors are indebted to the Endowment Fund of the Department of Philosophy at Colorado State University for financial assistance to prepare this chapter and present it at the 1990 Annual Convention of the American Psychological Association.

to McDermott's warning, one were to underplay the basic function of radical empiricism in these two aspects of his thought.

If one counts the chapters in the *Principles* that focus largely on psychological content and discounts the chapters that concentrate on the nervous system, then 15 of the 25 psychological topic areas are readdressed, sometimes briefly, sometimes at length, in *Essays in Radical Empiricism*. And if one considers the entire corpus of James's philosophical work, it will be seen that he returned to virtually every psychological topic covered in the *Principles*. He persistently revisited topics such as consciousness, the self, emotion, imagination, perception, will, experience, thinking, and reality, to adumbrate, alter, or extend earlier positions. Hence, areas covered in the *Principles* continued to thrive in James's philosophy, and his earlier psychological views were often enlarged and clarified by the development of his more mature philosophical perspectives, culminating in the philosophy of radical empiricism.

We address here, therefore, a fascinating and important question: What would a psychology that is radically empirical, in James's sense of the term, look like? After first interpreting what radical empiricism is in James's mature philosophy, we then will discuss earlier expressions of this outlook in the *Principles*. Finally, we will contemplate ways in which he might have revised that work in accordance with developments in his later thought.

THE PHILOSOPHY OF RADICAL EMPIRICISM

James's empiricism can be termed *radical* for at least the following reasons. These reasons show how fundamentally different his empiricism is from the traditional British empiricism that has persisted well into this century.

1. For James (1912/1976), "experience and reality come to the same thing" (p. 30). Experience is James's metaphysical ultimate. Everything real is an aspect and manifestation of this ultimate. Instead of focusing on the experience of reality, as most empiricists have tended to do, James focused on the reality of experience. Instead of talking about experience of the world, he talked about the world of experience.

2. The distinction between subject and object, knower and known is made *within* the field of experience. Experience does not presuppose a subjective experiencer, and it does not presuppose an objective world to be experienced. Thus, James did not buy into the subjectivist turn of modern philosophy, epitomized by the famous cogito, ergo sum of René Descartes, nor did he accept the correspondence theory of truth, which interprets truth to

mean representation of an in-itself world thought to lie behind experience and to be its ultimate cause. Instead, truth for James meant adequacy to experience or workability in practice. He made no attempt to look behind experience as such for its putative causes; experience is the given, and it is pointless to try to probe beyond that given, because experience is the sole warrant for any of our claims.

James construed both the self and the world as interconnected aspects of experience, each of which functions in certain distinctive ways, rather than conceiving of them in substantialist terms. His view of the self was closer to that of Buddhism than to that of Aristotle, Descartes, or John Locke. No substantial self can be found in experience, nor can any substantial thing, as even Locke (an advocate of substantialism) had to admit, referring to substance, whether mental or physical, as "something he knew not what" (Locke 1690/1959, pp. 391–392).

3. All kinds of experience are relevant to the truth of claims in philosophy, psychology, and other domains, not just to sensate experience. That is, our claims to truth need to be brought before the court of emotional, recollective, inquisitive, deliberative, judgmental, and evaluative, as well as sensate experience. For example, in his essay, "The Dilemma of Determinism," James (1884) rejected both hard and soft determinism on the ground that neither is adequate to our moral experience, and in his *Varieties of Religious Experience* (1902/1925), he carefully assessed the truth of claims resting on religious experience. Furthermore, he agreed with Henri Bergson that an adequate understanding of issues relating to time, causality, chance, and freedom cannot be founded merely on sensate experience in the manner of David Hume. It must be based, instead, on the felt influences of the past and the lures of an open future, as reflected in experiences of continuity, novelty, memory, habit, anticipation, effort, and aim.

4. Relations are as real in experience as the things that are related. James rejected the strong nominalistic tendencies of traditional British empiricism. Hence, no "transexperiential agents of unification, substances, intellectual categories and powers, and selves" (James, 1912/1976, p. 23) are needed to account for the connectedness of the experienced world. This is in keeping with James's (1912/1976) contention that "to be radical, an empiricism must neither admit into its constructions any element that is not directly experienced, nor *exclude* [italics added] from them any element that is directly experienced" (p. 22). Relations are an integral part of our experience, characterizing it at the very outset and at every turn. Hume and other empiricists were wrong to

exclude them, that is, to assume that experience presents itself in separate bits devoid of any relations.

5. Although there is unity or relatedness in our experience, it is not the through and through unity of metaphysical monism. Experience exhibits what James called *concatenated unity*, that is, a multiplicity of irreducibly particular occurrences in the midst of intricate patterns of relatedness (James, 1912/1976). It contains elements of order combined with elements of chaos, of upsurging novelty as well as predictable continuity. Thus, although no conceptual account can do full justice to the elusive diversity, complexity, and dynamism of experience, there is sufficient connectedness and intelligibility in it to make it amenable to conceptual systematization and understanding. Such understanding can best be gained, however, when we make allowances for a variety of methods of inquiry, hypothetical models, and ways of thinking. "There is no possible point of view," said James (1897/1979), "from which the world can appear as an absolutely single fact" (p. 6).

6. In any conflict of concepts and experience, experience must take precedence. James did not assume that experience can be completely separated from linguistic, cultural, or historical conceptualizations. Even though he talked of "pure experience," he hastened to remind us that "its purity is only a relative term, meaning the proportional amount of unverbalized sensation which it still embodies" (James, 1912/1976, p. 46). The contrast of experience and concepts is, therefore, a relative one, not an absolute one. But the relative distinction is crucial, for it means that we must always strive to put our intellectual constructions (e.g., monism, pluralism, materialism, idealism, theism, and naturalism) to the test of our experiences and to take fully into account obdurate limits imposed by those experiences. Even the "most assured conclusions concerning matters of fact," wrote James, are to be regarded "as hypotheses liable to modification in the course of future experience" (James, 1897/1979, p. 5). We must be extremely careful, therefore, to stick with the concreteness of experience and not to be seduced by mere verbal or intellectual abstractions.

ANTICIPATION OF RADICAL EMPIRICISM IN THE *PRINCIPLES*

Statements suggestive of each of these six traits of radical empiricism can be found in the *Principles*. However, some of the traits are more strongly adumbrated than others, and the relevant texts often contain ambiguities, uncertainties, and hedgings that contrast with the more forthright formulations of James's later philosophy.

The first trait—the idea that experience and reality come to the same thing—is not clearly set forth in the *Principles*, but the seed of the idea is certainly present. For example, in the chapter, "The Perception of Reality," James argued for a functional, pragmatic, contextual vision of reality. Throughout the chapter, he spoke of reality as lived, reality in relation to us and to our needs and interests, rather than of an absolute, independently existing world. He insisted that experiences and conceptions will be accorded more or less objective reality, depending on the extent to which they take account of and terminate in sensations (especially tactile sensations, because he held these to be the least fluctuating types of sensate experiences and the ones most vital for the exigencies of life), posses immediacy or vividness, cohere with other experiences and conceptions, and have practical, emotional, and valuative interest for the perceiver or thinker. "What are things?," he asked in the chapter, "The Stream of Thought." He answered, "Nothing . . . but special groups of sensible qualities which happen practically or aesthetically to interest us, to which we therefore give substantive names, and which we exalt to this exclusive status and dignity" (James, 1890/1981, p. 274). He contended that reality, thus understood, is fluid and changeable, capable of varying from time to time, situation to situation, person to person, and culture to culture.

"The fons et origo of all reality," James (1890/1981) concluded, "is thus subjective, is ourselves" (p. 925). Or as he put it in another place, "existence is . . . no substantive quality when we predicate it of any object; it is a relation, ultimately terminating in ourselves, and at the moment when it terminates, becoming a *practical* relation" (James, 1890/1981, p. 919). This emphasis on *ourselves* admittedly has a more subjectivist tone than that in James's later writings, for there he talked of both the self and the world as functional distinctions drawn within a neutral field of pure experience. But the emphasis in this chapter of the *Principles* on reality as thoroughly relational and experiential is congruous with his later view.

The second trait of radical empiricism—that the distinction between subject and object ought to be regarded as purely functional and contextual (in opposition to the traditional picture of two fundamentally different, and yet somehow interacting, types of substantial entities, the one mental and the other physical)—is also anticipated in the *Principles*. But this foreshadowing exists alongside of, and in tension with, texts asserting a version of mind–body dualism.

James (1890/1981) flatly declared in the chapter, "The Relations of Minds to Other Things," that the psychologist's attitude toward cognition must be that of "a thoroughgoing dualism." This dualism "supposes two elements, mind knowing and thing known, and treats them as irreducible" (p. 214). He also seemed to assume, in at least one part of the *Principles*, something very much like the traditional correspondence view of truth, that beliefs are true to the extent that they duplicate or mirror aspects of a self-subsisting external reality (see James, 1890/1981, pp. 1226–1227).

James gave at least two reasons for his espousal of mind–body dualism in his psychological treatise. First, he thought it entirely appropriate that psychology, as a science, simply assume the common view that knowledge is possible and that it is a representation of objects external to the self. Psychology need not concern itself with the perplexing issues posed when we subject this common view to philosophical scrutiny. Second, James saw psychology as being in the business of trying to understand how "the mind's *own brain*" (James, 1890/1981, p. 212) relates to mental experiences and, thus, of exploring the interactions of two worlds—the one physical and the other mental. He puzzled in one place over relations between what he called the *nerve world* and the *mind-world* (James, 1890/1981, p. 157), wondering whether the fusion of initially discrete blows or taps into a single tone takes place in the former or the latter. He concluded that the integration must take place in the brain, and he asserted in another passage that "to every brain-modification, however small, must correspond a change of equal amount in the feeling which the brain subserves" (James, 1890/1981, p. 227). Although acknowledging that philosophical problems about actual causal relations of the putatively separate domains of mind and brain "are of a unique and utterly mysterious sort" (p. 212) (an admission betraying his own deep misgivings about the philosophical adequacy of metaphysical dualism), James contended that psychology, by its very nature, has the task of exploring regular correlations of physical structures and occurrences, most particularly those of the brain, with mental phenomena such as thought and emotion (James, 1890/1981). Hence, by his reckoning in the *Principles*, psychology is committed to a kind of dualism, but entitled by its restricted status as a natural science to bracket more ultimate questions of epistemology and metaphysics raised by this dualism.

There would seem to be no in-principle inconsistency between the guarded, generally methodological dualism espoused in the *Principles* and James's later rejection of philosophical mind–body dualism in favor of the second trait of radical empiricism now under discussion. In fact, in the *Principles*, James conceived of the mind as a stream of passing thought appropriating previous thoughts, rather than as a substantial ego standing against the world. And, as we already mentioned, James frequently spoke of extramental reality in functionalist, relational terms, rather than in those of an in-itself, substantialist material world. Moreover, James anticipated in the *Principles* his later notion of "pure experience," regarded as a field of awareness prior to the distinction between subject and object, when he discussed the significance of nonreflective experiences in which objects are perceived "as simple *beings*, neither in nor out of thought" (James, 1890/1981, p. 263; see Wild, 1969, p. 73).

Passages of the *Principles* that interpret the self and the world in this way erode the rigid barriers between the two which is the dubious legacy of philosophies of the seventeenth and eighteenth centuries. The passages foreshadow James's later, more fully developed perspective of radical empiricism that refuses to sharply separate mind from body or to make either or both of them prior to experience. These passages also open the way to his later rejection of the correspondence theory of truth, with its strong overtones of metaphysical dualism (see Crosby, 1988, pp. 174–185), in favor of the pragmatic theory.

The third trait of James's philosophy of radical empiricism—that many types of experiences and not just sensate experiences are directly relevant to assessments of the truth of claims in various fields of investigation—is also prefigured in the *Principles*. James assigned a certain priority to sensate experiences there, insisting that a "conception, to prevail, must *terminate* in the world of orderly sensible experience" and "hang together with . . . facts of sense" (James, 1890/1981, pp. 929–930). But he also argued that acceptance of the truth of propositions and theories depends on the extent to which they accord with our aesthetic, emotional, practical, and thus moral and religious experiences and needs.

Materialistic philosophies, for example, will and should "fail of universal adoption," for they deny "reality to the objects of almost all the impulses which we most cherish" (James, 1890/1981, p. 940). Similarly, although external matter may be sincerely doubted by philosophical idealists "minds external to our own are never doubted. We need them too much, are too essentially social to dispense with them" (James, 1890/1981, p. 45). And although James conceded that "so-called 'scientific' conceptions of the universe have so far gratified the purely intellectual interests more than the mere sentimental conceptions have," he also noted that "they leave the emotional and active interests cold." (James, 1890/1981, pp. 944–945). We cannot help aspiring, therefore, to worldviews that can include these scientific conceptions, but also provide larger frameworks wherein our emotional and active interests can find satisfaction. In these ways, James clearly anticipated the wider empiricism, ranging beyond the deliverances of the five senses and seeking to encompass all important dimensions of human sensibility and aspiration for which his later philosophy is noted.

Evidence of this wider empiricism in the *Principles* is the remarkable scope of the work. For James, empiricism could not be restricted or exclusive. Whatever is found in experience must be included in the subject matter of psychology. The enormous breadth of his treatise is brought home to us when we contrast it with other psychological texts of the day. For example, over 55 percent of Titchener's *A Textbook of Psychology* (1910) is devoted to sensation, perception, and conception. By contrast, only 13 percent of James's *Principles* is devoted to these topics. The content of the latter strays from the familiar topical areas that lent themselves easily to the methodologies of the day. For this reason, James was accused by some of his contemporaries of compromising the scientific status of psychology. An example of the wide-ranging character of his work is cited by Daniel Bjork (1983), who pointed out that James was "the only first-generation American experimental psychologist to incorporate the unconscious mind into psychology" (p. 145). James was also interested in paranormal phenomena, abnormal psychology, the "mind cure" movement, and the psychology of religion. He believed that all of these topics had some place in the stream of experience and, therefore, should not be ignored by psychology. As Bjork (1983) observed, James believed that his colleagues "had compromised experimental psychology; they had abandoned the scientific frontier for safer, stale psychologies" (p. 146).

The fourth trait of radical empiricism—that relations are as fundamental and real in experience as the things that are related—constitutes one of James's main lines of attack on standard British empiricism. This trait is pervasively present in the *Principles*, as is illustrated in this typical statement:

> Most books start with sensations, as the simplest mental facts, and proceed sympathetically, constructing each higher stage from those below it. But this is abandoning the empirical method of investigation. No one ever had a simple sensation by itself. Consciousness, from our natal day, is of a teeming multiplicity of objects and relations, and what we call simple sensations are results of discriminative attention, pushed often to a very high degree. (James, 1890/1981, p. 219)

James contrasted his view with British empiricism's *atomism*, which he called "a brickbat plan of construction" (James, 1890/1981, p. 195) and held that a "pure sensation is an abstraction" (James, 1890/1981, p. 653). Because relations are omnipresent in our experience, there is no need for the traditional empiricist doctrine of association to account for them or to serve as a kind of glue for the units of sensation, "each separate, each ignorant of its mates" (James, 1890/1981, p. 334), as was erroneously assumed by thinkers such as Hume, David Hartley, and James Mill.

James cited a striking example testifying to the original connectedness of experience. A sharp clap of thunder may appear to be a discrete event, but more adequate introspection demonstrates that we do not hear "thunder *pure*, but thunder-breaking-upon-silence-and-contrasting-with-it." The "feeling of the thunder," he pointed out, "is also a feeling of the silence as just gone." Ordinary language misleads us by referring to our sensations as if they occurred in isolation, whereas experience exhibits the relations of each of them to "perhaps a thousand other things" (James, 1890/1981, p. 234). James's point was not that every detail of the complex patterns of relatedness suffusing experience is present vividly to the mind. Of most of the relations of any discriminated sensation, we are only dimly aware "in the penumbral nascent way of a 'fringe' of unarticulated affinities about it" (James, 1890/1981, p. 250). His point was rather that relations are already profuse in experience, meaning that there is no demand for them to be externally imposed by a supposed substantial self, by putative laws of association, or—as for the Kantians—by the mysterious operations of a *transcendental ego*. The fourth trait of James's later doctrine of radical empiricism is, therefore, straightforwardly proclaimed and developed at considerable length in the *Principles*.

The fifth trait—that experience is not a through-and-through unity, but only a concatenated one, and that a variety of methods of inquiry and ways of thinking are required even to begin to do justice to its richness—is at least implicitly contained in the *Principles*. James commented frequently on how chaotic and unwieldy experience would be if it were not for the fact that our activities of sensing, conceiving, naming, organizing, and theorizing are working constantly to simplify it. But these activities are also highly selective. "Out of the infinite chaos of movements, of which physics teaches us that the outer world consists, each sense organ picks out those which fall within certain limits of velocity" (James, 1890/1981, p. 273). Moreover, the "mind chooses to suit itself and decides what particular sensation shall be held more real and valid than all the rest" (James, 1890/1981, p. 275). Reasoning and ethical decision making are but other forms of the selective activity of the mind.

James maintained that the mind works with the materials provided to it by experience much as the sculptor works on a block of stone, rejecting certain portions of it and highlighting and shaping others.

> Other minds, other worlds from the same monotonous and inexpressive chaos! My world is but one in a million, alike embedded, alike real to those who may abstract them. How different must be the worlds in the consciousness of ant, cuttle-fish, or crab! (James, 1890/1981, p. 277)

The outlook of nineteenth-century science, with its devotion to the model of the machine, was for James one such selective perspective on experience, useful in some ways, but not in others, and not to be confused with the totality of the world. He described the nervous system as a machine and compared it to a telephone switchboard, but he was quick to refer to this characterization as a "mere scheme" (James, 1890/1981, p. 38). When James was a mechanist in the *Principles*, he tended to be a methodological mechanist, not a metaphysical one. He pointed out that "psychology will be psychology, and science will be science" (James, 1890/1981, p. 1179), suggesting that, for him, psychology is not merely a science, or at least not in the nineteenth-century sense.

James mused (1890/1981) that science "may be enveloped in a wider order, on which she has no claims at all" (p. 1179). He labeled as "utterly absurd" the "popular notion that 'Science' is forced on the mind ab extra, and that our interests have nothing to do with its constructions." Science, like other theoretical constructions, is rooted in a "craving to believe that the things of the world belong to kinds which are related by inward rationality together." Interest, need, and assumption contribute to the selectivity of science. The "original investigator always preserves a healthy sense of how plastic the materials are in his hands" (James, 1890/1981, p. 1260).

James's keen sensitivity to the selective, partial nature of any given perspective on experience is shown by the fact, noted by Myers (1981), that in the *Principles*, James approached some topics almost from the viewpoint of a behaviorist, others from that of a biologist, and still others from that of a philosopher or a phenomenological psychologist. He repeatedly refused to be used by any particular methodology; rather, he appropriated various methodologies in the service of a larger vision. He was not, however, a mere eclectic. Self-conscious organizing conceptions are at work in the *Principles*, which kept James from a piecemeal, hit-or-miss approach to the discipline of psychology.

The upshot of these considerations is that the *Principles* exhibits a sense of what James was later to call *concatenated unity*, as opposed to the complete order and knowability of the world often assumed by more rationalistic thinkers and encapsulated in a favorite rationalistic principle, the law of sufficient reason. According to James, conjunctions are real in experience, but disjunctions are real as well. The experienced world is a blend of order and chaos, intelligibility and mystery. Different perspectives can illuminate different facets of experience, but only at the price of casting others into shadow. No single perspective can hope to capture the whole or even to do complete justice to a part of the whole. The spirit of methodological and metaphysical pluralism that breathes in the *Principles* was later to find explicit expression in what we are calling the fifth trait of radical empiricism.

The sixth trait—that in any conflict of concepts, beliefs, or theories with experience, experience must be given precedence—is simply a concise statement of the creed of empiricism. But James's radical empiricism took this creed seriously in a way that, according to James, ordinary British empiricism did not (as his attack on the latter's uncritical assumption of epistemological atomism demonstrated). Another dogma of traditional empiricism that James rejected on empirical grounds is the notion that each of the five senses is so irreducibly unique that there can be no analogies with which we can pass from one to another. John Locke, William Molyneaux, and George Berkeley argued, for example, that a person blind from birth who suddenly regains sight could not make a visual discrimination between a cube and a sphere without touching them. In opposition to the claim that there are no intersensory analogies, James called attention to numerous metaphors of common speech, which were presumable reflective of ordinary experience. If there are no such analogies, then why are terms such as " 'sweet' and 'soft' used so synonymously in most languages?" Other examples cited by James are "rough sounds, heavy smells, hard lights, cold colors" (James, 1890/1981, p. 844). Although the doctrine of the irreducible heterogeneity of the senses was deeply entrenched in James's day and accepted by some of the leading luminaries in the field, James's stubborn empiricism called it into question. He wrote "although in its more superficial determinations the blind man's space is very different from our [visual] space, yet a deep analogy remains between the two" (James, 1890/1981, p. 841).

As opposed to the various forms of rationalism, which give a fundamental role in knowing to what Kant called "synthetic a priori" judgments and propositions, that is, judgments and propositions that are alleged to be informative about the world although not dependent on experience, James insisted that no judgments or propositions ought to be accepted as true that do not pass the test of experience. In the final chapter of the *Principles*, entitled "Necessary Truths and the Effects of Experience," James admitted that there are such things as necessary truths (e.g, in logic and mathematics), but argued that they are necessary in a formal or mental sense only. They become synthetic or informative about the world only when they can be confirmed experientially, meaning that they must then be regarded as empirical hypotheses. To the extent that supposed necessary truths lack such confirmation, they have no right to be regarded as true except in a purely definitional or formal sense. Such conceptions "stand waiting in the mind," as James put it in this chapter, "forming a beautiful ideal network; and the most we can say is that *we hope* to discover outer realities over which the network may be flung so that ideal and real may coincide" (James, 1890/1981, p. 1258). This chapter of the *Principles* gives unequivocal endorsement, then, to the sixth trait of radical empiricism, and it does so by taking issue with a central tenet of rationalism. James championed the priority of experience over theory throughout his treatise, even though he fully recognized the selective and constructive role of the ever-active, purposeful human mind.

RADICAL EMPIRICISM AND POSSIBLE REVISIONS
OF THE *PRINCIPLES*

How might James have revised the *Principles* in accordance with his later thought? We can only speculate, but we want to suggest several possible ways. One is that he would probably have purged the *Principles* of any traces of metaphysical dualism, subjective idealism, or the correspondence theory of truth, revising it in the direction of the first and second traits of radical empiricism. All talk of the brain, of the external world, of other minds, and of one's own mind, and all discussion of our knowledge of the world could now be brought within the purview of James's later philosophical outlook, which had already been anticipated in the *Principles*—where the distinction between mind and body becomes functional and relative, made within the larger field of experience, and where correspondence to an in-itself world gives way to pragmatic methods of assessing truth. James would have lost nothing of great importance with these translations of his psychology into the sphere of his later philosophy, and he would have gained a great deal in clarity and coherence.

Another line of possible revision for the *Principles* is suggested by James's conviction that relations in experience are as real as the things related. If he had lived just a few more years, he would have encountered the Gestalt psychologists who offered specific practical examples and convincing experimental research on the fundamental role of relations. The Gestaltists filled out part of the intellectual map that was so central to James's psychological and philosophical work, and there can be little doubt that he would have found much to admire in their program.

Myers (1986) pointed out that "James would have welcomed the collapse of material objects into fields, a theory which agrees precisely with the spirit of radical empiricism; in fact, he himself employed the term *field*" (p. 131). James also used the term *Gestaltqualität* (James, 1912/1976, p. 83) in discussing the experience of activity. He would have been especially receptive to Gestalt field-theoretical approaches to brain activity. Such approaches are clearly more consistent with radical empiricism than earlier nineteenth-century connectionist views of the structure and workings of the brain.

It is intriguing to speculate how much a revision of the *Principles* might have been influenced by Gestalt psychology had James lived a bit longer. There are similarities between the two systems, but also important differences. Wolfgang Köhler (1947/1970) acknowledged the major contention of radical empiricism that conjunctions and disjunctions are both matters of direct experience. He argued however, that radical empiricism as envisioned by James adduces relations lacking certain qualities that Gestaltists emphasize. For example, James failed, in Köhler's judgment, to show clearly why a given whole or relation is important or meaningful or why it should hold our attention. Moreover, in the Gestalt view, the whole is fundamentally and qualitatively different from the parts. It is not a mere aggregate or conjunction. The whole precedes part processes, and part processes are governed by the nature of the whole. Köhler did not find such a rigorously wholistic view of relations in James's work. James might have responded to these criticisms by giving more attention to the concept of wholes and more importance to wholes in relation to their parts, but he would not have allowed this emphasis to swamp his pluralistic empiricism. He would have strongly resisted, in other words, any monistic tendencies in Gestalt psychology, where particular aspects of experience come to be seen as insignificant in their subordination to wholes.

An additional way that a revision of the *Principles* might have brought it closer to Gestalt thinking is suggested by Köhler's (1947/1970) observation that "James was most anxious to give felt determination its share in the description of experience" (p. 340). This was important for Köhler, because felt determination is a key concept in Gestalt psychology and is viewed as one of the components of insight. A continuing theme in James's philosophical works is an emphasis on experience of active manipulations, of exertions of effort against obstacles, and of being now triumphant, now defeated forces in the field of activity. In a letter to Shadworth H. Hodgson in 1885, James criticized monistic and deterministic views for their inability to make a real distinction between activity and passivity. James complained that these views cannot differentiate between " 'impediments from within' and 'impediments from without'!—between being fated to do the thing *willingly* or not!" They provide us with "a wrong complement to the rest of life," a "monstrous indifferentism which brings forth everything *eodem jure*," although our "nature demands something *objective* to take sides with" (H. James, 1920, p. 246). James was deeply sensitive, then, to our feelings of effortful striving, to our awareness of focused activity, and to our encounters with forces that sometimes resist and sometimes complement our labor. In light of this persistent emphasis on felt determination or effort already present in his work, we conclude that he might have wanted to give more attention to the intimate connections between effort and insight argued for by Gestalt psychologists and then revised his *Principles* accordingly.

James's insistence on the fundamental importance of feeling in works such as *Talks to Teachers: And to Students on Some of Life's Ideals* (1899/1983) and *Essays in Radical Empiricism* (1912/1976) suggests another direction for a revision of the *Principles*. He did not neglect this topic in his psychological treatise, but it became even more crucial for him later, and he might well have given greater stress to feeling's pervasive role in experience in a revision of the work. His mature psychology would have been especially marked, we surmise, by concerted attention to the interrelations of cognition and feeling.

In his introduction to the recent Harvard edition of the *Principles*, Myers (1981) noted that James often used the terms *thought* and *feeling* interchangeably and that his "famous 'stream of thought' is equally a stream of feeling, sensations, or images" (p. xxviii). In *Talks to Teachers*, James asserted that the primal or immediate fact that psychology must study is that human beings have fields of consciousness. These fields are

> always complex. They contain sensations of our bodies and of the objects around us, memories of past experiences and thoughts of distant things, feelings of satisfaction and dissatisfaction, desires and aversions, and other emotional conditions, together with determinations of the will, in every variety of permutation and combination. (James, 1899/1983, pp. 19–20)

There is no such thing, then, as sensation or cognition denuded of feeling.

James observed in "On a Certain Blindness in Human Beings" (one of the "Talks to Students" included in the 1899 edition of *Talks to Teachers*) that if "we were radically feelingless, and if ideas were the only things our mind could entertain, we should lose all our likes and dislikes at a stroke, and be unable to point to any one situation or experience in life more valuable or significant than any other" (James, 1899/1983, p. 132). The blindness to which the title of this lecture refers is that which can result from taking, or trying to take, a purely intellectual view of things, devoid of sympathetic insight or emotion. This attitude becomes especially harmful when it cuts us off from experiences of value that are mediated largely by feeling or makes us oblivious to the feelings and concerns of others. In *Essays in Radical Empiricism*, James (1912/1976) insisted that feelings "may be as prophetic and anticipatory of truth as anything else we have, and some of them more so than others" (p. 143).

A radically empirical psychology would be deeply suspicious, therefore, of any system that neglects or diminishes the central role of affect in thinking. It might even argue that cognition is parasitic to affect more often than the reverse. Indeed, one of James's criticisms of rationalistic absolutism, as contrasted with empiricism, is that it will not admit that "all philosophies are hypotheses, to which all our faculties, *emotional as well as logical* [italics added], help us" (James, 1912/1976, p. 143). James was already well aware in the *Principles* of the role of emotion in thinking. As we have seen, emotion enters into the selectivity of thinking, and emotional satisfaction is an important empirical test of the adequacy of worldviews in that work. But in a revision of the *Principles*, James might have explored in more depth and detail the intimate relations between affect and cognition in keeping with his emphasis on such relations in his later thought.

A revision of the *Principles* might also have placed more emphasis on the practical side of the central role of feeling in human life. In *Talks to Teachers*, James offered advice about how to manipulate emotion by manipulating activity. He argued that activity is more subject to effortful striving than feeling. "To wrestle with a bad feeling only pins our attention on it" (James, 1899/1983, p. 118). To change a feeling, focus on actions or behaviors that are its opposite. James's advice was remarkably similar to Viktor Frankl's paradoxical intention or to behavioral manipulation of moods.

Another characteristic of a revised *Principles* that we can imagine is the further development of a psychology with a strong social–environmental flavor. James's well-known pluralistic concern for the uniqueness and importance of individuals does not imply an insensitivity to social or environmental contexts. Like Sigmund Freud, in his exchange of letters with Albert Einstein entitled "Why War?" (see Freud, 1932), James was deeply troubled by the dishonesty, artificiality, and alienating effects of some aspects of civilization and its institutions. One of his best known essays, "The Moral Equivalent of War" (James, 1910), displays informed awareness of the dangerous social and political tendencies of the time. Furthermore, according to James's radical empiricism, the very significance of life is in its relations, and there is no such thing as an autonomous Cartesian self that draws from innate reservoirs of truth and is isolated from other selves and the rest of the world.

Because the self, for James, is through and through a social self, social and environmental contexts must play key roles, along with biological or physiological correlates, in any adequate investigation of the complexities of behavior and the routes to mental health. In an essay entitled "The Need for Social Psychology," John Dewey (1917) acknowledged the landmark contributions of James in the *Principles* to the emerging field of social psychology—particularly his theories of the social self and instincts—and then pointed out the need to transfer attention in current psychology "from vague generalities regarding social consciousness and social mind to the specific processes of interaction which take place among human beings, and to the details of group-behavior" (p. 270). The central task of such a social psychology, as Dewey conceived it, is investigation of ways in which instinctive behavior is related to socially acquired capacities and habits. A revision of the *Principles* by James might have steered the work in at least some of the directions outlined by Dewey's article, directions anticipated by the *Principles*'s discussions of the socially interrelated, inherently dynamic and responsive self.

A final feature of a revised *Principles* would probably have been a pronounced emphasis on subconscious or unconscious process. The powerful role of these processes in human experience was already recognized by James in the 1890 work. He referred to gaps in consciousness brought about by anesthesia, sleep, lapses of attention, and insensibilities to commonplace noises. He quoted the studies on hysteria by Pierre Janet and Alfred Binet and saw such studies as demonstrating that "the total possible consciousness may be split into parts which coexist but mutually ignore each other" (James, 1890/1981, p. 198). He also reviewed the early work on posthypnotic suggestion and accepted it as evidence for the operation of unconscious processes.

The James of the *Principles* was deeply interested in finding an explanation for the workings of the unconscious. He was curious about whether one must believe, as did the Cartesians, that it is the very essence of the mind to think. If so, then a priori explanations solve the problem of the unconscious, interpreting it as "lapses of ordinary memory, or . . . the sinking of consciousness to a minimal state, in which all it feels is a bare existence which leaves no particulars behind to be recalled" (James, 1890/1981, p. 198). On the other hand, one can follow the lead of Locke and "take the appearances for what they seem to be," allowing "that the mind, as well as the body, may go to sleep" (James, 1890/1981, p. 198). So far as the specific operations of the unconscious are concerned, James affirmed (1890/1981) that "on the whole it is best to abstain from a conclusion. The science of the near future will doubtless answer this question more wisely than we can now" (p. 210).

James's intense interest in unconscious processes continued to manifest itself more than a decade after publication of the *Principles* in his classic *Varieties of Religious Experience* (1902/1925), although by this time, he preferred the vaguer terms *subconscious* and *subliminal*. In this book, James suggested that the subliminal mind may be open to influences that cannot produce effects in ordinary consciousness. His pragmatism was also influencing his approach to subconscious phenomena at this time, for he argued that these phenomena must be judged by their effects (James, 1902/1925, pp. 242–243). In the final chapter of the *Varieties*, James (1902/1925) observed that "the *subconscious self* is nowadays a well-accredited psychological entity [and that] there is actually and literally more life in our total soul than we are at any time aware of" (p. 511). Given his obvious and abiding enthusiasm about what could be learned from ongoing research into subconscious phenomena, it seems likely that James would have devoted a great deal of space to this important topic in a revision of the *Principles*.

As yet, there is no psychological system known to us that is radically empirical in the fullest Jamesian sense. William James only pointed in the direction of such a psychology and identified some of its cardinal traits. The leads he provided are as relevant today and worthy of pursuit among psychologists as they were in 1890.

REFERENCES

Bjork, D. W. (1983). *The compromised scientist: William James in the development of American psychology*. New York: Columbia University Press.

Crosby, D. A. (1988). *The specter of the absurd: Sources and criticisms of modern nihilism*. Albany, NY: State University of New York Press.

Dewey, J. (1917). The need for social psychology. *Psychological Review, 24,* 266–277.

Freud, S. (1932). Way War? In James Strachey (Ed. and Trans.), *The standard edition of the complete psychological works of Sigmund Freud* (Vol. 22, pp. 197–215). London: Hogarth Press.

James, H., Jr. (Ed.). (1920). *The letters of William James* (Vol. 1). Boston: Atlantic Monthly Press.

James, W. (1884). The dilemma of determinism. *Unitarian Review, 22,* 193–224.

James, W. (1910). The moral equivalent of war. *Popular Science Monthly, 77,* 400–412.

James, W. (1925). *The Varieties of religious experience: A study in human nature*. New York: Longmans, Green. (Original work published in 1902)

James, W. (1976). *Essays in radical empiricism*. Cambridge, MA: Harvard University Press. (Original work published 1912)

James, W. (1979). *The will to believe*. Cambridge, MA: Harvard University Press. (Original work published 1897)

James, W. (1981). *The principles of psychology* (3 vols.). Cambridge, MA: Harvard University Press. (Original work published 1890)

James, W. (1983). *Talks to teachers on psychology: And to students on some of life's ideals*. Cambridge, MA: Harvard University Press. (Original work published 1899)

Köhler, W. (1970). *Gestalt psychology*. New York: Liveright. (Original work published 1947)

Locke, J. (1959). An essay concerning human understanding (Vol. 1). New York: Dover Publications. (Original work published 1690)

McDermott, J. J. (Ed.). (1977). *The writings of William James*. Chicago: University of Chicago Press.

Myers, G. E. (1981). Introduction: The Intellectual Context. In W. James, *Principles of psychology* (pp. xi–xx). Cambridge, MA: Harvard University Press.

Myers, G. (1986). *William James: His life and thought*. New Haven, CT: Yale University Press.

Titchener, E. B. (1910). *A textbook of psychology*. New York: Macmillan.

Wild, J. (1969). *The radical empiricism of William James*. Garden City, NY: Doubleday and Company.

8

A PHENOMENOLOGICAL REINTERPRETATION OF THE JAMESIAN SCHEMA FOR PSYCHOLOGY

AMEDEO GIORGI

Over 100 years after its publication, William James's *Principles of Psychology* (1890/1950), continues to provoke considerable reflection on Jamesian themes, and deservedly so. A work that is still rewarding to read a century after its original publication must be addressing some perennial problems. The problem addressed in this chapter is the issue of the subject matter of psychology. As is well known, psychology has had several competing definitions of its field during the last century—consciousness, behavior, the unconscious, and the field of experience—to name only the most popular ones. The issue, of course, remains unresolved, and so long as it does, the possibility of conceiving of psychology as a coherent discipline will also remain unresolved. James, himself, was deeply concerned about both psychology's scientific status and a proper understanding of psychology's subject matter.

A case can be made that James's schema for approaching and defining the subject matter of psychology is still the best place to start despite its century old status. James presented his schema in the chapter, "The Methods and Snares of Psychology," and he spoke of the natural-science perspective that psychology must adopt. He (1950/1890) wrote

> It is highly important that this natural-science point of view should be understood at the outset. Otherwise more may be demanded of the psychologist than he ought to be expected to perform. A diagram will exhibit more emphatically what the assumptions of Psychology must be:

1	2	3	4
The Psychologist	The Thought Studied	The Thought's Object	The Psychologist's Reality

> These four squares contain the irreducible data of psychology. No. 1, the psychologist, believes Nos. 2, 3, and 4, which together form *his* total object, to be realities, and reports them and their mutual relations as truly as he can without troubling himself with the puzzle of how he can report them at all. About such *ultimate* puzzles he in the main need trouble himself no more than the geometer, the chemist, or the botanist do, who precisely make the same assumptions as he. (p. 184)

In this chapter, I will attempt to show that although James was logically correct in dividing the "irreducible data" of psychology into four categories, it is not psychologically defensible. On the basis of phenomenological thought, an alternative schema will be proposed for the science of psychology. I will suggest instead an experiential basis for the schema that will consist of two complex factors that incorporate James's four, but are understood differently. The schema would look as follows:

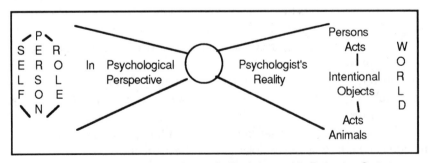

Figure 1: The Phenomenologically Modified Schema for Psychology and Its Explanatory Context.

The outer line refers to the fact that, in human affairs, one is always dealing with complex relationships: person–world, person–person, person–animal, and person–self. When persons or animals relate to objects or others, a minimum condition for psychological phenomena is satisfied, but not a sufficient one. In addition, the person who is a psychologist assumes a psychological attitude (role) toward the expressed (intentional) relationships, which constitutes the psychologist's reality. The psychologist can also constitute the psychologist's reality with respect to oneself. The lines demarcating the psychological perspective and the psychologist's reality are also meant to indicate that the psychological perspective is neither absolute nor exhaustive. With respect to James's schema, one could say that the psychologist (1) assumes a psychological perspective with respect to the intentional object, which intrinsically includes the relationship between the thought studied (2) and the thought's object (3) and, thus, constitutes the psychological reality (4). Descriptively, and trying to be as comprehensive as possible, the alternative schema could be the following: A person who is a psychologist assumes the posture of the phenomenological reduction and also assumes a psychological perspective, thus constituting the psychologist's reality, with respect to an expression of the consciousness or behavior of the other, or oneself, as it is intentionally related to its object, and then observes and describes it.

Although this schema took only a few lines to describe, the issues are so complex that it will take the rest of the chapter to explicate them. I will use a dialogue with the Jamesian schema to make the issues more understandable.

APPROACHING THE JAMESIAN SCHEMA

Before elaborating on my alternative schema, I want to clarify the intention of this chapter. My purpose is to use the Jamesian schema as the basis for developing another schema that might more accurately capture the subject matter or *irreducible data* of psychology. I still believe that James's schema is the best to date, but that it falls short. I am not claiming that my own schema solves the problem; my only hope is that it might further advance the discussion of the key issues.

However, another point needs to be clarified: I am *not* reducing James's perspective on psychology to the schema. James clearly exceeded the categories of the schema in his multiple discussions of psychology and offered many illuminating points that are sympathetic to phenomenology. In fact, I agree with Linschoten's (1959/1968) assessment that James was on the way to a phenomenological psychology among many other things. However, to be on the way also means that he was not there yet, and his schema reflects this incompleteness. Consequently, I will try to show what a schema for psychology would look like if one were fully ensconced in a phenomenological perspective.

It might also be helpful to indicate some of the contextual factors that influenced James at the time of writing the *Principles*, which in turn, had an influence on the construction of his schema. The articulation of these factors might help to elucidate the difference between a partial phenomenological stance and a complete one. The following were the major factors:

1. James (1890/1950) was trying to introduce psychology as a natural science. Granted, his interpretation of natural science was broad and liberal (Giorgi, 1990), but from the perspective of phenomenology, it was still restrictive with respect to the totality of psychological phenomena.

2. James was trying to be nonmetaphysical. For him, this was the great value of psychology as a natural science. This value is so important to this discussion that I will quote an extensive passage from James where he made his position abundantly clear. James (1890/1950) wrote,

> This book, assuming that thoughts and feelings exist and are vehicles of knowledge, thereupon contends that psychology where she has ascertained the empirical correlation of the various sorts of thought or feeling with definite conditions of the brain, can go no farther—can go no farther, that is, as a natural science. If she goes farther she becomes metaphysical. All attempts to *explain* our phenomenally given thoughts as products of deeper-lying entities (whether the latter be named "Soul," "transcendental Ego," or "Ideas," or "Elementary Units of Consciousness") are metaphysical. This book consequently rejects both the associationist and the spiritualist theories; and in this strictly positivistic point of view consists the only feature of it for which I feel tempted to claim originality. Of course this point of view is anything but ultimate. Men must keep thinking; and the data assumed by psychology, just like those assumed by physics and the other natural sciences, must some time be overhauled. The effort to overhaul them clearly and thoroughly is metaphysics; but metaphysics can only perform her task well when distinctly conscious of its great extent. Metaphysics fragmentary, irresponsible, and half-awake, and unconscious that she is metaphysical, spoils two good things when she injects herself into a natural science. (p. vi)

In addition to clarifying his nonmetaphysical stance, James also remained open to the overhauling of the metaphysical presuppositions of psychology, and he insisted that it is better to be explicit about metaphysical or philosophical assumptions than to be constrained by unclarified ones. The revised schema I will introduce is precisely a change in the assumptions concerning the phenomena of psychology.

3. In addition to the schema, James made other positive assumptions about the field of psychology. For example, he stated "I have therefore treated our passing thoughts as integers, and regarded the mere laws of their coexistence with brain-states as the ultimate laws for our science" (James, 1890/1950, pp. vi–vii). This Cartesian expression can be maintained by James because "Every natural science assumes data uncritically, and declines to challenge the elements between which its own 'laws' obtain, and from which its own deductions are carried on" (James, 1890/1950, pp. v–vi). As mentioned earlier, James stated that the psychologist (Square 1) believed Squares 2, 3, and 4, which "form *his* total object, to be realities" (James, 1890/1950, p. 184). In the name of a nonmetaphysical stance, might James not unwittingly have let a "Metaphysics fragmentary, irresponsible and half-awake" (James, 1890/1950, p. vi) into his perspective, despite his caution? This question has to be raised because one can wonder to what extent a thought or certain types of thoughts' objects are realities.

4. James was equally concerned with limiting the scope of psychology, that is, determining the characteristics of phenomena so that they can be identified with the field of study. James's opening sentence of the *Principles* defined the field: "Psychology is the Science of Mental Life, both of its phenomena and their conditions. The phenomena are such things as we call feelings, desires, cognitions, reasonings, decisions, and the like" (1890/1950, p. 1); further on in the same chapter, James described the criterion of mentality: *The pursuance of future ends and the choice of means for their attainment are thus the mark and criterion of the presence of mentality* in a phenomenon" (James, 1890/1950, p. 8). Thus, mind is the field and teleology is the criterion.

5. James was primarily descriptive in his approach to psychology. The justification was the following: "*Introspective Observation is what we have to rely on first and foremost and always*" (1890/1950, p. 185). After a lengthy discussion of the pros and cons of introspection, he concluded "*Introspection is difficult and fallible; and that the difficulty is simply that of all observations of whatever kind*" (1890/1950, p. 191). James again used the specter of metaphysics to avoid discussing the thornier problems involved with the use of introspection.

6. Finally, in the context of his discussion of the merits of introspection, James noted in passing that the psychologist has a

"peculiar point of view—that of being a reporter of subjective as well as of objective facts" (1890/1950, pp. 184–185). This peculiarity has bedeviled psychology perennially, and its status as a science cannot be resolved without resolving the issue of psychology's peculiarity.

I shall now briefly contrast a phenomenological perspective with these six Jamesian points. However, I want to stress that these points cannot be defended or argued. They are not included to convince the reader; they are here to make communication of the phenomenological perspective clearer. One would have to go to primary sources to be exposed to their legitimating context. Consequently, the contrasting phenomenological framework would be of the following:

1. Psychology is conceived of as a nonnatural science. Presently, this has to be expressed negatively because there is not yet an accurate positive term to communicate accurately the complex differential perspective required for all of psychology's legitimate phenomena. Thus, psychology is a human science when human phenomena are its subject matter, and it is an animal science when animal phenomena are its focus; however, *animal* cannot be reduced to a biological or a zoological perspective. The presence of consciousness differentiates the two.

2. James strived to be nonmetaphysical, and so do phenomenologists; however, their strategies for avoiding metaphysics are different. For James, the avoidance of metaphysics was achieved by keeping to a natural-science perspective, which implied as he said "that psychology, when she has ascertained the empirical correlation of the various sorts of thoughts or feeling with definite conditions of the brain, can go no farther" (1890/1950, p. vi). It also meant that James avoided terms with spiritualistic connotations (e.g., *Soul*), but not terms with naturalistic connotations. Almost simultaneously with the appearance of the *Principles*, Ladd (1892) objected to this bias and wondered why a metaphysics of physics was permitted, whereas a metaphysics relating to experience and consciousness was banned. Thus, one must be aware of the extent to which James's strategy was successfully practiced. According to Ladd, it was only selectively applied. In any case, for phenomenology, metaphysics is avoided by practicing the phenomenological reduction.

3. In addition to a repetition of his nonmetaphysical, natural-science stance, the important feature of the third point was that the thought, the thought's object, and the psychologist's reality are considered by James to be realities that can be known. He stated that, like in all sciences, one simply has to assume that this is possible without interrogation, otherwise, one becomes

metaphysical. For phenomenologists, to say that thoughts, the thought's object, as well as the psychologist's reality are real becomes equivocal. From a Husserlian perspective, the real is what exists in space, time, and with causal regularity, broadly understood. To be sure, conscious phenomena can be shown to be dependent on the real in some sense, but not exhaustively (i.e., not in every sense) because such a perspective accounts for the fact of conscious phenomena, but not for their meaning. For phenomenologists, whether conscious phenomena are essentially understood by a realistic perspective is dubious and so, in order to be faithful to the essential characteristics of conscious phenomena, a perspective other than a real one as defined earlier would be necessary.

4. James defined psychology as the science of mental life and distinguished mental life in terms of purposiveness. From a phenomenological perspective, the definition of psychology as the study of mental life simpliciter is too broad, so further delimitation would be necessary, and intentionality is the essence of consciousness, not purposiveness.

5. For James, whatever the difficulties, introspection was necessary. For phenomenologists, a descriptive approach to psychological subject matter is necessary. The difference between *introspective* and *descriptive* approaches lies in the theory of description and the types of reality toward which it is directed. Phenomenology situates itself within the purview of descriptive science, regardless of the type of reality (e.g., inner or outer) and, thus, uses the broader term *descriptive science*.

6. That psychology has a peculiar point of view is also affirmed by phenomenology and that is why psychology's irreducible data cannot uncritically be appropriated by a natural-science perspective. The realm of subjectivity or consciousness presents itself so radically differently from material reality that a different mode of access is called for, precisely, in the name of science.

With these contextual matters articulated, this chapter will now return to the phenomenologically modified schema.

THE PSYCHOLOGIST'S REALITY BASED ON CONSCIOUSNESS'S INTENTIONAL RELATION TO ITS OBJECTS

Earlier, I presented a one-sentence description of the meaning of psychology as well as a schema with a brief explicatory paragraph. Both were highly condensed and meant to serve merely as orientations for further discussion. I will now try to elaborate on that description. I will begin with the intentional relation between acts of consciousness (whether personal or animal) and their objects, or according to the Jamesian schema, Squares 2 and 3, although he logically divided what I believe should have been kept together.

To say that mental life is the subject matter of psychology should be an introductory statement rather than one of closure. It directly leads to the question: What is mental life and just what makes it psychological? From a phenomenological perspective, one cannot study mental life without including the mind's object because of the intentional relationship. To make two factors out of this relationship, as James did, is to accept the Cartesian heritage and its host of unsolvable problems. The only way to overcome Cartesian problems is to avoid them by starting anew.

Intentionality is a Husserlian contribution to the investigation of consciousness. Brentano resurrected the term as used by the scholastics, and then Husserl took the term from Brentano, but radicalized its meaning (Mohanty, 1972). From a Husserlian phenomenological perspective, intentionality is the essence of consciousness, and it refers to the fact that acts of consciousness or experience require an object and that the object always transcends the acts to which it is related. Later phenomenologists (e.g., Merleau-Ponty, 1945/1962) have argued that behavior, as action on the world, equally partakes of intentionality.

The major implication of the discovery of intentionality for psychology is that if one is interested in the mind or consciousness, one is automatically interested in the mind's object. This means that psychology's subject matter is intrinsically relational, which implies that its analyses have to be relational analyses. Logically separating the terms of the relationship is not best for psychological analyses because it severs what is experientially unified. One could, perhaps, argue that what is logically separated can be related again; thus, the separation is only temporary. But another implication of the intentional relationship would be missed: What is given to the thought or consciousness of the other has to be described precisely as it presents itself. This is a fundamental premise of psychology that is in dispute here. Things or events are not given initially logically or as substantives, but are awakened precisely because they become related to consciousness. If psychology is to be an exact science, then the things and events have to be known and communicated precisely as they present themselves to the consciousness of the experiencer. Another way of saying this is that the only legitimate way of studying the things and events of the world from a psychological perspective is through the other's experience of or behavior toward it. That this very first step is fraught with difficulties is attested to by the history of psychology. Official warnings and cautions such as "the stimulus error" or "psychologist's fallacy" have been designated to alert practicing psychologists, even though the warnings are seldom heeded.

For example, staying within a Jamesian perspective, if the psychologist were to substitute his or her own experience of the object for the other's experience of it where possible, he or she would be guilty of one version of the psychologist's fallacy. James (1890/1950) described this as "The *great snare of the psychologist* [which] is the *confusion of his own standpoint with that of the mental fact* about which he is making his report (p.196). If, on the other hand, the psychologist adds his or her own knowledge about the object, whether theoretical or from past experience, to the other's experience of it, he or she would be equally guilty, but of another version of the psychologist's fallacy. James described the other version of the psychologist's fallacy as

> the assumption that the mental state studied must be conscious of itself as the psychologist is conscious of it. The mental state is aware of itself only from within; it grasps what we call its own content, and nothing more. The psychologist, on the contrary, is aware of it from without, and knows its relations with all sorts of things. (p. 197)

This version of the fallacy warns the psychologist that he or she should not foist features onto the intentional object and then describe them as intrinsically belonging to the object as experienced. Ultimately, the psychologist's fallacy rests on a confusion of standpoints (Giorgi, 1981), and the clear implication is that only the standpoint of the experiencer counts as a point of departure, but the thing or event experienced must be captured precisely as it is for the experiencer. Thus, if the intentional relationship is precisely what must be captured, then the minimum that is required on the part of the psychologist is a receptive attitude toward an expression of the intentional relationship on the part of the other. As an aside, it should be noted that James was often descriptive and frequently practiced the point I am making, but for some reason, in presenting his schema, he chose a logical rather than a descriptive perspective.

Another additional feaure introduced with the explicit acknowledgment of the intentional relationship is that all modes of consciousness's relationship to a thing or state of affairs is included. One should recall that James had limited the relationship to a cognitive one. Again, in his descriptions, James clearly went beyond such a limitation, but his schema did not explicitly account for this. However, by explicitly calling the relationship between acts of consciousness and their objects *intentional,* one avoids the problem of how to account for noncognitive relationships. Thus, conative, affective, and unconscious relationships are equally included, as are behavioral relationships.

Of course, implicit in this discussion is the assumption that one can already discriminate mental or conscious phenomena. This raises a difficult problem that cannot be completely resolved here; however, at least the lines of the phenomenological approach to the issue can be delineated. The scope of psychology is at stake when one talks about the possibility of discriminating intentional relationships. James, it will be recalled, used purposiveness as the criterion of the mental life, which in turn, defined his subject matter. Phenomenologists use the intentional relationship as the minimum feature that a phenomenon must have in order to allow a psychological phenomenon to show itself, but it is not sufficient in and of itself. The intentional relationship presupposes life, but in order not to reduce psychology to biology, the proper object of psychology must demonstrate more than sheer life, just as the biological phenomenon must demonstrate more than mere physical existence. The intentional relationship is the *more* that is perceived, and it is distinguished by the fact that creatures possessing sensory-mobile openness to environments can create phenomenal worlds whose structures guide their actions. The constituted structures imply that such creatures can be present to a given in ways other than as the raw energy that is the basis of the stimulation and that ordered or integrated actions are possible that go beyond the impulsive response to the energy. In other words, a distinction becomes possible between presences (or contents) and environments, on one hand, and between directed responses and mere reactions, on the other. A phenomenal world of perception and action with its own meanings rises on the ground of the physical relationships. James's (1890/1950) discussion of the difference between mechanism and purpose parallels this description.

But psychology also needs a boundary on the higher side in order to differentiate its phenomena. James, for example, also admitted that there are necessary or a priori judgments that no amount of experience can modify, whether individual, social, or cultural (1890/1950, pp. 617–618). This, then, is what I propose as a boundary for psychology at the upper level. When the intentional object of awareness presents itself as transcending modifiability by experience, individual or collective, then it, or at least the aspects of it that transcend experiential modifiability, are beyond the domain of psychology. Examples that are beyond this domain would be strict logical conclusions or mathematical or geometric axioms. The psychic is correlated with phenomenal presences or contents that are identifiable by all sorts of experiences and that exhibit structures that are contextually dependent and temporally vulnerable.

If one identifies the mental life with the intentional, rather than with purposiveness, then one can see that the mental life exceeds the psychological. Thus, other qualifications have to be described in order to guarantee identification of the proper object of psychology, and I have tried to indicate one of those characteristics earlier: presences or actions correlated with individual subjectivity that are modifiable by experience. This qualification implicitly refers to the other parts of my schema, so I will now elaborate on the latter. But, of course, the reader should appreciate that the schema is really a structural unity with each constituent playing a complex role, so that, ultimately, multiple referencing of the same constituents is inevitable.

A PERSON WHO IS A PSYCHOLOGIST ASSUMES A PSYCHOLOGICAL PERSPECTIVE WITH RESPECT TO INTENTIONAL RELATIONSHIPS

The other two terms of the Jamesian schema are *psychologist* and *psychologist's reality*. Curiously, James does not elaborate on these two factors, perhaps because he thought he might be encroaching on metaphysics if he did. In any event, it is clear that a psychologist is first a person in the everyday world who has to assume a special attitude or perspective that is more restricted than his personal identity in order to function as a psychologist, and when he or she does so, the psychologist's reality is constituted. I cannot imagine anyone functioning effectively as a psychologist without being sensitive to the psychologist's reality, and this cannot happen if one does not assume a psychological perspective, which in turn, constitutes the psychologist's reality. Again, several remarks elaborating on the implications of this are called for.

We are all aware that no one is born a psychologist. One becomes a psychologist through education and training, and even then, such a role does not replace the individual's identity. (One sometimes hears that a person is a "born psychologist," which means that he or she has special talents with respect to the discrimination of psychological reality, but such a person still receives training, or else, only uses the talent avocationally.) This point is relatively obvious, but still needs to be mentioned so that no hidden assumptions play a devastating role in the analysis. Phenomenologists have stressed the primary role of the Lifeworld and the derivative role of science at length. Here, we are simply applying that insight. But, of course, this is the crucial question: How does one become a psychologist? To say that one is trained or educated to become one, merely postpones critical questions: What does it mean to become a psychologist? What is the proper training and education? Is the de facto education what it ought to be? The fact that one can challenge psychological training implies that a certain theory of psychology must accompany its existence. There should be a rationale as to why such a science should exist in the world—some motive or reason that would sustain the hope that the knowledge produced would be of value. This then leads to the fundamental question of why and how sciences are created in the first place. What is psychology's proper object, how does it proceed, what is its method, what kind of knowledge does it produce, what can one expect from it, and to which cultural institution does it belong?

All of these questions lead directly to the issue of the psychologist's reality and how it is established. We must regress back to the very origins of science, back to its very first steps, back to the phenomena of the Lifeworld and the set of problems that motivate it. Gurwitsch (1974), following Husserlian guidelines, wrote on this issue more extensively than most phenomenological philosophers, and he described it as the beginning of *theoria*—a special perspective that begins to see a range of problems in a certain way. A host of questions surround this step, and James clearly saw them, which is why he wanted to avoid metaphysical issues.

In order to appreciate the phenomenological modification of the Jamesian schema, it is important to keep in mind that one of James's problems was how to describe precisely the psychologist's reality without being metaphysical. That is why he conceived of psychology as a natural science. His goal was to describe its phenomena without making assumptions about their ultimate nature. Because James was philosophically sophisticated, he used common sense expressions for many of his initial descriptions. This is one reason why James wrote so well. However, phenomenologically speaking, this meant that James described from within the natural attitude, and at times, even used what can only be called *naturalistic descriptions*. The latter interpretation can be evidenced when James (1892) wrote, "As constituting the inner life of individual persons who are born and die, our conscious states are temporal events arising in the ordinary course of nature—events, moreover, the conditions of whose happening or unhappenings from one moment to another, lie certainly in large part in the physical world" (pp. 147–148). So complex was James, however, that he also produced brilliant descriptions that withstand phenomenological criticism and can also be conceived as being implicitly phenomenological. But this chapter concentrates on the theoretical assumptions that surround his schema for psychology.

It is at this point, within the context of the constitution of the psychologist's reality, that the phenomenological reduction becomes important. To assume the phenomenological reduction means that one puts aside all unwarranted assumptions or past knowledge about the phenomenon in brackets and that one also withholds existential claims about what appears. The use of the term *unwarranted assumptions* means that only those dimensions of the phenomenon that withstand the criteria of phenomenological evidence are relevant to the presence of the phenomenon. In addition, the withholding of existential attribution to the phenomenon does not mean that the modes of being of what presents itself disappear, only that no statement is made to affirm the modes of being. The content of the experience within the reduction does not change; simply, one does not say that things *are* as they present themselves as one would normally do within an everyday perspective. The ultimate outcome of all this is that descriptions are metaphysically neutral, although ontologically inviting. The refusal to remove the brackets limits one to a discussion of things or states of affairs as presences.

But how does a nonmetaphysical stance help psychology? Let's recall the problems psychology has had in accessing its subject matter. The psychologist's fallacy has already been discussed—How psychology confuses standpoints. Rather than rigorously staying with the thing or event as it presented itself to the consciousness of the experiencer, the psychologist would substitute his or her own experience of the object, or past knowledge of the object, or a theoretically laden definition of the object, or a logical or other reconstruction of the object, or finally, a physical description of the object. All of these substitutions were usually motivated by some sense of natural-science or metaphysical precomprehension. But the question never raised was whether these substitutions were not made too soon. Were the transformations faithful to the essential characteristics of psychological phenomena? Perhaps one had to dwell longer on the proper object of psychology before transforming it in order to be sure that all relevant aspects of it had been noted. But how could one know the limits of psychology if its essence was not clarified? And how could one clarify the essence of psychology nonmetaphysically?

This was James's problem. He wanted to stick with psychology as such, but needed to use language that was neutral with respect to metaphysics. Clearly, terms like *transcendental* and *soul* were heavily weighted, so he did not want to use them. But are physiological and neurological terms not equally metaphysical? The traditional usage of such terms makes them appear more scientific than metaphysical. In the physical sciences, a leniency with regard to metaphysics had developed, but with the language of consciousness, the ties with philosophy were still too visible during James's time.

Husserl's contribution was to figure a way out of this dilemma, not by seeking another language, but by an attitudinal shift whereby the meanings of the words would undergo a change of sense. The natural attitude would no longer be maintained, so one could now use the same words as in everyday language, but *the given* referred to as understood, not as existent. Thus, all that the given contained would still be present, but one could now speak of the meaning with which the given was taken up by the person. The phenomenological reduction is a device that helps the researcher to grasp the phenomenological object precisely as it is given to the experiencer. Of course, Husserl (1913/1962) was not unaware of the problem of language, and he complained that he had only the language of the natural attitude to describe a wholly different sense of the given as it appears within the reduction. Nevertheless, he felt that if one were carefully aware of the attitudinal differences, one could proceed with one's work.

A further implication becomes apparent here that is highly important to psychology. Under the influence of empiricism, and especially positivism, psychology had always presupposed that it was dealing with the real. James also shared this conviction. But has psychology ever questioned the sense of the real with which it is dealing? Is psychological reality the same as physical reality? If so, why does one often speak of reductionism if the psychological is reduced to the physical? Just what kind of reality is the psychological? Is it simply the opposite of physical—the spiritual? Does the metaphysical really fall in only two categories? James said it was mental life, but then was hesitant to probe it for fear of being metaphysical. But as Ladd (1892) already asked, why is physical reality less metaphysical than mental life?

Again, this is where the reduction might help. Because no metaphysical claims are made within the reduction, but nevertheless, the observing consciousness is full of presences of all sorts, one can at least describe the presences that appear. One might even begin to notice a commonality to all these phenomena that we could label *psychological*. If one understands that the precise meaning of psychology has not yet been resolved, then it is precisely the reduction that can free one sufficiently from past knowledge and biases in order to describe freshly what presence to the givens of psychology means. This freedom must be radically exercised for it could even be that the physical is not so much a reality or a positivity as it is a presence, but a presence that would not be spiritual. It could be that psychological phenomena are neither full consciousness nor full physicality, but a type of being that has yet to be properly grasped in a positive way.

This leads us to the question of the psychologist's reality, but before exploring it in full, some more comments are needed about the attitude that the person who is a psychologist must assume. Not only would the phenomenological reduction be necessary, but also a psychological perspective. The psychological perspective is necessary to guarantee that the psychologist does not become a philosopher. The real difficulty at this stage of the development is that this attitude must be assumed at an unclarified intuitive level, practiced, and only then, clarified, reflectively. This step is often not understood by psychologists. James, for example, and many others, simply identified the psychological realm with mental life or consciousness simpliciter. This identification, however, is too coarse. After all, the intentional relation as such supports philosophical consciousness, historical consciousness, political consciousness, feminine consciousness, as well as naive consciousness. As Merleau-Ponty (1945/1962) said, there are many ways for consciousness to be consciousness, and psychological consciousness is but one of them. So one must press on, and although still tentative, I suggest that the psychologist's perspective concentrates on *the concrete meaningful expressions* of an individual subject with respect to the situations he or she encounters. If true, this is a way of limiting psychology's subject matter. *Expression* would depict the experiential–behavioral relations between a subject and an object or state of affairs, and the term *individual* is used rather than personal in order to allow for the functioning of an anonymous subjectivity. Implied as well is the idea that not everything expressed by the individual originates in the individual (e.g., social and linguistic realities could be expressed by individuals even though originated by others).

There is still another advantage to understanding psychological subject matter in terms of expression or expressiveness, which is that it helps liberate psychology from both objectivism and physicalism. This is why the freedom provided by the reduction proves to be so critical. The natural-science paradigm is weighted toward the establishment of facts of physical reality. It was mentioned earlier how, for Husserl, the real was understood to be that which was given in space, time, and causality, but it was also shown how psychological structures departed from such strict determination to engender phenomenal presences, meanings, and ordered actions, which although patterned and based on physicality, could not be completely subsumed under physical, or even rational, categories. The contributions of subjectivity to the structures could not be negated; thus, different principles of analysis would have to be introduced. What James called the *peculiarity* of psychology's subject matter has to be respected. Thus, in this approach, *objective* cannot mean statements without reference to subjectivity, nor can it mean merely physical statements or even quantifiable ones because these meanings would miss expressing the essence of psychological. For a phenomenological approach, *objectivity* refers to the faithful comprehension of a phenomenon; it is a means for capturing and expressing something with its essence intact; it is not a matter of reifying a phenomenon. Rather, phenomenologically, the science of psychology would be based on the phenomenal world of individuals, or more precisely, the subjectively construed meanings of things or events that the psychologist has to grasp in an objective way, that is, precisely as they are phenomenally expressed. In other words, without the phenomenological reduction, the practicing psychologist might still be arbitrarily tied to realistic, naturalistic, or common sense criteria.

There is still another important implication: Psychological reality is not ready-made but constituted. It has already been noted how a concrete consciousness could support other disciplines. Consequently, the initial encounter is with a richer, more concrete, pretheoretical experience. We do not simply open our eyes and see psychological reality; it appears only if a person assumes a special attitude. James was probably keenly aware of this fact, and this is why he included psychologist's reality as a factor in his schema. Only careful attention to the assumption of the attitude can help one avoid the snares of the psychologist's fallacy, which relates as we have seen, to standpoint confusion.

This chapter has covered many contextual issues—necessarily so in order to communicate phenomenological understanding properly—so I want to return to the key factors once again. The point of departure was that a person who is a psychologist must assume a psychological perspective toward intentional relationships in order to constitute the psychologist's reality. The person, therefore, must assume a scientific or professional role that is characterized by sensitivity to the expressed individuated meanings of persons as they relate to situated events in the world. The role assumed remains interactive with the person that assumes it, and the psychologist's reality that is constituted remains open to influence from other aspects of the intentional relationship that are not directly thematized. Thus, psychology is not autonomous, absolute, exhaustive, or closed off to other endeavors.

THE PSYCHOLOGICAL PERSPECTIVE APPLIED TO ONESELF

In all of the examples that have been presented, I have been speaking about a psychologist approaching his subject matter in terms of the other—the consciousness, behavior, or expressiveness of the other. However, all of the analyses could have been done with respect to oneself just as well. Recall how James wanted to preserve introspection, even though he admitted that it was flawed. He nevertheless argued for its inclusion by claiming that it could be as objective as any other scientific procedure in the sense of being impersonal. He placed the emphasis at the beginning of the introspective process and wanted the psychologist to be impersonal from the start. From a psychological, phenomenological perspective, however, I would argue that one begins with concrete, personal descriptions, and one progresses to their objective expression. In my reinterpretation, self-descriptive analyses, or *introspection*, can succeed because one can reflectively assume a psychological perspective toward one's own richer prereflective, pretheoretical experience and discover the actually lived meanings expressed there. In this sense, objectivity is not the translation of the personal into the impersonal, but a faithful rendering of the personal as lived. Thus, whether turned toward oneself or the other, what matters is the ability of the psychologist to constitute the psychologist's reality on the basis of concrete, prereflective, pretheoretical experience or behavior.

As mentioned earlier, when turned to the other, the psychologist observed the expression of an intentional relationship. There is a difference between the attitude toward oneself and the attitude toward the other. Even though James used the terms *feelings* and *thought*, he was aware that the thought or feeling of the other could not be directly observed, although they could for oneself. Thus, some mode of expression of the conscious stream or of the behavioral flow would be necessary for psychological analyses. Description could reveal the conscious stream as well as some behavioral aspects, although the latter could also be captured by observations. But, alternatively, expressiveness could also be described by others, and because it is expressive, some aspects of the consciousness of the subject are also captured. In brief, some form of concrete expression is required in order for the intentional relationship to manifest itself such that it could become a theme for analysis. But even then, it is not so much the intentional relationship as such, but the intentional relationships viewed from the psychological perspective, although initially, the entire concrete expression is analyzed. Psychological, phenomenological analyses move from the concrete to the thematized by working through all of the givens. In other words, although the intentional relationship may be epistemologically primary in the sense that one has to find it, describe it, and deal with it, it is not chronologically primary. One has to arrive at it and then use it, and this requires some concrete mode of expression on the part of the subject who is providing the database for psychological analysis.

Hence, from a phenomenological perspective, I have reduced James's logically constructed quadruple schema, but all of the features were retained. Consequently, I suggest the following framework for psychology: Persons assume a psychological perspective toward the other's or one's own expressiveness (experiential–behavioral relations) in a situation in the world, and one tries to describe this network of expressiveness (relationships) precisely as it is lived in order to discover the structure or meaningful patterns of the individually constituted expressions. It should be recalled that psychological analysis is not exhaustive because the psychologist's reality is a thematization arising from pretheoretical experience, and the assumption of the psychologist's perspective reflects personally (individually) lived experience oriented toward oneself or the other in a situation.

The ultimate test of the modified schema, of course, would be to demonstrate that all genuine psychological problems could be successfully approached in terms of it. For the sake of scientific validation, that claim is being made, but it would be impossible to show in a chapter of this size that psychological problems, from psychophysics to social psychology or from psychopathology to industrial psychology, could be precisely and comprehensively approached using this schema. It would not be surprising if such an exercise also produced changes in the schema, but obviously, such changes would be hard to predict.

REFERENCES

Giorgi, A. (1981). On the relationship among the psychologist's fallacy psychologism and the phenomenological reduction. *Journal of Phenomenological Psychology, 12*, 75–86.

Giorgi, A. (1990). The implications of James's plea for psychology as a natural science. In M. G. Johnson & T. B. Heneley (Eds.), *Reflections on the principles of psychology: William James after a century* (pp. 63–75). Hillsdale, NJ: Erlbaum.

Gurwitsch, A. (1974). *Phenomenology and the theory of science.* Evanston, IL: Northwestern University Press.

Husserl, E. (1962). *Ideas: General introduction to pure phenomenology* (W. R. B. Gibson, Trans.). New York: Collier Books. (Original work published 1913)

James, W. (1892). A plea for psychology as a 'natural science.' *Philosophical Review, 1*, 146–153.

James, W. (1950). *The principles of psychology* (Vol. I). New York: Dover. (Original work published 1890)

Ladd, G. T. (1892). Psychology as so-called natural science. *Philosophical Review, 1*, 24–53.

Linschoten, H. (1968). *On the way toward a phenomenological psychology: Psychology of William James.* Pittsburgh, PA: Duquesne University Press. (Original work published 1959)

Merleau-Ponty, M. (1962). *The phenomenology of perception* (C. Smith, Trans.). New York: Humanities Press. (Original work published 1945)

Mohanty, J. (1972). *The concept of intentionality.* St. Louis, MO: Warren H. Green, Inc.

III

JAMES'S DEBT TO DARWIN

9

SELECTION—
JAMES'S PRINCIPAL PRINCIPLE

JONATHAN SCHULL

One of the worst sins a historian can commit is called *presentism*—the interpretation of past events and documents as if they were written by our own contemporaries, for our own contemporaries.

I am about to commit that sin.

Fortunately, I am not a historian.

I am a biological psychologist and a learning theorist who is convinced that some of the most provocative and promising new ideas in evolutionary theory, learning theory, psychology, brain science, connectionism, philosophy of science, and philosophy of nature today are to be found in the writings of a man who died 80 years ago.

William James lived an extraordinary range of careers: art study, field biology, medicine, psychology, philosophy, and speculative theology. However, I hope to convince you that his life was actually an unwavering quest for a point of view that could encompass and advance modern science without denying the spiritual values and experiences that make life worth

I gratefully thank my friends and audience: Lola Bogyo, Sharon Duman, Ira Packer, and Betsy Wood.

living. One of the miracles of modern science is that we are only *now* in a position to understand, appreciate, and exploit James's academic contemporaries, they alienated many of his successors in psychology, biology, philosophy, and religion, and they will probably trouble many of today's scientists. But they demand our attention, if only because they are "live wires" whose power has neither been tapped nor extinguished.

The theoretical notions to which I refer range from neural cell assemblies and the discipline now called connectionism; to the study of personality, mind, and cognitive science; and beyond that to the study of biological evolution, cultural evolution, religious experience, and even theology. But the fundamental theoretical notion, and the one which pulls together all of these diverse topics, is that of selection—Darwin's theory of natural selection, generalized and extended in a characteristically Jamesian fashion to account for learning, neural development, and consciousness, as well as the evolution of species. Once we recognize James's underlying biopsychological theory of selection at multiple levels in a hierarchy of living things, his entire life's work can be seen as a prolonged effort in speculative biology that speaks to many of the most pressing scientific and metascientific issues of today.

A second theme in James's work that I want to emphasize in this chapter will be of special interest to psychologists of the personality and those of clinical and humanistic "persuasions." That theme is the story of James's lifelong struggle with depression and "philosophical hypochondria." For although James's writings deserve to be treated as serious (if radical) scientific work, they were also motivated by his personal psychology in a way that is just too germane to ignore. Briefly, then, at the age of 28, William James underwent a spiritual crisis that brought him to the brink of suicide. James (whose father was a Swedenborgian mystic) was tormented by the existence of evil and by the discouraging implications of monism and determinism. For if an all-powerful God is omnipotent then He is (alas) responsible for evil as well as for good. If such a God does *not* exist in a deterministic universe, then the universe is amoral and meaningless. And if all of our actions are predetermined by the physical causes operating within and upon our nervous systems, then our own moral struggles, our agonies of indecision and our seemingly hard-won decisions, are all deceptions. In a deterministic universe, we have no choice, we can do no good, and nothing matters.

For James, these seemingly abstract problems were literally matters of life and death and nearly did him in. Years later, he inserted a disguised account of his personal travails into his *Varieties of Religious Experience* (1902):

> Whilst in this state of philosophic pessimism and general depression of spirits about my prospects, I went one evening into a dressing room in

the twilight . . . when suddenly there fell upon me without any warning . . . a horrible fear of my own existence. Simultaneously there arose in my mind the image of an epileptic patient whom I had seen in the asylum, a black-haired youth with greenish skin, entirely idiotic, who used to sit all day on one of the benches. . . . That shape am I, I felt, potentially. (pp. 166–167)

"It was like a revelation," he wrote. By his own account, he owed the preservation of his sanity to religious professions of faith, and the escape from incapacitating indecision to a philosophical resolution inspired by his reading of Renouvier, a French philosopher of free will, and (I will suggest) of psychology's own Gustav Fechner, whose writings James was reading at the time of his recovery. At that time he wrote in his diary, "My first act of free will shall be to believe in free will" (Perry, 1935, p. 323). He elaborated,

I will voluntarily cultivate the feeling of moral freedom. Hitherto, when I have felt like taking a free initiative, like daring to act originally, without carefully waiting for contemplation of the external world to determine all for me, suicide seemed the most manly form to put my daring into; now, I will go a step further with my will, not only act with it, but believe as well; believe in my individual reality and creative power. (James's diary, quoted in Allen, 1967, p. 169)

This might have been the happy ending to a fairly uninteresting story, if not for the fact that James was a materialist with a deep commitment to science. In order to sustain the happy ending, he would have to reconcile the facts of science with a world in which life and its travails could be of real consequence. (It is here, by the way, that Fechner will eventually make his reappearance in this story.)

Thus, the second theme I want to highlight is the way in which James's very survival depended on his "construction of a workable reality." The phrase is a modern one frequently used by clinicians today, but it is entirely applicable to James. Indeed, considering James's multifarious roles as philosopher, scientist, psychologist, and psychological sufferer, the phrase was never more apt.

James's "first act" of free will was in fact only the first act in a lifelong drama. Although there were many preliminary intimations of the drama's essential themes, they were explicitly stated for the first time in the opening pages of James's *Principles of Psychology* (1890/1952).

JAMES'S PRINCIPAL PRINCIPLE

The first chapter of the *Principles of Psychology* defines the phenomena of psychology through a description of purposiveness. James contrasted the attraction of iron filings to a magnet with the attraction of Romeo to Juliet, or of a frog to the conditions that will allow it to breathe. The important difference is revealed when an impediment is placed between the agent and its object of attraction:

> Romeo wants Juliet as the filings want the magnet; and if no obstacles intervene he moves towards her by as straight a line as they. But Romeo and Juliet, if a wall be built between them, do not remain idiotically pressing their faces against its opposite sides like the magnet and the filings with the card. (James, 1890/1952, p. 4)

Rather, they, the frog, and indeed all systems to which observers attribute mentality share one crucial characteristic: They adapt their behavior to suit their purposes. James wrote,

> *The pursuance of future ends and the choice of means for their attainment are thus the mark and criterion of mentality in a phenomenon.* We all use this test to discriminate between an intelligent and a mechanical performance. We impute no mentality to sticks and stones, because they never seem to move for *the sake* of anything, but always when pushed, and then indifferently, and with no sign of choice. So we unhesitatingly call them senseless. (1890/1952, p. 5)

And then, in what might have seemed a rhetorical flourish but was not, he continued,

> Just so we form our decision upon the deepest of all philosophic problems: Is the Kosmos an expression of intelligence rational in its inward nature, or a brute external fact pure and simple? If we find ourselves, in contemplating it, unable to banish the impression that it is a realm of final purposes, that it exists for the sake of something, we place intelligence at the heart of it and have a religion. If, on the contrary, in surveying its irremediable flux, we can think of the present only as so much mere mechanical sprouting from the past, occurring with no reference to the future, we are atheists and materialists. (James, 1890/1952, p. 5)

Now, the rest of the *Principles* deals with individuals, not the "Kosmos," but the theoretical explanation James offered to explain purposive intelligence is in fact one which will throw considerable light on James's later attempts to deal with this "deepest of all philosophical problems."

It overstates things only slightly to assert that the *Principles* was devoted to showing that selection was the essential mechanism of mentality. In his chapter on the automaton theory, for example (the chapter which both *anticipates* and *refutes* behaviorism), he wrote that

> The study of the phenomena of consciousness which we shall make throughout the rest of this book will show us that consciousness is at all times primarily a *selecting agency*. Whether we take it in the lowest sphere of sense, or in the highest sphere of intellection, we find it always doing one thing, choosing one out of several of the materials so presented to its notice, emphasizing and accentuating that and suppressing as far as possible all the rest. The item emphasized is always in close connection with some *interest* felt by consciousness to be paramount at the time. (James, 1890/1952, p. 91)

But what did James mean by selection? He meant natural selection writ large, and natural selection writ small. James steeped himself in the new ideas of Darwinism from his first days at Harvard. He studied field biology in the Amazon with Louis Agassiz, studied evolution with Jeffries Wyman, and dealt with the subject in his very first publications and in his first lectures at Harvard. Yet, from the start, his conception of Darwin's theory was uniquely his own. Even in those first publications, a review of Darwin's *Variation of Animals and Plants Under Domestication* and an essay titled "Great Men, Great Thoughts and the Environment," James had already introduced four critical points.

First, while crediting Darwin with the distinction between variation and selection, James argued that variation was crucial but largely unexplained. Darwin called such variations "random," but James pointed out that this might only mean "unpredictable" or due to processes other than selection. In any case, evolution had to be seen as a probabilistic rather than a deterministic process, and James had taken a first step toward his later discussions of how mindlike processes might be able to influence events by tipping the balance ever so slightly.

Second, James had an interactive view of evolution—the environment selects variants *and* selected variants affect the environment. This also adds an indeterminacy to evolution and allows for the possibility that the *products* of natural selection might themselves *influence* natural selection.

Third, something like natural selection operates not only in evolution but also (a) within the mind of the individual and (b) in society. Society preserves or destroys aberrant individuals (and calls them geniuses or madmen), and whenever it adopts and preserves the great man, it becomes modified by his influence in an entirely original and peculiar way. He acts as a ferment, and changes its constitution, just as the advent of a new zoological species changes the faunal and floral equilibrium of the region in which it appears. (James, 1889/1897, p. 226)

And so James's fourth critical extension of Darwinism was the realization that selection is a multileveled and arguably integrated process, spanning from the intraneural to the supraindividual. In James's hands, this extended generic selectionism afforded a theory that could encompass the phenomena as well as the phenomenology of mind, brain, and behavior. But because James himself never discussed his conception of selection independent of the issues to which he applied them (and I don't claim to understand why he kept his cards so close to his chest), he is known for his far-ranging interests and near-miraculous insights, rather than for the theory from which they may well have been derived. It is perhaps for this reason, and also because his ideas were so far ahead of their time in both content and temperament, that his theory has never been adequately spelled out.

THE IMPORTANCE OF SELECTION IN THE *PRINCIPLES OF PSYCHOLOGY*

In his chapter "The Automaton Theory," James argued that although the extreme excitability of neural tissue makes it a fine source of random variations, this also creates the need for some kind of determining influence to select the variant neural events that will best advance the needs of the individual. Consciousness seems to be, and may well be, this determining influence. Although James was thus launching an attack on reductionism and asserting the causal efficacy of mind, he was explicitly *not* trying to separate mind from brain. Rather, in an easily overlooked thread of cross-references in the *Principles*, he repeatedly attempted to show that the brain is a structure in which selection is mediated, needed, and exploited and that consciousness is nothing other than the subjective experience of these activities. Occasionally, he explicitly supposed that "feeling, may be likened to a cross-section of the chain of nervous discharge, ascertaining the links already laid down, and groping among the fresh ends presented to it for the one which seems to fit the case" (James, 1890/1952, p. 93). But more generally and more persuasively, he showed that the patterning and conditions of occurrence of consciousness all make sense in light of the hypothesis that consciousness is the subjective manifestation of intraneural selective processes.

The Neurology of Selection

At the end of the introductory chapter in the *Principles*, James described a phenomenon to which he would repeatedly revert: "If . . . the right knee of a headless frog be irritated with acid the right foot will wipe it off. When, however, this foot is amputated, the animal will often raise the left foot to the spot and wipe the offending material away" (James, 1890/1952, p. 5). As the book progresses, James showed that this particularly impressive example of "the choice of means for the pursuance of ends" is in fact also explicable in neurological terms. By dwelling on it as he did, James was able to show both that (a) such phenomena argue for the causal efficacy of mind and (b) physiology is at least as amenable to a neural–selectionist interpretation as it is to the (more commonly applied) deterministic and reflexological one.

For example, after a review of vertebrate neuroanatomy in the next chapter, James argued that after brain damage, recovery of function occurs because new functions are acquired by brain areas that did not formerly perform those functions. His account of how this occurs was clearly a precursor of his student Thorndike's principle of reinforcement. The brain, wrote James,

> is essentially a place of currents, which run in organized paths . . . and a current that runs in has got to run out *somewhere*; if it only succeeds by accident in striking into its old place of exit again, the thrill of satisfaction which the consciousness connected with the whole residual brain then receives will reinforce and fix the paths of that moment and make them more likely to be struck into again. The resultant feeling that the old habitual act is at last successfully back again, becomes itself a new stimulus which stamps all the existing currents in." (James, 1890/1952, p. 47)

It is but a small step from here to a physiological theory of reinforcement, and James made this step in a later chapter on the will. There, he provided (complete with diagrams of neural networks) an account of how reinforcement strengthens neural connections in the requisite manner to explain recovery of function as well as instrumental learning (as we call it today). Students of today's revolution in cognition, connectionism, and neuroscience will recognize the remarkable prescience of these theoretical concerns.

A Hierarchy of Selective Processes

The "multileveledness" of James's notion of selection can hardly be overestimated. We have already seen that biological evolution, social evolution, mental selection, and neural selection all received explicit treatment in James's writings. But mental selection was itself conceived as multileveled, as spelled out for psychological levels ranging from sensation to action to the formation of character. In the conclusion of the chapter in *Principles* on "the stream of thought," James summarized

> The mind is at every stage a theatre of simultaneous possibilities. Consciousness consists in the comparison of these with each other, the selection of some, and the suppression of the rest by the reinforcing and inhibiting agency of attention. The highest and most elaborated mental products are filtered from the data chosen by the faculty next beneath, out of the mass offered by the faculty below that, which mass in turn was sifted from a still larger amount of yet simpler material, and so on. (James, 1890/1952, p. 187)

Similarly, in his chapter on the will, James argued that the essential act of will is the selection of a particular goal as the object of attention. This goal then acts as a selector of those acts (one level down) that can accomplish the goal. Within this framework, then, James could reduce the whole issue of free will to the question of whether our *efforts* at sticking to some goal have even a slight influence on our tendency to actually pursue that goal. Common sense says that they do, and in James's hierarchical selective theory that is enough to allow for the possibility, however slight, of causal efficacy.

A Hierarchy of Selves

James discussed the interrelations of these varieties of selective processes relatively explicitly in the *Principles*. Much less explicitly did he identify a parallel hierarchy of entities, or "selves," made possible by these processes. On the one hand, the latter hierarchy can be seen as James's demonstration of the power of his theoretical innovations. At the same time, its grandeur and scope (ranging from neurological selves to quasi-theistic Selves) may explain why James (evolutionist, physiologist, defender of free will and of the will to believe) cared so much about these issues.

The Personal Self

In his chapter on the self, James assayed a description of the "spiritual self," that nexus of mind "felt by all men as a sort of innermost centre within subjective life as a whole" (James, 1890/1952, p. 192). He asked, "*Can we tell . . . in what the feeling of this central active self consists?*" (James,

1890/1952, p. 193). Drawing on his own introspections, he wrote, "First of all, I am aware of a constant play of furtherances and hindrances in my thinking, of checks and releases, tendencies which run with desire and tendencies which run the other way" (James, 1890/1952, p. 193).

As this last quote illustrates, many of James's celebrated descriptions of introspected consciousness can almost be read as personalized accounts of natural selection in action. Although we must therefore recognize that these self-reports may have been substantially more theory laden than originally met the eye, they nonetheless provided James with still more grist for his thesis that consciousness is the experiential manifestation of a physical system that mediates a multileveled natural-selectionlike process. As we have seen, James offered this position as a possible alternative to spiritualistic as well as reductionistic accounts of mind, and he buttressed it with arguments and evidence from philosophy, physiology, and evolutionary theory, as well as from introspection. But for James this thesis was more significant still, for it allowed him to ask whether other physical systems whose modes of operation are importantly selective might also be seats of "selves" or purposive consciousnesses.

In fact, the "spiritual self" just discussed was of intermediate scope in a hierarchy of selves discussed over the course of James's career. This nested hierarchy of selves is nowhere considered as a totality, neither in James's own writing nor in the secondary literature), but in conjunction with his theorizing on the importance of selection, it reveals the coherence underlying his seemingly diverse projects.

Subcortical Consciousnesses

These were discussed in a few curious pages of the *Principles* under the heading, "*Man's Consciousness Limited To The Hemispheres. But is the consciousness which accompanies the activity of the cortex the only consciousness that man has? or are his lower centres conscious as well?*" (James, 1890/1952, p. 43).

The question is a strange one, but not unreasonable. After all, human brains contain subcortical centers that are as large and complex as the brains of birds and rodents who may well be possessed of some kinds of consciousness. James judiciously doubted that the question could ever be answered, so he refused to answer the question negatively.

Subpsychological Selves

Much more tractable than this neurological question is an analogous one concerning subpsychological selves (presumably mediated by the cortex). In the *Principles*, James reviewed "a lot of curious observations made on hysterical and hypnotic subjects" (1890/1952, p. 132), which suggest that "the total possible consciousness may be split into parts which coexist but mutually ignore each other, and share the objects of knowledge between them" (James, 1890/1952, 134–135).

This was the main issue taken up in James's Lowell Lectures, delivered in 1896 and only recently reconstructed and published by Eugene Taylor (1984). These lectures provide a missing link between James's psychological and theological writings, and in them James moved perceptibly closer to a theoretical framework. "In all of this we notice *dissociation*, polyzoism, or polypsychism" (Taylor, pp. 33–34). [Polyzoism had been defined by F. W. H. Meyers as "the property in a complex organism, of being composed of minor quasi-independent organisms" (Taylor, 1984, p. 34).]

Because James felt that such speculation brought one to the verge of supernaturalism, he carefully discussed appearances and skirted premature claims about underlying realities. But he was clearly fascinated with the notion that, just as there are multiple ongoing processes of selection going on in each of us, there might also be multiple selves coexisting in parallel within each of us, with little intercourse with, or knowledge of, each other. In the context of his theoretical work, this idea cannot be dismissed lightly.

Similarly, because James argued that the hierarchy of selective processes extends beyond the individual into "the race" and society, and because this process of selection is the essence of mentality, intelligence, and self, the hypothesis emerges inexorably that there might be "larger selves" of which we are ourselves mere parts, even though we may know little of them or of our mutual involvement in them. Here, then, is the reappearance of the religious themes that so bedeviled James at the beginning of his nearly abortive career.

Transpersonal Selves, or "Gods"

James's study, *The Varieties of Religious Experience*, provided strong support for the hypothesis of larger selves, even though the theoretical bases for the ideas themselves were barely hinted at.

> The only thing that [religious experience] unequivocally testifies to is that we can experience union with *something* larger than ourselves and in that union find our greatest peace. All that the facts require is that the power should be both other and larger than our conscious selves. . . . It need not be infinite, it need not be solitary. It might conceivably even be only a larger and more godlike self, of which the present self would then be but the mutilated expression, and the universe might conceivably be a collection of such selves, of different degrees of inclusiveness, with no absolute unity realized in it at all. Thus would a sort of polytheism return upon us. (James, 1902, p. 413)

It is little wonder, therefore, that James resonated so strongly to Gustav Fechner's now-forgotten speculations on transpersonal cosmic consciousnesses. Toward the end of his career, James summarized Fechner's views as follows:

> In ourselves, visual consciousness goes with our eyes, tactile consciousness with our skin. But although neither skin nor eye knows aught of the sensations of the other, they come together and figure in some sort of relation and combination in the more inclusive consciousness which each of us names his self. Quite similarly then, says Fechner, we must suppose that my consciousness of myself and yours of yourself, although in their immediacy they keep entirely separate and know nothing of each other, are yet known and used together in a higher consciousness, that of the human race, say, into which they enter as constituent parts. Similarly the nonhuman and the animal kingdom at large are members of a collective consciousness of still higher grade. This combines with consciousness of the vegetable kingdom, in the Soul of the Earth, which in turn contributes its share of experience to that of the whole solar system; and so on. (James 1909, pp. 283–284)

Thus, just as James had extended evolutionary selectionism into the domain of psychology, so had Fechner advanced a psychological theory about the mixing of elements of consciousnesses into the domain of evolutionary biology. And then for good measure, James, the great authority on mechanisms of mind, took it on himself to defend Fechner against the complaint that the earth lacks the nerves that consciousness might seem to require. James wrote,

> But if [nerve] fibers are indeed all that is needed to do that trick [in animals], has not the earth pathways, by which you and I are physically continuous, more than enough to do for our two minds what the brain-fibers do for the sounds and sights in a single mind? (James, 1909/1977, p. 75)

The irony here is that because James had taken pains to show that the brain was the kind of place that could host a process analogous to natural selection, he could hardly fail to assert that it was at least a "legitimate hypothesis" that the ecological systems could host processes analogous to those mediated by the brain.

Thus, James's unconventional interpretations of religious experience, abnormal personality states, and the pluralistic pantheism of his last works were almost inevitable outcomes of a lifetime of theorizing about brain physiology, mind, and evolution by natural selection (broadly conceived).

In general terms, James did make exactly this point toward the end of his career:

> The analogies with ordinary psychology and with the facts of pathology, with those of psychical research, so called, and with those of religious experience, establish, when taken together, a decidedly *formidable* probability in favor of a general view of the world almost identical with Fechner's. (James, 1909/1977, p. 140)

But because James did not show how his own past theoretical innovations were particularly supportive of this vision, he left to posterity the task of "taking it all together" to arrive at the general view he espoused. In an ensuing era of reductionism and behaviorism, posterity did not take James's invitation. But the invitation seems no less valid today. And the party may not be over.

EPILOGUE

In fact, recent developments in a variety of disciplines suggest that some of James's ideas may just now be coming into their own (and our own). The natural selection metaphor for brain function is currently undergoing a renaissance, as evidenced by books with titles such as *Neural Darwinism* (Edelman, 1987). Similarly, an information processing conception of evolution today seems hardly even controversial. (One need only think about the significance of the fact that replicas of owls' eyes show up on butterfly wings to realize that selection pressures are more than adequate to provide "pathways" of the sort James insisted on. Add to this realization the old idea that evolution is like learning and the new idea that species (or biological lineages) are real biological entities or individuals, and it is no longer easy to dismiss the idea that species are the intelligent entities that deserve credit for the existence of design and purpose in the biological "Kosmos." Furthermore, if one adds to this brew the notion of organic selection formulated by James's friend James Mark Baldwin or the notion of interdemic selection formulated later by Sewall Wright, then evolving species may have much the same kind of multileveled hierarchical organization and integration that James so forcefully argued was the essence of mentality. All of these issues are elaborated in Schull, 1989, 1990, and 1992.)

And so what of James's "ecological theology"? I am personally inclined to think that such ideas still loom just beyond the horizon of today's science, but their time may yet come. Certainly James's overarching conception of the individual as causal agent embedded in a biosocial world has much to offer in the context of today's ecological crisis and the embarrassingly parochial arguments about creationism versus evolutionism. James's own life may also demonstrate how these ideas can bridge the gap (personally as well as theoretically) between spiritual and scientific "ways of knowing."

We are still far from clear about the implications of selectionism and about the character of the systems that are based on selectionistic processes. William James was one of the first great thinkers to work these implications through from top to bottom, and incredibly, he is also one of the last. For that reason, a contemporary reassessment of his work may not only contribute to the history of such ideas, it may also contribute to their future.

REFERENCES

Allen, G. W. (1967). *William James: A biography*. New York: Viking Press.

Edelman, G. M. (1987). *Neural Darwinism: The theory of neuronal group selection*. New York: Basic Books.

James, W. (1868). Review [unsigned] of Charles Darwin's *The variation of animals and plants under domestication*. *North American Review, 107*, 362–368.

James, W. (1897). Great men, great thoughts, and the environment. In *The Will to Believe*. New York: Longmans, Green. (Original work published 1880)

James, W. (1902). *The varieties of religious experience: A study in human nature*. New York: Longmans, Green.

James, W. (1909). The doctrine of the earth-soul and of beings intermediate between man and God. An account of the philosophy of G. T. Fechner. *Hibbert Journal, 7*, 279–294.

James, W. (1952). *The principles of psychology*. Chicago: Great Books of the Western World. Encyclopedia Britannica, Inc. (Original work published 1890)

James, W. (1977). *A pluralistic universe*. Cambridge, MA: Harvard University Press. (Original work published 1909)

Perry, R. B. (1935). *The thought and character of William James* (Vols. 1–2). Boston: Little, Brown.

Schull, J. (1989). Are species intelligent? *Behavioral and Brain Sciences, 13*, 68–113.

Schull, J. (1990). Evolution and learning: Analogies and interactions. In E. Laszlo (Ed.), *The evolution paradigm*. New York: Gordon & Breach.

Schull, J. (1992). *Life as it knows us*. Manuscript in preparation.

Taylor, E. (1984). *William James on exceptional mental states: The 1896 Lowell Lectures*. Amherst: University of Massachusetts Press.

10

JAMES'S EVOLUTIONARY EXPISTEMOLOGY: "NECESSARY TRUTHS AND THE EFFECTS OF EXPERIENCE"

WILLIAM R. WOODWARD

EPISTEMOLOGICAL BEHAVIORISM

In 1979, Richard Rorty led the return to pragmatism in our time. He contended that William James showed that the correspondence theory of truth is dead. The ideas of the mind do not necessarily correspond to the order and arrangement of the way things are. Rorty called this view *epistemological behaviorism*, because the truth becomes grounded in behavior and language games (p. 174). Lacking objective "foundations," the criterion of truth becomes coherence or convenience: A dog is what we refer to it as; morality is the way persons behave. Some call Rorty's position *anti-foundationalism*.

I thank Margaret E. Donnelly for instigating this chapter and helping to bring the volume to fruition. The original paper was presented at the 98th Annual Convention of the American Psychological Association on August 12, 1990, in Boston, Massachusetts. I also wish to thank Thomas Carlson, Paul Croce, Deborah Johnson, Gerald Myers, Charlene Haddock Siegfried, Fernando Vidal, and Sandra Webster for helpful comments. A Fulbright Lecturer Award from the Council for International Exchange of Scholars supported my revision of the chapter while I was at Humboldt University in East Berlin, Germany, during 1990 and 1991.

But other philosophers have rallied against him on several counts, first wishing to claim that Rorty has gone too far and second seeking to rescue the good name of James. The general strategy has been to return to the German ontological tradition of hermeneutics. The idea is to show that we do indeed have foundations for knowledge, but not of the reductionist sort that analytic philosophy sought in the first half of the twentieth century. Instead, one seeks structures "between objectivism and relativism" (Bernstein, 1983) that are embedded in experience and nature and shared by more than one observer.

The return to James thus has new meaning for philosophers. James Edie (1987) thought Rorty viewed James "in a Deweyan manner," emphasizing functions and overlooking real touchstones of truth and meaning that only a phenomenological realism can explain. In her book *Speculative Pragmatism*, Sandra Rosenthal (1986) reinterpreted the truths of science as "regulative" or "hypothetical," showing that when we verify our knowledge we need to have "intentional relationships of meanings" (p. 53). Observation is thus theory laden. She referred specifically to James's final chapter of *The Principles of Psychology* (1890/1981) claiming that James refused to adhere to Kant's distinction of two kinds of knowledge, analytic and synthetic.

James's last chapter of the *Principles* has special significance to psychologists because it offers a kind of Piagetian genetic epistemology. It is about our different kinds of knowledge and how we acquire them. It ranges from knowledge of numbers to knowledge of morality. It poses the epistemological question of a priori versus empirical truth in its title, "Necessary Truths and the Effects of Experience." The term *effects* links this theory to evolution, for the surviving effects of our actions become the ones we live by.

Rorty is fond of contrasting pragmatism with Kantian epistemological foundations. A reverse move by philosophers and literary critics in the hermeneutic tradition emphasizes praxis and pragmatic criteria of meaning. Hence, they claim Henry James and William James for their own (Armstrong, 1983). The issue turns on how one construes evidence. To be meaningful, the evidence must have a content that can be verified. For Husserl, the meaning of an intentional act required objective reference, namely, the experience of evidence. For Heidegger, meaning came from the practical context. A hammer must bring about a successful shelter if it is to count as meaningful. In either case, we judge an act by the state of affairs that it brings about (Okrent, 1988).

Charlene Haddock Seigfried (1990) has creatively combined both the German hermeneutic and the British evolutionary views of James. She called James's method of natural history observation a "seeing as 'feeling with' " (p. 169). Elsewhere, she referred to his combination of artistic with scientific seeing as a "concrete hermeneutics" (p. 183). She denied that his "pragmatic evolutionism" is either mechanistic or sociobiological, terming it a "trans-formation of some idealist presuppositions" (p. 169). She compared James's "proliferation of hypotheses and the determination of their fitness in solving the problem" with Darwin's spontaneous variations (p. 38). However, the center of James's vision becomes a "reconstructed realism" in which we are at home in the world. We humans construct order and bear responsibility for disorder. This, I think, James shared with Hermann Lotze, Charles Peirce, and the German hermeneutic tradition.

Psychologists tend to have topical interests in various chapters or problems of the *Principles*, whereas philosophers largely study the later works. But they may have more common ground than they know. Toward that end, I want to call attention to the Kantian sources of the important but neglected last chapter of the *Principles*. I will present Gerald Myers's (1986) summary and then explore how the chapter developed in James's life and writing. By connecting psychologists' interests in cognitive development with philosophers' theories of truth, belief, and meaning, I hope to situate James's evolutionary epistemology in history and in theory.

ORIGINS OF FALLIBILISM

I begin by sketching briefly one aspect of pragmatism and then trying to link it historically to the development of the central strand of the *Principles*. *"True ideas are those that we can assimilate, validate, corroborate and verify. False ideas are those that we cannot"* (James, 1975, p. 97; 1907, p. 133). If nothing else, this is a statement of fallibilism. Fallibilism is the notion that we define science by those propositions that survive the test of *modus tollens*: if not *q*, then not *p*. Fallibilism originated on the North American side with the Cambridge pragmatists Chauncey Wright, Charles Sanders Peirce, and William James (Madden, 1963). Less well known, it stems on the German side from Jakob Friedrich Fries (Popper, 1959), Ernst Friedrich Apelt (Laudan, 1968), and Hermann Lotze (Woodward, 1985). This tradition of hypothesis testing came to prominence through Karl Popper's *Logik der Forschung* in the 1934: it appeared in English as *The Logic of Scientific Discovery* in 1959. James synthesized German rational introduc-tion with British empiricism.

Myers (1986) recognized this synthesis without tracing its historical sources. As a consequence, the strong links to Kantian thought go unde-tected. Myers discussed the quoted fallibilistic passage in the same chapter "Knowledge," that treated James's chapters in the *Principles* on "Necessary Truths" and "The Perception of Reality" (1890), his essay, "The Function of Cognition" (1885), and his books, *Pragmatism* (1907) and *The Meaning of Truth* (1909). These writings—from 1885 to 1909—all have pragmatism in common. Myers has successfully pushed back the origins of James's pragmatism from 1907 when it is conventionally dated to some 22 years earlier, 1885. I think it can be pushed back at least 20 more years to the 1860s. In so doing, one comes face to face with the German sources of James's critique of Spencer (Kraushaar, 1936, 1938, 1939, 1940).

Myers further argued that James combined empiricism with rationalism by basing truth on the testing of beliefs. James wrote in "The Perception of Reality" that *"any object which remains uncontradicted is ipso facto believed and posited as absolute reality"* (1981, Vol. 2, p. 981; 1890, Vol. 2, p. 289). Knowing has to do with states of mind, and it is akin to emotion. Myers ascribed to Bain James's insight that Mill made belief too intellectual. I want to show that this insight on James's part also came from the Kantians, especially Charles Peirce and Hermann Lotze.

RECEPTION OF DARWIN IN
CAMBRIDGE, MASSACHUSETTS

The *Origin of Species* appeared just 2 years before James entered the Lawrence Scientific Laboratory in 1861. Among James's scientific mentors, anatomist Jeffries Wyman supported evolution, whereas naturalist Louis Agassiz opposed it. Referring to the prevailing "theistic and idealistic philosophy," John Dewey (1910) noted that "the Darwinian principle of natural selection cut straight under this philosophy" (p. 11). In 1935, Ralph Barton Perry reported that "evolution was the first scientific problem to which James devoted himself systematically"; more recent commentators seem to agree (Wiener, 1949; Ford, 1982; Richards, 1987). Although this consensus about the inspiration of evolutionary ideas is still popular, the details of it are by no means clear.

I think the Cambridge pragmatists engaged in more critique of Darwin and more borrowing from the German tradition than they let on. To what extent, then, did they appropriate German rationalist models of the mind? Granted, James protested about Kant's "elaborate machine-shop" (James, 1890, Vol. 1, p. 363) and Hegel's "raging fever" of speculation (James, 1890, Vol. 1, p. 366). All the while, he was studying the models of judgment and the theories of scientific method of the Kantians. But he had to work through the empiricist positions of Chauncey Wright and Herbert Spencer first.

CHAUNCEY WRIGHT AND THE EMPIRICAL
JUSTIFICATION OF INDUCTION

Before casting my lot with those who say Darwin's theory of evolution was central to James, I wish to examine him in his community (Fisch, 1964;

Murphy, 1968). One preeminent figure in James's early career was a shy mathematical physicist for the *Nautical Almanac*, who was an essayist and above all a companion at the Quincy Street residence—a man singled out by Darwin to introduce his ideas in the United States. Chauncey Wright (1830–1875) shared with others in James's circle a preoccupation with the nature of scientific laws and their empirical versus a priori status. According to Edward Madden, "Wright believed what Peirce later denied, that the universality of causality is a postulate of scientific inquiry" (1955–1956, p. 422). Causality refers here to the empirical justification of cause and effect.

In 1864, Wright published a review of a theory of the origin of the universe whereby stars arose from nebulae. The nebular hypothesis stated that mechanical contraction of the gases in rotary motion led to formation of planets. Pierre Simon de Laplace, William Hershel, and Herbert Spencer all supported this mechanical hypothesis. Yet Wright, admirer of Mill and critic of Spencer, was eager to refute it. "The gist of this argument is to prove simplicity in the antecedents of the solar system," wrote Wright. "It is not from the regularities of the solar system, but from its complexity, that its physical origin is justly inferred . . . The appearance of accident among the manifestations of law is proof of the existence of complex antecedent conditions and of physical causation" (1864/1971 p. 9).

Thus, Wright staked out a position close to that of John Stuart Mill and David Hume. He believed that we have to postulate an empirical justification of inductive inferences because the necessary connection is not provided by any a priori principle. James wrote from Brazil; "Would I might hear Chauncey Wright philosophize for one evening" (July 23, 1865, in Perry, Vol. 1, p. 222). James at 23 years of age was still under the sway of empiricism.

HERBERT SPENCER AND EQUILIBRATION

Although he cited Spencer's *Principles of Psychology* of 1855 and 1872 in his own *Principles* in 1890, James was initially infatuated by Spencer's *First Principles* of 1862:

> I . . . was carried away with enthusiasm by the intellectual perspectives which it seemed to open. When a maturer companion, Mr. Charles S. Peirce, attacked it in my presence, I felt spiritually wounded, as by the defacement of a sacred image or picture, though I could not verbally defend it against his criticisms. (James, 1912/1968, p. 125, cf. Fisch, 1947, p. 364)

The reasons for the popularity of Spencer are not far to seek. Spencer, at least as much as Darwin, was the focus of new efforts to reconcile science and religion on a secular foundation.

Spencer's *First Principles* would eventually sell 162,000 copies, and his other 25 books some half a million more (Fisch, 1947, p. 360). Edward Youman's aggressive recruiting of scientific authors and the competitive spirit of his publisher, the Appleton Company, would do much for the spread of Spencer and "evolutionism" in the United States. Although Spencer authored the phrase "survival of the fittest," he actually believed in Lamarckian use-inheritance. In his theory of mental evolution, he retained from his *Principles of Psychology* the mechanism of equilibration whereby the mind evolves by reproducing in its "internal relations" the "external relations" of objects in the world (Bowler, 1989, pp. 288–290).

Wright wrote in his review of Spencer in 1865 that "Mr. Spencer proposes to formulate the phenomena of mind as well as those of matter in terms of matter, motion, and force . . . These are only formulating terms, entirely abstract . . . Experiment must establish these presumptions" (1865/1971, pp. 75 and 79). The notion of experimentation is critical to the thinking of the American opponents of Spencer. In his first publication, a review of Darwin's plant book in 1868, 24-year-old James commented on the impossibility of experimenting on Darwin's hypothesis of pangenesis, "For, in the present state of science, it seems impossible to bring it to an experimental test" (p. 366).

Of course, Wright and James were not first and foremost experimental scientists. We might say that they were experimental philosophers, for they looked to scientific method as a model of scientific thought. Their understanding of laws and how we come to know them linked up with their conception of the experiment. A way to refute Spencer was dawning on James. Indeed, in the same review of 1868, James already noted two prime factors: variability and fitness enabling survival. He would soon discover a logical mechanism in Peirce and Lotze. Subscribing to Lamarkian use-inheritance, Spencer lacked the biological variation-and-selection mechanism and the logical hypothesis-testing one. James combined both into a theory of mental evolution, or "psychogenesis."

CHARLES S. PEIRCE DISTINGUISHES HYPOTHESIS FROM INDUCTION

Peirce's articles of 1868 reveal why Spencer's epistemology was so distasteful to him. The psychologistic foundation of Spencer's convictions did not square with Peirce's logicism, his firm belief that logical truths are independent of experience. Peirce began to distinguish induction from hypothesis as follows:

Induction is where we generalize from a number of cases of which something is true, and infer that the same thing is true of the whole class . . . . Hypothesis is where we find some surprising fact which would be explained by supposing that it was a case of a certain general rule, and thereupon adopt that supposition. The sort of inference is called "making a hypothesis." (2.623–2.624, quoted in Fann, 1970, p. 21)

Did Peirce's theory of hypothesis inspire James's theory of truth? We do not know for sure, because we lack manuscripts from the period of 1868 to 1878. But we do know that James started from biology and the effects of experience on reasoning, whereas Peirce began with logic and necessary truths. One area of convergence involved the formation of hypotheses.

WILLIAM JAMES INTRODUCES VARIABILITY AND SURVIVAL IN PSYCHOGENESIS

To sum up so far, I have compared Spencer, Wright, Peirce, and James up to 1868, when James was only 26 years old and Peirce, 29. I have found broad agreement on the problem to be solved: the explanation of logical inference by physiological mechanisms. I have found dissatisfaction on the part of the latter three men with Spencer's account. And I have seen the beginnings of an original solution on the part of James: variability and survival of ideas through fitness or adaptation.

James was not the only one of the four to adopt this account. Wright was interested in the variability and selection of self-consciousness, whereas Peirce was "always lukewarm about the Darwinian position" (Hookway, 1985, p. 5). W. B. Gallie (1965) observed that "Peirce must be given credit for emphasizing the virtually statistical character of Darwinian theory—a character that rests on its initial assumption of an inherent tendency to variation in the offspring of every breeding-group" (p. 235). But in another respect, Peirce was critical of Darwin's emphasis on individuals in competition, which he compared with the lawlike atomism of Ockham, Descartes, Hobbes, and Newton: "Evolutionism must eventually restore the rejected idea of reasonableness energizing the world (no matter through what mechanism of natural selection or otherwise)" (quoted in Gallie, 1965, p. 234).

My remaining account takes a running survey of James's treatment of reasoning, memory, comparison, and a priori and empirical knowledge. I will just mention a few signposts in James's development of a genetic epistemology beginning in 1878, when he contracted with the Holt Company, the competitor of Appleton. By 1885, James's argument for "psychogenesis" was in place, with only a coda in support of Weismann's rejection of Spencer's transmission of acquired characteristics.

JAMES USES LOTZE TO REVISE SPENCER'S THEORY OF EQUILIBRATION

In 1876, James adopted the second edition of Spencer's *Principles of Psychology* to use in his third year of teaching; the course was called Natural History 2. Physiological Psychology (Stern, 1965). Those who have traced the Darwinian side of James have characteristically limited their view to his chapters on emotion, instinct, and will—the behavioral chapters, so to speak—or to his pragmatism (Richards, 1987; Thayer, 1981). If one bears in mind the mechanism of random variation and selection, and the importance of chance for James's understanding of both, then I think one will get the gist of his answer to Spencer on a broad range of psychological problems.

An unpublished lecture on "Spencer's Law of Intelligence" tells how he used Spencer. Because Richards covers it well, I can be brief (Richards, 1987, pp. 426–427). James was critical of Spencer's passive account of the mind. Spencer held that the way the environment molds the organism is not a direct one, as he maintained by his correspondence of inner and outer relations. James answered that spontaneous mental variations occur, and we choose from among them. He knew that Darwin distinguished the causes of variation, which we cannot know, from the mechanism of selection. James simply transferred this operation to the mind.

James was also reading Hermann Lotze's *Logik* (1874), as we know from marginal notes in his own excellent German on virtually every page of his original exemplar (signed with the address, "20 Quincy St"). James finally summarized in English on the back flyleaf:

> The two words *gelten* [to be valid] and *zusammengehören* [to belong together] express a great deal of Lotze's philosophy. The conclusion he works at all thro' the book is that of showing how *zusammengehören* can be made to appear possible. He leaves it vague. For him the essential form of rational connection in thought is S + x = P in which x is the condition or ground of S becoming P, but in which P is itself identical. This question Lotze answers by pointing to the *Anschauungsformen* [forms of intuition] of number, space, the operations of subtraction, of measuring, the demands of justice, & by submitting to which, as a matter of fact "things" actually succeed in appearing under different forms. And the "a priority" of the *Anschauung* consists in instantaneous seeing that any simple truth which these forms make possible is universally valid. (James, note on Lotze, 1874, back flyleaf)

We recognize throughout that James wanted to learn from Lotze how we acquire and justify perceptual, mathematical, and moral truths. Lotze provided him with the rationale that in judgment we make a selection of the empirical conditions x under which S = P. This became his empirical mechanism of cognitive and moral development, if not mental evolution.

In other marginalia to Lotze's *Logik*, James wrote in mixed German and English that "the 'conceptual order' ist nicht the real order, doch passen sie zusammen" [yet they agree] (note on Lotze, 1874, p. 550). "Practically considered," James wrote in German, "analysis and induction flow together. The use of symbolically very simple objects allows us to make very wide inductions" (note on Lotze, 1874, p. 349). Despite his heavy criticism of Lotze, James found reassurance in Lotze's *Logik* for a fallibilist theory of scientific method. However, James was "broadening and deepening the definition of experience" (Kraushaar, 1938, p. 522).

In "The Feeling of Effort" (1880/1983). James cited Lotze' *Medizinische Psychologie* (1852) to establish that testing the effects of action guides voluntary ideas through a reflexive feedback loop (Woodward, 1984). This mechanism became known as the James–Lange theory of emotions (Kraushaar, 1936). In his articles, Kraushaar carefully demonstrated that in the 1880s James "was full of the Lotzean text." He used Lotze to oppose associationism in "The Sentiment of Rationality" (1879/1986) and "The Association of Ideas" (1880/1986). He displayed how the mind reconstructs "the given order into the order of conception" in "Reflex Action and Theism" (1881; reprinted in 1897/1979, cited in Kraushaar, 1939, p. 461). Practical interests and results steer mental association and reflex physiology.

JAMES ADAPTS PEIRCE'S SIGN THEORY AS MENTAL SELECTION

Gradually during the 1870s, beginning with logical truths, Charles Peirce had begun to identify three forms of inference: induction, deduction, and hypothesis—later termed *abduction* (Fann, 1970). With the strong claim that all mental action is inference, he accounted for human irrationality by false premises, weak inductions, and deficient hypotheses, respectively. His sign theory linked mental states, including sensations, to the objects or images to which they refer, for example, "We can see a speckled surface without seeing it as having a definite number of speckles" (Hookway, 1985, p. 35). A community of observers induces reality "in the long run." Here was another source of James's theory of cognition.

In 1878, for example, James published the essay "Brute and Human Intellect" (1878/1983) that would become his chapter on "Reasoning" in the *Principles*. (Woodward, 1983, pp. xiv–xv). James addressed the way a dog would respond to its master's request for a dipper to empty water from a rowboat. The dog might leap to a gesture signaling it to fetch a sponge. But a human might contemplate and return with a dipper or a mop. This illustrates how human reasoning is able to select the partial character, in logical terms, suited to its interests on that occasion.

Again in his essay "Are We Automata?" (1879/1983) replying to Huxley's essay on that topic, James foreshadowed parts of chapters in the *Principles* on the automaton–theory, attention, and the stream of thought. He countered Huxley's physiological determinism with the argument that consciousness has in fact survived, hence it must have had a utility. Again, he reasoned in terms of Darwinian selection.

Did James's selection account of reasoning differ from Peirce's? Karl-Otto Apel (1967/1981) argued that it did so, because Peirce maintained the more objective criterion that "in the long run" truth is that on which many observers converge. By 1877, Peirce wrote, "The most that can be maintained is, that we seek for a belief that we shall think to be true. But we think each one of our beliefs to be true, and, indeed, it is a mere tautology to say so" (cited in Apel, 1967/1981, pp. 60–61). Whereas James defined the true as that which is useful, that which realizes our ends—hence individual selection—Peirce stressed the group.

Next, in 1880, James's "Great Men, Great Thoughts, and the Environment" presaged his genetic epistemology from the side of moral and cultural evolution. Here he attacked a disciple of Spencer, Grant Allen, for his contention that the physical conditions alone account for "nation making" in different cultures (James, 1880/1979, p. 450). James credited William Stanley Jevons's *Philosophy of Science* (1877) for the recognition that random guesses underlie scientific discovery. Concluded James, "I think that all who have had the patience to follow me thus far will agree that the Spencerian 'philosophy' of social and intellectual progress is an obsolete anachronism" (James, 1880, p. 459).

THE JAMESIAN SYNTHESIS

Close to the logic of mental evolution, but on the level of mental development, came James's "The Feeling of Effort" (1880/1983). His terms *effect-theory (effektsbild)* and *effects of experience* came from reflex physiology, but James gave them a distinctly evolutionary twist. An "effect" is a variation on what I call the psychophysiological level, because in choosing actions one selects from previous effects. The action of will, the choice, embodies the metaphor of natural selection.

James was only 38 years old; he would not write the key chapter on knowledge in the *Principles* until he was 43, and the book would appear in his 48th year. In the final chapter on "Necessary Truths and the Effects of Experience," as Gerald Myers (1986) emphasized, James "makes the spectacular claim that the act of comparing exclusively underpins the pure science of logic and mathematics and results not from experience but from the brain's native or innate structure" (p. 264). This act of comparison is akin to judging in the German logical tradition. This is the analytic side of thought, the deductive process. But insofar as James recognized particular sensations from which we synthesize rules, we have the inductive side.

Let us see how James actually put these ideas and others together in his chapter on "Necessary Truths and the Effects of Experience," drawing a few comparisons with his contemporaries.

First, he acknowledged that sensations are primary. "The *elementary qualities* of cold, heat, pleasure, pain, red, blue, sound, silence, etc., are original, innate, or *a priori* properties of our subjective nature" (1890/1981, Vol. 2, p. 1216; 1890, Vol. 2, p. 618). Reality, in fact, consists in sensations. In this claim he resembled Ernst Mach, Henri Poincaré, and Karl Pearson.

Second, as a picture of the brain bombarded by little *o*'s in Figure 1 shows, the outer relations impose order on the inner relations, marked *x*. The *o*'s work directly, the *x*'s indirectly, to modify the mind. The *o*'s refer to experiences. They include time and space relations. Allying himself with

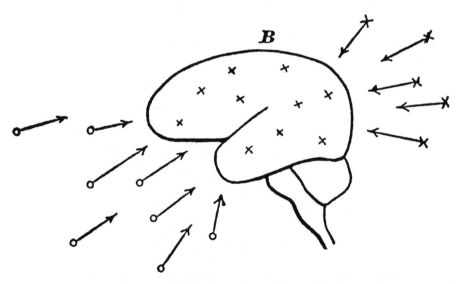

Figure 1: Evolution of Brain Structure: "B stands for our human brain in the midst of the world. All the little *o*'s with arrows proceeding from them are natural objects (like sunsets, etc.), which impress it through the senses. . . . All the *x*'s inside the brain and all the little *x*'s outside of it are other natural objects and processes (in the ovum, in the blood, etc.) which equally modify the brain, but mould it to no cognition of *themselves*. . . . No one can successfully treat of psychogenesis, or the factors of mental evolution, without distinguishing between these two ways in which the mind is assailed. . . . I will then, with the reader's permission, restrict the word 'experience' to processes which influence the mind by the front-door-way of simple habits and associations" (James, 1890/1981, 626–628).

Bishop George Berkeley and Carl Stumpf, James held that space comes to us ready made in the experience itself. With this he touched off a controversy (Woodward, 1983).

Third, invoking Shadworth Hodgson, Hermann Lotze, and Christoph Sigwart and quoting his own reflex action essay on mental evolution, James wrote that "what we *think* is an abstract system of hypothetical data and laws" (1890/1981, Vol. 2, p. 1231; 1890, Vol. 2, p. 634). Here his ideas resemble Hans Vaihinger's philosophy of "as if" as well as the philosophies of the logicians just named.

Fourth, the so-called pure sciences of mathematics, logic, and classification do not require experience. They come from comparison but outside of the order of time and space (James, 1890/1981, Vol. 2, p. 1237; 1890, Vol. 2, p. 641). Doubtless he followed Peirce here.

Fifth, drawing from F. H. Bradley's logic, he discussed predication and various series: classification, reasoning, and mathematics, which are "the basis of rationality" (James, 1890/1981, Vol. 2, p. 1253; 1890, Vol. 2, p. 659; cf. Wollheim, 1959/1969, p. 27). His distinction between existence and validity originated from Lotze, whom he read and annotated extensively:

> Arithmetic does not tell us where her 7's, 5's, and 12's are to be *found*; geometry affirms not that circles and rectangles are *real*. All that these sciences make us sure of is, that if these things are anywhere to be found, the eternal verities will obtain of them. (James, 1981, Vol. 2, p. 1890: Vol. 2. p. 663)

Sixth, regarding the analytic–synthetic distinction, James refused to take a position (1981, Vol. 2, p. 1235; 1890, Vol. 2, p. 639). Willard van Orman Quine (1981) called this "the abandonment of the analytic–synthetic dualism," and he noted that "James rejected the distinction." Quine himself agreed: "I would expect it to waver likewise in any far-reaching theory of man-made truth" (p. 35).

Notice that what unites these features of knowledge is irreducible. Some truths are found in introspective experience, others are analytically valid. Some are the product of evolution, and others are hypothetical. Many, like the truths of science, are man-made constructions, yet others are wired in, such as the evolution and variation of brain structures. As James put it in *Pragmatism* (1907/1975), "Truth happens to an idea. It becomes true, is made true by events . . . . It converts the absolutely empty notion of a static relation of 'correspondence' between our minds and reality, into that of a rich and active commerce . . . between particular thoughts of ours" (1975 [1907], p. 37). It is a "sketch," wrote H. S. Thayer, or an "inquiry" for Peirce and Dewey (Thayer, 1975, p. xxxi).

RECENT LITERATURE SUPPORTS
NON-DARWINIAN INFLUENCES

I would like to draw to a close by saluting a recent dissertation and an undergraduate thesis that further help situate James and his community in nineteenth-century thought. The first by Thomas Carlson, a student of Hilary Putnam, chastens Richard Rorty for hailing pragmatism as a reform of Kant's philosophy. Rorty unfairly treated "the Kantian conception of philosophy as foundational instead of viewing Kant as a 'proto-Jamesian' " (1990, p. 13).

Although Carlson's claim seems historically absurd, it serves to highlight a feature of Kant that the Neo-Kantians and Rortyans neglected. Kant's three critiques, bringing together knowledge, morality, and faith, contain passages that suggest the founding of truth on belief. I will show how the inherent selection required in judgment and hypothesis testing also requires belief. This selection appears full-blown in Charles Peirce's theory of hypothesis and in Lotze's Kantian theory of scientific method. Of course, James's "survival of the fittest among beliefs" went beyond both in his adoption of Darwin's language. However, I contend that the resort to German thought was required because Darwin offered no mechanism of how the mind develops knowledge in a lifetime.

Paul Croce's (1990) undergraduate thesis at Brown University (directed by historian of mathematics Joan Richards) directs attention to the probabilistic side of James, in keeping with new literature on the probabilistic revolution (Krüger, Daston, & Heidelberger, 1987). It follows on the earlier work of Charlene Haddock Siegfried (1978) on chaos, a superbly argued work that suggests further support for an evolutionary interpretation and emphasizes chaos in the sense of experience that is not structured. I take this as support for James's insistence on the variability of ideas in mental development.

Consider the final two paragraphs of the *Principles* in 1890, amounting to a parting critique of Spencer:

> I must therefore end this chapter on the genesis of our mental structure by reaffirming my conviction that the so-called Experience-Philosophy has failed to prove its point. No more if we take ancestral experiences into account than if we limit ourselves to those of the individual after birth, can we believe that the couplings of terms within the mind are simple copies of corresponding coupling impressed upon it by the environment. (James, 1890/1981, Vol. 2, p. 1280; 1890, Vol. 2, p. 688)

James sought to explain the truths of science and morality with something more rational that mere learning from experience, what philosophers term a correspondence theory between mind and nature.

But James also rejected a pure coherence theory that logical relations alone guarantee truth. Nature must remain our guide in checking our hypotheses. He drew extensively from Lotze's *Logik* in 1874, as we saw, as well as from the Hegelian T. H. Bradley's *Principles of Logic*. For example, when we engage in comparison by classifying animals, by doing mathematics and logic, our thoughts

> would form a merely theoretic scheme and be of no use for the conduct of life. But our world is no such world. . . . Some of the things are of the same kind as other things. . . . The flight to this last kind over the heads of the intermediaries is the essential feature of the intellectual operation here. (1890/1981, Vol. 2, pp. 1246–1247; 1890, Vol. 2, pp. 651–652)

James's reply to Spencer has to do with how we come to know propositions of aesthetics, ethics, science, metaphysics, time, and space. There could scarely be a higher calling for the "New Psychology" than to account for the origins of knowledge and beauty, of action and being. James ended the *Principles* with a critique of Spencer's and Bradley's accounts of psychogenesis. Ideas are not mere copies; their origin is not merely empirical. Nor are they merely rational in origin. Clearly, James sought an alternative to experience-philosophy and to the so-called Neo-Hegelians. Clearly, a lot was riding on the answer. From today's perspective, our collective responsibility for the further evolution of humanity is at stake.

REFERENCES

Apel, K.-O. (1981). *Charles S. Peirce: From pragmatism to pragmaticism.* Amherst: University of Massachusetts. (Original work published 1967)

Armstrong, P. (1983). *The phenomenology of Henry James.* Chapel Hill: University of North Carolina Press.

Bernstein, R. J. (1983). *Beyond objectivism and relativism: Scicne, hermeneutics, and praxis.* Philadelphia: University of Pennsylvania Press.

Bowler, P. (1983). *The eclipse of Darwinism: Anti-Darwinian evolution theories in the decades around 1900.* Baltimore, MD: Johns Hopkins, University Press.

Bowler, P. (1989). *Evolution: The history of an idea.* Berkeley: University of California Press.

Carlson, T. B. (1990). *The pragmatic individual: From Kant to James.* Unpublished doctoral dissertation, Harvard University, Cambridge, MA.

Croce, P. J. (1990, June). *Finding the role of chance in science: William James's scientific education and the probabilistic revolution*. Paper presented at Cheiron: Society For the History of the Behavioral and Social Sciences, Westfield, MA.

Dewey, J. (1910). *The influence of Darwin on philosophy*. New York: Holt.

Edie, J. (1987). *William James and phenomenology*. Bloomington: Indiana University Press.

Fann, K. T. (1970). *Peirce's theory of abduction*. Dordrecht, The Netherlands: Martinus Nijhoff.

Fisch, M. H. (1947). Evolution in American philosophy. *Philosophical Review, 56,* 357–373.

Fisch, M. H. (1964). Was there a metaphysical club in Cambridge? In E. C. Moore & R. S. Robin (Eds.), *Studies in the philosophy of Charles Sanders Peirce* (pp. 3–32). Amherst: University of Massachusetts Press.

Ford, M. (1982) *William James's philosophy*. Amherst: University of Massachusetts Press.

Gallie, W. B. (1965). *Peirce and pragmatism*. New York: Dover.

Hookway, C. (1985). *Peirce*. London: Routledge & Kegan Paul.

James, W. (1868). Review [unsigned] of Charles Darwin's *The variation of animals and plants under domestication. North American Review, 107,* 362–368.

James, W. (1975). *Pragmatism*. Cambridge, MA: Harvard University Press. (Original work published 1907)

James, W. (1975). *The meaning of truth*. Cambridge, MA: Harvard University Press. (Original work published 1909)

James, W. (1979). Great men, great thoughts, and the environment. In F. H. Burkhardt, F. Bowers, & I. K. Skrupskelis (Eds.), *The will to believe and other essays in popular philosophy* (pp. 163–189). Cambridge, MA: Harvard University Press. (Original book published 1897; original essay published 1880)

James, W. (1979). *The will to believe and other essays in popular philosophy*. Cambridge, MA: Harvard University Press. (Original work published 1897)

James, W. (1981). *The principles of psychology*. Cambridge, MA: Harvard University Press. (Original work published 1890)

James, W. (1983). Brute and human intellect. In F. Burkhardt, F. Bowers, & I. K. Skrupskelis (Eds.), *Essays in psychology* (pp. 1–37). Cambridge, MA: Harvard University Press. (Original work published 1878)

James, W. (1983). The feeling of effort. In F. H. Burkhardt & I. K. Skrupskelis (Eds.), *Essays in psychology* (pp. 83–124). Cambridge, MA: Harvard University Press. (Original work published 1880)

James, W. (1983). Are we automata? In F. H. Burkhardt, F. Bowers, & I. K. Skrupskelis (Eds.), *Essays in psychology* (pp. 38–61). Cambridge, MA: Harvard University Press. (Original work published 1879)

James, W. (1986). The sentiment of rationality: Remarks on Spencer's definition of mind as correspondence. In F. H. Burkhardt, F. Bowers, & I. K. Skrupskelis (Eds.), *Essays in philosophy*. Cambridge, MA: Harvard University Press. (Original work published 1879)

James, W. (1986). The association of ideas. In F. H. Burkhardt, F. Bowers, & I. K. Skrupskelis (Eds.), *Essays in philosophy*. Cambridge, MA: Harvard University Press. (Original work published 1880)

Jevons, W. S. (1877). *The principles of science* (2nd ed.). New York: Macmillan.

Kraushaar, O. F. (1936). Lotze's influence on the psychology of William James. *Psychological Review, 43*, 235–257.

Kraushaar, O. F. (1938). What James's philosophical orientation owed to Lotze. *Philosophical Review, 48*, 517–526.

Kraushaar, O. F. (1939). Lotze as a factor in the development of James's radical empiricism and pluralism. *Philosophical Review, 48*, 455–471.

Kraushaar, O. F. (1940). Lotze's influence on the pragmatism and practical philosophy of William James. *Journal of the History of Ideas, 1*, 439–458.

Krüger, L., Daston, L., & Heidelberger, M. (1987). *The probabilistic revolution*. Cambridge, MA: MIT Press.

Laudan, L. (1968). Theories of scientific method from Plato to Mach: A bibliographical review. *History of Science, 7*, 1–63.

Lotze, H. (1852). *Medicinische Psychologie*. Leipzig, Germany: Weidmann.

Lotze, H. (1874). *Logik*. Leipzig, German: S. Hirzel [W. James's personal copy in Houghton Library, Harvard University, Cambridge, MA.]

Madden, E. H. (1955–1956). Chance and counterfacts in Wright and Peirce. *Review of Metaphysics, 19*, 420–432.

Madden, E. H. (1963). *Chauncey Wright and the foundations of pragmatism*. Seattle: University of Washington Press.

Murphey, M. (1968). Kant's children: The Cambridge pragmatists, *Transactions of the Charles Peirce Society, 4*, 3–33.

Myers, G. (1986). *William James: His life and thought*. New Haven, CT: Yale University Press.

Okrent, M. (1988). *Heidegger's pragmatism: Understanding, being, and the critique of metaphysics*. Ithaca, NY: Cornell University Press.

Peirce, C. S. (1869). Grounds and validity of the laws of logic; Questions concerning certain faculties claimed for man; Some consequences of four incapacities. *Journal of Speculative Philosophy, 2*, 193–208.

Perry, R. B. (1935). *The thought and character of William James* (Vols. 1–2). Boston: Little, Brown.

Popper, K. (1959). *The logic of scientific discovery*. London: Routledge & Kegan Paul. (Author, Trans.) (Original work published 1934)

Popper, K. (1979). *Die beiden Grundprobleme der Erkenntnistheorie*, [The two basic epistemological problems]. Tübingen: J. C. B. Mohr. (Original work published 1930–1933)

Quine, W. V. (1981). The pragmatists' place in empiricism. In R. J. Mulvaney &

P. M. Zeltner (Eds.), *Pragmatism, its sources and prospects* (pp. 21–40). Columbia: University of South Carolina Press.

Richards, R. J. (1987). *Darwin and the emergence of evolutionary theories of mind and behavior*. Chicago: University of Chicago Press.

Rorty, R. (1979). *Philosophy and the mirror of nature*. Princeton, NJ: Princeton University Press.

Rosenthal, S. B. (1986). *Speculative pragmatism*. Amherst: University of Massachusetts Press.

Seigfried, C. H . (1978). *Chaos and context: A study in William James*. Athens: Ohio University Press.

Seigfried, C. H. (1990). *William James's radical reconstruction of philosophy*. Albany: State University of New York Press.

Spencer, H. (1860). *First principles*. New York: Appleton & Co.

Spencer, H. (1870–1872). *Principles of psychology*. London: Williams & Nargete. (Original work published 1855)

Stern, S. (1968). William James and the new psychology. In P. Buck (Ed.), *The social sciences at Harvard* (pp. 175–222). Cambridge, MA: Harvard University Press.

Thayer, H. S. (1975). Introduction. In W. James, *Pragmatism* (pp. xi–xxxviii). Cambridge, MA: Harvard University Press.

Thayer, H. S. (1981). *Meaning and action: A critical history of pragmatism*. Indianapolis, IN: Hackett.

Wiener, P. (1949). *Evolution and the founders of pragmatism*. Cambridge, MA: Harvard University Press.

Wollheim, R. (1969). *F. H . Bradley*. Baltimore: Penguin. (Original work published 1959)

Woodward, W. R. (1983). Introduction. In W. James, *Essays in psychology* (pp. xi–xxxix). Cambridge, MA: Harvard University Press.

Woodward, W. R. (1984). William James's psychology of will: Its revolutionary impact on American psychology. In J. Brozek (Ed.), *Explorations in the history of psychology in the United States* (pp. 148–195). Lewisburg, PA: Bucknell University Press.

Woodward, W. R. (1985). Hermann Lotze's concept of function: Its Kantian origin and its impact on evolutionism in the United States. In G. Eckardt, W. G. Bringmann, & L. Sprung, (Eds.). *Contributions to a history of developmental psychology* (pp. 576–593). Amsterdam/Berlin: Mouton.

Wright, C. (1971). A physical view of the universe. In C. Wright (Ed.), *Philosophical discussions* (pp. 1–34). New York: Burt Franklin. (Original work published 1864)

Wright, C. (1971). The philosophy of Herbert Spencer. In C. Wright (Ed.), *Philosophical discussions* (pp. 43–96). New York: Burt Franklin. (Original work published 1865)

IV

FURTHER THOUGHTS
ON THE SELF

11

WILLIAM JAMES AND THE PSYCHOLOGY OF SELF

M. BREWSTER SMITH

William James wrote so directly and vividly on psychologically pro-vocative and important subjects that reading him today goes far toward restoring our damaged convictions about the human centrality of psychology and its intellectual challenges. I can give personal testimony from rereading the chapter in *The Principles of Psychology* (1890/1981), "The Consciousness of Self," and a chapter in "The Self in 'Jimmy'" (as students in the century called *Psychology: Briefer Course* [1892/1984]). There have been several excellent recent discussions of James's treatment of self, for example, by Gerald Myers (1981) in his introduction to the definitive Harvard edition of the *Principles*, by David Leary (1990), and by Hazel Markus (1990) in the *Psychological Science* symposium on the *Principles*. What, I wondered, could I possibly add? I began to curse the day that I agreed to submit this paper. But then I did my homework, reread the *Principles*, *Briefer Course*, and the recent appraisals. I discovered, to my reassurance, that there is plenty to say. James provided so rich a stimulus that not only is there little overlap among the commentaries that I have cited, but none of the commentators elected to say what immediately occurred to me as relevant! Depending on what one brings to James, one finds different things provocative.

JAMES ON SELFHOOD

I want, first, to reinstate what James said about selfhood. In these classic chapters in the *Principles*, he did not merely summarize and criticize, but he invented on a grand scale. Second, rather than emphasizing what has been drawn directly from James, I will focus on some problems visible in his formulations from my retrospective vantage point, which bear the current uses of his germinal ideas. Fad and fashion have made the recent literature on self and identity so proliferated and confusing that one needs to struggle to get his or her bearings. My reconsideration of James is part of my attempt to do so.

For James, selfhood inhered in the very nature of thought. He began his famous chapter, "The Stream of Thought" (which immediately precedes "The Consciousness of the Self") with an exemplary statement of the phenomenological attitude—the deliberate setting aside of presuppositions to attend as faithfully as possible to the presenting phenomena. The presuppositions he particularly wanted to avoid had to do with elementary sensations, which in the nineteenth century functioned as building blocks in a mechanistic theoretical psychology much as elementary responses or stimulus–response (S–R) connections functioned in the mid twentieth century. James wrote,

> Most books start with sensations, as the simplest mental facts, and proceed synthetically, constructing each higher stage from those below it. But this is abandoning the empirical method of investigation. No one ever had a simple sensation by itself. Consciousness, from our natal day, is of a teeming multiplicity of objects and relations, and what we call simple sensations are results of discriminitive attention, pushed often to a very high degree. It is astonishing what havoc is wrought in psychology by admitting at the outset apparently innocent presuppositions, that nevertheless contain a flaw. The bad consequences develop themselves later on, and are irremediable, being woven through the whole texture of the work. The notion that sensations, being the simplest things, are the first things to take up in psychology is one of these suppositions. The only thing which psychology has a right to postulate at the outset is the fact of thinking itself, and that must first be taken up and analyzed (p. 1890/1981, 219)

So James took thinking as the starting point. He noted five characteristics of thought that, from another perspective, set the terms of selfhood in conscious experience:

1. Every thought tends to be part of a personal consciousness.

2. Within each personal consciousness thought is always changing.

3. Within each personal consciousness thought is sensibly continuous.

4. It always appears to deal with objects independent of itself.

5. It is some parts of these objects to the exclusion of others, and welcomes or rejects—chooses from among them, in a word—all the while. (1890/1981, p. 220).

In discussing the first of these points, James wrote,

> It seems as if the elementary psychic fact were not *thought* or *this thought* or *that thought*, but *my thought*, every thought being *owned*. . . . On these terms the personal self rather than the thought might be treated as the immediate datum in psychology. The universal conscious fact is not "feelings and thought exist," but "I think" and "I feel". No psychology, at any rate, can question the *existence* of personal selves. The worst a psychology can do is so to interpret the nature of these selves as to rob them of their worth. (1890/1981, p. 221) [Subsequent psychology *has* often done its worst.]

At the end of "The Stream of Thought," James summed up the selectiveness of consciousness and reintroduced the preeminent importance of selfhood in its organization.

> The mind is at every stage a theatre of simultaneous possibilities. Consciousness consists in the comparison of these with each other, the selection of some, and the suppression of the rest. . . . In my mind and your mind the rejected portions and the selected portions of the original world-stuff are to a great extent the same. . . . There is, however, one entirely extraordinary case in which no two men are ever known to choose alike. One great splitting of the whole universe into two halves is made by each of us; and for each of us almost all of the interest attaches to one of the halves; but we all draw the line of division between them in a different place. When I say that we all call the two halves by the same names, and that those names are "me" and "not me" respectively, it will at once be seen what I mean. The altogether unique kind of interest which each human mind feels in those parts of creation which it can call *me* or *mine* may be a moral riddle, but it is a fundamental psychological fact. (1890/1981, pp. 277–278)

James began his chapter, "The Consciousness of Self," with a distinction that subsequent theorists have generally adopted: between the experiencing *I* and the empirical self or *me*—the self as the object in reflexive self-consciousness. In this chapter, James first discussed the *me*, which is what psychology has focused on most frequently. I will start here with the *I*, because if one is persuaded by James's extensive argument that whether or not there is a substantial soul makes no difference to empirical psychology, there is not very much to be said about the *I* in James's theory. For psychological purposes, he asserted, the *I* is the momentary, passing thought in the stream of consciousness, which, as it occupies the center of the stage, appropriates with a sense of identity memories of the preceding thoughts in the stream, looks ahead to the future, and *is* the thought of the present. Phenomenologically, this rings true. George Herbert Mead (1934), a direct intellectual descendant of James who thought of himself as a social behaviorist while launching the symbolic interactionist tradition in sociology, also conceived of the *I* in much the same insubstantial way.

Of course, Freud and his successors stepped out of the subjective, phenomenological frame without James's felt obligation to confute the relics of religious philosophy—the substantial soul of the Scottish school and the transcendental ego of Kant and Hegel. Freud and many subsequent personality theorists conceived of a central system of directive or causal processes linked to the *I* of experience, but far from identical with it. Freud's (1927/1961) ego and Erikson's (1959) identity are concepts applied from the outside to account for stabilities in self-perception, in internal coordination, and in the organization of a person's actions in the world; they do not originate in the flow of experience. Although James's account of the appropriative passing thought seems just right phenomenologically, his frame of reference is hard to integrate in contemporary theories.

The *me* or empirical self is the center of James's attention. He wrote,

> The Empirical Self of each of us is all that he is tempted to call by the name of *me*. But it is clear that between what a man calls *me* and what he simply calls *mine* the line is difficult to draw . . . the same object being sometimes treated as part of me, at other times as simply mine, and then again as if I had nothing to do with it at all. *In its widest possible sense, however, a man's Self is the sum total of all that he can call his*, not only his body and his psychic powers, but his clothes and his house, his wife and children, his ancestors and friends, his reputation and works, his land and horses, and yacht and bank account. All these things give him the same emotions. If they wax and prosper, he feels triumphant; if they dwindle and die away, he feels cast down,—not necessarily in the same degree for each thing, but in much the same way for all. (1890/1981, pp. 279–280)

The empirical self has three divisions. The *material self* is one's body, one's clothes, one's property, which are all part of the me and mine when one's passing thought—*I* the subject—thinks of oneself as the object. A person's *social self* is the "recognition which he gets from his mates" (1890/1981, p. 281), as James put it, but he meant more. As he said in expansion, "Properly speaking, *a man has as many social selves as there are individuals who recognize him* and carry an image of him in their mind (1890/1981, pp. 281–282). This still is not exactly what he meant, as becomes clear from his illustrations. The social self—or selves—does not really exist in other people's recognition, but in the person's own regard for it. So James's conception of the multiplicity of the social self anticipated the social situationism of much modern sociological theory (without saying that there is nothing more to the self) and foreshadowed reference-group theory as initiated by Hyman (1942) and Merton (1957), according to which we judge ourselves in relation to standards that arise from the groups (or persons) we identify with and also guide what we do by the norms we attribute to them. The elaborated modern ideas seem present implicitly in James's account, without his erecting a partial truth about human nature into an imperialistically competitive theory.

The third aspect of the *me* is the spiritual self, by which James meant "a man's inner or subjective being, his psychic faculties and dispositions, taken concretely; not the bare principle of personal Unity, or 'pure' Ego. . . . These psychic dispositions are the most enduring and intimate part of the self, that which we most verily seem to be" (1890/1981, p. 283). Awareness of self in this sense requires truly reflective consciousness, "thinking ourselves as thinkers" in James's words, with all its puzzles, which James did not clarify. As people attempt to abstract from the stream of consciousness a core or a self of selves, James said,

> Probably all men would describe it in much the same way up to a certain point. They would call it the *active* element in all consciousness; saying that whatever qualities a man's feelings may possess, or whatever content his thought may include, there is a spiritual something in him which seems to *go out* to meet these qualities and contents, whilst they seem to *come in* to be received by it. It is what welcomes and rejects. It presides over the perception of sensations, and by giving or withholding its assent it influences the movements they tend to arouse. It is the home of interest,—not the pleasant or the painful, not even pleasure or pain, as such, but that within us to which pleasure and pain, the pleasant and the painful, speak. It is the source of effort and attention, and the place from which appear to emanate the fiats of the will. (1890/1981, p. 285)

James then went on to say, however, that

> all men must single out from the rest of what they call themselves some central principle of which each would recognize the foregoing to be a fair general description,—accurate enough, at any rate, to denote what

is meant, and keep it unconfused with other things, the moment . . . they came to closer quarters with it, trying to define more accurately its precise nature, we would find opinions beginning to diverge. Some would say that it is a simple active substance, the soul, of which they are thus conscious; others, that it is nothing but a fiction, the imaginary being denoted by the pronoun I; and between these extremes of opinion all sorts of intermediaries would be found. (1890/1981, p. 285–286)

These divergences, of course, concern the crucial relation between the *me* as object and the *I* as subject: Is what one thinks one knows about *me* at all informative about the *I* as knower and thinker? An empiricist in psychology, who was in the process of developing radical empiricism in philosophy, James noted, but avoided, the issue. He reported that in his own introspections, the core of the spiritual self, of this central active self, lies in feelings of bodily processes, taking place mostly in the head—a parallel to his famous theory of the bodily basis of emotion. Some people may feel let down at this point—I do—with his reduction of the *I* to the appropriative passing thought. I will return to this problem shortly.

Self-seeking and *self-love* pertain to the person's various empirical selves, as do the *self-feelings* of self-esteem versus despair, shame, and guilt. Self-feelings, thus, depend on relation among one's empirical selves, on which James's comments are classic:

> I am often confronted by the necessity of standing by one of my empirical selves and relinquishing the rest. . . . [Many] different characters may conceivably at the outset of life be *possible* to a man. But to make any one of them actual, the rest must more or less be suppressed. So the seeker of his truest, strongest, deepest self must review the list carefully, and pick out the one on which to stake his salvation. All other selves thereupon become unreal, but the fortunes of this self are real. Its failures are real failures, its triumphs real triumphs, carrying shame and gladness with them. This is as strong an example as there is of that selective industry of the mind on which I insisted some pages back. Our thought, incessantly deciding, among many things of a kind, which ones for it shall be realities, here chooses one of many possible selves or characters, and forthwith reckons it no shame to fail in any of those not adopted expressly as its own. I, who for the time have staked my all on being a psychologist, am mortified if others know much more psychology than I. But I am contented to wallow in the grossest ignorance of Greek. (1890/1980, pp. 295–296)

It is in this connection that James introduced his famous formula for self-esteem, which lay fallow for many years until, in my own time, Kurt Lewin (1935) and his students and successors resurrected it in research on the new topic of level of aspiration.

So our self-feeling in this world depends entirely on what we *back* ourselves to be and do. It is determined by the ratio of our actualities to our supposed potentialities; a fraction of which our pretensions are the denominator and the numerator of our success: thus, Self-esteem=Success/Pretensions. Such a fraction may be increased as well by diminishing the denominator as by increasing the numerator. To give up pretensions is as blessed a relief as to get them gratified; and where disappointment is incessant and the struggle unending, this is what men will always do. (James, 1890/1981, pp. 296–297)

James suggested and then dropped one of his interesting typologies, which divides people according to their characteristic strategies for dealing with this formula: stoics, who proceed by exclusion, seeking to reduce the denominator, versus sympathetic people, who proceed by expansion and inclusion. For most people, the different selves are arranged in a hierarchical scale of worth, *"with the bodily Self at the bottom, the spiritual Self at the top, and the extracorporeal material selves and the various social selves in between"* (1890/1981, p. 299). With each kind of self, people distinguish between the immediate and actual and between the more remote and potential.

Of all these wider, more potential selves, the *potential social self* is the most interesting, by reason of certain apparent paradoxes to which it leads in conduct, and by reason of its connection with our moral and religious life. When for motives of honor and conscience I brave the condemnation of my own family, club, and "set". . . I am always inwardly strengthened in my course and steeled against the loss of my actual social self by the thought of other and better *possible* social judges than those whose verdict goes against me now. The ideal social self which I thus seek in appealing their decision may be very remote: it may be represented as barely possible. (1890/1981, p. 300)

James saw moral progress in the social self in terms of such "substitution of higher tribunals for lower" (1890/1981, p. 301) with God as the highest. The social self, for James, did not necessarily imply "other directedness"—far from it.

SOME PROBLEMS IN JAMES'S FORMULATIONS

This very partial sampling of William James on selfhood must surely have conveyed some of the intrinsic appeal of his ground-breaking account. James's account is the point of origin of all subsequent consideration of self by psychologists and sociologists. I could have gone on at much greater length, especially if I were to indicate how his treatment of the divided self that is reflected in multiple personality and in hypnotic phenomena fore-shadowed most of the issues that have surfaced during the revival of interest in hypnosis in recent decades (Kihlstrom & McConkey, 1990) and, also, how his opening the door to the possibility of mystical cosmic consciousness anticipated themes of transpersonal psychology. In the remainder of this chapter, however, I want to take advantage of the hindsight that is available because of the contributions of later psychologists and sociologists in order to look at some problems in James's formulations that could not have been fully apparent to him. Attending to these problems should put psychologists in a better position to continue to build on James's foundations for a psychology of selfhood.

Problems Arising From the Phenomenological Basis

One set of problems arises from the phenomenological basis on which James constructed his account. "The Consciousness of Self" is intrinsic to his characterization of "The Stream of Thought," the chapter that precedes it in the *Principles*. I, as my momentary thought that appropriates the preceding stream in memory (and thus maintains continuity in my sense of identity), splits the universe that I know in the stream that I remember into me and not me. The distinction between I and me is the familiar duality of subject and object in the relation of intentionality beloved by phenomenologists; the bifurcation of me and not me is phenomenologically identified with the special emotional quality with which all that concerns me is invested. So far, there are no problems.

Note, however, that in this treatment, the I serves a purely cognitive function. It would be redundant, as James insisted, to introduce a substantive soul or a transcendental ego to account for the psychological subject if the only function to be considered were that of knower. But of course, knowing is not the only function with which one must be concerned. Our subject also feels and chooses and decides and acts; Gordon Allport (1943a), a good successor to James at Harvard along with his complement, Henry Murray (1938), had a longer list in his classic paper on the ego. If these functions are to be joined to the knowing consciousness of self and world, a more substantive, inferred construct is called for; hence, the various post-Jamesian conceptions of ego and identity.

As is commonly known, James's view of the mind emphasized its activity, its selectivity in attention and in constituting its experience from the plenum of potentiality. In his sorting out of selfhood into I and me—the appropriative passing thought and its reflexive object—the odd thing is that he packed these active features into the empirical me, the self as object, especially into his account of the spiritual self. Do they not belong as well in the I, the psychological subject? Phrasing the problem a little differently, how do the I and the me of James's phenomenological analysis get from knowledge into action? Of course, other chapters in the *Principles*, for example, those on attention and the will, address the issue, and this is still a problem for modern cognitive psychology. All the same, there is something oddly lopsided about locating the active features of the psyche in the me and leaving them out of the I. The awkwardness seems the more fundamental now that the severe limitations inherent in our self-consciousness are understood. Nisbett and Wilson (1977) probably overstated their case, but not by much. James seemed to have actually lost sight of his I–me distinction when he was caught up in his discussion of the spiritual self (also in his treatment of dissociation and multiple personality). He was talking about inferentially derived functional aspects of personality, not just about self as an object of consciousness. The same goes for aspects of his treatment of the social self.

My critical point here is that although James began his treatment of selfhood from a phenomenological standpoint, he was drawn into non-phenomenological considerations by intrinsic requirements of the human realities he had to deal with. So his actual treatment seems inconsistent with his starting point. In my own attempts to formulate selfhood (Smith, 1950; 1978; 1991), I have concentrated on the necessity of maintaining complementary perspectives in joint focus if justice is to be done to the distinctively human phenomena: phenomenological givens versus inferential constructs and meaningful, interpretative or hermeneutic approaches versus causal, functional, explanatory ones. The tensions of inconsistency in James's treatment point to problems that remain unresolved in our contemporary psychology of personality. My concern will become clearer after I examine a related limitation in James's classic analysis, his only partial grasp of the significance of the reflexivity of human self-consciousness.

Post-Jamesian Insights Into the Reflexivity of Selfhood

James was keenly aware of the mystery of human reflexivity:

Whether we take it abstractly or concretely, our considering the spiritual self at all is a reflective process, is the result of our abandoning the outward-looking point of view, and of our having become able to think of subjectivity as such, *to think ourselves as thinkers*. This attention to thought as such, and the identification of ourselves with it rather than with any of the objects which it reveals, is a momentous and in some respects a rather mysterious operation, of which we need here only say that as a matter of fact it exists; and that in everyone, at an early age, the distinction between thought as such, and what it is "of" or "about," has become familiar to the mind. (1890/1981, p. 284)

But it remained for his successors who took a social and developmental perspective—James Mark Baldwin in psychology and Charles H. Cooley and George H. Mead in sociology—to lay the foundation from which the fuller implications of reflexive consciousness for selfhood became apparent. Baldwin (1897), a contemporary of James and his colleague in the early leadership of American psychology, offered a surprisingly modern dialectical conception of the emergence of understanding of self and other in early childhood. Cooley's (1902) conception of the *looking-glass self* elaborated on James's ideas about the social self to suggest ways in which the content of our self-conception is derived from processes of reflected appraisal by significant others. And Mead (1934), in the most important post-Jamesian contribution, proposed that the mind, in the sense of reflective consciousness, emerges in the social process of empathic role taking, through which human organisms become people capable of taking themselves as objects, as a by-product of developing increasingly well-attuned communicative interaction with others. For Mead, the Jamesian I and me became participants in internalized dialogue in his conception of the source of spontaneity and novelty in human nature. (But Mead's I is as intangible and evanescent as James's momentary appropriative thought.)

Baldwin, Cooley, and Mead enriched and grounded James's conception of selfhood as reflexive consciousness in ways that made it natural to regard people's self-conceptions as formative in important aspects of their personalities as social participants—as involving self-fulfilling prophecies (Jones, 1977; Merton, 1957). Elsewhere (e.g., Smith, 1980; 1991), I noted that attribution theory in social psychology and labeling theory in sociology concern complementary facets of a process in which what people come to believe about themselves potentiates or limits what they are. Research on the popular topics of locus of control (Rotter, 1966), self-efficacy (Bandura, 1977), and learned helplessness (Abramson, Seligman, & Teasdale, 1978) has yielded ample evidence that people's self-interpretations are enormously consequential. To deal with the literature of consequential reflexivity requires a conceptual framework different from James's, however, one in which self-conceptions or understandings relate not only to the momentary thought of self-perception, but to inferred structures of personality that phenomenology does not provide.

Does Personality Theory Need The Self?

These considerations raise frontally the question of how William James's century-old treatment of selfhood can best be integrated into our contemporary psychology of personality, a field of psychology that emerged in its present academically institutionalized form only after the publication of the textbooks by Allport (1937) and Stagner (1937), and the *Explorations in Personality* by Murray and his collaborators (1938; Smith, 1990). After long decades in which selfhood was an almost exclusively sociological topic, the spate of publications on the self during the 1980s—a torrent that shows no sign of abating—has produced little clarity; indeed, the terms *self* and *identity* have been used so loosely in such a variety of contexts as to risk losing their usefulness. In this field of confusion, it may be constructive to rise to the challenge of trying to find where James's original ideas belong.

James, himself, must bear part of the blame for this confusion. In the transition from the James of the *Principles* (1890) to the Jimmy of the *Briefer Course* (1892), James changed his chapter title from "The Consciousness of Self" to simply "The Self"—at the same time that he omitted the long critique of soul, associationist, and transcendental views of self that helped in the understanding of the motivation of his phenomenological analysis. The self, thus, became established in the literature as a substantive term, ambiguously referring to I and me, along with the conflation of phenomenological and functional conceptions that I have already noted. The modal, normative practice in psychology and sociology probably identifies self with James's me—self as object—as in self-concept (Wylie, 1974, 1979), self-theories (Epstein, 1973), and self-understanding (Damon & Hart, 1982). Even when the reference to me is clear, however, one can still get into trouble when referring to the self. One is tempted by reification. The passing thought as conscious of self—what might be called *self-perception*—with which James began is not the same thing as relatively more stable, inferred constructs such as self-concept, self-theories, self-understanding, and self-attributions, which are all subjective constructs with somewhat different connotations and at some distance from the phenomenological bases in which they are somehow rooted. I don't see how the self can be dissected from the structures and processes of personality.

A number of years ago (Smith, 1980; reprinted in Smith, 1991), I therefore proposed some appropriate terminological conventions. My proposal had no influence, so I repeat it hoping for better luck this time.

> There are a number of terms in the domain of selfhood [the term I use to refer to the distinctive human characteristic of self-awareness and its cluster of momentous consequences] that give me no trouble, or seem potentially useful. There is the *person*, the actual, concrete participant in symbolically construed and governed social relations. There is *personality*, the psychologist's formulation or construction of the person, a construction of organized processes, states, and dispositions. . . . There is Erikson's (1959) rich but slippery concept of *identity*—some

trouble here to disentangle and pin down the meanings. There is a set of terms in the reflexive mode—*self-perceptions* and *self-attributions*, *self-concepts*, *self-theories* . . .—in which the prefix "self-" implies reflexive reference but does *not* imply a surgically or conceptually separable object of reference—other than the person. People—persons—may reify "I" and "me," but psychologists shouldn't, except as they take into account the causal-functional importance of people's own reifications. . . . There is Jung's (1966) *Self-as-archetype*—an ideal of integration, perhaps a template for integration, a symbolization of it. . . . I don't see a place for *the self* in such a list. It is not a term that designates an entity or an agency, except in usages that treat it as synonymous with the *person*—in which case one or the other term is superfluous. (1991, pp. 69–70)

Is there a place in our conceptions of personality for a self-system? Harry Stack Sullivan (1946) thought so, conceiving it in entirely defensive terms. Gardner Murphy (1947) agreed, using the term *ego* for the personality system organized around the self or reflexive awareness. Allport (1943a) began with the ego, but later turned to his own neologism, the *proprium* (Allport, 1955). Hazel Markus (1990) found the term useful in her suggestive examination of the present relevance of James's treatment of self. I think the question is open, so long as the formulations of personality provide for the substantial role of reflexive self-attribution in constituting essential features of who we are.

The self may not be needed, but the conceptions of personality will surely continue to feature the aspects of self-awareness that James brought so vividly into psychology. However, the metatheoretical muddle that was inherited from James must still be resolved: How can psychologists integrate an intentional, phenomenological psychology of meaning with a causal, explanatory psychology? James's brilliant treatment near the beginning of the discipline has provided psychologists with major grounds for thinking that any adequate psychology of selfhood must be rooted on both sides of that philosophical divide.

JAMES'S FERTILE INCONSISTENCIES

I have dwelt on some inconsistencies in William James's rich and fruitful treatment of selfhood, inconsistencies in the contribution of our greatest psychologist that bring to mind even more spectacular inconsistencies in the writings of his peer in the intellectual history of this discipline, Sigmund Freud (Holt, 1972, 1989). Nearly half a century ago in the midst of World War II, Gordon Allport (1943b) honored James at the centennial of his birth with a masterful essay, "The Productive Paradoxes of William

James"—an essay in which he identified inconsistencies and ambivalences in James's treatment of all the major persistent riddles of psychology. In closing my contribution to another centennial celebration, I can do no better than to quote my former teacher. Allport wrote the following in his conclusion:

> It was [James's] passion to face up to all phenomena of mental life, and to exclude none. . . . He opened channels that would admit to the domain of psychology the "big fears, loves, and indignations" of mankind and the penetrating appeal of "the higher fidelities, like justice, truth, or freedom." And he wanted psychologists to confront the fundamental moral fact that by their own theories of human nature they have the power of elevating or degrading this same human nature. Debasing assumptions debase the mind; generous assumptions exalt the mind. His own assumptions were always the most generous possible.
>
> The message of James for psychology today is this: narrow consistency can neither bring salvation to your science, nor help to mankind. Let your approaches be diverse, but let them in the aggregate do full justice to the heroic qualities in man. If you find yourself tangled in paradoxes, what of that? . . . . To accommodate the whole of human experience keep layers of space and air and vision in your scientific formulations. (1943b, pp. 117–119)

Like James and like Allport, I continue to hope for a psychology that is at once humanistic and scientific. James's writings on human selfhood remain central to that aspiration. Our own internal pressures toward consistency should not dampen the lively openness to everything human that is found in James's thought.

REFERENCES

Abramson, L. Y., Seligman, M. E. P., & Teasdale, J. D. (1978). Learned helplessness in humans: Critique and reformulation. *Journal of Abnormal Psychology*, 87, 49–74.

Allport, G. W. (1937). *Personality: A psychological interpretation*. New York: Holt.

Allport, G. W. (1943a). The ego in contemporary psychology. *Psychological Review*, 50, 451–478.

Allport, G. W. (1943b). The productive paradoxes of William James. *Psychological Review*, 50, 95–120.

Allport, G. W. (1955). *Becoming: Basic considerations for a psychology of personality*. New Haven, CT: Yale University Press.

Baldwin, J. M. (1897). *Social and ethical interpretations in mental development*. New York: Macmillan.

Bandura, A. (1977). Self-efficacy: Toward a unifying theory of behavioral change. *Psychological Review, 84,* 191–215.

Cooley, C. H. (1902). *Human nature and the social order*. New York: Scribner.

Damon, W., & Hart, D. (1982). The development of self-understanding from infancy through adolescence. *Child Development, 53,* 841–864.

Epstein, S. (1973). The self-concept revisited: Or a theory of a theory. *American Psychologist, 28,* 404–416.

Erikson, E. H. (1959). Identity and the life cycle. *Psychological Issues* (Whole No. 1).

Freud, S. (1961). *The ego and the id,* (J. Strachey, Trans.). London: Hogarth. (Original work published 1927)

Holt, R. R. (1972). Freud's mechanistic and humanistic images of man. In R. R. Holt & E. Peterfreund (Eds.), *Psychoanalysis and Contemporary Science, 1,* 3–24.

Holt, R. R. (1989). *Freud reappraised: A fresh look at psychoanalytic theory*. New York: Guilford.

Hyman, H. H. (1942). The psychology of status. *Archives of Psychology,* 269.

James, W. (1981). *The Principles of Psychology* (3 vols). Cambridge, MA: Harvard University Press. (Original work published 1890)

James, W. (1984). *Psychology: Briefer course*. Cambridge, MA: Harvard University Press. (Original work published 1892)

Jones, R. A. (1977). *Self-fulfilling prophecies: Social, psychological, and physiological effects of expectancies*. Hillsdale, NJ: Erlbaum.

Jung, C. G. (1966). *Two essays on analytical psychology*. (2nd ed.; R. F. C. Hull, Trans.). Princeton, NJ: Princeton University Press.

Kihlstrom, J. F., & McConkey, K. M. (1990). William James symposium: William James and hypnosis: A centennial reflection. *Psychological Science, 1,* 174–178.

Leary, D. (1990). William James on the self and personality: Clearing the ground for subsequent theorists, researchers, and practitioners. In M. G. Johnson & T. Henley (Eds.), *William James: The Principles at 100*. Hillsdale, NJ: Erlbaum.

Lewin, K. (1935). *A dynamic theory of personality* (D. K. Adams & K. E. Zener, Trans.). New York: McGraw-Hill.

Markus, H. (1990). William James symposium: On splitting the universe. *Psychological Science, 1,* 181–185.

Mead, G. H. (1934). *Mind, self and society*. Chicago: University of Chicago Press.

Merton, R. K. (1957). *Social theory and social structure* (rev. ed.). New York: Free Press.

Murphy, G. (1947). *Personality: A biosocial approach to origins and structure*. New York: Harper.

Murray, H. A. (1938). *Explorations in personality*. New York: Cambridge University Press.

Myers, G. E. (1981). Introduction: The intellectual context. In W. James, *Principles of psychology* (Vol. 1, pp. xi–xx). Cambridge, MA: Harvard University Press.

Nisbett, R. E., & Wilson, T. D. (1977). Telling more than we know: Verbal reports on mental processes. *Psychological Review, 84*, 231–279.

Rotter, J. R. (1966). Generalized expectancies for internal versus external control of reinforcement. *Psychological Monographs, 80*, (1, Whole No. 609).

Smith, M. B. (1950). The phenomenological approach in personality theory: Some critical remarks. *Journal of Abnormal and Social Psychology, 45*, 516–522.

Smith, M. B. (1978). Perspectives on selfhood. *American Psychologist, 33*, 1053–1063.

Smith, M. B. (1980). Attitude, values and selfhood. In H. E. Howe & M. M. Page (Eds.), *Nebraska Symposium on Motivation 1979*. Lincoln, NE: University of Nebraska Press.

Smith, M. B. (1990). Personology launched. Retrospective review of H. A. Murray et al. (1938), *Contemporary Psychology, 35*, 537–539.

Smith, M. B. (1991). *Values, self and society: Toward a humanist social psychology*. New Brunswick, NJ: Transaction Books.

Stagner, R. (1937). *Personality*. New York: McGraw-Hill.

Sullivan, H. S. (1946). *Conceptions of modern psychiatry*. (2nd ed.). Washington, DC: The William Alanson White Psychiatric Foundation.

Wylie, R. C. (1974). *The self-concept, Vol. 1* (rev. ed.). Lincoln, NE: University of Nebraska Press.

Wylie, R. C. (1979). *The self-concept, Vol. 2* (rev. ed.). Lincoln, NE: University of Nebraska Press.

12

WILLIAM JAMES AND CONTEMPORARY RESEARCH ON THE SELF: THE INFLUENCE OF PRAGMATISM, REALITY, AND TRUTH

MICHAEL J. STRUBE, JOHN H. YOST, AND JAMES R. BAILEY

Americans have always had a love affair with adventure. The pioneer spirit that fueled our march across the western frontier now fuels our assaults along many other fronts. William James's *Principles of Psychology* was written by an American adventurer. His bold intellect carved out an expansive, exciting landscape from the American psychological frontier. In the generations that have followed, social scientists have replaced the survey markers laid down by James with impressive structures of their own, but their debt of gratitude for the intellectual groundwork is evidenced by James's continuing popularity. Indeed, the popularity of James's work among seasoned scholars and lay public alike attests to the simple enduring truths he proclaimed and his ability to communicate them in so compelling a fashion.

Recently, we have witnessed many examinations of key research topics in light of William James's writings (e.g., the William James Symposium in *Psychological Science* [1990] and the special issue in *Personality and Social Psychology Bulletin* [Arkin, 1990]). In some ways this chapter will be no different. We, too, will suggest how a consideration of William James's views can provide new direction to current problems. We, too, will focus our attention on a particular substantive area, in our case the self, and point to some ways that James's views can shed new light on some old puzzles. But our intent is a bit broader as well. We will argue that a consideration of James's views on psychology are necessarily bound to a consideration of his broader philosophical views. To borrow one and ignore the other is a disservice to the intellectual endowment that James left us, and it ignores that psychology and philosophy were largely indistinguishable at the turn of the century. Indeed, the highly selective and often gratuitous citation of his work suggests that James may be the scientist's favorite inkblot. We hope to tell more about James than about ourselves in this chapter. Although we, too, will have to be selective in our coverage, we hope to represent fairly the broader sweep of James's thinking and the more general guidance it provides for contemporary researchers.

In the presentation that follows, we first outline some key philosophical points that are critical to understanding James's psychological views. We then describe how these points and James's psychological views on the self allow new insights into contemporary problems in the study of the self. Our coverage is very selective, and we focus primarily on what James called *self-seeking*. We focus on the self so that our suggestions have specificity, but the general principles underlying the suggestions may be of use in other areas as well. Finally, we offer some general advice for research on the self and social processes.

A PHILOSOPHICAL OVERVIEW

William James lived in a time of great change. Many social orders were toppled, western expansion was a driving force, and the first industrial generation was born (Kallen, 1953). In sum, there were so many revolutions in the way Western civilization conducted its affairs that to survive one could not rely solely on knowledge handed down from past generations. Life for James's generation, more than for any generation until that point, had to be experienced and interpreted first hand. Henry Adams (1918/1964) summed up the transitional nature of the period when he claimed that the best American education available prepared him only for the seventeenth and eighteenth centuries but left him totally unprepared for the twentieth century.

The nature of the times in which William James lived shaped his philosophy of life. It is a philosophy that reflects the personal struggles of a man living in a time of great flux. As Horace Kallen has argued, it remains a viable philosophy for the twentieth century:

> The philosophy of William James opens for the children and victims of this civilization in the twentieth century, a clear way out of its

levelings and enslavements. It is a map of life for us modern men, a lamp to light our steps upon the hillroad of freedom, courage, and creative endeavor. It expresses what is most deeply inward in our nature, and shows us how to meet the untoward event in hope without illusion. (1953, p. 44)

McDermott has likewise argued that "if James's originality constituted a stage of the national self-consciousness in his time, his vision now replies to the needs of man today, who confront an endless but increasingly controllable cosmos" (1967, p. xvii). Although the times have changed dramatically since 1890, and no one's thinking can escape the social and historical climate in which it develops, there are parallels between the late nineteenth century and the late twentieth century that make James's views quite relevant today. The industrial revolution has been replaced by technological and social revolutions, yet the same national character that pushed back frontiers then is pushing them back now. The same core individualism is as valued today as it was then (cf. Spence, 1985).

James's general philosophy of experience, which later became his radical empiricism, fit well the ethos of the period. His belief that there were no givens, no absolutes, but only experience influenced greatly his wide-ranging philosophical views. We focus on three essential elements of that philosophy that are particularly relevant for the study of the self: James's views on pragmatism, truth, and reality.

Pragmatism, Reality, and Truth

Within philosophy, James is perhaps best known for his views on pragmatism. Along with Peirce, Dewey, and Schiller, James initially viewed pragmatism as a *method* for settling metaphysical disputes, but its applications proved to be much broader. The pragmatic method is to interpret each of two conflicting ideas by tracing their respective practical consequences:

What difference would it practically make to any one if this notion rather than that notion were true? If no practical difference whatever can be traced, then the alternatives mean practically the same thing, and all dispute is idle. Whenever a dispute is serious, we ought to be able to show some practical difference that must follow from one side or the other's being right. (James, 1907/1924, p. 199)

From a pragmatist's standpoint, a thought's meaning is determined by the "conduct it is fitted to produce," its "rule for action" (James, 1907/1924, p. 200). According to James,

You must bring out of each word its practical cash-value, set it at work within the stream of your experience. It appears less as a solution, then, than as a programme for more work, and more particularly as an indication of the ways in which existing realities may be *changed*. (James, 1907/1924, p. 203)

For James, then, meaning was grounded in practical consequences.

James's views on reality and truth were a natural outgrowth of his pragmatism. Because pragmatism is grounded in the "cash-value" an idea has in one's experience, reality and truth are not equivalent. James felt that "realities are not *true*, they *are*; and beliefs are true *of* them" (1909/1978, p. 272). This distinction is well stated in James's essay "What Pragmatism Means," in which he points out that theories (ideas about reality) are only selective and convenient approximations to reality:

No theory is absolutely a transcript of reality, but that any one of them may from some point of view be useful. Their great use is to summarize old facts and to lead to new ones. They are only a man-made language, a conceptual shorthand, as some one calls them, in which we write our reports of nature; and languages, as is well known, tolerate much choice of expression and many dialects. (James, 1907/1924, p. 205)

For James, truth was not an inherent property of reality but was instead a property of one's ideas about reality.

In addition to distinguishing reality from truth, James used the term *reality* in two apparently different ways. He often referred to a reality "out there" that was independent of the observer, but he also referred to a reality as experienced. This has been a source of confusion in his writing because it has been interpreted as advocating both a constant reality and also a varying subjective reality. Because experiences vary, reality is not the same for all individuals or of constant importance for the same individual (see James, 1907, p. 203). What James meant was that there is a reality "out there" for anyone to experience and believe, but the beliefs in reality may vary and it is ultimately those beliefs that govern our relations toward reality. In this sense, reality is both constant (really "out there") but also relative (subject to individual experience and interpretation). James clearly emphasized the latter aspect. In the *Principles*, he argued that the *real* is what excites us and what intimately invokes the self. In his chapter "The Perception of Reality" in the *Principles*, James wrote

Whichever represented objects give us sensations, especially interesting ones, or incite our motor impulses, or arouse our hate, desire, or fear, are real enough for us. Our requirements in the way of reality terminate in our own acts and emotions, our pleasures and pains. These are the

ultimate fixities from which . . . the whole chain of our beliefs depends
. . . until . . . the supporting branch, the Self, is reached and held.
(James, 1890/1981, p. 939)

The real is thus defined by the pleasures and pains that the self experiences. This view demands a subjective, experiential, and individual orientation to reality. Not all stimuli are real in the experiential sense for all individuals; reality exists "out there" only so far as it has a hold on the self. Although objects may exist in a physical sense, they are real for the individual only in a phenomenological sense. James made a similar point earlier in the *Principles* when he referred to the "one great splitting of the whole universe into two halves": the "me" and the "not me" (James, 1890/1981). We attach a special significance to that side of the universe that we call "mine." What we call "mine" is what produces unique pleasures and pains for us; it is for us our reality.

Because reality for us is, in a sense, an extension of the self, we strive to know and understand that reality. We try to come in closer contact with it. For James, this meant that we strive to hold beliefs about that reality that are *true*. According to James, it is vital for us to understand what so intimately touches the self, indeed what ultimately defines the self. Truth, then, is a practical matter, consisting of the worth of an action plan for bringing the self in closer contact with the real. In *Pragmatism*, James wrote

The possession of true thought means everywhere the possession of invaluable instruments of action; and that our duty to gain truth, so far from being a blank command from out of the blue, or a 'stunt' self-imposed by our intellect, can account for itself by excellent practical reasons. The importance to human life of having true beliefs about matters of fact is a thing too notorious. We live in a world of realities that can be infinitely useful or infinitely harmful. Ideas that tell us which of them to expect count as the true ideas in all this primary sphere of verification, and the pursuit of such ideas is a primary human duty. The possession of truth, so far from being here an end in itself, is only a preliminary means toward other vital satisfactions. (James, 1907, pp. 202–203)

Ideas or beliefs are thus true to the extent that they allow a better contact or commerce with objects or ideas that are important to us (cf. James, 1909/1978). James used the phrase *cash-value* to describe the truth of an idea. True ideas have a cash-value because they make a real difference in our daily pursuits. Accordingly, there is no one truth about reality; no absolute truth "out there." Instead, "truth happens to an idea," and there are as many truths as there are practical consequences for an idea. "What works is true and represents a reality, for the individual for whom it works"

(James, 1909/1978, p. 298). In sum, an individual's struggle for survival is inherently a struggle to achieve a useful working knowledge of the self in relation to the physical world.

Criticisms of Pragmatism

James spent nearly as much time defending his philosophical views as he did promoting them (e.g., James, 1909/1978). It is useful to consider some of the major criticisms of his philosophy in order to dispel misunderstandings that persist today and to highlight several additional philosophical points.

Perhaps no aspect of James's pragmatism was as harshly criticized and misunderstood as its conception of truth. It has been equated with a mindless, completely self-interested hedonism that calls true whatever gives current satisfaction. Instead, what James had in mind with his use of the term *satisfaction* was an understanding of reality that was better than if the idea were not held. True ideas "agreed" with reality. By this James meant,

> To 'agree' in the widest sense with a reality *can only mean to be guided either straight up to it or into its surroundings, or to be put into such working touch with it as to handle either it or something connected to it better than if we disagreed.* . . . Any idea that helps us to *deal*, whether practically or intellectually, with either the reality or its belongings, that doesn't entangle our progress in frustrations, that *fits*, in fact, and adapts our life to the reality's whole setting, will agree sufficiently to meet the requirement. It will hold true of that reality. (James, 1907, p. 212–213)

In these terms, true ideas might very well expose a reality fraught with displeasure, but one that would be better understood and better negotiated in the future. Regarding satisfactions, then, the pragmatist refers only to the satisfaction of "knowing truly" (James, 1909/1978, p. 272).

The criticism that pragmatism advocates a heinous self-interest also fails to consider that truths held by others are an important source of our own truths. As James argued, most of our truths live on a "credit system." We accept others' verifications and they accept ours. "We trade on each other's truths. But beliefs verified concretely by *somebody* are the posts of the whole superstructure" (James, 1907, p. 208). Thus, the social context within which our beliefs exist cannot be ignored and imposes an important constraint on what passes for true.

Critics of pragmatism have also claimed that it espouses a "here-and-now" philosophy that makes present satisfaction the only criterion for truth.

A careful reading of James, however, clearly indicates the error in this interpretation. James held that any new idea had to be consistent with the larger corpus of ideas that we hold:

> This new idea is then adopted as the true one. It preserves the older stock of truths with a minimum of modification, stretching them just enough to make them admit the novelty, but conceiving that in ways as familiar as the case leaves possible. An *outrée* explanation, violating all our preconceptions, would never pass for a true account of a novelty. We should scratch around industriously till we found something less eccentric. The most violent revolutions in an individual's beliefs leave most of his old order standing. . . . New truth is always a go-between, a smoother-over of transitions. It marries old opinion to new fact so as ever to show a minimum of jolt, a maximum of continuity. . . . The point I now urge you to observe particularly is the part played by the older truths. Failure to take account of it is the source of much of the unjust criticism levelled against pragmatism. Their influence is absolutely controlling. Loyalty to them is the first principle. (James, 1907/1924d, p. 207)

The emphasis that James placed on the consistency of truth also helps explain why we do not follow a rule that equates truth with goodness. James's own words are again the most convincing:

> If we practically did believe everything that made for good in our personal lives, we should be found indulging all kinds of fancies about this world's affairs, and all kinds of sentimental superstitions about a world hereafter. . . . What is better for us to believe is true *unless the belief incidentally clashes with some other vital benefit.* Now in real life what vital benefits is any particular belief of ours most liable to clash with? What indeed except the vital benefits yielded by *other beliefs* when these prove incompatible with the first ones? In other words, the greatest enemy of any one of our truths may be the rest of our truths. (James, 1907/1924d, p. 216)

The importance of consistency in our beliefs is evident in *The Meaning of Truth*, in which James elevated its status to a particularly lofty level:

> After man's interest in breathing freely, the greatest of all his interests (because it never fluctuates or remits, as most of his physical interests do) is his interest in *consistency*, in feeling that what he now thinks goes with what he thinks on other occasions. We tirelessly compare truth with truth for this sole purpose. (James, 1909/1978, p. 279)

The central thesis of James's pragmatism then is not the self-serving "if it feels good, do it" or the "anything goes" doctrine that so many have called it. Instead, it argues for an individual orientation to reality, a reality that is admittedly defined differently for different individuals but that is always grounded in practical consequences and guided by a concern for consistency. In summary, James's pragmatism admits variability in the interpretation and experience of reality, but it also requires a coherence that transcends individuals. Our dependence on others' experiences demands a loosely held consensus on truth that prevents the chaos predicted by critics.

Pragmatism and Evolution

It should be clear that James embraced the notion that humans act in ways that serve some purpose. Indeed, he was a firm believer in the evolutionary principles espoused by Darwin (cf. Yost, Strube, & Bailey, 1990), and a consideration of his views on this topic serves as a final prelude to our treatment of the self.

In melding his pragmatism with the functionalism of evolutionary principles, James saw the banishment of uncertainty (the attainment of truth) as being a central principle of animal behavior (James, 1897). In his essay "The Sentiment of Rationality," James wrote

> It is of the utmost practical importance to an animal that he should have prevision of the qualities of objects that surround him, and especially that he should not come to rest in the presence of circumstances that might be fraught either with peril or advantage—go to sleep, for example, on the brink of precipices, in the dens of enemies, or view with indifference some new-appearing object that might, if chased, prove an important addition to the larder. Novelty *ought* to irritate him. All curiosity has thus a practical genesis. (James, 1897/1924b, p. 138)

James held, in fact, that social evolution was modified by individual choice and action. In this sense, social evolution was both a selection by the environment and a selection by society or individuals. This view suggests a very proactive role on the part of individuals and societies and not a mindless, inevitable rush to a model society. In fact, James alluded to the *creation* of favorable conditions in his essay "Great Men and Their Environment": "If anything is humanly certain it is that the great man's society, properly so-called, does *not* make him before he can remake it" (James, 1897/1924a, p. 180). Similar hints at the importance of initiative can be found in the chapter on will in the *Principles* and in the essay "The Will to Believe" (James, 1907).

James claimed in addition that the resolution of uncertainty (the attainment of truth) was not a cold, calculated affair of reason but was an experience laden with affect. Indeed, this "sentiment of rationality" is the mark that tells us that truth has been attained. It is the "pleasure at finding that a chaos of facts is the expression of a single underlying fact" and "is like the relief of the musician at resolving a confused mass of sound into melodic or harmonic order" (James, 1897/1924b, pp. 125–126). The sentiment of rationality is thus a feeling of the "sufficiency of the moment" and marks or identifies the truth of an idea. More important, it points to an intimate bond between affect and the search for truth.

To summarize the key philosophical points, James held that reality was essentially self-centered: What affects us is what we call real. Because of the importance of knowing about what affects us, there is an adaptiveness to having true beliefs. This truth, however, is not a property of the physical world but of our ideas about the physical world. Beliefs that allow one to engage in more effective commerce with the physical world are true for that person. Furthermore, the drive to know the self and its relation to the physical world is not merely a reactive process. Instead, we seek to create circumstances that are true. In this sense, James believed we molded the environment in addition to being molded by it. This idea of freedom and will was one of the more popular aspects of his philosophical framework.

A MODERN VIEW OF SELF-SEEKING

The general philosophical views of William James take on particular meaning when applied to specific problems within psychology today. Accordingly, we turn to some problems that have confronted contemporary researchers of the self. In his seminal chapter on the self in the *Principles*, James outlined his now-famous tripartite division of the empirical self into the material self, the social self, and the spiritual self. The material self includes our bodies and material possessions, the social self involves the recognition that we get from others, and the spiritual self is composed of the most enduring and intimate parts of the self (e.g., traits). James held that "self-seeking" occurred at each level. According to James, humans had an innate propensity to collect material goods and to get themselves noticed by others. These desires include "higher level" pursuits as well. We receive social sanctions for our ideas and creations just as much as for our material possessions and physical features. Thus, self-seeking can be seen to represent a basic hedonistic drive. From the philosophical points raised earlier, however, this striving can be seen to have a functional basis. The active striving for pleasures and the active avoidance of pains validate the beliefs we have about the relation of the self to the environment. They banish uncertainty from the future and verify beliefs about reality. Thus, there are both hedonistic and knowledge-based components to James's self-seeking.

Contemporary research on the self has also had a major interest in self-seeking. However, the hedonistic and knowledge-driven features of self-seeking that James saw as being intimately tied together have been curiously split in contemporary work.[1] Indeed, there have been two traditional camps in the study of how individuals transact with their social worlds. On the one hand, there is a strong tradition in social psychology that favors a rational, accuracy-driven approach to self-seeking. This approach holds that humans are motivated by a drive to acquire as accurate an appraisal of their capabilities and limitations as is possible, regardless of the self-esteem or hedonic implications (e.g., Trope, 1986). This view is motivated by the belief that an accurate assessment of abilities allows for a more adaptive organism. Many traditional theories in social psychology are based on this type of assumption (e.g., social comparison theory, Festinger, 1954; traditional attribution theory, Heider, 1958; Jones & Davis, 1965; Kelley, 1967; competence motivation, White, 1959).

On the other hand, an alternative view holds that self-seeking is, in fact, quite biased toward favorable appraisal of the self. The well-known self-serving attributional bias is a classic example (e.g., Bradley, 1978; Snyder, Stephan, & Rosenfield, 1976), and the more recent description of proactively constructed self-handicapping strategies (Jones & Berglas, 1978) suggests the great lengths to which people will go to protect their self-conceptions (e.g., Arkin & Baumgardner, 1985; Higgins & Snyder, 1990). For many years, the two sides have simply ignored each other, with one self-seeking aspect being emphasized over the other but no attempt to claim the priority of one over the other. More recently, however, the different camps have engaged in border disputes about the priority of the two apparent motives (e.g., Strube, Lott, Le, Oxenberg, & Deichmann, 1986; Trope, 1980).

A return to James provides some useful insights into this debate (Strube, 1990). The question of accurate self-assessment *versus* biased self-enhancement would seem odd to William James. To him, the two were complementary. The "debate" between the self-assessment and the self-enhancement camps can be seen to be more apparent than real when it is recognized that accurate self-appraisal is necessary to carry out effective self-enhancement.[2] James suggested this connection in his famous formula

---

[1] The reason for this split is itself an interesting issue. It may reflect a rejection of the simple and sovereign theories that predominated early in the history of psychology and of which hedonism was a common example (Allport, 1985). Nonetheless, hedonistic assumptions are still quite common (e.g., see recent reviews by Abelson & Levi, 1985; Berscheid, 1985; Jones, 1985; Ross & Fletcher, 1985), although perhaps not as explicit as in James's time.

[2] For an alternative view, see Swann, Pelham, and Krull (1989).

from the *Principles* that equates self-esteem with the ratio of successes to pretensions. The acquisition of accurate information about one's abilities and limitations allows the careful selection or construction of performance arenas in which abilities and situational demands are well matched. Self-appraisal thus tempers our pretensions and enhances the likelihood that we strive for realistic goals. Accordingly, self-enhancement can be carried out with greater efficiency.

This resolution, claiming that self-appraisal assists self-enhancement, provides a convenient means of integrating two apparently different literatures, but as Strube (1990) notes, it is not without some apparent problems. One objection is that the self-appraisal aspect is inconsistent with existing data. Research indicates that people harbor many illusions about the self and that they are not completely accurate in identifying the objective markers of ability. For example, most normal healthy individuals have an illusion of control or competence that argues against any truly accurate self-appraisal process (e.g., Langer, 1984; Taylor & Brown, 1988). Indeed, those who are accurate in their beliefs about ability–outcome contingencies may be more depressed than their more biased counterparts (Alloy & Abramson, 1979; Alloy, Abramson, & Viscusi, 1981). Furthermore, the characteristics of tasks that are so crucial to ability appraisal (e.g., diagnosticity) are not perceived veridically and are often confused with irrelevant task features (e.g., Strube & Roemmele, 1985; Strube et al., 1986). Finally, self-serving distortions are most apparent when events are important or threatening (e.g., Greenwald, 1981), conditions in which accurate self-appraisal would seem most necessary. Thus, overall, accurate self-appraisal appears to be the exception, not the norm.

Strube (1990) argued, however, that this puzzle can be resolved by recognizing that accuracy-driven self-appraisal is a *process* that produces self-enhancement as an *outcome*. As information about abilities is acquired, individuals should become more adept at selecting performance arenas in which their abilities and environmental demands are well matched. They can identify and avoid those settings in which failure is certain or success is achieved without challenge. They can thus select themselves into, or construct, performance settings that maximize the demonstration of capabilities and minimize the display of liabilities. Consequently, individuals should possess a biased sample of performance outcomes that promote an illusion of competence. These distorted perceptions cannot stray too far from the mark, however, or they cease to provide good guidance for future self-seeking. They fail to be true in the Jamesian sense. The self-seeking system, thus, has a built-in quality control.

A consideration of William James's views contains several important lessons for research on self-seeking. It emphasizes, for example, that self-seeking is very idiographic. All tasks or performance settings may not touch the selves of all individuals in a similar manner. We need to ask, *for this individual*, what constitute the hedonically relevant stimuli. Some headway has been made with expectancy-value models (e.g., Fishbein & Ajzen, 1975; Ajzen & Fishbein, 1980; for a general review, see Abelson & Levi, 1985), but even in those cases a nomothetic bias is usually evident.

The criterion for an accurate or *true* self-view must also be considered carefully. It is not the accuracy of ability perceptions following self-appraisal that should interest us primarily. Rather, we should focus on the adequacy of the strategies for selecting situations that allow self-seeking. Those strategies represent ideas that are true or accurate to the extent that they have a cash-value for the strategist, that is, to the extent that they are hedonically pragmatic from that individual's perspective. This view of accuracy requires knowledge of individual goals and the extent to which action plans meet those goals.

The importance of the match between individual goals and outcomes underscores an additional aspect of James's thinking: the construction of social reality. Just as James emphasized the evolutionary interplay between genius and environment, so too the success of self-seeking depends as much on the making of the environment by the individual as it does on the shaping of the individual by the environment. Self-seeking is clearly a transactional affair, and the constructive aspects require as much attention as the reactive aspects. Similarly, James recognized that self-seeking was as much a process of self-exclusion as it was a process of self-expansion. In other words, not only could the discovery of new abilities assist in the attainment of material and social ends (i.e., success), but the realization of limitations could allow for disengagement from unfruitful self-seeking: "To give up pretensions is as blessed a relief as to get them gratified. . . . Thank God! We say, *those* illusions are gone. Everything added to the Self is a burden as well as a pride" (James, 1890/1981, pp. 296–297). In other words, a narrowing and better resolution of the self, a self-entrenchment, may be quite normal and adaptive. Self-esteem is thus enhanced by seeking settings that allow success and by avoiding those with little prospect thereof.

The relief experienced with the abandonment of pretensions resembles closely the sentiment of rationality mentioned earlier and underscores the importance of affect in self-seeking. However, although the abandonment of pretensions is a resolution of uncertainty and should have the mark of truth to it, James reminded us that the abandonment may not be a wholly pleasant experience. For example, I will not make a fool out of myself on the golf course in view of my abandoned pretension, but I am less than pleased about my meager abilities all the same. This is why James sometimes referred to the sentiment of rationality as relief having a negative character. The emotional experiences that accompany self-seeking thus are not likely to be uniformly positive. Our obtained successes are mixed with the admission of possible but unlikely successes that must be abandoned.

Finally, James's description of self-seeking underscores the importance of possibility to the self (see also Markus & Nurius, 1986; Markus & Ruvolo, 1989). In the self-esteem formula, pretensions represent possibilities about future action. In the self-appraisal sense, they represent testable propositions about the self that have cash-value or are true to the extent that they allow successful situational choice or construction. They are essentially plans for the gratification of self-seeking. In general, then, *pretensions* are ideas about reality that might be true or are verifiable, *self-appraisal* is the process of verification, *true* are the beliefs thus verified, and *self-esteem* is the consequence of truth applied successfully.

GENERAL PRESCRIPTIONS

The self-seeking example highlights several points that deserve additional mention because they have more general implications. For example, James's emphasis on experience and subjective reality reminds contemporary researchers that our striving for objective measures can never completely replace getting inside the heads of those we study (cf. Strube, 1989). We need to understand the subjective reality from the actor's standpoint, in addition to our observer's standpoint. We must, as scientists, be aware of what James called a "certain blindness in human beings" (James, 1899).

We must also assess the value or truth of information, beliefs, or ideas against a pragmatic criterion. Too often we use accuracy criteria that fail to consider the success of a plan or strategy from the actor's standpoint, in addition to our observer's standpoint. We must, as scientists, be aware of what James called a "certain blindness in human beings" (James, 1899).

We must also assess the value or truth of information, beliefs, or ideas against a pragmatic criterion. Too often we use accuracy criteria that fail to consider the success of a plan or strategy from the actor's standpoint. For example, in the social cognition literature, social perceivers have been described as inaccurate or irrational because their judgments do not coincide well with statistical criteria (for reviews, see Alloy & Tabachnik, 1984; Abelson & Levi, 1985; Crocker, 1981; Nisbett & Ross, 1980; Nisbett, Krantz, Jepson, & Kunda, 1983). Yet social perceivers get along quite capably, obviously being able to abstract the important contingencies in their lives in order to survive. A Jamesian perspective suggests that we need to shift the question from "In what ways are social perceivers inaccurate?" to "In what ways are social perceptions true?" (cf. Swann, 1984). We must admit that different perceptions may be true of the same reality. A particular judgment may not be accurate from the observer's standpoint, but it may be accurate *enough* from the actor's standpoint. The challenge is in understanding how the perception is rational or accurate in the pragmatic sense.[3]

James also emphasized a free-will component to human action that we often fail to appreciate. The self is active and constructive (cf. Yost et al., 1990). It both extends and limits the range of its possibilities. We need to include accounts of these transactions in our attempts to study social processes. One particularly intriguing example is the link between will and reality that James held to exist. In the *Principles*, he wrote

> *We need only in cold blood* ACT *as if the thing in question were real, and keep acting as if it were real, and it will infallibly end by growing into such a connection with our life that it will become real.* (James, 1890/1981, p. 949)

James implied that actions are not always based on truth but in fact may be motivated to bring about a truth, to impose a truth. These are conditions in which "truths cannot become true till our faith has made them so" (James, 1897/1924b, p. 153; see also the essay *The Will to Believe*, James, 1907/1924c). In "The Sentiment of Rationality," James gave a vivid example:

> Suppose, for example, that I am climbing in the Alps and have had the ill-luck to work myself into a position from which the only escape is by a terrible leap. Being without similar experience, I have no evidence of my ability to perform it successfully; but hope and confidence in myself make me sure I shall not miss my aim, and nerve my feet to execute what without those subjective emotions would perhaps have been impossible. But suppose that, on the contrary, the emotions of fear and mistrust preponderate. . . . Why, then I shall hesitate so long that at last, exhausted and trembling, and launching myself in a moment of despair, I miss my foothold and roll into the abyss. . . . *There are then cases where faith creates its own verification.* (James, 1897/1924b, p. 153)

Thus, we need to explore the differences between cases in which truth can be verified in the absence of belief and those in which belief is necessary

---

[3]This Jamesian perspective on truth is reminiscent of Simon's (1955) bounded rationality view, which argues that we don't need to be perfectly rational to survive in the world. Our decisions, according to this model, need not be optimal. Instead, they need only be "good enough." This notion of rationality is nicely captured by the following anecdote: Two people were walking in the woods when they noticed a bear approaching. One of the two immediately bent down and began to put on a pair of running shoes. The other replied "I don't know why you are bothering with those, you can't outrun that bear." To which the well-shod partner replied, "I know, but I don't have to outrun the bear, I just have to outrun you."

to get the verification process started (cf. self-efficacy theory; e.g., Bandura, 1986).

We also need to account for how humans grapple with the realities of unyielding environments in which no amount of belief can make a reality so. At some level, we must recognize that there are some things we cannot do and that circumstances often have more to do with the broad direction of our behavior than does any conscious choice. Perhaps we focus on the choices possible within the constraints. That would be a view consistent with James's philosophy and suggests that the perspective we take on self-seeking or general behavioral freedom can shift in the breadth of its focus. We need to be wary of the different levels of analysis on which the self-seeker operates. Although we readily acknowledge different levels of analysis in our theories of social behavior (e.g., Carver & Scheier, 1985; Scheier & Carver, 1983; Wegner & Vallacher, 1986), we have failed to consider this perspective from the social perceiver's standpoint. We need to consider the self-seeker as a lay social philosopher who grapples with different levels of reality.

Finally, at the epistemological level, we might profitably apply the pragmatic method to constructs and theories. Quite a bit of muddy thinking, for example, has crept into work on the self. Contemporary researchers argue, and James would have agreed, that relevance to the self is a central construct in discussing human behavior. But is self-relevance different from task importance, familiarity, ego-involvement, or a host of other adjectives applied in this area? Are there any *practical* differences among these terms? The exercise alone of carrying out the pragmatic method might force useful specification. Similarly, we seem flooded with self-hyphenated theories: self-assessment, self-appraisal, self-evaluation, self-verification, self-enhancement, self-etc. Again, a hard-headed search for the practical scientific consequences of the distinctions may alert us to truths that are more apparent than real. In sum, application of William James's philosophical views might assist in the clearer use of constructs and operations and lead to more efficient theory development.

We end with one final quote. On the occasion of the 100-year anniversary of William James's birth, his son Henry remarked

> My father's search for truth was not a mere cool exercise of reason. It was the quest of a passionate pilgrim. What's more, he felt that his findings, to be worth recording, must help other puzzled or perhaps distressed souls to find more truth. (1942, pp. 4–5)

One hundred years after the publication of the *Principles*, we believe that modern puzzled souls can still turn to William James for that kind of inspiration.

REFERENCES

Abelson, R. P., & Levi, A. (1985). Decision making and decision theory. In G. Lindzey & E. Aronson (Eds.), *Handbook of social psychology* (3rd ed., Vol. 1, pp. 231–309). New York: Random House.

Adams, H. (1964). *The education of Henry Adams.* New York: Time. (Original work published 1918)

Ajzen, I., & Fishbein, M. (1980). *Understanding attitudes and predicting social behavior.* Englewood Cliffs, NJ: Prentice-Hall.

Alloy, L. B., & Abramson, L. Y. (1979). Judgment of contingency in depressed and nondepressed students: Sadder but wiser? *Journal of Experimental Psychology: General, 108,* 441–485.

Alloy, L. B., Abramson, L. Y., & Viscusi, D. (1981). Induced mood and the illusion of control. *Journal of Personality and Social Psychology, 41,* 1129–1140.

Alloy, L. B., & Tabachnik, N. (1984). Assessment of covariation by humans and animals: The joint influence of prior expectations and current situational information. *Psychological Review, 91,* 112–149.

Allport, G. (1985). The historical background of social psychology. In G. Lindzey & E. Aronson (Eds.), *Handbook of social psychology* (3rd ed., Vol. 1, pp. 1–46). New York: Random House.

Arkin, R. M. (Ed.). (1990). Centennial celebration of *The Principles of Psychology. Personality and Social Psychology Bulletin, 16,* 597–773.

Arkin, R. M., & Baumgardner, A. H. (1985). Self-handicapping. In J. H. Harvey & G. Weary (Eds.), *Attribution: Basic issues and applications* (pp. 169–202). San Diego, CA: Academic Press.

Bandura, A. (1986). *Social foundations of thought and action: A social cognitive theory.* Englewood Cliffs, NJ: Prentice-Hall.

Berscheid, E. (1985). Interpersonal attraction. In G. Lindzey & E. Aronson (Eds.), *Handbook of social psychology* (3rd ed., Vol. 2, pp. 413–484). New York: Random House.

Bradley, G. W. (1978). Self-serving biases in the attribution process: A reexamination of the fact or fiction question. *Journal of Personality and Social Psychology, 36,* 56–71.

Carver, C. S., & Scheier, M. F. (1985). Aspects of self, and the control of behavior. In B. Schlenker (Ed.), *The self and social life* (pp. 146–174). New York: McGraw-Hill.

Crocker, J. (1981). Judgment of covariation by social perceivers. *Psychological Bulletin, 90,* 272–292.

Festinger, L. (1954). A theory of social comparison processes. *Human Relations, 7,* 117–140.

Fishbein, M., & Ajzen, I. (1975). *Belief, attitude, intention, and behavior: An introduction to theory and research.* Reading, MA: Addison-Wesley.

Greenwald, A. G. (1981). The self and memory. In G. H. Bower (Ed.), *The psychology of learning and motivation* (Vol. 15, pp. 201–236). San Diego, CA: Academic Press.

Heider, F. (1958). *The psychology of interpersonal relations.* New York: Wiley.

Higgins, R., Snyder, C. R., & Berglas, S. (Eds.). (1990). *Self-handicapping: The paradox that isn't.* New York: Plenum Press.

James, H. (1942). Remarks on the occasion of the centenary of William James. In H. M. Kallen (Ed.), *In commemoration of William James, 1842–1942* (pp. 3–10). New York: Columbia University Press.

James, W. (1897). *The will to believe. And other essays in popular philosophy.* New York: Longmans, Green.

James, W. (1899). *Talks to teachers on psychology: And to students on some of life's ideals.* New York: Holt.

James, W. (1907). *Pragmatism: A new way for some old ways of thinking.* New York: Longmans, Green.

James, W. (1924a). Great men and their environment. In E. Rhys (Ed.), *Selected papers on philosophy by William James* (pp. 165–197). New York: Dutton. (Original work published in *The will to believe. And other essays in popular philosophy,* 1897)

James, W. (1924b). The sentiment of rationality. In E. Rhys (Ed.), *Selected papers on philosophy by William James* (pp. 125–164). New York: Dutton. (Original work published in *The will to believe. And other essays in popular philosophy,* 1897)

James, W. (1924c). The will to believe. In E. Rhys (Ed.), *Selected papers on philosophy by William James* (pp. 99–124). New York: Dutton. (Original work published in *The will to believe. And other essays in popular philosophy,* 1897)

James, W. (1924). What pragmatism means. In E. Rhys (Ed.), *Selected papers on philosophy by William James* (pp. 198–217). New York: Dutton. (Original work published in *Pragmatism: A new way for some old ways of thinking,* 1907)

James, W. (1978). *The meaning of truth: A sequel to "Pragmatism."* Cambridge, MA: Harvard University Press. (Original work published 1909)

James, W. (1981). *The principles of psychology* (3 vols.). Cambridge, MA: Harvard University Press. (Original work published 1890)

Jones, E. E. (1985). Major developments in social psychology during the past five decades. In G. Lindzey & E. Aronson (Eds.), *Handbook of social psychology* (3rd ed., Vol. 1, pp. 47–107). New York: Random House.

Jones, E. E., & Berglas, S. (1978). Control of attributions about the self through self-handicapping strategies: The appeal of alcohol and the role of under-achievement. *Personality and Social Psychology Bulletin, 4,* 200–206.

Jones, E. E., & Davis, K. E. (1965). From acts to dispositions: The attribution process in person perception. In L. Berkowitz (Ed.), *Advances in experimental social psychology* (Vol. 2, pp. 219–266). San Diego, CA: Academic Press.

Kallen, H. M. (Ed.). (1953). *The philosophy of William James*. New York: Random House.

Kelley, H. H. (1967). Attribution theory in social psychology. In D. Levine (Ed.), *Nebraska Symposium on Motivation* (pp. 192–238). Lincoln: University of Nebraska Press.

Langer, E. J. (1984). *The psychology of control*. Beverly Hills, CA: Sage.

Markus, H., & Nurius, P. (1986). Possible selves. *American Psychologist, 41*, 954–969.

Markus, H., & Ruvolo, A. (1989). Possible selves: Personalized representations of goals. In L. A. Pervin (Ed.), *Goal concepts in personality and social psychology* (pp. 211–241). Hillsdale, NJ: Erlbaum.

McDermott, J. J. (Ed.). (1967). *The writings of William James*. New York: Random House.

Nisbett, R. E., Krantz, D. H., Jepson, C., & Kunda, Z. (1983). The use of statistical heuristics in everyday inductive reasoning. *Psychological Review, 90*, 339–363.

Nisbett, R. E., & Ross, L. (1980). *Human inference: Strategies and shortcomings of social judgment*. Englewood Cliffs, NJ: Prentice-Hall.

Ross, M., & Fletcher, G. J. O. (1985). Attribution and social perception. In G. Lindzey & E. Aronson (Eds.), *Handbook of social psychology* (3rd ed., Vol. 2, pp. 73–122). New York: Random House.

Scheier, M. F., & Carver, C. S. (1983). Two sides of the self: One for you and one for me. In J. Suls & A. Greenwald (Eds.), *Psychological perspectives on the self* (Vol. 2, pp. 123–157). Hillsdale, NJ: Erlbaum.

Simon, H. A. (1955). A behavioral model of rational choice. *Quarterly Journal of Economics, 69*, 99–118.

Snyder, M. L., Stephan, W. G., & Rosenfield, D. (1976). Egotism and attribution. *Journal of Personality and Social Psychology, 33*, 435–441.

Spence, J. T. (1985). Achievement American style: The rewards and costs of individualism. *American Psychologist, 40*, 1285–1295.

Strube, M. J. (1989). Assessing subjects' construal of the laboratory situation. In N. Schneiderman, S. M. Weiss, & P. G. Kaufmann (Eds.), *Handbook of research methods in cardiovascular behavioral medicine* (pp. 527–542). New York: Plenum Press.

Strube, M. J. (1990). In search of self: Balancing the good and the true. *Personality and Social Psychology Bulletin, 16*, 699–704.

Strube, M. J., Lott, C. L., Le, H., Oxenberg, J., & Deichmann, A. K. (1986). Self-evaluation of abilities: Accurate self-assessment versus biased self-enhancement. *Journal of Personality and Social Psychology, 51*, 16–25.

Strube, M. J, & Roemmele, L. A. (1985). Self-enhancement, self-assessment, and self-evaluative task choice. *Journal of Personality and Social Psychology, 49*, 981–993.

Swann, W. B., Jr. (1984). Quest for accuracy in person perception: A matter of pragmatics. *Psychological Review, 91*, 457–477.

Swann, W. B., Jr., Pelham, B. W., & Krull, D. S. (1989). Agreeable fancy or disagreeable truth? Reconciling self-enhancement with self-verification. *Journal of Personality and Social Psychology, 57,* 782–791.

Taylor, S. E., & Brown, J. D. (1988). Illusion and well-being: A social psychological perspective on mental health. *Psychological Bulletin, 103,* 193–210.

Trope, Y. (1980). Self-assessment, self-enhancement, and task preference. *Journal of Experimental Social Psychology, 16,* 116–129.

Trope, Y. (1986). Self-enhancement and self-assessment in achievement behavior. In R. M. Sorrentino & E. T. Higgins (Eds.), *Handbook of motivation and cognition: Foundations of social behavior* (pp. 350–378). New York: Guilford Press.

Wegner, D. M., & Vallacher, R. R. (1986). Action identification. In R. M. Sorrentino & E. T. Higgins (Eds.), *Handbook of motivation and cognition: Foundations of social behavior* (pp. 550–582). New York: Guilford Press.

White, R. W. (1959). Motivation reconsidered: The concept of competence. *Psychological Review, 66,* 297–333.

William James Symposium. (1990). *Psychological Science, 1,* 149–185.

Yost, J. H., Strube, M. J, & Bailey, J. R. (1990, August). *An evolutionary view of self-construction.* Paper presented at the 98th Annual Convention of the American Psychological Association, Boston, MA.

V

EMOTION:
"HERE'S WHAT'S HAPPENED TO EMOTION, MR. JAMES"

13

SILVAN TOMKINS'S THEORY OF EMOTION

E. VIRGINIA DEMOS

It is a daunting prospect to address William James over the time span of 80 years and to describe what has happened to emotion in that time. The problem is how to relate the mentality of the late nineteenth and early twentieth century, when James sat in his armchair and engaged in introspection about the nature of emotional and religious experiences, to the zeitgeist of today, with our radically increased repertoire of methodologies, including the innovation of video and computer technologies; a broadened range of conceptual models borrowed from biology, neurology, physics, ethology; a more sophisticated version of evolution; and a markedly diverse and enlarged data base, all providing the context in which today's controversies about emotion take place. Although this increase in the sheer amount of information and diversity of approaches sounds like progress, it has at the same time led to more specialization and segregation of researchers than perhaps would have been imaginable in an earlier era. To increase communication in the field, the International Society for Research in Emotions was founded in 1985, but there is still little theoretical unity or consensus in the field.

THE COGNITIVE APPROACH TO THE
STUDY OF EMOTION

Many of the parameters of emotional experiences that James discussed, such as perception, motor responses, physiological responses, and cognitive interpretations, are still part of the discourse, and all have been elaborated on with a variety of new technologies and cross-cultural and cross-species data. There are also continuing efforts to understand the relationships between these various components and to articulate the precise nature of the quantitative and qualitative aspects of emotion. But perhaps the most dominant trend today is to describe emotion as a function of cognition, whether it be as in James's original theory—an appraisal or an interpretation of physiological and motor responses—or as in today's versions—social and cultural constructions that the child learns through socialization. Today, for example, emotional development is seen as merely another aspect of cognitive development, following the same stages and utilizing the same processes (Fischer, Shaver, & Carnochan, 1990).

One can hardly hold James responsible for the continuing dominance of this cognitive bias in the study of emotion. Nor can one deny that such an approach accounts for some important kinds of emotional experiences. But a cognitive approach tends to disregard the physiological components of emotion and thereby underestimates the biological determinants of emotional processes. Thus, such an approach cannot account for equally important kinds of emotional experiences, namely, those occasions when one feels an emotion for no particular reason, or those instances when emotion influences cognition, or those emotional experiences of infants, who are assumed to be not cognitively capable of anything but global states or expressive behaviors that are seen as precursors to emotion. Now to talk about the emotional experiences of infants might have sounded astonishing to James, but that is the topic I propose to focus on here, partly because it represents my area of specialization and partly because it allows me to present perhaps the only truly novel theory of emotion since the work of James and Darwin.

TOMKINS'S THEORY OF AFFECT

Silvan Tomkins is the only theorist to argue that emotion can occur independently of cognition and to focus our attention on the unique characteristics of emotion. He argues that the human organism has evolved as a "multimechanism system in which each mechanism is at once incomplete but essential to the functioning of the system as a whole." (Tomkins, 1981, p. 320). In other words, each mechanism is distinct, with its particular components, characteristics, and functions; and each mechanism is capable of acting independently, dependently, and interdependently with any or all of the other mechanisms in this system. The affect mechanism is therefore distinct from the sensory, motor, memory, cognitive, pain, and drive mechanisms; and although it frequently enters into dependent and interdependent relationships with these other mechanisms, it can operate independently of them as well.

What are the distinctive features of the affect mechanism, and what is its distinctive function? Tomkins has differentiated 13 components of the affect system, paying special, but not exclusive, attention to the face as the primary locus of the affect response. He argues that each affect operates as a specific correlated set of responses that includes facial muscles, vocal, respiratory, and blood-flow changes, heightened skin receptor sensitivity, and other autonomic responses. These correlated sets of responses are thought to be innately programmed and to operate involuntarily, but they are at the same time amenable to voluntary control and thus open to all of the effects of learning. Nevertheless, we never gain complete control over our emotions (Tomkins, 1962, 1963).

What are the correlated sets of responses designed to do? What is their function in the larger system? In Tomkins's paradigm, the affect mechanism is the primary motivational system. It is activated both innately and through learning by three classes of stimulation change—stimulation increase, stimulation level, and stimulation decrease. The correlated sets of responses are designed to replicate by analogous bodily responses these stimulus characteristics. Thus, affect acts as an analogue amplifier of anything that is increasing rapidly, as in fear; or remaining the same at a nonoptimal level, as in distress; or decreasing, as in enjoyment, thereby making bad things worse and good things better (Tomkins, 1978). By amplifying stimulus characteristics through bodily responses, affect creates a specific punishing or rewarding qualitative state in the organism that combines urgency, abstractness, and generality, and causes the organism to care about what is happening. Thus, for example, a rapid rate of stimulus increase will activate fear, which involves a rapid increase in heart rate, a rapid intake of breath, an eye widening, a bilateral pulling back of the corners of the mouth, one's hair standing on end, and a drop in skin temperature—all combining to create a qualitatively urgent, abstract, general, amplified experience of something happening "too fast!" When affect combines with perception and cognition, that abstract, general something can become quite specific, such as a speeding car or a charging lion heading in one's direction. However, it is not the verbal labeling of the object, nor one's knowledge of the consequences of being hit or attacked by the object that activates the fear, but rather the rate of change in the approach of the object that triggers the fear. Such specific knowledge is not irrelevant, because it may enable one to act to escape disaster. Thus, although affect supplies the urgency for action, it does not dictate the specific adaptive solution. It must combine with perceptual, cognitive, memory, and motor mechanisms to produce an effective escape. Nevertheless, one must be clear about what is contributed by affect and what is achieved by a coordination of the affect mechanism with other mechanisms. This distinction between affect and affect coordinations, or *affect complexes*, as Tomkins calls them, is blurred when affect is defined as a function of cognition, and this confusion has clouded the question of what the primary affects are and how many there are. Here I would like to quote Tomkins's answer to this question.

> This is a basic question, primarily biological in nature, that is treated more and more as though it were a psychosocial question. Affect mechanisms are no less biological than drive mechanisms. We do not argue for a Chinese hunger drive and an American hunger drive as two kinds of hunger drives. Subserving these taste preferences, we speak of a small and limited number of taste receptors and do not invent new primary taste receptors with every new food recipe. Nor do we postulate new sensory color receptors with every new color combination in painting. Nor do we postulate new pain receptors with each discovery of a new disease or new instruments of torture. If each innate affect is controlled by inherited programs that in turn control facial muscle responses, autonomic blood flow, respiratory, and vocal responses, then these correlated sets of responses will define the number and specific types of primary affects. The evidence I have presented plus the cross-cultural consensus demonstrated by Ekman (1972) and Izard (1968) suggests strongly, if not conclusively, that there are a limited number of such specific types of responses. There are, I believe, nine such responses: interest, enjoyment, surprise, fear, anger, distress, shame, contempt, and disgust. These are discriminable distinct sets of facial, vocal, respiratory, skin, and muscle responses. The decisive evidence for this will, I think, require conjoint specific patterned brain stimulation with moving and thermographic pictures of the face. This is a project for the future. In the meantime we must not assume that we can solve this problem by an analysis of the cognitions that are combined with each of these affects. (Tomkins, 1981, p. 325)

This theory has been of enormous value to those of us interested in infants' emotions. If the affect mechanism is governed by innate programs that do not require learning for their activation, then the cries, smiles, frowns, and laughs of young infants can be taken seriously as emotions. For example, consider the hungry crying neonate. This ordinary event has captured the imagination of many a theorist who felt it required some explanation. Freud, who postulated drives as the primary motivator, argued that hunger created an overwhelming drive tension in the newborn and that the cry represented a physiological release of this tension and functioned as a safety valve. Observers of infant states, such as Wolff (1969) and Sander and Julia (1966), who articulated states along a sleep–wake continuum, have simply labeled this as the crying state. Child development researchers, such as Sroufe (1979) and Emde (1976), have argued that because the activator is physiological and there is no cognitive activity involved, the cry represents a precursor to emotion but is not emotion itself. And attachment model theorists and researchers would argue that the infant's cry functions as a signal to the caregiver to approach and take some action, but they do not say anything about how the cry is activated or how it functions within the infant and within the mother (Bowlby, 1969). So what does Tomkins's theory contribute to our understanding of the hungry, crying neonate?

First, it focuses our attention on the characteristics of the cry itself and on the pattern of responses that are occurring with the cry. There have been a number of studies that have analyzed the acoustical features of the newborn's cries (Wolff, 1969; Wasz-Hockert, Link, Vuorenkoski, Partanen, & Valanne, 1968). They describe the basic cry, or hunger cry, as a rhythmical cry with a frequency of somewhere between 350 and 470 Hz, and they also report what they call a pain cry, which is a long initial cry that may be followed by breath holding and then an inspiration and breath. None of these researchers reported with any precision other features of the response, such as facial expressions or bodily responses that may have occurred with the cries. I have reported data on one hungry 9-day-old infant who was being given a bath (Demos, 1988). Her cries alternated between the rhythmical cry and the long cry reported by others, and as her cries changed, so too did her face and body. With the rhythmical cry, her face showed the distress pattern described by Tomkins—the corners of her mouth were turned down, with lips loose and open; the inner corners of her brows were raised and pulled together; and her limbs were flailing. But with the long cry, when more air is forced through the vocal cords, her mouth was squared and tight; her brows were lowered and pulled together; her face was red; and her body was stiff, with legs kicking—all manifestations of the facial and motor pattern for anger.

These facial, vocal, and motor responses are *not* random. They are clearly patterned and coordinated with each other. They are also *not* learned. Every neonate knows how to cry in distress or in anger. Nor do they operate in a reflexlike manner. They are exquisitely responsive to subtle changes in the environment. We do not yet have a complete picture of the full innate affect program for distress and anger, because no one has done a simultaneous recording of the facial, vocal, motor, skin temperature, and autonomic responses of a crying neonate. The evidence we do have, however, on facial and vocal expressions of infants is in agreement with the patterns described by Tomkins. On the strength of this evidence then, it is possible to assert that these correlated sets of responses observed in the newborn are emotions. If we now return to our hungry infant, we can say that the cry and face and body of that infant indicate the emotion of distress and that that state feels distressing to the infant. The infant knows neither why he or she is crying nor that anything can be done about it. There is no cognitive and memory information coassembled with the affect. The hungry neonate is experiencing distress in its pure form.

Second, Tomkins's theory helps us understand what is activating the distress and why it is distress and not some other affect that is activated. Hunger represents a source of a continuous, nonoptimal level of stimulation that fits the innate profile for activating distress. And the distress affect program, with rhythmical crying and the facial pattern and motor responses described earlier, amplifies that nonoptimal level of stimulation, making a bad situation worse and causing the infant to feel the punishing quality of distress. With the infant I was observing, when the mother added a bath on top of an already distressing level of stimulation, the increase in the level of nonoptimal stimulation activated the innate anger response, which in turn, with its facial, vocal, and motor pattern, amplified this higher level, producing the punishing quality of anger. In these amplified states of distress and anger, the infant is primed to pay attention to anything that improves the situation. In other words, the infant cares about what happens next, and the capacity for learning is greatly enhanced.

The third contribution of Tomkins's theory is to focus attention on the antecedents and consequences of these emotional states experienced by the infant. Because the infant not only possesses affect programs but also all of the other mechanisms, she will very quickly begin to enlist her memory, her cognition, her motor patterns, and her perception in an effort to lower the level of distress and return to a more comfortable state. The infant then becomes actively engaged in creating what Tomkins has called affect complexes, which are coordinations of multiple mechanisms in order to connect antecedents and consequences with affect states. For example, every mother knows that within a week or two after birth, the infant will stop crying as soon as he or she sees the bottle or the breast. At low intensities of distress, infants have some capacities for self-soothing. If they can get their fist to their mouth, the regular pattern of sucking will override the distress pattern. Or if they can find something interesting to look at, the calm, focused affect pattern of interest will override the distress pattern. This was illustrated by the infant–mother pair I described earlier. When the mother held the infant in an *en face* position after the bath, this hungry infant quieted down and gazed with intense interest at her mother's face. Of course, sooner or later, the hunger will reassert itself, because that source of stimulation will continue to increase until the infant is fed. And indeed, at more intense levels of distress, the affect dynamic of amplification will cause distress to evoke more distress in a positive feedback loop, continuing to escalate, and thereby compounding intensity with duration and producing a high density of negative affect. At such intensity levels, infants are dependent on caregivers to modulate, soothe, and bring them back to more moderate intensity levels.

The fourth contribution of Tomkins's theory is that it provides a way to explore and understand the caregiver's response to the crying infant. The amplifying function of affect not only evokes more of the same affect in the person experiencing the affect but also tends to evoke that affect in the listener. And infant affect is full-blown and unsocialized and thus is even more contagious and compelling. A number of studies using rating scales or physiological measures have shown that adults experience infant crying as arousing, distressing, aversive, grating, and irritating in varying degrees, depending on the type of cry and on several adult variables (Lester & Zeskind, 1982), such as other competing affects, the context and meaning for the observer of the infant's distress, the degree of responsibility felt by the observer for doing something about the infant's distress, and the degree of defensiveness of the observer with regard to distress. For example, Wiesenfeld, Malatesta, and DeLoach (1981) reported that mothers showed more autonomic responsivity to their own infant's distress cries than did fathers, and more than they did to an unfamiliar infant's distress cry; Frodi and Lamb (1980) reported that abusive mothers showed greater autonomic arousal and produced more negative emotional ratings than did controls; and Boukydis (1979; as cited in Lester & Zeskind, 1982) reported that new parents showed their highest levels of arousal to average cries, whereas experienced parents and nonparents showed their highest levels of arousal to difficult cries and their lowest levels to easy cries. Hence, there is no simple, direct relationship between the intensity and kind of affect expressed by the infant and the intensity and kind of affect evoked in the observer. Nevertheless, because of the amplifying function of affect and the relatively higher intensity and density of affect expressed by infants, it is likely that a caregiver who is engaged with a crying infant will experience a variant of the affect expressed by the infant. When this happens, then the caregiver's ability to soothe and help the infant will depend on the caregiver's response to his or her own affective experience at that particular moment. Thus, our research should begin to focus on the range of meanings such a moment can have for a caregiver and on the caregiver's unique personal history of learning in relation to the evoked affect.

The fifth and final contribution of Tomkins's theory to be discussed here is his assertion that the newborn possesses the full range of innate primary affects. Thus, instead of assuming that such emotions cannot exist in the young infant, researchers can begin to look systematically at what is actually going on with the infant. I have reported instances of distress and anger in infants (Demos, 1986, 1988); Brazelton (1973) and his co-workers have reported smiles of enjoyment in newborns. Oster (1978) and Langsdorf, Izard, Rayias, and Hembree (1983) have described the state of interest in young infants. And Gaensbauer (1982) has reported the fear responses of a 3-month-old infant with a history of physical abuse by her father during the first 2 months of her life. Our evidence is scanty, but consistent, and therefore encouraging; whenever researchers make the effort to look carefully at the very young infant, a rich and complex picture emerges. Tomkins's theory has opened the door to such explorations, and I would like to think that William James would be excited and pleased by these new possibilities.

REFERENCES

Bowlby, J. (1969). *Attachment and loss: Vol. I. Attachment.* New York: Basic Books.

Brazelton, T. B. (1973). *Neonatal Assessment Scale.* London: Heinemann Medical Books.

Demos, E. V. (1986). Crying in early infancy: An illustration of the motivational function of affect. In T. B. Brazelton & M. Yogman (Eds.), *Affective development in early infancy* (pp. 39–73). Norwood, NJ: Ablex.

Demos, E. V. (1988). Affect and the development of the self: A new frontier. In A. Goldberg (Ed.), *Frontiers in self psychology: Progress in self psychology* (Vol. 3, pp. 27–53). Hillsdale, NJ: Analytic Press.

Ekman, P. (1972). Universal and cultural differences in facial expression of emotion. *Nebraska Symposium on Motivation, 19,* 207–283.

Emde, R. N., Gaensbauer, T., & Harmon, R. (1976). Emotional expression in infancy: A biobehavioral study. *Psychological Issues, Monograph No. 37.* Madison, CT: International Universities Press.

Fischer, K. W., Shaver, P. R., & Carnochan, P. (1990). How emotions develop and how they organize development. *Cognition and Emotion, 4*(2). 81–127.

Frodi, A. M., & Lamb, M. E. (1980). Child abusers' responses to infant smiles and cries. *Child Development, 51,* 238–241.

Gaensbauer, T. (1982). The differentiation of discrete affects. *Psychoanalytic Study of the Child, 37,* 29–65.

Izard, C. E. (1968). The emotions and emotion constructs in personality and culture research. In R. B. Cattell (Ed.), *Handbook of modern personality theory.* Chicago: Aldine.

Langsdorf, P., Izard, C. E., Rayias, M., & Hembree, E. A. (1983). Interest expression, visual fixation, and heart rate changes in 2- and 8-month-old infants. *Developmental Psychology, 19,* 373–386.

Lester, B. M., & Zeskind, P. S. (1982). A biobehavioral perspec
early infancy. In H. Fitzgerald, B. Lester, & M. W. Yogma
and research in behavioral pediatrics (Vol. I, pp. 133–180). Ne
Press.

Oster, H. (1978). Facial expression and affect development. In M.
Rosenblum (Eds.), *The development of affect* (pp. 43–75). New
Press.

Sander, L., & Julia, H. L. Continuous interactional monitoring in
Psychosomatic Medicine, 28, 822–835.

Sroufe, L. A. (1979). The ontogenesis of emotion in infants. In J. O;
Handbook of infant development (pp. 462–490). New York: Wiley.

Tomkins, S. (1962). *Affect, imagery, consciousness: Vol. I. The positive a*
York: Springer.

Tomkins, S. (1963). *Affect, imagery, consciousness: Vol. II. The negative af*
York: Springer.

Tomkins, S. (1978). Script theory: Differential magnification of affects.
Symposium on Motivation, 26, 201–263.

Tomkins, S. (1981). The quest for primary motives: Biography and autobi,
of an idea. *Journal of Personality and Social Psychology, 41,* 306–329.

Wasz-Hockert, O., Link, J., Vuorenkoski, V., Partanen, T., & Valanne, E. (
The infant cry. London: Heinemann Medical Books.

Wiesenfeld, A. R., Malatesta, E. Z., & DeLoach, L. L. (1981). Differential pai
response to familiar and unfamiliar infant distress signals. *Infant Behavio
Development, 4,* 281–295.

Wolff, P. (1969). The natural history of crying and other vocalizations in ε
infancy. In B. M. Foss (Ed.), *Determinants of infant behavior* (pp. 81–1(
London: Methuen.

14

WILLIAM JAMES'S OTHER
THEORY OF EMOTION

JAMES R. AVERILL

In Shakespeare's play *Julius Caesar*, Mark Antony proclaimed to the crowd, "We have come to bury Caesar, not to praise him." Now more than 100 years after the publication of William James's *The Principles of Psychology* (1890), it would seem appropriate to praise James, not to bury him. Still, I would like to take a cue from Mark Antony. It is time to give a decent burial to James's famous theory of emotion as it was presented in the *Principles* (and earlier, in 1884, in the journal *Mind*). I will refer to this as "James's first theory," for he had a second, less well-known theory of emotion. This other theory has not received the attention it deserves, in part, because it was never explicitly formulated or labeled as a theory of emotion by James. Rather, it is largely implicit in a work, the topic of which is peripheral to the interests of most psychologists, namely, *The Varieties of Religious Experience* (James, 1902/1961). Drawing on another distinction made famous by James (1907/1955), his first theory appeals to the tough-minded empiricist; his second theory is more attuned to the tender-minded rationalist. But like most dichotomies, this one conceals as much as it reveals. In this chapter, I will try to give explicit formulation to James's second theory, and I will argue that it is actually closer to the facts (more empirically based) than is his first.

JAMES'S FIRST THEORY

"My theory . . . is that *bodily changes follow directly the perception of the exciting fact, and that our feeling of the same changes as they occur IS the emotion.*" (James, 1890, p. 449)

To be perfectly blunt, this theory has been a dead end. Or, more accurately, it has been an arduous detour leading to a dead end; along the way, it has exacted a terrible toll in time and resources. This may seem like a harsh assessment, considering all the research the theory has generated over the past century. But in their time, alchemy and astrology also generated much research—some of it quite valuable. As theories, however, they led nowhere.

James's theory is a dead end for two main reasons: First, it is irrefutable, and a theory that is irrefutable is empirically meaningless; second, by focusing attention on bodily changes during emotion, it has led investigators to ignore two important facts about human emotions, namely, (a) emotions are intimately related to a person's sense of self, both in terms of eliciting conditions and consequences, and (b) emotions can be understood only in the context of broader interpersonal and social relations.

A central tenet of James's theory is that feedback from bodily changes adds a certain emotional quale to an otherwise cold perception of the exciting event. Although this seems like a reasonable empirical hypothesis, it is irrefutable for three main reasons:

1. Although James emphasized the viscera as the primary source of feedback, any kind of feedback will do—if not feedback from the viscera, then from the striated muscles involved in posture and movement; if not from them, then from facial expressions. Discredit one source, and an appeal can be (and often is) made to one of the others. In James's own words,

   If we wish to conquer undesirable emotional tendencies in ourselves, we must assiduously, and in the first instance cold-bloodedly, go through the *outward movements* of those contrary dispositions which we prefer to cultivate. . . . Smooth the brow, brighten the eye, contract the dorsal rather than the ventral aspect of the frame, and speak in a major key, pass the genial compliment, and your heart must be frigid indeed if it do not gradually thaw! (1890, p. 463)

2. The feedback need not be from bodily change. The nervous system can, in a sense, perceive its own activity. Thus, the mere

intention to respond, or the fantasy that one is responding, can, according to James, meet the requirements of his theory:

> Under all these conditions [e.g., dreams, hallucinations, trance, ecstasy] one may have the liveliest subjective feelings, either of eye or ear, or of the more visceral and emotional sort, as a result of pure nerve-central activity, and yet, as I believe, with complete peripheral repose. (1890, p. 459)

3. In fact, there need not be even the intention to respond, real or fancied. The most fundamental assumption behind James's theory is that feelings of emotion can be accounted for in terms of simple sensory processes. Sensory processes may be exteroceptive as well as interoceptive. It follows that the perception of certain configurations in the environment, and not just the perception of one's own bodily responses, may be sufficient to elicit emotional feelings. This helps account for subtler emotions, for example, aesthetic feelings. Edmund Gurney (1884) in a critique of James's initial (1884) publication of his theory, stated that he (Gurney) experienced much emotion when listening to, or even imagining a musical score. This presents no real problem, James responded,

> In organizations as musical as Mr. Gurney's, purely acoustic form gives so intense a degree of sensible pleasure that the lower bodily reverberation is of no account. . . . I see nothing in the facts which Mr. Gurney cites, to lead one to believe in an emotion divorced from *sensational processes* of any kind. (1890, p. 470)

In other words, to disprove, James's theory, we would need a person who is completely insensitive to all bodily changes, who is not aware of his or her own motor impulses, and who is blind, deaf, and devoid of sensory processes of any kind. If such a person could experience emotion, the theory would be disproved. Such a person was unimaginable to James, and I presume to anybody else. (James did entertain the notion that disembodied spirits, which presumably have no sensory processes of the regular kind, might experience emotion. The theoretic raptures of ordinary human beings, he implied, might approach this disembodied ideal, thus providing a test of his theory.)

In addition to being irrefutable, James's theory is severly limited in scope. Bodily changes, according to the theory, presumably "follow directly the perception of the exciting fact." But what makes the fact exciting? The theory gives no clue. If a woman comes home one evening, and her husband says, as she walks in the door, "I am really angry with you tonight." Is he simply giving a report of bodily changes as they occur? I think not. Something is obviously missing from the theory, namely, the meaning of the emotion.

Given that the theory is irrefutable and that it fails to account for important aspects of emotion, this question arises: Why has the theory remained so popular? The reasons are fivefold:

1. The theory has a grain of truth. The perception of bodily changes does add a certain quale to our experience. The problem is that bodily change (beyond that which accompanies any psychological activity) is neither sufficient nor necessary for the experience of emotion.

2. The theory fits with our popular conception of emotions as uncontrollable, primitive responses. Emotions are, colloquially speaking, gut reactions. This conception can be traced back to the ancient Greeks (Averill, 1974). Plato, for example, placed reason in the head, because the head is round, and rational thought, Plato believed, involves circular motion. Having localized reason in the head on largely symbolic grounds, Plato then placed emotions in the gut far away from the head so that they might interfere with reason as little as possible. Thus, in some respects, James's theory has both intuitive appeal and historical precedent.

3. In other respects, however, the theory is counterintuitive. For example, most people believe we run because we are afraid. To turn this sequence around seems like a real discovery. Psychologists like nothing better than seemingly counterintuitive discoveries. It demonstrates to skeptics that psychology is a science after all!

4. The theory fit the emerging behaviorist paradigm in American psychology. If feelings are the product of bodily changes, rather than the cause, they can be ignored without loss of explanatory power.

5. The theory is simple. James claimed that he was surfeited by too much reading of classic works on emotion. He would "as lief read verbal descriptions of the shapes of the rocks on a New Hampshire farm as toil through them again" (1890, p. 448). Nowhere do such works give the kind of deductive or generative principle that is "the beauty of all truly scientific work" (p. 448). His theory, he believed, provided that generative principle. And "having the goose which lays the golden eggs, the description of each egg already laid is a minor matter" (p. 449).

This last point deserves brief elaboration. James recognized that description and classification are propaedeutic to any science. Yet, he found such endeavors tedious. Many others evidently have agreed. As a result, our theories of emotion have been built on a very narrow base. Fear, anger, grief, and love have been the primary emotions investigated, yet literally hundreds of other emotions are recognized in ordinary language. James, himself, did not even mention in his *Principles* such states as hope, pride, and guilt, all of which have at one time or another been considered basic (or fundamental) human emotions.

James made prominent mention of Darwin in his chapter on emotion. What if Darwin had been equally surfeited on descriptions of barnacles and finches, and instead had, from his armchair, searched for a generative principle of biological evolution? Good theory, particularly in the human and biological sciences, must rest on the kind of detailed observation that James found boring, but that Darwin found fascinating.

Fortunately, the situation is changing. During the past decade, a considerable amount of research has been devoted to the classification of the hundreds of emotions recognized in ordinary language (e.g., Ortony, Clore, & Collins, 1988; Storm & Storm, 1987) and to a broader sampling of emotions for investigation. Such a broadening of the empirical base is one of the most important things that has happened to the field of emotion since James discovered his goose that lays the golden eggs.

To summarize the discussion thus far, James's theory of emotion as presented in the *Principles* is both irrefutable and limited in scope. In recent decades, a number of attempts have been made to overcome these short-comings and, in one form or another, neo-Jamesian approaches are still among the most popular in psychology (cf. the facial feedback theory of Tomkins, 1962–1963, or the autonomic feedback theory of Schachter, 1964). My own opinion is that the theory should be laid to rest. We should not waste time trying to repair it, for that will only distract us from more important tasks. At most, we should pay passing homage to it, and then move on. In doing so, we would, ironically, be following in the path of James.

JAMES'S SECOND THEORY

"A foolish consistency," Emerson (1841/1968) asserted, "is the hobgoblin of little minds." No one can accuse James of foolish consistency or of being hostage to hobgoblins. Perhaps in a few years, we will celebrate the centennial of *The Varieties of Religious Experience*, which was published in 1902, for the *Varieties* contains a far richer and more insightful theory of emotion than does the *Principles*.

At the outset of the *Varieties*, James warned against the dangers of physiological reductionism:

There is not a single one of our states of mind, high or low, healthy or morbid, that has not some organic process as its condition. Scientific theories are organically conditioned just as much as religious emotions are; and if we only knew the facts intimately enough, we should doubtless see "the liver" determining the dicta of the sturdy atheist as decisively as it does those of the Methodist under conviction anxious about his soul. (1902/1961, p. 30)

The *Varieties* is a very discursive work. It is impossible to summarize its main insights with a few short propositions. To provide the gist of James's second theory, therefore, I will pick one thread that runs through the entire work. That thread has to do with creativity, but on the emotional rather than on the intellectual level. "When a person has an inborn genius for certain emotions, his life differs strangely from that of ordinary people, for none of their usual deterrents check him" (1902/1961, p. 215).

Einstein was a genius in science; Mozart, in music; Jefferson, in politics; Napoleon, in warfare. But what does it mean to be a genius in emotion? James focused on a lack of "usual deterrents," which is a characteristic feature of creative people in general (Albert & Runco, 1986). To be creative, a person must be willing not only to innovate and change, but also to pursue single-mindedly a vision, even at the risk of personal misfortune and social censure. But there is more to creativity than that.

Following Wallas's (1926) work, it is common to divide creative activity into four phases: preparation, incubation, illumination, and verification. Although James antedated Wallas by several decades, he used some of the same terminology in his second theory of emotion.

How small an additional stimulus will overthrow the mind into a new state of equilibrium when the process of preparation and incubation has proceeded far enough. It is like the proverbial last straw added to the camel's burden, or that touch of a needle which makes the salt in a supersaturated fluid suddenly begin to crystallize out. (1902/1961, p. 151)

The incident that occasioned these remarks involved a young man who gave up his religious faith on hearing a minor remark from his brother. James believed that similar processes can be observed in more commonplace emotional reactions, such as falling in (and out of) love: "Falling in love also conforms frequently to this type, a latent process of unconscious preparation often preceding a sudden awakening to the fact that the mischief is irretrievably done" (1902/1961, p. 152).

This "sudden awakening" is the equivalent of Wallas's phase of illumination. The person feels overcome by emotion, as though struck by the proverbial bolt of lightening. But the feeling is more illusion than fact.

Emotions do not just happen any more than scientific or artistic inspiration just happens. The development of effective emotional responses typically requires a good deal of preparation and incubation. After repetition, of course, an emotional response can become habitual and unthinking, just like any other kind of response. But if we want to understand underlying processes, the habitual is probably not the best place to begin.

What might correspond to Wallas's fourth phase, verification, in the case of emotions? A scientific insight is verified if it meets certain standards of logic and empirical test. A work of art is verified if it meets standards of aesthetics and public acceptance. An emotional response is verified if it is adaptive, that is, if it proves to be a viable solution to the problems facing an individual or society.

Emotions can be adaptive (verified) in a variety of different ways, depending on the type of emotion and the context. In the *Varieties*, the kinds of verification of most concern to James were those "in which the sand and grit of selfhood incline to disappear" (p. 225), and the person enters into more harmonious relationships with his or her environment. Although this is only one possible outcome, it does reflect a broader truth. Emotions necessarily involve the self. In fear, the self is perceived as threatened; in anger, as affronted; in grief, as diminished; and in love, as reaching out to another. It follows that there can be no fundamental change in the emotional life of a person without a corresponding change in the self and vice versa (Morgan & Averill, 1992).

But relating the emotions to the self is only a first step. As Mead (1934) emphasized, the self derives its meaning, in large part, from its embeddedness in a broader social network, and so, too, do the emotions. Every culture has emotions that are considered basic within the culture, but seem relatively incomprehensible to members of other cultures. A wealth of detailed cross-cultural comparisons is another of the most important things that has happened to the field of emotion since the time of James (e.g., Levy, 1984; Lutz, 1988; Rosaldo, 1980; Shweder, 1985).

Although James did not explicitly relate emotions to culture, the dependency of emotion on broader belief systems is implicit in his second theory. The religious convert, for example, knows that he or she has arrived, not when there is an intellectual acceptance of the new belief system, but when the emotions defined by the system are experienced.

To summarize, I have analyzed one thread in James's complex analysis—the thread having to do with emotional innovation and change. I have chosen this particular thread because it happens to coincide with some of my own research interests at the moment (Averill & Nunley, 1992; Averill & Thomas-Knowles, 1991). I could have analyzed other threads, but the conclusion would have been the same. Namely, it is misleading to claim, as James did in the *Principles*, that bodily changes "follow directly the perception of the exciting fact." Typically, the exciting fact is itself the end product of a long process of preparation and incubation. It is even more misleading to claim that the emotion is "our feeling of the same changes as they occur," for this assertion robs the emotions of much of their meaning and significance. Closer to the truth is James's contention that

> The best thing is to describe the condition [emotion] integrally as a characteristic affection to which our nature is liable, a region in which we find ourselves at home, a sea in which we swim; but not to pretend to explain its parts by deriving them too cleverly from one another. (1902/1961, p. 225)

If this passage sounds a bit mystical—it is, because James was referring to such states as religious rapture, moral enthusiasm, ontological wonder, and "cosmic emotion." However, the statement applies mutatis mutandis to emotions of all sorts. Indeed, if we read it figuratively yet carefully, it can serve as a brief summary of James's second theory of emotion. As emotion is "a sea in which we swim"—an ever changing sea, I might add, whose contours are shaped by three entities: the body, self, and society. Particular note should be taken of James's admonition "not to pretend to explain [the] parts by deriving them too cleverly from one another." That is precisely what he tried to do in his first theory of emotion.

I will conclude with an observation from James's own conclusion to the *Varieties*. James commented that, on rereading the manuscript, he was "almost appalled at the amount of emotionality" it contained (p. 377). Why should that have appalled him? He was, after all, writing a book on varieties of religious *experience*, not varieties of religious *thought* (i.e., a book on theology). I suspect that one thing that bothered James was the apparent irrelevancy of the generative principle that he had so forcefully advanced 12 years earlier in the *Principles*. Stated most baldly, the "goose which lays the golden eggs" turned out to be a sterile turkey when it came to the analysis of actual emotional experiences. In saying this, I am not criticizing James, who seemed to have recognized the limits of his first theory. On the contrary, I am suggesting that we follow James's lead. Let us give his first theory a decent burial; then let us get on with the task of analysis. There is no better place to begin that task than with the insights and wisdom of James's other theory.

REFERENCES

Albert, R. S., & Runco, M. A. (1986). The achievement of eminence: A model based on a longitudinal study of exceptionally gifted boys and their families.

In R. J. Sternberg & J. E. Davidson (Eds.), *Conceptions of giftedness* (pp. 332–357). New York: Cambridge University Press.

Averill, J. R. (1974). An analysis of psychophysiological symbolism and its influence on theories of emotion. *Journal for the Theory of Social Behavior, 4*, 147–190.

Averill, J. R., & Nunley, E. P. (1992). *Voyages of the heart: Living an emotionally creative life.* New York: The Free Press.

Averill, J. R., & Thomas-Knowles, C. (1991). Emotional creativity. In K. T. Strongman (Ed.). *International review of studies on emotion* (Vol. 1). New York: Wiley.

Emerson, R. W. (1986). Self-reliance. In *The complete works of Emerson: Vol. 2. Essays.* New York: AMS Press. (Original work published 1841)

Gurney, E. (1884). What is an emotion? *Mind, 9*, 421–426.

James, W. (1884). What is an emotion? *Mind, 9*, 1–26.

James, W. (1890). *The principles of psychology* (2 vols.). New York: Holt.

James, W. (1955). *Pragmatism.* Cleveland: Merridian Books. (Original work published 1907).

James, W. (1961). *The varieties of religious experience.* New York: Collier Books. (Original work published 1902)

Levy, R. I. (1984). The emotions in comparative perspective. In K. R. Scherer & P. Ekman (Eds.), *Approaches to emotion* (pp. 397–412). Hillsdale, NJ: Erlbaum.

Lutz, C. A. (1988). *Unnatural emotions: Everyday sentiments on a Micronesian atoll and their challenge to Western theory.* Chicago: University of Chicago Press.

Mead, G. H. (1934). *Mind, self, and society.* Chicago: University of Chicago Press.

Morgan, C., & Averill, J. R. (1992). True feelings, the self, and authenticity: A psychosocial perspective. In D. D. Franks & V. Gecas (Eds.), *Social perspectives on emotion* (Vol. 1, pp. 95–124). Greenwich, CT: JAI Press.

Ortony, A., Clore, G. L., & Collins, A. (1988). *The cognitive structure of emotions.* Cambridge, England: Cambridge University Press.

Rosaldo, M. Z. (1980). *Knowledge and passion: Ilongot notions on self and social life.* Cambridge, England: Cambridge University Press.

Schachter, S. (1964). The interaction of cognitive and physiological determinants of emotional states. In L. Berkowitz (Ed.), *Advances in experimental social psychology* (Vol. 1, pp. 49–80). New York: Academic Press.

Shweder, R. A. (1985). Menstrual pollution, soul loss, and the comparative study of emotions. In A. Kleinman & B. Good. (Eds.), *Culture and depression* (pp. 182–215). Berkeley, CA: University of California Press.

Storm, C., & Storm, T. (1987). A taxonomic study of the vocabulary of emotions. *Journal of Personality and Social Psychology, 53*, 805–816.

Tomkins, S. S. (1962–1963). *Affect, imagery, consciousness* (2 vols.). New York: Springer Publishing.

Wallas, G. (1926). *The art of thought.* New York: Harcourt, Brace.

15

A PHENOMENOLOGICAL RESPONSE TO JAMES'S VIEW OF EMOTION

DAMIAN S. VALLELONGA

Anyone who investigates the field of emotion inevitably encounters the radical ambiguity of the language used to denote it. The English language, for example, uses three principal terms to refer to this domain: *feeling*, *affect*, and *emotion*. Although one might appreciate the denotative richness of English, there are a number of problems associated with the availability of several labels to denominate this phenomenon.

First of all, there is no consensus as to whether these terms are synonymous or not. Some authors (e.g., Izard, 1977; Meadows, 1975; Zajonc, 1980) appear at times to use all three interchangeably. Others distinguish among the three terms (e.g., Vallelonga, 1986) or between various pairs of the three (e.g., Buytendijk, 1962; Ewert, 1970; Izard, 1982; McDougall, 1928; Sartre, 1962; Shibles, 1974).

Second, each of these three terms has multiple referents. An example of this is the word, *feeling*, which is used variously in everyday life to refer to (a) opinions or beliefs, as in "I feel Gorbachev was a great leader;" (b) the affective impact of events or situations on us, as in "I feel ashamed of myself for failing;" (c) physical sensations, as in "I feel cold;" and (d) the hedonic quality of experiences, as in "That feels pleasant."

It is my own personal preference to use *affect* to denote the overall domain rather than either *feeling* or *emotion*. Feeling has a long etymological association with touch, sensation, and the physiological dimension, whereas emotion has a similar long association both with physiological arousal and motivated action. Affect more neutrally conveys the meaning of simply being influenced or impacted on by circumstances. Nevertheless, precisely because of differences among authors in preferences regarding the usage of these terms, one must be careful in reading the literature to ascertain their concrete referents. The literature on emotion cannot be read uncritically; it must be *exegeted* (to borrow a term from biblical studies).

Furthermore, I would posit that the very ambiguity of the affect–feeling–emotion phenomenon has occasioned many of the ongoing disagreements in the emotion literature. However, rather than argue, as James and his opponents did, over whether or not the physiological events or their awareness constitutes the emotion, I suggest that this very ambiguity offers a way to integrate the various opposing positions into a synthesis or more comprehensive understanding of the feeling–affect–emotion phenomenon. I propose that this ambiguity is itself a clue to that essential character of the phenomenon that we have overlooked, that is, its *multidimensionality*.

The problem with most, if not all, of the extant theories of emotion (including James's) is that they are reductionistic to one extent or another. They all constrict the total phenomenon to one or two or, occasionally, three of its constituent dimensions. These theorists (like the six blind men of Indostan in John Godfrey Saxe's poem, 1948) do not stand back far enough, so to speak, to be able to embrace the total phenomenon within their view. I suggest that the only way to take such a panoramic view is to focus, not on decontextualized and atemporal events within the person, but on certain person–world interactions as they unfold within a particular situation across some portion of time. That focal field, which alone is broad enough to disclose the total phenomenon, is what I call the *affective situation*, rather than either affect, feeling, or emotion. Only from the perspective of this affective situation, can one grasp the several dimensions that make up the complete phenomenon denominated variously by the terms, affect, feeling, and emotion.

Having said this much in preface, what remains is to sketch out the five dimensions that constitute the affective situation. These five dimensions are (a) the appetitive, (b) the cognitive, (c) the feeling or corporeally based, (d) the inchoate conative, and (e) the dialectical.

THE APPETITIVE DIMENSION

The basic dimension that underlies all the others and makes possible the occurrence of affects or emotions is the *appetitive dimension*. This is the dimension of values or desires or what phenomenologists are wont to call *projects*. Unless one values, desires, or wants something, one cannot be affected or undergo emotion. Without the appetitive dimension, one can experience physiological sensations or neutral cognitions, but not affects or emotions. We are affected by what matters to us, even if only on the vital or biological level. Buddha recognized this when he taught that desire (*tanha*) is the source of suffering (*dukkha*) (Rahula, 1974). Likewise, common wisdom has captured this truth in the saying, "He who expects nothing, shall never be disappointed." What these beliefs overlook, however, is that desiring or valuing is also the source of joy and not just of suffering. In other words, it founds the occurrence of the positive emotions or affects and not just of the negative ones.

Many of the theorists of emotion implicitly recognize this truth, that is, that affects or emotions are founded on values or desires. Unfortunately, they do not explicitly integrate it into their theoretical conceptualizations. James was one of these theorists.

Thus, in the *Principles* (1890), in a section on self-feelings, James discussed pride and shame and, in effect, said that they depend on the self one chooses to be. He stated "Our thought incessantly deciding which one for it shall be realities, here chooses one of many possible selves or characters, and forthwith reckons it no shame to fail in any of those not adopted expressly as its own" (p. 310). He went on to say the following: "I, who for the time have staked my all on being a psychologist, am mortified if others know much more psychology than I. But I am contented to wallow in the grossest ignorance of Greek. My deficiencies there give me no sense of personal humiliation at all" (p. 310). In effect, James was asserting that the experiences of pride and shame depend on the success or failure of the self-projects we value and adopt, that is, on who we want to be.

James's understanding of the relevance of the appetitive dimension (i.e., of values and desires) to the affective event came out also in his assertion that our self-esteem is a product of a ratio between our success and our pretensions (p. 310). For James, thus, our experiences of shame or pride are a matter of the relation between what we want (our pretensions) and what is or what occurs (our success). This is a profound insight and applicable to the entire range of affects and emotions and not just to what James called the *self-feelings*. Unfortunately, James never integrated this insight into his theory of emotions. He defined emotion too narrowly to permit the integration of the appetitive and feeling (or corporeally based) dimensions.

Of all the theorists of emotion, however, the one who seems to have come the closest to explicitly acknowledging the role of the appetitive dimension in constituting the affective event is Hillman. He stated, "Through the feeling function we appreciate a situation, a person, an object, a moment in terms of value. A prerequisite for feeling is therefore . . . a set of values, to which the event can be related" (1970, p. 127). In an earlier work (1960), he also declared that "emotion cognizes values" (p. 191) and indicated that "a concept of love or desire has been put forward time and again as the single root of all emotions" (p. 160).

Others have alluded to this dimension. Thus, Arnold (1970) described McDougall's conception of certain emotions as "reactions to experienced success or failure of any desire or striving" (p. 170). Likewise, Tronick (1989), describing emotion in infants, made the point that "infants, like all other creatures, have a multiplicity of goals" (p. 113) and that their emotional states are a product of their evaluations as to whether they are succeeding in accomplishing those goals.

Despite these insights, few if any theorists have explicitly acknowledged the role of the appetitive dimension in making possible the occurrence of the affective event.

THE COGNITIVE DIMENSION

The core of the affective situation is co-constituted by two tightly integrated dimensions: the cognitive and the feeling or corporeally based dimensions. It is my position that these two dimensions constitute a unitary felt-perception. Although they can be logically distinguished, they are psychologically integrated, at least in phenomenal experience. I will first discuss each of them separately, and later, I will again address their essential integration in experience.

The cognitive dimension of the affective event (which is the core of the affective situation) consists of the perception or intuitive grasp of the vicissitudes of our values, desires, or projects. It is a perception (but *not* necessarily a thematically aware perception) of how our desires or projects (or the things that matter to us) are faring in any particular situation or circumstance. It is the perception or intuitive grasp of the personal relevance of situations or circumstances, that is, of the relevance of situations and circumstances to the achievement or maintenance of our personal desires or projects. The affects or emotions are the felt-perceptions of the ratio between what one wants and what is (or, as James put it, the ratio between our success or failure and our pretensions). Hillman (1970) put it succinctly when he declared that "feeling tells us how things are with us" (p. 128).

Positive affects or emotions are the felt–perceptions of the congruence between circumstances and situations and our desires or projects (i.e., of their faring well or of their fulfillment). Negative affects or emotions, on the other hand, are the felt–perceptions of the discrepancy between circumstances and situations and our desires or projects (i.e., of their faring poorly or of their failure).

It is important to note at this juncture, however, in response to Zajonc's point regarding the relation between the cognitive and the affective, that this perception can be completely unthematic. It is not necessarily an act of thematic consciousness or discursive or worded consciousness. That is what is intended by also characterizing this dimension as an intuitive event. Solomon (1976) supported this understanding when he characterized emotions as judgments that are "undeliberated, unarticulated and unreflective" (p. 192).

This dimension has by no means been overlooked by James or other theorists of emotion. Even though James declared that emotion is the feeling of the bodily changes as they occur, he also indicated that these "bodily changes follow directly the perception of the exciting fact" (1890, p. 449). James, thus, was aware of the cognitive aspect of this event. He simply did not integrate it into emotion on an equal footing with the feeling of the bodily changes. Shibles said that "James' theory seems to reduce emotions to only one factor in emotion," but is, in fact, "a covert cognitive theory of emotion" (p. 123).

Most of the theories of emotion can be characterized as cognitive ones. Thus, Leeper (1970) described emotions as "perceptual processes" that have "definite cognitive content" (p. 156); whereas Arnold characterized emotion as an "immediate intuitive estimate" and as an "appraisal of 'good or bad for me' " (p. 174).

Similarly, Shibles (1974) stated "Knowledge precedes emotion or feeling in many ways. To fear an object implies that we know about it and assess it in a certain way" (p. 54). He also declared, "One's emotional reaction *is* how one sees a situation" (p. 55) and "cognition is part of emotion" (p. 127).

Solomon made similar observations. He said that our emotions are "dependent upon our opinions and beliefs" and declared that "an emotion is an evaluative (or a 'normative') judgment, a judgment about my situation" (p. 187).

Likewise, Lazarus, Averill, and Opton (1970) spoke of a person "as an evaluating organism, one who searches his environment for cues about what he needs and wants, and evaluates each stimulus as to its personal relevance and significance. Emotions should be recognized as a function of such cognitive activity" (p. 217).

Finally, Tronick declared that even "infants process information about their current state in relation to their goal" (p. 113), and went on to say that "an evaluation by the infant that the goal is being accomplished results in a positive emotional state—joy or interest. . . . When the infant's evaluation is that the goal is not being accomplished, the infant experiences negative emotions" (p. 113).

THE FEELING OR CORPOREALLY BASED DIMENSION

This dimension consists in the felt aspects or qualities of the perception or intuition. It is mediated by what James called the *organic reverberations* to the perception of the exciting fact and is similar to what he called the emotion.

I was originally inclined to call this dimension the *corporeal* or *physiological* dimension until I realized that the events that are referred to by it are not just events in the body or physiological events, but are experiential ones as well or events in consciousness, even if not necessarily thematic or reflective consciousness. The feeling is an experiential event that is based on the whole complex of corporeal and physiological events (whether of the peripheral or central kind) that accompany the perception or intuition. These physiological events mediate the experience of the perception or intuition as pleasant or unpleasant, as constrictive or expansive, or as uplifting or depressive. James, too, was clear that what he called emotion (and what I am calling feeling or the feeling dimension) is not the bodily changes in themselves, but the awareness or experience of these bodily changes. To wit, James said that it is "our feeling of the same changes as they occur" that "IS the emotion" (1890, p. 449).

There is no doubt that this feeling dimension is essential to the affective event. The problem is that several theorists, including James, conceived of it as the affective event in isolation from the perception or intuition with which it forms a unitary reality. Neither the organic reverberations nor the awareness of them are decontextualized events. Both occur in the context of and simultaneously with certain perceptions. They are the way in which certain situations (i.e., the ones with relevance to one's personal projects) are perceived. As Hillman said, "Emotion signifies the value of objects. As such it is a way of perceiving, a way of knowing" (1960, p. 188).

Again, what James and others overlooked is that the cognitive and corporeally based dimensions interpenetrate in phenomenal experience as a unitary event—that is, as a felt–perception. The unitary character of this felt–perception corresponds to the unitary character of the human person as a *body–subject* (as the phenomenologists call it). James split the unitary felt–perception in two in order to emphasize the physiological involvement in the affective event as well as in the life of consciousness. Unfortunately, like Descartes's "res cogitans" and "res extensa," once they are split, it is difficult to put them back together.

The feeling and the perceiving that make up the unitary felt–perception are very much like Aristotle's matter and form. They are both essential principles or constituents of all objects, but neither exists without the other. They are co-constituents of real objects. Thus, without the feeling or corporeally based component, the perception would be, as James pointed out, a cold, neutral cognition and not an affect or emotion. Likewise, experienced physical arousal, as Schachter's and Singer's (1962) experiments cogently suggested, makes no sense and is not experienced as any particular emotion or affect without a context to inform it, that is, without the perception of a state of affairs that matters to us.

To illustrate the point, without the perception of a potential or actual negative exposure of oneself to another, a facial flush is simply a flush and not a blush. To undergo a flush in itself is not to feel embarrassed. Thus, the perceived personal meaning of situations is like Aristotle's form, and the experienced bodily reverberations or resonance are like Aristotle's matter. Together, they make up the felt–perception that is the core of the affective or emotional event. Affects or emotions, thus, are neither feelingless cognitions nor cognitionless feelings, but are felt–cognitions. With them, we simultaneously grasp the personal meaning of situations and are grasped by it.

The domain of affects or emotions and that of cognitions are not mutually exclusive. They overlap. Affects or emotions also entail cognitions—even if only prethematic, intuitive, and unworded ones. Likewise, they affect us feelingly precisely because they entail a physiological resonance and because they are cognitions regarding matters about which we care.

THE INCHOATE CONATIVE DIMENSION

The fourth dimension of the affective situation is the inchoate conative dimension. It consists in the experience of an impulse or tendency to do something (usually not clearly specified) about the just-perceived state of affairs relative to our desires or projects. In negative affects or emotions, it consists in the experience of an impulse to undo or end in some way the pain or discomfort of the feelingly perceived discrepancy between circumstances and desires. In positive affects and emotions, it consists in the experience of an impulse to continue or expand in some way the pleasantness of the feelingly perceived congruence between circumstances and desires.

I call this the *inchoate* conative dimension to highlight that what is entailed, is not necessarily some actual behavior, but rather an impulse or experienced vector inclining us toward such behavior or action.

James was cognizant of this dimension as well, even though, as with the appetitive and cognitive dimensions, he did not explicitly integrate it with the feeling dimension to produce a more comprehensive view of the affective event. Thus, James spoke of certain events as exciting in us both "emotions and *tendencies to action* [italics added]" (1890, p. 320). Likewise, he asked, "Can anyone fancy the state of rage and picture no ebullition in the chest, no flushing of the face. . . , no *impulses to vigorous action* [italics added]?" (1890, p. 452).

Other theorists have also acknowledged the incipient motivational thrust inherent in the affective event. Most prominent among these theorists is Arnold (1970) who defined emotion as a "felt tendency to action based on appraisal" (p. 178). She also described it as "an immediate intuitive estimate which inevitably produces an impulse to action" and as an "appraisal of 'good or bad for me' " that produces "an impulse toward or away from the thing appraised" (p. 174).

Likewise, Arieti (1970) said of feelings and affects that they "become motivational factors because the awareness of what is pleasant elicits behavior aimed at searching for or retaining pleasure. On the other hand, the awareness of what is unpleasant elicits behavior which tends to avoid or discontinue the experience" (p. 136). Even Tronick (1989) alluded to this dimension in his characterization of infant emotion as entailing an evaluation that the infant uses "to guide actions aimed at accomplishing their goal" (p. 113).

THE DIALECTICAL DIMENSION

The last dimension constituting the affective situation is the dialectical dimension. It consists in the experience of certain pulls or vectors toward undergoing spontaneous correlative transformations of the meaning of one's past, present, or future self or world as a result of what one has just feelingly perceived. In other words, each affect or emotion entails pulls toward undergoing correlative modes of being feelingly affected.

Thus, in being affected, it is not just our bodies that are changed in the perception of certain personally significant situations. Our mode of living the past and the future is also changed (i.e., our memories along with our hopes and expectations are also changed). In addition, our stance toward our self and world also changes.

An illustration of this can be found in my phenomenological investigation (1986) of being embarrassed and being ashamed of oneself. In being ashamed of oneself, one feelingly perceives oneself as the kind of person one does not want to be or must not be. This perception has a painful quality to it and is tinged with a certain felt distaste for or disgust with the self. One also experiences the impulse to hide or escape from this distasteful self or to change it into something more palatable. In this felt–perception, thus, one lives a negative transformation of one's present self. That negative transformation dialectically evokes a correlative negative transformation of one's present world or environment, which in being ashamed is lived as the correlative experience of being self conscious or being embarrassed, that is, as the experience that others are potentially or actually seeing this negative self and disesteeming it. Likewise, these negative transformations of one's present self and world call forth correlative negative transformations of one's past self or world and future self or world. Thus, the negative transformation of one's future world is lived as the experience of being anxious in the face of anticipated rejection or harm. Likewise, the negative transformation of one's past self is lived as the experience of being disillusioned in oneself and the belief that one has been a phony. These correlative pulls are the ties that bind together our affective moments into a meaningful but complicated tapestry.

No author, besides myself, has articulated the role of this dialectical dimension as an essential constituent of the affective situation. Arieti, however, alluded to it when he said, "The loss has been sustained. Indeed, not only the present but the future seems affected by this loss. Whatever happened to make the individual feel depressed seems to him to have an impact on the future, too" (1970, pp. 140–141).

Only in grasping the interrelation of these five dimensions can one grasp the structure and complexity of the affective event and the affective situation as a gestalt. Although James was aware of four of the five dimensions, he failed to integrate them explicitly into a meaningful larger reality. James and other theorists of emotion mistook a part for the whole and, thus, like John Godfrey Saxe's six blind men of Indostan,

> Though each was partly in the right,
> And all were in the wrong!" (1948, p. 42)

REFERENCES

Arieti, S. (1970). Cognition and feeling. In M. B. Arnold (Ed.), *Feelings and emotions: The Loyola symposium* (pp. 135–143). New York: Academic Press.

Arnold, M. B. (1970). Perennial problems in the field of emotion. In M. B. Arnold (Ed.), *Feelings and emotions: The Loyola symposium* (pp. 169–185). New York: Academic Press.

Buytendijk, F. J. J. (1962). The phenomenological approach to the problem of feelings and emotions. In H. M. Ruitenbeek (Ed.), *Psychoanalysis and existential philosophy* (pp. 155–178). New York: Dutton.

Ewert, O. (1970). The attitudinal character of emotion. In M. B. Arnold (Ed.), *Feelings and emotions: The Loyola symposium* (pp. 233–240). New York: Academic Press.

Hillman, J. (1960). *Emotion: A comprehensive phenomenology of theories and their meanings for therapy.* London: Routledge & Kegan Paul.

Hillman, J. (1970). C. G. Jung's contributions to "feelings and emotions": Synopsis and implications. In M. B. Arnold (Ed.), *Feelings and emotions: The Loyola symposium* (pp. 125–134). New York: Academic Press.

Izard, C. E. (1977). *Human emotions.* New York: Plenum.

Izard, C. E. (1982). Comments on emotion and cognition: Can there be a working relationship? In M. S. Clark & S. T. Fisher (Eds.), *Affect and cognition.* Hillsdale, NJ: Erlbaum.

James, W. (1890). *The principles of psychology* (2 vols.). New York: Holt.

Lazarus, R. S., Averill, J. R., & Opton, E. M., Jr. (1970). Towards a cognitive theory of emotion. In M. B. Arnold (Ed.), *Feelings and emotions: The Loyola symposium* (pp. 135–143). New York: Academic Press.

Leeper, R. W. (1970). The motivational and perceptual properties of emotions as indicating their fundamental character and role. In M. B. Arnold (Ed.), *Feelings and emotions: The Loyola symposium* (pp. 151–163). New York: Academic Press.

McDougall, W. (1928). Emotion and feeling distinguished. In M. L. Reymert (Ed.), *Feelings and emotions.* Worcester, MA: Clark University Press.

Meadows, C. M. (1975). The phenomenology of joy: An empirical investigation. *Psychological Reports, 37,* 39–54.

Rahula, W. (1974). *What the Buddha taught* (2nd ed.). New York: Grove Press.

Sartre, J.-P. (1962). *Sketch for a theory of the emotions* (P. Mairet, Trans.). London: Methuen. (Original work published 1939)

Saxe, J. G. (1948). The blind men and the elephant. In L. Untermeyer (Ed.), *An anthology of the New England poets from colonial times to the present day.* (p. 42). New York: Random House. (Original work published 1861)

Schachter, S., & Singer, J. (1962). Cognitive, social and physiological determinants of emotional state. *Psychological Review, 69,* 379–399.

Shibles, W. (1974). *Emotion: The method of philosophical therapy.* Whitewater, WI: Language Press.

Solomon, R. C. (1976). *The passions.* Garden City, NY: Anchor Press/Doubleday.

Tronick, E. Z. (1989). Emotions and emotional communication in infants. *American Psychologist, 44*, 112–119.

Vallelonga, D. S. (1986). *The lived structures of being-embarrassed and being-ashamed-of-oneself: An empirical phenomenological study.* Unpublished doctoral dissertation, Duquesne University, Pittsburgh.

Zajonc, R. B. (1980). Feeling and thinking: Preferences need no inferences. *American Psychologist, 35*, 151–175.

16

A STUDY OF EMOTION
IN THE CONTEXT OF
RADICAL EMPIRICISM

WAYNE VINEY

Throughout his life, William James was deeply interested in the place of emotion in the world of experience. James's early article (1884/1983), "What is an Emotion?" which was later incorporated into *The Principles of Psychology* (1890), is only the beginning of James's work on a topic that, according to Myers (1986), "commanded more interest than any of his other psychological contributions" (p. 215). Indeed, the extensive interest and criticism generated by the 1884 article prompted James (1894/1983) to revisit the subject under the title, "The Physical Basis of Emotion." This paper clarified and amplified the original statement, responded to critics, and marshaled evidence in support of the theory.

James's first philosophical work, *The Will to Believe* (1897/1979), returned to the topic with special reference to the emotional effects of expectation. James's continuing interest in emotion is evident in his *Talks to Teachers on Psychology* (1899/1983) where he spoke of the value of emotions and offered practical suggestions for their control. James's treatment of emotion in *The Varieties of Religious Experience* (1902/1985), as correctly noted by James Averill in this volume, placed emphasis on the crucial role of emotions in belief systems. James's interest, however, did not stop there. He repeatedly returned to the subject of emotion in works published after the *Varieties*. For example, his article on the mental effects of earthquakes (James, 1906/1983) described the paradoxical emotions he experienced during the famous 1906 San Francisco Earthquake. The topics of affect and emotion are recurring themes in James's posthumously published *Essays in Radical Empiricism* (1912/1976), and he discussed "the stream of feeling" in his book, *Some Problems of Philosophy* (1911/1979). Thus, James the philosopher was as interested in emotion as James the psychologist. Indeed, I will argue that James's approach to emotion is understood only in the context of his larger philosophical vision. Any account of James on emotion, based exclusively on early publications such as the 1884 article or the 1894 paper may amount to little more than a caricature.

In response to the chapters on emotion in this volume, I sketch some of the insights that James, the mature philosopher, brought to this field of study. Next, I will explore how those insights might articulate with selected modern developments. I will now turn to some of the marks of James's philosophical vision and their implications for the role of emotion in experience.

First, James embraced a thoroughgoing methodological pluralism. In his paper, "The Physical Basis of Emotion," James (1894/1983) expressed regret about the contradictory findings that came out of introspective studies on emotion, and he welcomed methods that provide "a more objective sort of umpire" (p. 310). He even suggested the possibility that a more objective method was already available in his day and that the method was highly relevant to his theory. Referring to cases of generalized anesthesia, James (1894/1983) noted that "if a patient could be found who, in spite of being anaesthetic inside and out, could still suffer emotion, my case would be upset" (p. 310). He made the same point in his article, "What is an Emotion?" where he wrote, "The persistence of strong emotional feeling in such a case would completely overthrow our case" (James, 1884/1983, p. 184). James was deeply aware of the methodological problems associated with the study of hysterical anesthesia or hypnotically induced anesthesia. The types of anesthesia induced by injuries are also problematic because there are often degrees of visceral and muscular innervation left intact. James was intrigued by the case of a middle-aged man who suffered extensive anesthesia, but who could talk with difficulty. The man claimed to be indifferent to interests, likes and dislikes, love and hate. He did, however, feel a "stroke in the stomach" when his wife walked into his room, and he expressed fears about the welfare of his daughter (see James, 1894/1983, p. 312). James saw the case as largely supportive of his theory, but he also recognized its limitations. He would have been keenly interested in the induction of acute pharmocological paralysis and the possible implications of studies using such techniques for his theory.

In his search for an ever "more objective sort of umpire" James welcomed objective observation, but he also based some of his thought on introspective studies. Indeed, it was his own introspections that led him to raise questions about the existence of a *mind-stuff emotion* or an emotion that is completely bodiless. James was also a pioneer in phenomenological studies of emotion and, as a process philosopher, he would have shared Virginia Demos's enthusiasm in this volume for developmental approaches. He would have been no less impressed with the explosion of knowledge about emotions coming out of the neurosciences. James would undoubtedly have enjoyed the diversity of late-twentieth-century psychology. He repeatedly and emphatically referred to himself as a pluralist (James, 1909/1975, 1909/1977, 1912/1976). He also defined philosophical study as "the habit of always seeing an alternative" (James, 1876, p. 178).

A second implication for the study of emotion encountered in James's mature philosophical work also grows out of his pluralism. Paradoxically, one of the advantages of a Jamesian brand of pluralism is that it permits, even encourages, a quest for unities. As an all-form philosophy, monism denies any theoretic disconnectedness. Pluralism, as a more moderate philosophy, accepts a great deal of connection in the world. It is not defeated when unities and connections are discovered, but monism is defeated if there are genuine nonconductors. As a pluralist, James was free to search for unities and, where emotion was concerned, he embarked on a passionate quest for the unity of mind and body. Nevertheless, as noted by Charlene Seigfried (1990), James refused "to allow the drive toward harmony to erode the legitimacy of particular angles of vision" (p. 116).

James's search for unity in this arena was partly a protest against primarily descriptive psychologies that did little more than make long lists of the shades and varieties of feelings and emotions. He did not believe that such lists, however ingeniously devised, advanced the discipline of psychology. According to Myers (1986), "The issue that dominated James's thinking was to define emotion" (p. 216). This definition attempted a marriage of psychological and biological events, if only in a narrowly defined arena. In the mature philosophy, neither set of events could be more basic or fundamental if the terms from each are clearly definable in terms drawn from experience. James called attention to the narrowness of the unity he sought. He was dealing primarily with strong feelings of excitement occurring when "a wave of bodily disturbance of some kind accompanies the perception" (James, 1884/1983, p. 169). James's pluralism clearly encouraged integrative efforts, although his preference was for the search for modest unities in limited domains. He had a deep suspicion of grand unities in which everything is supposedly related to everything else.

A third implication for the study of emotion found in James's philosophy is encountered in his rejection of any all-encompassing reductionism.

Myers (1986) pointed out that James was not denying "causality to emotions by downgrading them to epiphenomena. In connecting emotion and instinct, he meant not only to corroborate but to deepen the common sense assumption that human behavior is constantly the effect of human emotion" (pp. 226–227). James's larger philosophical vision always stood opposed to concepts marked by expressions and words such as *nothing but, all,* and *every.* The chapter in the *Varieties,* entitled "Religion and Neurology," is a classic statement reflecting James's deep opposition to reductionism. To be sure, he was enthusiastic about neurophysiological studies, but in his view, the error begins when the claim is made that a psychological process is nothing but neurophysiology. In that regard, James never did intend to say that emotion is nothing but a physiological process. James also drew attention to the genetic fallacy or the tendency to dismiss the legitimacy of a psychological claim because of the nature of its neurophysiological underpinnings.

In his 1894 article, "The Physical Basis of Emotion," James argued against those who viewed his theory of emotion as materialistic. He believed that his theory was born in introspection and, thus, had a solid empirical basis. It was not materialistic. The theory "assumes (what probably everyone assumes) that there must be a process of some sort in the nerve-centres for emotion, and it simply defines that process to consist of afferent currents" (James, 1894/1983, p. 306). James was often prepared to give temporary or practical privilege to a unique vantage point as he did in his theory of emotion, but as a radical empiricist, he repeatedly returned to experience. Experience itself is radically pluralistic. It inevitably accentuates alternative organizations, and James was willing to give each one a fair hearing.

A fourth characteristic of James's mature philosophical vision is that it elevates the centrality of emotion in human experience and, therefore, in psychology. Emotion is elevated because it is involved even in our higher order beliefs. In *Essays in Radical Empiricism,* James (1912/1976) pointed out that "all of us have feelings [and] they may be as prophetic and anticipatory of truth as anything else we have, and some of them more so than others . . . all philosophies are hypotheses, to which all our faculties, emotional as well as logical, help us" (p. 143). James's view of the roles of the affective and emotional dimensions was underscored when he declared that we should "frankly confess to each other the motives of our several faiths. I frankly confess mine—I cannot but think that at bottom they are of an aesthetic and not of a logical sort" (James, 1912/1976, p. 142).

Barzun (1983) called attention to the fact that, for James, there is a fringe of feelings around each object of thought and that "mind and emotion, head and heart, are not contending parties" (p. 65). A careful reading of the *Principles* and the later philosophical works shows that James recognized the artificiality of sharp distinctions between emotion and thinking. Each was parasitic on the other. Emotions are laden with a fringe of thought, and thought is laden with a fringe of emotions. Even rationality, James described as a sentiment and the mark of the transition from puzzle to solution as "full of lively relief and pleasure" (James, 1897/1979, p. 57). Emotion, for James, is not an isolated process, it is woven into the stream of experience as a part of everything else.

A fifth and final insight that James, as a mature philosopher, brought to the study of emotion is related to his view of experience. Experience itself, the lived world, is James's metaphysical ultimate. One of the most central features of experience is that it is a process. In *Essays in Radical Empiricism*, James (1912/1976) declared that "our fields of experience have no more definite boundaries than have our fields of view. Both are fringed forever by a *more* that continually develops and that continuously supercedes them as life proceeds" (p. 35). Such a view of experience argues against the possibility of capturing phenomena in their wholeness. Reality itself, according to James, is dynamic, growing, changing, and full of real novelty. He once asked a difficult and compelling question. Quoting the author Benjamin Paul Blood, he asked, "What has concluded that we might conclude in regard to it?" (James, 1910/1978, p. 190).

Even if reality were not growing, if it were static and respectable, James would have been curious about the epistemological grounds that would warrant the big claim. For his part, he was content to discover truth or rather truths with a small *t* and he was suspicious of those who claimed to see the whole. Drawing from the story of the blind subjects and the elephant, in John Godfrey Saxe's poem, which Damian Vallelonga used in the last chapter, James would have accorded generous space for the claims of each of the blind subjects exploring the elephant. He would then have encouraged each participant to try a different vantage point. It is conceivable that, after trying many vantage points, they might have achieved a unified account of what the elephant is, but that would have come about only through the excellence of their empirical work. If a unified account did surface, James would accord it only provisional status.

JAMES AND MODERN DEVELOPMENTS IN EMOTION

The chapters in this book illustrate the extreme diversity of ongoing research and theory in contemporary studies of emotion. James would have applauded the diversity because it gives birth to ideas. He would also have applauded the increased repertoire of methodologies noted by E. Virginia Demos. The materials I have presented thus far have already included some comments on various points raised by the other authors. A few additional comments are now in order.

First, modern studies demonstrating emotional effects of central stimulation to the brain (e.g., Olds & Milner, 1954; Stellar & Stellar, 1985) appear superficially, at least, to deliver a death blow to James's theory. If a weak electrical stimulus applied to the lateral hypothalamus produces pleasure why is that not powerful evidence against the somatic theory? Commenting on this problem, A. C. Papanicolaou (1989) pointed out that artificial impulses delivered to the brain "echo well beyond the target area to which they are delivered" (p. 117). When human subjects receive artificial stimulation to the brain, they sometimes report tingling sensations in many other parts of their bodies, often contralateral to the area of the brain, stimulated. Commenting on studies on central stimulation, Papanicolaou argued that "no evidence is now available indicating that the body is not a necessary condition of emotion . . . reports of affect, when detailed, are also reports of somatic sensations (p. 127).

On another topic, James would be particularly interested in Tomkins's notion that fear is triggered by the rate of change of the provoking stimulus. James was aware of the importance of the context of a stimulus, and he might have wondered how rate of change and context would interact. An anecdote illustrates the power of rate of change independent of context. A visitor to the Denver zoo recently presented an image of complete relaxation, even defiance, as he placed himself somewhat ostentatiously next to a glass wall separating observers by a few inches from the underground polar bear pool. A large polar bear was submerged immediately on the other side of the glass seemingly oblivious to her visitor, who was now posturing as if to convey some special virtue of bravery in his close proximity to the large animal. Then in an unbelievably lightning-like move, the bear slapped her giant paw at the glass with an enormous force. Context was completely trumped by rate of change and, to the joy of the crowd, the once secure visitor was appropriately downsized by his startled response and leap backward. James linked instinct and emotion and would most assuredly have been friendly to the idea that many affect mechanisms are governed by innate programs. He never denied that emotional behavior was linked to strong stimuli. The man saw the bear and jumped. After the jump, he was undoubtedly feeling emotion.

Averill's chapter presented the most direct challenge to James's early theory. If James were here, he would find it amusing that Papanicolaou's new book, *Emotion: A Reconsideration of the Somatic Theory* (1989), found James's peripheral theory to be the one most consistent with modern clinical and experimental data. James would, however, appreciate Averill's recognition of the additional vantage points he introduced in the *Varieties*. I think James would agree that emotional expression cannot be understood apart from the sense of self and interpersonal and social relations. Such a position is entirely consistent with James's radical empiricism. He would find it most unfortunate if his privileging of a particular vantage point had somehow blocked other approaches. That goes against everything in the Jamesian spirit.

Several tales of Edgar Allan Poe, such as "The Premature Burial," "Ligeia," and "Loss of Breath," reveal Poe's fear of being buried alive. In his day, it was apparently not a completely unrealistic fear. My fear is that if we attempt to bury James's theory of emotion, as proposed by Averill, we might be burying something that is very much alive. A modest counterproposal is that we seek an integration of James's psychological and philosophical work in an attempt to capture a newer and broader, radically empirical theory of emotions.

REFERENCES

Barzun, J. (1983). *A stroll with William James*. New York: Harper & Row.

James, W. (1876, September 21). The teaching of philosophy in our colleges. *The Nation*, pp. 178–179.

James, W. (1890). *The principles of psychology* (2 Vols.). New York: Holt.

James, W. (1975). *The meaning of truth*. Cambridge, MA: Harvard University Press. (Original work published 1909)

James, W. (1976). *Essays in radical empiricism*. Cambridge, MA: Harvard University Press. (Original work published 1912)

James, W. (1977). *A pluralistic universe*. Cambridge, MA: Harvard University Press. (Original work published 1909)

James, W. (1978). A pluralistic mystic. *Essays in philosophy* (pp. 172–190). Cambridge, MA: Harvard University Press. (Original work published 1910)

James, W. (1979). *Some problems of philosophy*. Cambridge, MA: Harvard University Press. (Original work published 1911)

James, W. (1979). *The will to believe*. Cambridge, MA: Harvard University Press. (Original work published 1897)

James, W. (1983). The physical basis of emotion. *Essays in psychology* (pp. 299–314). Cambridge, MA: Harvard University Press. (Original work published 1894)

James, W. (1983). On some mental effects of the earthquake. *Essays in psychology* (pp. 331–338) Cambridge, MA: Harvard University Press. (Original work published 1906)

James, W. (1983). *Talks to teachers on psychology: And to students on some of life's ideals*. Cambridge, MA: Harvard University Press. (Original work published 1899)

James, W. (1983). What is an emotion? *Essays in psychology* (pp. 168–187) Cambridge, MA: Harvard University Press. (Original work published 1884)

James, W. (1985). *The varieties of religious experience*. Cambridge, MA: Harvard University Press. (Original work published 1902)

Myers, G. E. (1986). *William James: His life and thought*. New Haven, CT: Yale University Press.

Olds, J., & Milner, P. (1954). Positive reinforcement produced by electrical stimulation of septal area and other regions of rat brain. *The Journal of Comparative and Physiological Psychology, 47*, 419–427.

Papanicolaou, A. C. (1989). *Emotion: A reconsideration of the somatic theory*. New York: Gordon and Breach Science Publishers.

Seigfried, C. (1990). Poetic invention and scientific observation: James's model of sympathetic concrete observation. *Transactions of the C. S. Peirce Society, 26*, 115–130.

Stellar, J. R., & Stellar, E. (1985). *The neurobiology of motivation and reward*. New York: Springer-Verlag.

VI

SELECTED TOPICS: MINING THE JAMESIAN LODE

17

WILLIAM JAMES AND GUSTAV FECHNER: FROM REJECTION TO ELECTIVE AFFINITY

HELMUT E. ADLER

When William James wrote *The Principles of Psychology* (1890/1981), he was very negative in his evaluation of Gustav Fechner's contribution to psychological measurement, and, in fact, was one of his severest critics. Yet it is a paradox in William James's life that his earlier unqualified rejection of Fechner's psychophysics later turned into enthusiastic support for Fechner's metaphysics.

What James discovered was the close affinity of his own philosophical approach to Fechner's wide-ranging speculations. It is customary to divide Fechner's work into two phases: his empirical and mathematical studies, which laid the foundation of experimental psychology, and his philosophical writings, which contained what can best be described as his *Weltanschauung* (see Myers, 1986; Sprung & Sprung, 1978). For Fechner, these distinctions did not exist; to him, psychophysics grew out of the philosophical roots of his treatment of the mind–body relationship, as exemplified by the fact that the outline of psychophysics first appeared in the decidedly philosophical *Zend-Avesta* of 1851, 9 years before publication of the *Elements of Psychophysics* (1860/1966).

Although James never met Fechner who was 41 years older than himself, they shared a number of background factors. Both were the product of families in which the father or his surrogate—an uncle in the case of Fechner—was interested in religion. William James's father was devoted to Swedenborgianism, a mystic Protestant sect. Fechner was the son of a Lutheran minister and, after his father's early death, was brought up by his uncle, who was also a minister. They both developed their own individualistic religious convictions. Fechner's *Zend Avesta* and James's *Varieties of Religious Experience* (1902) express the iconoclastic mysticism in their approach to religion.

Similarly, both Fechner and James were plagued by health problems. Fechner had injured his eyes in early experiments on visual afterimages. He developed severe symptoms of photophobia, as well as other symptoms and, in 1840, had to resign his position as professor of physics at Leipzig University. He retired on his pension and after his recovery, in 1843, returned to lecture at the university, but only on a part-time basis and on subjects that interested him.

James also had problems with his eyes as the result of smallpox that he contracted in Rio de Janeiro, Brazil, on a collecting trip in which he accompanied Louis Agassiz in 1865. On his return to Boston, he also found himself the victim of severe back pain. He went off to Germany, seeking a cure, but although his eyesight improved, his back did not. In 1870, he went into a deep depression. His recovery was miraculously initiated by reading an essay on free will by the French philosopher, Charles Renuvier, leading to his decision that his "first act of free will shall be to believe in free will" (Myers, 1986, p. 46).

Fechner and James also shared an interest in sensation and perception, but here there were fundamental differences. James approached sensations from a philosophical stance, whereas Fechner, whose approach was that of a physicist, looked for measurable characteristics. Fechner was able to measure simple sensations looking at them in isolation. Using the psychophysical methods described in his *Elements of Psychophysics* (Fechner, 1860/1966), he determined absolute and difference thresholds in several sense domains. He then proceeded to derive his psychophysical law, now known as *Fechner's law*. James disagreed strongly with Fechner's approach. He felt that sensations could not be elements that could be quantified. James called this assumption unjustified. Sensations were indivisible phenomena; they could not be summed or subtracted from each other.

James kept abreast with the developments of psychology in Europe. Although he did not agree with the technical details, he included them in his *Principles* in considerable detail. He wrote in the *Principles*,

> In 1860 Professor G. T. Fechner of Leipzig, a man of great learning
> and subtlety of mind, published two volumes entitled "Psychophysik,"

devoted to establishing and explaining a law called by him the psy-chophysik law, which he considered to express the deepest and most elementary relation between the mental and physical worlds. It is a formula for the connection between the amount of our sensations and the amount of their outward causes. Its simplest expression is, that when we pass from one sensation to a stronger one of the same kind, the sensations increase proportionally to the logarithms of their essential causes. (p. 504)

James had purchased his own copy of the *Elements of Psychophysics* in Berlin in 1867. He also had available to him the German literature, as well as such American reports as Charles S. Peirce's first American psychophys-ical experiment on the Bezold-Brücke effect, the apparent changes in hue with increased luminance (Cadwallader, 1974), and G. T. Ladd's full ac-count of psychophysical methods in his *Elements of Physiological Psychology* (1887). James was very skeptical about these developments from the start. In an article in the *Nation*, James (1876/1978) devoted to the teaching of philosophy, he wrote the following:

It is more than doubtful whether Fechner's "psychophysical law" (that sensation is proportional to the logarithm of the stimulus) is of any great *psychological* importance. . .There is indeed something touching in the helpless way in which Fechner's law is beginning to be hawked about, as it were, in popular philosophic literature, by writers who do not know in the least what to do with it, but who evidently feel persuaded that somehow or other it must be of tremendous import. (p. 6).

By the time the *Principles* appeared in 1890 James devoted considerable space to a full description of psychophysical methods, cited the *Massformel* (measurement formula), and added two methods not due to Fechner: Delboeuf's (1883) *equal appearing intervals* and Merkel's (1888) *ratio scaling*. These led to functions that differed from the logarithmic relationship pro-posed by Fechner. They both follow the *power law*, which, in essence, states that it is the sensation ratios that are proportional to stimulus ratios rather than magnitudes (See Adler, 1980). James did not comment on this dis-crepancy, either because he was not aware of it or because he ignored it. He liked Fechner's treatment of attention, discrimination, and perception. He also looked favorably at Fechner's notion of consciousness and the unconscious, but he was strongly opposed to Fechner's law and the whole idea of mental measurement. Sensations must be whole phenomena, not compounds, according to James. To quote *Psychology: Briefer Course* (1892/1984), also known as "Jimmy," James argued for the uniqueness of our sensations, "Our sensation of an electric arc-light. . . does not contain many smoky tallow candles in itself" (pp. 25–26). (This is concrete writing at its best.) But despite his negative opinion of the measurement of sensation, his private copy of the *Briefer Course* is annotated with the three psychophysical methods in German (eben mklh/mittlere fehler/falsch and richtige falle) (=just noticeable differences/average error/false and right cases=constant stimuli).

James's attack on Fechner's psychophysics in the *Principles* took the form of polemics—short on *facts*, but most appealing in their formulation. To quote a few, James wrote,

> Fechner's book was the starting point of a new department of literature, which would be perhaps impossible to match for the qualities of thoroughness and subtlety, but which in the humble opinion of the present writer, the proper psychological outcome is just *nothing*. (p. 504)

> The only amusing part of it is that Fechner's critics should always be bound, after smiting his theories hip and thigh and leaving not a stick of them standing, to wind up by saying nevertheless to him belongs the *imperishable glory* of first formulating them and thereby turning psychology into an exact science. (p. 518)

> But it would be terrible if even such a dear old man [Fechner had died in 1887] as this would saddle our Science forever with his patient whimseys, and, in a world so full of more nutritious objects of attention, compel all future students to plough through the difficulties not only of his own works, but of the still drier one written in his refutation. Those who desire this dreadful literature can find it. . ., but I will not even enumerate it in a footnote. (p. 518)

And James concluded his chapter on discrimination and comparison with this little poem:

> "And everybody praised the duke
> Who this great fight did win."
> "But what good came of it at last?"
> Quoth little Peterkin.
> "Why, that I cannot tell," said he,
> "but 'twas a famous victory!" (p. 518)[1]

Turning now to James's attitudes toward Fechner's philosophical writings, it is apparent that James had been aware of Fechner as early as 1870, when he wrote a letter to Henry Bowditch, who was later a professor of physiology at Harvard and then in Leipzig, thanking him for a picture of Fechner for his physiognomic collection (H. James, 1920). (Bowditch had

---

[1]From "The Battle of Blenheim" by Robert Southey (1774–1843).

allowed James's students, such as G. S. Hall, to work in his laboratory.) Hall himself wrote from Leipzig, where he spent some time with Wundt and lived next to the Fechners, in a letter dated December 27, 1876: "Fechner is a curiosity... He has forgotten all his *Psychophysik*; and is chiefly interested in theorizing how knots are tied in endless strings, and how words are written on the inner side of two slates sealed together" (Perry, 1936, Vol. 2, p. 18). The latter part referred to Fechner's interest in psychic phenomena, an interest shared by James.

Even in his attack on Fechner's theories in the *Principles*, James did not direct his polemics *ad hominem*. He praised Fechner, writing the following: "Fechner himself indeed was a German Gelehrter of the ideal type, at once simple and shrewd, a mystic and an experimentalist, homely and daring, and as loyal to facts as to his theories" (James, 1890/1981, p. 518).

James discovered his intellectual kinship with Fechner late in his career, when he returned to philosophy after the publication of the *Principles*. There were two major areas of affinity: Fechner's panpsychism and their shared interest in psychic phenomena. James was intrigued by Fechner's metaphysical scheme of attributing consciousness to the entire universe: The earth has its consciousness; so does the solar system; God is the consciousness of the totalized scheme. There is a parallel attribution of consciousness of a sort to the vegetable kingdom and in the world of inanimate matter. The current "Gaia" hypothesis (Lovelock, 1988) has much in common with Fechner's scheme.

By 1905, James had read Fechner's *Die Tagesansicht gegenüber der Nachtansicht* (1879) and *Über die Seelenfrage* (1861). In 1907, he read his own copy of *Zend-Avesta* in Chocorua[2]. The Hibbert Lectures at Oxford, the basis for *A Pluralistic Universe*, were given in 1908 and 1909. One lecture was devoted to Fechner (1909/1967). Fechner's *day view* (*Tagesansicht*, called *daylight view* by James) appealed to James. Here was a monistic idealism to oppose the materialistic mechanistic worldview of his day. He tried hard to make Fechner's complex scheme accessible to his audience. In the course of doing so, he revealed his admiration for Fechner the man, as well as for his theories. James wrote,

> (Fechner) was the pattern of the ideal german [*sic*] scholar, as daringly original in his thought as he was homely in his life, a modest, genial, laborious slave to truth and learning, and withal the owner of an admirable literary style of the vernacular sort. (1909/1967, p. 148)

James no longer criticized psychophysics and, instead, gave Fechner credit for having "practically founded scientific psychology." (1909/1967,

---

[2]James's summer home in New Hamphire.

p. 148). He liked Fechner's intense concreteness and the fertility of detail that he provided.

> For altho [sic] the type of reasoning he employs is almost childlike in its simplicity, and his bare conclusions can be written on a single page, the *power* of the man is due altogether to the profuseness of his concrete imagination, to the multitude of the points which he considers successively, to the cumulative effect of his learning, of his thoroughness, and of the ingenuity of his detail, to his admirably homely style, to the sincerity with which his pages glow, and finally to the impression he gives of a man who doesn't live at second hand, but who *sees*, who in fact speaks as one having authority, and not as if he were of the common herd of professional philosophers. (1909/1967, pp. 154–155)

In James's opinion: "few professional philosophers have any vision," (1909/1967, p. 165) in comparison to Fechner.

The second area of James's affinity to Fechner was their mutual interest in psychic phenomena. In the "Report on Mrs. Piper's Hodgson-Control"[3] in *Proceedings of the Society for Psychical Research* (1909/1961), James wrote,

> Fechner in his Zend-Avesta and elsewhere assumes that mental life and physical life run parallel, all memory-processes being, according to him, coordinated with material processes. If an act of yours is to be consciously remembered hereafter, it must leave traces on the material universe such that when the traced parts of said universe systematically enter into activity together, the act is consciously recalled. (p. 16)

James, here, followed Fechner's ideas, as expressed in *Zend-Avesta* and elsewhere. The traces left by every act on the material universe change the structure of the cosmos to some degree—however slight. After death, these traces remain. James (1909/1961) wrote the following:

> Now, just as the air of the same room can be simultaneously used by many different voices for communicating with different pairs of ears, or as the ether of space can carry many simultaneous messages to and from mutually attuned Marconi-stations [i.e., radio], so the great continuum of material nature can have certain tracts within it thrown into emphasized activity whenever activity begins in any part. . . in which the potentiality of such systematic activity inheres. The bodies (including of course the brains) of Hodgson's friends who come as sitters, are naturally parts of the material universe which carry some of the traces

---

[3]Richard Hodgson (1855–1905) was born in Australia and was secretary-treasurer of the American Society for Psychical Research. He had dropped dead while playing handball.

of his ancient acts. They function as receiving stations. . . If now, the *rest* of the system of physical traces left behind by Hodgson's acts were, by some mutual induction throughout its extent, thrown into gear and made to vibrate all at once, by the presence of such human bodies to the medium, we should have a Hodgson-system active in the cosmos again and the "conscious aspect" of this vibrating system might be Hodgson's spirit redivivus, and recollecting and willing in a certain momentary way. (pp. 208–209)

When James was asked to write "A Few Words of Introduction" to the 1904 translation by Mary C. Wadsworth of Fechner's *Little Book of Life after Death*, he gladly complied. In his introduction, James mentioned Fechner's achievements in physics, in psychology where "it is a commonplace to glorify him as the first user of experimental methods and the first aimer at exactitude in facts" (p. 116), in cosmology, in literature, where "he has made his mark by, certain half-humoristic, half-philosophical essays published under the name of Dr. Mises" (p. 116), and in aesthetics, where "he may lay claim to be the earliest systematically empirical student" (p. 116). Finally, "in metaphysics, he is not only the author of an independently reasoned ethical system, but of a theological theory worked out in great detail" (p. 116). James felt a particularly strong affinity with Fechner's daylight view, his antimaterialistic philosophy. He considered Fechner's ideas to be promising solutions for the future progress of our understanding of some of the most basic questions of consciousness and the unconscious. Like Fechner, James attended séances and wrestled with the questions of immortality. In the Ingersoll lecture at Harvard in 1897 (published as "*Human Immortality*," 1898/1982), James relied on Fechner's *wave theory* of consciousness, an analogy of how our conscious experiences leave their traces permanently in the world memory. When one talks of James and Fechner, one is resurrecting traces of their actual presences, according to this theory.

To sum up this chapter, it is clear that James, in his later philosophical writings, was most enthusiastic about the same Fechner whom he had rejected in his discussion of the earlier psychological Fechner of the psychophysical law and mental measurement. As James wrote to his boyhood friend, Thomas Sergeant Perry, in 1909, "Fechner is indeed a dear, and I am glad to have introduced, so to speak, his speculations to the English world" (H. James, 1920). He also wrote to his fellow philosopher, Henri Bergson, "Are you a reader of Fechner?. . . He seems to me of the real race of prophets and I cannot help thinking that you, in particular, if not already acquainted with this book [i.e., *Zend-Avesta*], would find it very stimulating and suggestive. His day, I fancy, is still to come? (H. James, 1920).

This is indeed high praise. But Fechner's philosophy did not have the staying power of his psychophysics and aesthetics. According to a survey of

Fellows of the American Psychological Association's Division 26, (History of Psychology), Fechner rated among the top 10 in all-time importance and so did James, of course. Fechner is tied for the last three spots with Skinner and Binet, whereas James is an undisputed number two. (Korn, Davis, & Davis, 1991).

Similarly, a citation analysis (1966–1985) by Scheerer and Hildebrandt (1987) showed Fechner the psychophysicist with 245 citations leading Fechner the philosopher and metaphysician with only 30 citations. (His aesthetics were second highest with 66 citations.) Was James's estimate of Fechner's importance wrong? James, as always, was idiosyncratic and must be judged in a historical context.

REFERENCES

Adler, H. E. (1980). Vicissitudes of Fechnerian psychophysics in America. In R. W. Rieber & K. Salzinger (Eds.), *Psychology: Theoretical-historical perspectives* (pp. 11–23), NY: Academic Press.

Cadwallader, T. (1974). Charles S. Peirce (1839–1914): The first American experimental psychologist. *Journal of the History of Behavioral Sciences, 10,* 293–296.

Delboeuf, J. (1883). *Éléments de psychophysique générale et spéciale.* Paris: Baillière.

Fechner, G. T. (1851). *Zend-Avesta, oder über die Dinge des Himmels und des Jenseits. Vom Standpunkt der Naturbetrachtung.* Leipzig, Germany: L. Voss.

Fechner, G. T. (1861). *Über die Seelenfrage* [On the question of the soul]. Leipzig, Germany: Breitkopf und Härtel.

Fechner, G. T. (1879). *Die Tagesansicht gegenüber der Nachtansicht* [The dayview compared with the nightview]. Leipzig, Germany: Breitkopf und Härtel.

Fechner, G. T. (1966). *Elements of psychophysics* (Vol. 1, H. E. Adler, Trans., E. G. Boring & D. Howes, Eds.) NY: Holt, Rinehart & Winston. (Original work published 1860)

James, H. (1920). *The letters of William James.* Boston, MA: Atlantic Monthly Press

James, W. (1902). *The varieties of religious experience.* NY: Longmans, Green.

James, W. (1961). Report on Mrs. Piper's Hodgson—Control (*Proceedings of the Society for Psychical Research, 28*). In G. Murphy & R. O. Ballou (Eds.), *William James on psychical research.* London: Chatto and Windus. (Original work published 1909)

James, W. (1967). *Essays in radical empiricism and a pluralistic universe.* Gloucester, MA: P. Smith. (Original work published 1909)

James, W. (1978). The teaching of philosophy in our colleges. In F. H. Burkhardt,

F. T. Bower, & I. K. Skrupskelis (Eds.), *Essays in philosophy* (pp. 5–6), Cambridge, MA: Harvard University Press. (Original work published 1876)

James, W. (1981). *The Principles of psychology* (3 vols.). Cambridge, MA: Harvard University Press. (Original work published 1890)

James, W. (1982). Human immortality. In F. H. Burkhardt, F. T. Bower, & I. K. Skrupskelis (Eds.), *Essays in religion and morality*, Cambridge, MA: Harvard University Press. (Original work published 1898)

James, W. (1982). Introduction to Fechner's "Life after Death," (Mary C. Wadsworth, Trans.). In F. H. Burckhardt, F. T. Bower, & I. K. Skrupskelis (Eds.), *Essays in religion and morality* (pp. 116–119), Cambridge, MA: Harvard University Press. (Original work published 1904)

James, W. (1984). *Psychology: Briefer course.* Cambridge, MA: Harvard University Press. (Original work published 1892)

Korn, J. H., Davis, R., & Davis, S. F. (1991). Historians' and chairperson's judgment of eminence among psychologists. *American Psychologist, 46,* 789–792.

Ladd, G. T. (1887). *Elements of physiological psychology.* NY: Scribner's.

Lovelock, J. (1988). *The ages of Gaia: A biography of our living earth.* NY: Norton.

Merkel, J. (1988). Die Abhängigkeit Zwischen Reiz und Empfindung [The dependency of stimulus and sensation]. *Philosophische Studien, 4,* 541–594.

Myers, G. E. (1986). *William James: His life and thought.* New Haven, CT: Yale University Press.

Perry, R. B. (1936). *The thought and character of William James* (2 vols.). Boston, MA: Little Brown.

Scheerer, E., & Hildebrandt, Z. (1987). Was Fechner an eminent psychologist? In J. Brovek & H. Grundlach (Eds.), *G. T. Fechner und die Psychologie*, Passau, Germany: Passavia Universitätsverlag.

Sprung, L., & Sprung, H. (1978). Gustav Theodor Fechner—Wege und Abwege in der Begründung der Psychophysik [Gustav Theodor Fechner—Ways and byways in the founding of psychophysics]. *Zeitschrift für Psychologie, 186,* 439–454.

18

WILLIAM JAMES AND INSTINCT THEORY REVISITED

DONALD A. DEWSBURY

The flood of centennial publications to celebrate William James's *Principles of Psychology* (1890) revealed the extent to which he is noted for his contributions to such lofty topics as epistemology, consciousness, the will, the self, and ethics. Rather little was addressed to the issue of instinct. It seems paradoxical that a writer such as James also would be numbered among the most important instinct theorists. Yet on James's death, James Rowland Angell (1911, p. 80) wrote

> Following closely in the footsteps of Darwin, he made instinct an essential part of the study of the human mind in a way no other psychologist had done. He took a large, flexible, dynamic view of instinct which gave it a place in the very forefront of human life and so of human psychology, instead of relegating it to the limbo of "left-overs" from our animal ancestry for which apologies must be made and moralizing indulged.

I thank Paul Jerome Croce and Eugene Taylor for comments on a draft of this paper.

I will explore what James wrote about instinct, why he wrote it, and what influence he exerted.

WILLIAM JAMES AND THE TWO CULTURES

James was a thoroughgoing pluralist with his feet firmly planted in each of C. P Snow's (1959) "two cultures." Yet these two sides of James needed resolution.

A consuming passion among James scholars is the determination of a focus for the thought of this very pluralistic man—as coined by Bjork (1988), "the center of his vision" (see also Feinstein, 1984; Myers, 1986; Perry, 1935). Virtually all authors place James's focus on the humanistic side of the two cultures. Bjork (1988) placed the center of his vision in James's preoccupation with pure experience and the introspective exploration of his own mind. The essence of James's interest lay in the study of consciousness. What are deemed to be James's most original contributions—the stream of consciousness, the will to believe, and pure experience—may be tied to that endeavor. For Myers (1986), "The more one studies his thought, the more one understands that he was at heart more a metaphysician than anything else" (p. 293).

The complement to the humanistic aspect of the complex psyche of James lay in James's science—the aspect seized on by generations of positivists. James played an important role in introducing both British evolutionary biology and French and German physiological psychology into American psychology. His travels in Europe, then the focus of scientific activity, brought him into contact with these approaches and developments. James studied at the Lawrence Scientific School at Harvard and at the Harvard Medical School. In 1869, he received his MD—the only degree he ever earned. In 1865 and 1866, James participated in a research expedition to Brazil with Louis Agassiz. He was influenced by Jeffries Wyman, Henry P. Bowditch, and James Jackson Putnam. James was proud of his role in the establishment of experimental psychology (e.g., James, 1895).

Problems arose for James in developing a philosophy of free will, morals, and consciousness within the framework of his scientific persona—a task of little concern to one residing on just one side of the two cultures. James conceived of a mind exerting will and adjusting to environmental contingencies, but these were viewed as evolved and adapted traits (see Richards, 1987). Will rested atop a biological base. The Jamesian superstructure was built on a complex foundation of instincts. For James, it was always the loftier processes that ruled those of biology. The problem was to integrate them into a single worldview—or at least into as much of a single worldview as possible. I shall not argue that instincts lay at the center of his vision, but they did form the core of his psychology.

INSTINCT THEORY BEFORE JAMES

The necessity of placing a psychology of consciousness and will on a foundation of instinct was thrust on James by the developments of his time in the fields with which he was conversant. In his *Zoonomia* (1796/1974), Erasmus Darwin tried to explain away patterns that appeared to be instinctive as due to early learning, and thus affirm the role of volition as opposed to instinct. James, however, wrote after the publication of major works by Charles Darwin, T. H. Huxley, A. R. Wallace, G. J. Romanes, Herbert Spencer, G. H. Schneider, and Douglas Alexander Spalding and was influenced by these and similar writers. He had to find a different way to address the issue of instinct while retaining his focus.

I shall not trace the long history of the instinct concept, but I will refer the reader to Drever (1917), Wilm (1925), Diamond (1971), and Jaynes and Woodward (1974). However, consider the milieu in the period just before James wrote the *Principles*, which was first published in 1890. Darwin (1859/1896, 1871/1897, 1872/1897), Spencer (1880/1890), Romanes (1882, 1883), Chadbourne (1872), and Schneider (1880) all made important statements about instinct during this time. Spalding's work on instinct appeared during the 1870s. There was a spate of articles on instinct in the magazines and journals of the day (e.g., Bascom, 1871; Lewes, 1873). The problem of instinct was not one that a man of James's erudition had to seek out; it was prominent in the writings of the day.

The two most pressing issues relating to instinct were the problem of definition and the question of how instincts evolve. James was to become more concerned with the former than with the latter.

The Problem of Definition

C. Lloyd Morgan (1895) summarized differences among definitions with respect to a set of seven issues: the relation of instinct to consciousness, the relation of instinct to impulse, the relation of instinct to intelligence and volition, the relation of instinct to habit, the instincts of man, the plasticity and variability of instinct, and the periodicity and serial nature of instinct. Some of these issues go beyond the question of definition. Nevertheless, Morgan surely was correct that definitional differences were an important cause of miscommunication.

Herbert Spencer (1880/1890) defined *instincts* as "compound reflex action" (p. 432). Instincts differed from reflexes in that they had more complex eliciting stimuli and a more complex effective structure. Spencer believed that in higher forms instincts may be accompanied by consciousness.

Romanes took sharp issue with Spencer. For Romanes (1883), consciousness was intrinsic to instinct: "Instinct is reflex action into which there is imported the element of consciousness" (p. 159). He refined the concept noting that instincts are "concerned in conscious and adaptive action, antecedent to individual experience, without necessary knowledge of the relation between means employed and ends attained, but similarly performed under similar and frequently recurring circumstances by all the individuals of the same species" (Romanes, 1883, p. 159). Romanes was critical of Spencer for missing what he thought was a critical attribute of instincts—consciousness.

Some authors used definitions that seem strange today, as they included in their definitions instincts that were acquired during an individual's lifetime. Wilhelm Wundt, for example, used the term "to denote the more complex impulsive actions, which presuppose a long course of individual or generic practice" (Wundt, 1896, p. 388). He thus allowed for "*acquired* instincts," those that "have been developed . . . during the life of the individual" (p. 397). Wundt also opposed Spencer's view of instincts as compound reflex actions. Thus, for example, Wundt's statement that "man shares with the birds the instinct to live in wedlock" (p. 396) must be interpreted very differently than if it had been written by Spencer.

Morgan (1895) summarized the situation in a tortuous paragraph that merits quotation:

> Instinctive activities are unconscious (Claus), non-mental (Calderwood), incipiently conscious (Spencer), distinguished by the presence of consciousness (Romanes), accompanied by emotions in the mind (Wundt), involve connate ideas and inherited knowledge (Spalding); synonymous with impulsive activities (James), to be distinguished from those involving impulse proper (Hoffding, Marshall); not yet voluntary (Spencer), no longer voluntary (Lewes), never involuntary (Wundt); due to natural selection only (Weismann), to lapsed intelligence (Lewes, Schneider, Wundt), to both (Darwin, Romanes); to be distinguished from individually-acquired habits (Darwin, Romanes, Sully, and others), inclusive thereof (Wundt); at a minimum in man (Darwin, Romanes), at a maximum in man (James); essentially congenital (Romanes), inclusive of individually-acquired modifications through intelligence (Darwin, Romanes, Wallace). (p. 326)

Charles Darwin on Instinct

Darwin's ideas on instinct are presented in *The Origin of Species* (1859/1896) and in *Descent of Man* (1871/1897); some material deleted in the interest of condensation was published as a posthumous appendix by Romanes (1883). Darwin's goal seems to have been not to provide a complete explanation of instinct, but rather to show that the facts about instinct were consistent with his theory. Although he refused to define instinct, Darwin (1859/1896) noted that

> an action, which we ourselves require experience to enable us to perform, when performed by an animal, more especially by a very young one, without experience, and when performed by many individuals in the same way, without their knowing for what purpose it is performed, is usually said to be instinctive. (pp. 319–320)

However, Darwin pointed out that none of these characteristics are universal.

Like most authors, including James, Darwin was inconsistent in his application of this definition. For example, he wrote that in migration an instinct impels animals in a certain direction, thus introducing a motivational component that was not a part of his definition. Indeed, Beer (1983) characterized Darwin's treatment of instincts as "autonomous motivational systems," having "three distinguishable features: the urge or impulse to action; the behavior impelled; and the goal toward which the impulsion, and hence the behavior, are directed" (p. 73).

Darwin believed that most instincts evolve via the processes of natural selection that he had delineated. However, he was not confident that the principle of natural selection could explain all instances of instinct and proposed that some evolve as inherited habits. Romanes (1883) developed this dual origin of instincts more fully.

Darwin discussed many issues that were to be important for James and other later authors. Among the principles developed by Darwin were the following: instincts function for the welfare of the species, certain instincts cannot be considered absolutely perfect, and natural instincts can be lost under domestication. Darwin noted variability in instincts. He believed some instincts to be more complex than others; nidification and habitation, for example, were treated as more complex instincts (Romanes, 1883). Darwin postulated a social instinct, which he viewed as indispensable for some species. He (1871/1897) believed humans to have fewer instincts than closely related species; however, he opposed the view that there is an inverse relationship between instinct and intelligence across species. By treating instinct as prominently as he did, Darwin helped generate interest in its study. However, he did little to sort out the many confusions about the use of the term (see Beer, 1983).

The Evolution of Instincts

Perhaps the dominant issue of the day concerned the question of how instincts evolve. Romanes, following Darwin as usual, proposed two routes: *Primary instincts* originate via a process of natural selection as they are beneficial to the animals that display them. Such behavioral patterns never were performed intelligently; rather, they were the result of chance variation. *Secondary instincts*, by contrast, originate as habits, which originally were performed intelligently, but which become stereotyped into permanent instincts. Romanes presented various proofs for both processes and developed a conception of the complex interactions between primary and secondary instincts. Darwin also supported both views, although he believed primary instincts to be more common; Weismann was less accommodating. The essentially Lamarckian doctrine of *lapsed intelligence*, the process by which secondary instincts were supposed to evolve, was favored by G. H. Lewes (1873), G. H. Schneider (1880), Wundt (1896), and D. A. Spalding (1873a). In treating instinct, but stressing issues other than their evolution, James went against the trend in much of the literature of his day.

Spalding's Demonstrations of Innate Behavioral Patterns

Nineteenth-century authors writing on instinct generally wrote speculatively about broad issues, especially the evolution of instincts. Spalding shifted the emphasis in the study of instinct in two important ways. First, he was an experimenter, and thus a harbinger of the coming experimental approach in animal behavior. Second, he shifted emphasis from questions of evolution to questions of development, a shift that was important for James.

Although Spalding's contributions seem generally unappreciated today, he was not unappreciated in his time. Darwin (1873) called Spalding's (1873a) paper "admirable" (p. 281). Romanes (1883) called Spalding's research "brilliant" and proposed that it "placed beyond question the falsity of the view 'that all the supposed examples of instinct may be nothing more than cases of rapid learning, imitation, or instruction' " (p. 161). James wrote of "Mr. Spalding's wonderful article on instinct" (James, 1890,

p. 396). G. H. Lewes was prescient in his observation: "Mr. Spalding has . . . shown a rare ability in devising experiments, and we may fairly expect that his researches will mark an epoch" (Lewes, 1873, p. 437).

Though crude by today's standards, Spalding's (1872, 1873a, 1873b, 1875) studies had an elegance that was compelling (see Gray, 1962, 1967). In one series of experiments, Spalding reared young chicks with various types of hoods over their heads from the time they began to break through their shells until testing began several days later. When the hoods were removed, and the birds recovered from the initial shock of the light, often by the end of 2 min, they followed crawling insects with their eyes and soon pecked accurately with an apparently innate appreciation of distance. Similar results were obtained for auditory localization. In other research, Spalding reared unfledged swallows in a box so small that they could not even extend their wings. Although two birds showed some unsteady flight when released, two others engaged in intricate flight maneuvers immediately after they were released. Together, these studies established that some animal functions develop in the absence of specific experience.

If contemporary animal behaviorists know the name of Spalding, it is because he appears to have been the first to study the phenomenon of imprinting, although this phenomenon had been described by others before him. He developed a preliminary version of what is now known as the *critical period hypothesis*. Spalding noted that animals "can also forget—and very soon—that which they have never practiced" (Spalding, 1873a, p. 289). In essence, instincts must be used at the appropriate developmental stage or be lost. As examples of this phenomenon, Spalding used spoon-fed human infants that lost the ability to suck naturally, chicks that had not heard the call of a mother until 8 or 10 days old and had become unresponsive, a chick returned to its mother at 10 days of age that refused to follow her, and chicks that had been hooded for 4 days that displayed fear of Spalding, rather than following him. These ideas became focal for James's approach to instinct.

James would seize on several other aspects of Spalding's approach to instinct as well. Spalding viewed instincts as behavioral consequences of physical structure: "Instinct, looked at from its physical side, may be conceived to be, like memory, a turning on of the 'nerve currents' on already established tracks" (Spalding, 1873a, p. 290). Spalding's work may even have had an influence on James's decision to extend the scope of instinct into human psychology (see Gray, 1967). In essence, Spalding believed that the delayed postnatal appearance of behavior in humans was not because of the need to develop associations, but rather, "because the child comes into the world in a state of greater physical, and therefore mental immaturity" (Spalding, 1873c, p. 300).

James's approach to instinct was a product of its times and owed much to Darwin, Spencer, Romanes, and others. However, it is when James began to depart from the well-worn track in his approach to instinct that the influence of Spalding became especially clear.

HIERARCHICAL THEORIES OF INSTINCT

One more topic should be introduced before getting to the main body of James's writings on instinct. Several aspects of James's approach will be best understood in the context of twentieth-century hierarchical models of instinct; a brief digression is in order.

Appetitive Behaviors and Consummatory Acts

Psychologist–biologist Wallace Craig (1918) emphasized an important distinction in the study of species-typical behavior between appetitive behavior and consummatory acts. *Appetitive behavior* is the variable, searching behavior characteristic of animals in different drive states. A hungry tiger engages in a variety of behavioral patterns that function to increase the likelihood of a situation wherein it can kill and eat prey. The *consummatory acts* usually follow appetitive behavior and are the more stereotyped fixed-action patterns associated with discrete stimuli. Classical ethologists (e.g., Lorenz, 1950) adopted this distinction as a means of dealing with both the precisely coordinated motor patterns they wished to emphasize and the integrated apparent purposiveness of instinctive behavior they perceived as emphasized by vitalists and proponents of a purposive psychology.

Hierarchical Models

Craig's basic approach has been elaborated on, as researchers from embryology (e.g., Weiss, 1941), ethology (Baerends, 1976; Dawkins, 1976; Tinbergen, 1951), and learning psychology (e.g., Davey, 1989; Timberlake & Lucas, 1989) have converged on various forms of hierarchical models of instinctive behavior (see Figure 1). Essentially, such models suggest that animals display very stereotyped motor patterns, but that these are integrated at successively higher levels of organization in the same way that computer subroutines are nested within a complete program. Complete, integrated, and variable drive systems form the top of the hierarchy, and stereotyped motor patterns are at its bottom. A given lower level motor pattern may be part of several higher order units. At the higher levels, there are variability and purpose (e.g., alternative behavior toward similar ends in different

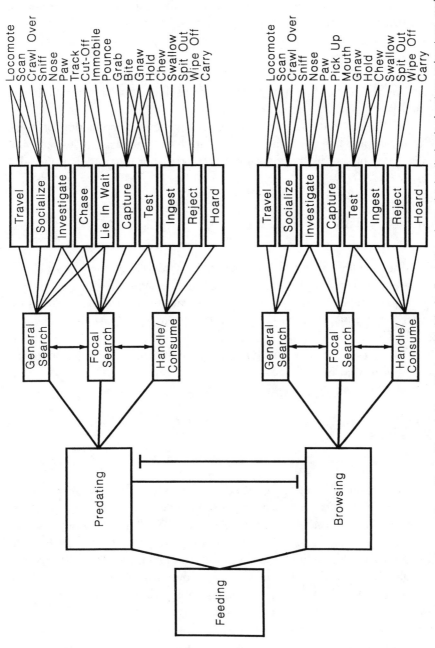

Figure 1: A schematic representation of Timberlake and Lucas's hierarchical model of the feeding system of rats, showing the levels of systems, subsystems, modes, and modules. From Timberlake & Lucas (1989). Copyright by Lawrence Erlbaum Associates, Inc. Reprinted with permission.

situations) lacking at the lower levels. In Timberlake and Lucas's (1989) version (Figure 1), there are four levels: *systems*, which organize behavior about functions such as feeding; *subsystems*, which are coherent strategies that sensitize the animal to certain stimuli and to make certain responses; *modes*, which are motivational substrates related to sequential and temporal organization of behavioral patterns; and *modules*, which are predispositions to respond to particular stimuli with particular responses. At even lower levels are the various motor patterns themselves that, in turn, have a hierarchical organization (see Weiss, 1941).

I will argue that (a) in places, James had some appreciation of hierarchical systems, but (b) some of his definitional inconsistencies led him to miss some of the distinctions apparent in the more hierarchical models.

JAMES'S INSTINCT CHAPTER

James began writing about instinct in a review of Lindsay's (1880) *Mind in the Lower Animals* (James, 1880). The chapter on instinct in the *Principles* is a reprinting, with minor modifications, of articles apearing in *Scribner's Magazine* (James, 1987a) and *Popular Science Monthly* (James, 1887b). The editor of *Science* greeted the former article as an excellent example of James's clarity and heartily recommended it to all intelligent readers ("Untitled Note," 1887).

The Nature of Instincts

Definitions

James began: "*Instinct is usually defined as the faculty of acting in such a way as to produce certain ends, without foresight of the ends, and without previous education in the performance*" (James, 1890, p. 383). This definition can be traced back at least as far as Hermann Reimarus (Jaynes & Woodward, 1974). James remained linked to the tradition of faculty psychology, which was probably inherited from the Scottish common-sense school.

James viewed instincts as producing ends without foresight. This was a common feature of definitions of the time (e.g., Romanes, 1883, p. 159). Later in the chapter on instinct in the *Principles*, James applied this feature in attacking Lindsay's voluntaristic interpretation of death feigning in birds, a theme he first addressed in his 1880 review of Lindsay's book. James pointed out that because nature builds animals to respond in the manner that is most often appropriate, humans can take advantage of the system, for example, by using worms and hooks to catch fish.

Instincts do not require previous education. James believed that animals learn such patterns as walking or flying by performing movements in an awkward manner at first. However, this is not due to the need to learn, but because "the animal is beginning his attempts before the co-ordinating centres have quite ripened for their work" (1890, p. 406).

For James, "The actions we call instinctive all conform to the general reflex type" (1890, p. 384). Here, although not acknowledging the point, James appeared to be siding with Spencer against Romanes; consciousness does not play an important role in this chapter. Reflexes grade into instincts, with reflexes generally affecting our own bodies and instincts affecting the outside world (1890, p. 403).

James believed, as did Spalding, that instincts are a consequence of the structure of an animal's nervous system. Thus, for example, the cat runs after the mouse, not because it has a clear purpose, but because he cannot help doing so; "his nervous system is to a great extent a preorganized bundle of such reactions" (1890, p. 384). Here, James followed such classics as Huxley's Belfast address (1874) and Spalding (as previously mentioned). The view of the nervous system as a preorganized bundle of responses introduces the structural complexity of instincts and, hence, of the nervous system, which becomes more apparent later. Further in this chapter (1890, p. 387), James used the term *a priori syntheses* in referring to instincts.

James dismissed the "older writings on instinct," those of authors who attributed to animals prophetic powers placed in them by the beneficence of God, as "ineffectual wastes of time" (1890, p. 384). James's theory is not concerned with clairvoyance or divine intervention, but with the consequences of structure.

Although accepting a Spencerian definition of instinct and repeatedly pointing to the advantages of his physiological conception, James postulated many instincts that would be difficult to squeeze into such a restrictive mold; consistency was not among the many Jamesian virtues. When listing human instincts, James included not only sucking, biting, and smiling, but resentment, sympathy, shyness, and modesty. So much for instincts as all conforming to the reflex type! This inconsistency, which is present in many writers' works, can be understood in relation to the hierarchical models discussed earlier (see also Dunlap, 1919). James needed to address not only what Timberlake called actions and modules, but also the more complex motivational units labeled as systems and subsystems in Figure 1. All are important in behavior. Although he had some developing concept of hierarchical structure, it was not clear enough to make this confusion and possible resolution apparent. James, like others, thus defined instinct in a fairly clear way, but was unable to use his definition consistently.

Instincts and impulses

Like many others, James tied instincts to impulses: "*Every instinct is an impulse*" (1890, p. 385); he sometimes used the terms interchangeably. In this regard, James followed in this tradition (see Diamond, 1971), along with authors in his own time such as Chadbourne (1872) and Morgan (1895).

It is in relation to this issue that James hinted at some hierarchical structure to "complex instinctive action" (1890, p. 385). In a passage not representative of the usual clarity of James's writing, following Schneider (1880), James distinguished among sensation impulses, perception impulses, and idea impulses. He discussed a hungry lion and the complex sequence in which it seeks, stalks, springs, and devours prey and quoted Schneider on the impulses of a hoarding hamster in picking up, carrying, and laying down corn. In both cases, these are patterns of muscular contraction set off only by the appropriate stimulus and integrated into complex instinctive actions. These are functionally integrated wholes, organized from bits of behavior.

As noted by Lorenz (1950) much later, the proximate end of appetitive behavior is not the object, but the display of the consummatory act. For James, "Every impulse and every step of every instinct shines with its own sufficient light, and seems at the moment the only eternally right and proper thing to do" (p. 387).

Instincts and emotions

To discuss the topic of instincts and emotions would take me out of James's instinct chapter and into his next one. I shall simply quote James's main statements: "*Instinctive reactions and emotional expressions . . . shade imperceptibly into each other. Every object that excites an instinct excites an emotion as well*" (1890, p. 442). James's treatment of the emotions is among the most famous of his proposals. James viewed the instincts as tied tightly to the emotions and, thus, through this linkage as through others, instincts lie near the core of James's psychology.

The proximate–ultimate distinction

An important and much-misunderstood topic in contemporary behavioral ecology and sociobiology is the distinction between proximate and ultimate causation. Animals are viewed as displaying behavior that accomplishes certain adaptive ends that benefit the long-term reproductive success of the individual. These can be viewed as evolutionary adapted behavioral patterns (ultimate causation) without any implication that the animal understands this connection (proximate causation). Failure to make this distinction leads to confusion.

James was clear with respect to this distinction. He noted that what appears to be useful is a conclusion drawn by science, not by the individual displaying the behavior: "Not one man in a billion, when taking his dinner, ever thinks of utility" (1890, p. 386), and again, "Nature . . . has left matters in this rough way, and made them act *always* in a manner that would be *oftenest* right" (1890, p. 392). With respect to sexual impulses, James wrote that "the teleology they contain is often at variance with the wishes of the individuals concerned; and the actions are performed for no assignable reason but because Nature urges just that way" (1890, p. 437). This distinction between what the individual and the observer know resembles James's views on the *psychologist's fallacy*, which is described elsewhere in the *Principles*. The bulk of James's approach is consistent with Weismann's evolutionary approach and subsequent developments in evolutionary biology and is not teleological in any problematical sense of the word (cf. Cravens, 1978).

The Variability of Instincts

The notion that instincts are not rigidly stereotyped had already gained some hold before James (e.g., Darwin, 1859/1896; Spalding, 1875). James considered this issue in a section of the chapter on instincts in the *Principles*, entitled "Instincts Not Always Blind or Invariable." Here, James began to both undermine the possibility of control of adult behavior by instincts and to start building a practical benefit for understanding instincts, which was another of his enduring concerns.

Having established that instincts are performed blindly, he introduced a major limitation; they are blind only on first occurrence: "It is obvious that every instinctive act, in an animal with memory, must cease to be 'blind' after being once repeated, and must be accompanied with foresight of its 'end' " (1890, p. 390). His example was a hen that, having hatched one brood, James viewed as unlikely to sit in perfect blindness on her second nest. Thus, one source of variability stems from effects of learning that are apparent on all but the first occurrence of an instinct.

A second source of variability comes from inhibition. Because instincts are defined as existing in physiologically defined nerve centers, James viewed them as being susceptible to inhibition, just as are all reflex arcs. If there are many instincts present, often they will conflict with one another, and it is this conflict that often engenders variability and the appearance of choice in behavior that is under the control of instincts. James wrote,

> The animal that exhibits them loses the 'instinctive' demeanor and appears to lead a life of hesitation and choice, an intellectual life; not, however, because he has no instincts—rather because he has so many that they block each other's path. (1890, p. 393)

These principles allowed James to make the controversial assertion that "man has a far greater variety of *impulses* than any lower animal" (1890, p. 390). Human behavior is variable because instincts are transformed by experience and because humans have so many instincts that their variability, due to inhibitory interactions among them, is greater than that in other species.

At this point, James introduced reason, again with a hierarchical flavor. Reason is capable of altering the occurrence of instinctive behavior. However, only other impulses, not reason, can inhibit impulses. Reason inhibits by using imagination to activate impulses counter to a given impulse.

Two Principles of Nonuniformity of Instincts

James developed these ideas further in what may be the most important part of the chapter on instincts—and the one with the greatest debt to Spalding. He proposed two principles with which he further explained variability in instincts, isolated them from higher processes, and developed the foundation for application in an educational setting—the inhibition of instincts by habits and the transitoriness of instincts. Sulloway (1979) viewed these principles as a synthesis of the experimental work of Romanes and Spalding into two laws of "instinctual perversion" (p. 266).

Inhibition of instincts by habits

James stated his first principle as follows: "When objects of a certain class elicit from an animal a certain sort of reaction, it often happens that the animal becomes partial to the first specimen of the class on which it has reacted, and will not afterward react on any other specimen" (1890, p. 394). Clearly, James based this principle on Spalding's work on imprinting, which he discussed prominently. James presented this principle in an energy model, noting than an impulse can "exhaust itself in its first achievements and to leave no surplus energy for reacting on new cases" (1890, p. 395). Once the instinct has been used, it seems that two factors restrict further use: (a) the depletion of energy from the impulse and (b) the restriction, applied by habits that are grafted onto instincts, that limits the ability to react to any but the habitual object. James used as examples the chicks that Spalding imprinted to himself, calves that wandered off into the wilderness and could not later be habituated to contact with humans, and some observations of Romanes on the rearing by hens of heterospecific animals. Later in the *Principles* (pp. 438–439), James used this concept to explain monogamy, as habits fix our preferences toward certain individuals.

The law of transitoriness

The law of transitoriness is based on Spalding's observations of critical periods: "Many instincts ripen at a certain age and then fade away" (1890, p. 398). Spalding's observations and several anecdotes are presented in support of this principle.

Having established the principle with examples from nonhuman animals, James applied it to humans: "There is a happy moment for fixing skill in drawing, for making boys collectors in natural history" (1890, p. 401). The ideas that men have are fixed by age 25. He then added, "To detect the moment of the instinctive readiness for the subject is, then, the first duty of every educator" (1890, p. 402).

What James Has Done

James, first, acknowledged the existence of instincts, consistent with the empirical demonstrations by Spalding of instincts in animals. In addition, as both Spalding and James (e.g., 1890, p. 148) believed in the continuity of species, James acknowledged the existence of instinct in humans as well.

However, James did not take the next step, as did William McDougall, of viewing the behavior of adult humans as instinct driven. Rather, he left instincts at the developmental core of his psychology, but wrapped that core with a protective blanket that kept instincts isolated from the critical faculties in which he was more interested and that enabled him to emphasize such topics as the will and the self that were at the center of his vision. In places, James was inconsistent with respect to the role of instincts in adult behavior. At this point, however, he was clear about the developmental function of instincts: "Most instincts are implanted for the sake of giving rise to habits, and . . . this purpose, once accomplished, the instincts themselves, as such, have no raison d'etre in the psychical economy, and consequently fade away" (1890, p. 402). This statement about the role of instincts in the development of animals can be used as an analogy for James's placement of instincts in his psychology; they are brought on the scene and have a function, but are quickly dispatched in the interest of loftier topics.

Although James may have wished to keep instincts buried once they had given rise to habits, he fell far short of this goal. From the statement quoted in the preceding paragraph, it is clear why Allport (1937) overstated James's argument in writing that "an instinct appears but once in a lifetime, whereupon it promptly disappears through transformation into habits" (p. 194). James was not that single-minded; instincts, though not in their pure form, were ascribed many functions after their first occurrence.

Special Human Instincts

The material covered thus far spans approximately 20 pages of the *Principles* and appeared in the first of the 1887 magazine articles (James, 1887a); the remaining material occupies some 39 pages and comes from the second article (James, 1887b). In this section, James presented his famous list of human instincts and discussed them, providing depth of coverage varying greatly with his interest in the topic. Because James was not concerned with generating an all-inclusive list, the instincts are presented in such a way as to be difficult to count. Some may be treated as one or several, depending on one's proclivity to lump or split; others grade into each other or are presented as clusters. It is a fair estimate that the number of instincts listed may lie somewhere in the 40s. I shall comment on only a few of them.

James began with some rather basic instincts, such as sucking, biting, and clasping, which were derived from Wilhelm Preyer. The hierarchical nature of James's thinking is apparent in the derivation of what appears to be a system or subsystem for eating out of a set of these simple, lower order instincts (modules?) (see Figure 1):

> This instinct (i.e., carrying objects to the mouth), guided and inhibited by the sense of taste, and combined with the instincts of biting, chewing, sucking, spitting-out, etc., and with the reflex act of swallowing, leads in the individual to a set of habits which constitute his *function of alimentation*, and which may or may not be gradually modified as life goes on (1890, p. 404).

In discussing the development of locomotion, James followed Spalding and disagreed with Bain, citing Spalding's observations that birds do not learn to fly. James predicted that if a human child were prevented from walking until past the normal age of occurrence, as Spalding's birds were prevented from flying, when released, the child would walk about as well as normal because the coordinating nerve centers would have matured in the absence of practice. The integration of the pattern of pressing downward with the foot, creeping, walking, and climbing into functional locomotion again suggests hierarchical organization.

When discussing pugnacity, anger, and resentment, James opined that "in many respects man is the most ruthlessly ferocious of beasts" (1890, p. 409). According to James, nine tenths of the world's work is done by emulation or rivalry (1890, p. 409). The retreat from the law of transitoriness of instincts should be apparent.

James provided a detailed discussion of fear and many of the things of which individuals are afraid. Many are ascribed teleological significance. Fear of the supernatural is explained as "the result of a combination of simpler horrors" (1890, p. 419).

Perhaps the most curious of the instincts is the antisexual instinct. This is an instinct of personal isolation and involves actual repulsion at the idea of intimate contact with most persons, especially those of our own sex. Thus, to most of us, it even is unpleasant to sit down in a chair still warm from occupancy by another person. Viewing the sexual and antisexual instincts together, James concluded that "there can be no better proof . . . that irregularity of behavior may come as well from the possession of too many instincts as from the lack of any at all" (1890, p. 438).

Although James's chapter in the *Principles* is most remembered for his list of human instincts, this is not the heart of the chapter or of James's thinking about instincts. Thus, when the *Principles* was condensed into the "Jimmy" (James, 1892), the first part of his chapter was kept reasonably intact; the section listing human instincts was cut severely.

SOME LOOSE ENDS

A number of additional issues merit attention.

Relation to the Rest of the Book

It is notable that the topic of instinct appears frequently in the *Principles*, beginning on page 5 of Volume I in a discussion on the scope of psychology. James underscored the importance he placed on the proximate–ultimate distinction by including a discussion in that same introductory chapter. It is discussed again in the chapter on the automaton theory.

In his second chapter, on the functions of the brain, the hierarchical nature of the nervous system and the use of the same muscles in different acts are both apparent. James noted that "it is like a general ordering a colonel to make a certain movement, but not telling him how it shall be done" (1890, p. 19). Later in the chapter, he discussed species differences in the hierarchical ordering of the nervous system and in the native tendencies of emotions and instincts.

As might be expected, instincts are mentioned repeatedly in his chapter on habits. James wrote, "the habits to which there is an innate tendency are called instincts" (1890, p. 104).

The placement of the instinct chapter is significant, as it appears in the *Principles* just before the important chapters on emotions and the will. In the "Jimmy," it is placed between those two chapters. As noted earlier, the link between instinct and the emotions is tight. Will plays a powerful role, especially via inhibition: "Inhibition is therefore not an occasional accident; it is an essential and unremitting element of our cerebral life" (1890, p. 583).

On the Evolution of Instincts

Consideration of the evolution of instincts was the outstanding issue of the day. However, James shifted the issue within genetic psychology from the question of evolution to that of development within the individual—a distinction not always made clear in the literature of this time. Finally, in the last major section of the *Principles*, James addressed the origin of instincts. Apparently, this odd placement is because James read Weismann's work, which countered Lamarckian inheritance, just before publication of the *Principles* (see Richards, 1987). He wrote in favor of Darwinian natural selection, as opposed to lapsed intelligence, as the route via which instincts are inherited, noting, in the penultimate paragraph of the entire work, that "the so-called Experience-philosophy has failed to prove its point" (1890, p. 688).

Instinct in Talks to Teachers

In 1899, James published his *Talks to Teachers on Psychology*, a much more pragmatic work than the *Principles*, which was aimed at making psychology more accessible in the classroom situation. Interestingly, James included a chapter entitled "Native Reactions and Acquired Reactions," and another called "What the Native Reactions Are." These roughly parallel the material that was in his original 1887 article. James applied his conception of instinct for teachers just as he did in the *Principles*, noting that his principle "underlies the whole process of acquisition and governs the entire activity of the teacher" (James, 1899, p. 38):

Every acquired reaction is, as a rule, either a complication grafted on a native reaction, or a substitute for a native reaction, which the same object originally tended to provoke.

The teacher's art consists in bringing about the substitution or complication, and success in the art presupposes a sympathetic acquaintance with the reactive tendencies natively there. (James, 1899, pp. 38–39)

James's nativistic approach to the development of habit was consistent throughout his work.

Perhaps the most interesting feature of the *Talks to Teachers*, for the present discussion, is the diagramming of his preliminary hierarchical model (see Figure 2). The context is a discussion underlying the process of teaching a child to beg nicely for a toy: If he begs nicely, he gets the toy; if he does not, he gets slapped. In James's first diagram (Figure 2a), which represents the situation before training, there are four instinctive centers coordinating reactions to particular stimuli: see-snatch, slap-cry, listen-beg, and get-smile. Each of these has a higher control center at the level of memory and will (1–4). After training (Figure 2b), the impression of seeing the toy leads, via the higher routes, only to begging and smiling; center 2 now inhibits

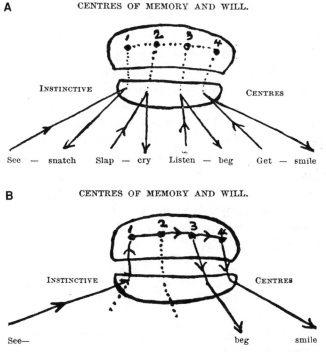

Figure 2: James's hierarchical model of the influence of the centers for memory and will on instinctive centers. (a) The system of a child before learning not to snatch at a toy. (b) The structure after training.

the response of snatching. This is the clearest statement of the hierarchical nature of James's views on the control of instinct.

Was James the First American to Propose Human Instincts?

House (1936) proposed that James was "the first American to assert specifically the thesis that human beings, like other animals, have instincts" (p. 210). This appears not to be the case. John Bascom (1871, 1878) acknowledged instincts in humans, although he viewed them as but "a very small remainder" (p. 188). Bascom discussed Spalding's work, which he called "noteworthy" (p. 149) and considered instincts as a basis for the formation of habits. Chadbourne (1872) proposed "that man has a wider range of Instinct than any other animal on the globe" (p. 212). At about the time of James's work, David Jayne Hill (1888) wrote that "there are in man, who also possess animal nature, certain tendencies to act, sufficiently universal and uniform to deserve the name of instincts" (p. 321). James acknowledged receipt of Hill's volume on January 21, 1888 (see Scott, 1986). These few instances suggest that the issue of instinct in pre-Jamesian American psychology merits further study.

Was the Topic of Instinct Important to James?

I have argued that the topic of instinct was not at the center of James's vision. Indeed, he seemed to have wrapped instinct in a developmental blanket that enabled him to address issues of will, metaphysics, and religion with minimal concern for instinct. Nevertheless, there are many indications that the topic of instinct was of at least some importance to him. First, the topic is woven throughout the *Principles*, beginning with the initial chapter and ending with the discussion of the evolution of instincts in the final chapter of the book. When the *Principles* was abridged, the section on the nature and dynamics of instincts was cut less than other sections. Instinct, as the progenitor of habit, even plays a significant role in the *Talks to Teachers*. Issues of epistemology were important to James, and his epistemology was based on Darwinian principles, with instinct serving as a part of that complex (see Richards, 1987).

THE INFLUENCE OF JAMES'S INSTINCT THEORY

The twentieth century has seen a long-lasting and often acrimonious debate over the instinct concept, especially as applied to humans. Although there never has been unanimity of opinion, patterns of ebb and flow have been discernable (Cravens, 1978; Degler, 1991; Dewsbury, 1984). It has been estimated that between 1900 and 1920 alone at least 600 articles and books advancing instinct theories were published in the United States and England (Cravens, 1978). What was the impact of James on this literature?

It would be difficult to sustain Harlow's (1969) opinion that "it is commonly conceded that one of William James's greatest contributions to psychology was his chapter on instincts in the *Principles of Psychology*" (p. 21). At the opposite extreme, however, Lindsley (1969) concluded that "James was not an instinct theorist" (p. 42). Lindsley based this view on the premise that to be a theorist one has to have influence as a theorist. He analyzed several textbooks on the history of psychology and found relatively few references to James's instinct theory. He concluded from this that "James's 59 pages of writing on instincts had almost no effect on historians of psychology and, therefore, almost no impact on others" (p. 39). Lindsley proceeded to a treatment of numerology in James's work. Rather than attack Lindsley's premises and approach, both of which were flawed, I shall consider some of the ways in which James's instinct theory influenced later work. I would not argue for a direct effect on James's views on instinct on contemporary psychology. However, there were important influences on those who shaped psychology in the twentieth century.

Edward L. Thorndike

Among those strongly influenced by James's instinct theory was a former student, Edward L. Thorndike. Although Thorndike is often portrayed only as a leader of the associationist–anti-instinct approach in American psychology (e.g., Thorpe, 1953), he actually promulgated an instinct theory very close to that of James (Thorndike, 1900, 1907, 1913). Thorndike proclaimed that instincts are unlearned expressions of the structure and function of the nervous system. They may be delayed or transitory and often are indefinite and inexact. Thorndike expressed his views in Jamesian prose: "Instincts are a fund of capital loaned to us by nature for a period, not given outright . . . they become our permanent property by being hardened into habits" (Thorndike, 1907, p. 188). Thorndike (1913) reprinted James's list of instincts, asserting that they provided the basis for all education. Thorndike (1907) predicted that, in the future, the list of human instincts would grow, not shrink; 35 years later, Thorndike (1942/1949) believed this to have been the case.

John B. Watson

Although Watson's approach to instinct changed over time, James's views on instinct were focal to Watson throughout his work. In the classic text in which Watson laid the foundation for behaviorism, he defined instinct as "a combination of congenital responses unfolding serially under appropriate stimulation" (Watson, 1914, p. 106). A case can be made that some of this text was written by Karl Lashley (Bruce, 1986). In the view of Herrnstein (1972), perhaps overstated, there is no appreciable difference between the conceptions of instinct of James and of Watson, except in their prose styles. Although he felt it impossible to provide a complete list of instincts, Watson provided a set of characteristic instincts that he expected to find in every species of vertebrates; these included obtaining food, shelter, rest, sleep, play, sex, defense and attack, and vocalization. In one of the many ways in which he anticipated later ethologists, Watson recommended field observation and deprivation experiments as the appropriate methods for the study of instincts. However, Watson challenged James's views on nonplasticity beyond critical periods.

By 1919, Watson was in transition—and at the peak of his interest in Jamesian thought. Much of his chapter on instinct is in response to James and Thorndike; Watson, at this stage, found much with which he could both agree and disagree. He wrote that "William James has made some statements about instinct which are as nearly true now as when he wrote them" (Watson, 1919, p. 232). Watson used seven pages to reprint Thorndike's list and treatment of human instincts, but concluded that "these asserted instincts are really consolidations of instinct and habit" (p. 261). Watson again disagreed with James's views on the transitoriness of instincts (p. 253) and accepted an inverse cross-species ratio between instinct and the capacity to form habits, a proposal so clearly rejected by James (p. 254). In 1919, then, Watson was reducing the importance of instincts in humans, but unwilling to drop them completely. His concluding statement owes a strong debt to James: "The principal role of all instinctive activity, neglecting the vegetative and procreative . . . is to initiate the process of learning" (p. 268).

Later, Watson rejected theories of human instincts; James, however, remained in Watson's focus. Watson (1930) wrote that "The behaviorist finds himself wholly unable to agree with James and other psychologists who claim that man has unlearned activities of these complicated kinds" (p. 110). Elsewhere, he wrote that "The behaviorist . . . says, 'I find none of the instincts listed by James'" (Watson, 1928, p. 28). Although Watson came to eschew the existence of instincts in humans, he never clearly reversed himself with respect to instincts in nonhumans (e.g., Watson, 1928). In order to accomplish this, he appeared to have reversed himself regarding the continuity of processes between humans and nonhumans (see Logue, 1978).

William McDougall

William McDougall was greatly influenced by James, writing that "James and Stout are the only two men of whom I have felt myself to be in some degree the disciple and humble pupil" (McDougall, 1930, p. 209). McDougall's reading of James's *Principles*, while he was a medical student, had an important effect on his future career. McDougall called a brief 1908 visit from James "one of the greatest pleasures of my life" (p. 208). In 1920, McDougall occupied the Harvard chair in psychology formerly held by James and Munsterberg. In *An Introduction to Social Psychology*, McDougall (1936) provided a full discussion of his instinct theory, citing Schneider and James and hoping that his book "may contribute in some slight degree to promote the recognition of the full scope and function of the human instincts" (McDougall, 1936, p. 21).

Instincts occupied a more prominent place in McDougall's psychology than in James's, Thorndike's, or the young Watson's. They were placed within the context of McDougall's purposive, or hormic, conception of behavior as "the prime movers of all human activity" (1936, p. 38). McDougall defined an instinct as

> an inherited or innate psycho-physical disposition which determines its possessor to perceive, and to pay attention to, objects of a certain class, to experience an emotional excitement of a particular quality upon perceiving such an object, and to act in regard to it in a particular manner, or, at least, to experience an impulse to such action. (p. 25).

Thus, for McDougall, instincts were distinctly nonmechanical mental processes that entailed perceptions, emotions, and, as James believed, impulses. McDougall's instincts would have to be at the highest level in Figure 1. McDougall followed James in writing of the late ripening of many human instincts and in viewing instincts as the basis of habits: "Habits are formed only in the service of instincts" (McDougall, 1936, p. 40).

Like James, McDougall formulated a list of human instincts, the exact number changing from time to time (see Woodworth, 1948). His disagreements with James were few; McDougall believed that James had erred in postulating instincts of emulation or rivalry, sympathy, and imitation.

McDougall applied the instinct concept to all complex social behavior, thus expanding the realm of instincts (see Krantz & Allen, 1967). Although he viewed instincts as less mechanical and more complex than other writers,

McDougall's treatment generally falls within the natural-science tradition. On occasion, however, he was capable of lapsing into vitalism, as when he wrote, "I hold that the instincts are essentially differentiations of the will to live that animates all organisms" (McDougall, 1910, p. 258). That McDougall's views are out of fashion today should not obscure his important place in the psychology of his day.

The Origins of Social Psychology

Another influence that James's instinct chapter in the *Principles* had was on the development of American social psychology, albeit a very different brand of social psychology from that extant in 1990. This development was traced most enthusiastically by House (1936). Included in James's list of instincts were such social instincts as sociability, shyness, secretiveness, cleanliness, modesty, shame, and love. Clearly, James viewed instincts as affecting not only the adjustments of individuals, but the social interactions as well. The influence of James on McDougall was noted earlier, and McDougall had great influence on the development of social psychology in his (1936) *Introduction to Social Psychology*. James also had a direct influence on Trotter's (1915) *Instincts of the Herd in Peace and War*.

House traced what he perceived as the two major schools of social psychology of his time to James's *Principles*—individualistic social psychology from the chapter on the self. As noted by John Dewey (1917),

> It would be ungrateful to engage in any discussion of the past and future of social psychology without recalling the few rich pages of the 'Principles' which are devoted to the social self, and, in the discussion of instincts, to the native reactions of human beings in the presence of one another. (p. 266).

Classical Ethology

Classical ethologists generally trace their roots to Charles Darwin, Charles O. Whitman, Wallace Craig, and Oskar Heinroth. It would seem as though James would merit some mention in the history of the development of ideas that were important to classical ethology. James generated a concept of instincts that are reflex-like, occur without previous education, and produce functional consequences without foresight. These are set off by "determinate sensory stimuli" (1890, p. 384), not unlike the sign stimuli of ethology. James attached great importance to the conflict between different instincts and the inhibition of instincts, which are important themes in classical ethology. He presented the beginnings of a hierarchical model of instincts.

Lorenz (1950) credited Craig with exploding "the myth of the 'infallibility of instinct'," as Craig proposed that the subject does not aim at the survival value of its activities, but at the discharge of consummatory acts. James deserves at least some of that credit. Eibl-Eibesfeldt (1989), an ethologist, credited James "who defined 'instinct' in fairly modern terms, as capacities of organisms based on innate neuronal organization" (p. ix).

Other Psychologists

James's influence is evident in the writings of other psychologists as well. Angell (1908) proposed a list of human instincts similar, in some respects, to James's, but balked at James's inclusion of cleanliness as an instinct. Warren (1919) also presented a list of human instincts. He viewed James's assertion of many instincts in humans as only partly correct; there are few pure instincts, but a great number of modified instincts. Other aspects of his treatment of instincts owe a clear debt to James.

Baldwin (1911) detailed the influence of James's instinct theory on education arguing that "James was the first educator to call direct attention to the native resources of the child and the place these native tendencies to reaction must necessarily have in any scheme of education" (p. 375). Baldwin detailed James's influence on writers such as John MacCunn, Henry C. King, and William Bagley. Even E. B. Titchener (1904) quoted James on instinctive action.

According to Sulloway (1979), James's principles of the inhibition of instincts by habits and of the transitoriness of instincts came to the attention of Sigmund Freud in the field of sexual pathology. Albert Moll applied James's laws to developmental disorders of the sexual libido, and Havelock Ellis applied the principle of transitoriness to psychosexual development.

A FINAL NOTE

The topic of instinct was not the driving force in William James's intellectual life. However, the instinct problem was so prevalent in the literature of his time that it could not be ignored. Building on the foundations provided by such writers as Darwin, Romanes, Spencer, Schneider, and especially Douglas A. Spalding, James constructed a psychology with instincts at its developmental core if not at the center of his vision. James especially developed his views on instinct as an ontogenetic process, and he attempted to come to grips with the changing role of instincts in the life of the organism. He had a notion of the hierarchical structure of instincts, but it was not developed sufficiently to prevent his inconsistent use of the term. James applied his ideas in the context of education; the effective teacher must be aware of instincts and the times at which they ripen. James's views on instinct influenced some of the major psychologists who shaped twentieth-century psychology. If only we all could make such significant contributions in areas in the periphery of our vision!

REFERENCES

Allport, G. W. (1937). *Personality: A psychological interpretation*. New York: Holt.

Angell, J. R. (1908). *Psychology: An introductory study of the structure and function of human consciousness* (4th ed.). New York: Holt.

Angell, J. R. (1911). Editorial. *Psychological Review*, 18, 80.

Baerends, G. P. (1976). The functional organization of behaviour. *Animal Behaviour*, 24, 726–738.

Baldwin, B. T. (1911). William James' contributions to education. *Journal of Educational Psychology*, 2, 369–382.

Bascom, J. (1871). Instinct. *Bibliotheca Sacra*, 28, 654–685.

Bascom, J. (1878). *Comparative psychology or, the growth and grades of intelligence*. New York: Putnam's.

Beer, C. (1983). Darwin, instinct, and ethology. *Journal of the History of the Behavioral Sciences*, 19, 68–80.

Bjork, D. W. (1988). *William James: The center of his vision*. New York: Columbia University Press.

Bruce, D. (1986). Lashley's shift from bacteriology to neuropsychology, 1910–1917, and the influence of Jennings, Watson, and Franz. *Journal of the History of the Behavioral Sciences*, 22, 27–44.

Chadbourne, P. A. (1872). *Instinct: Its office in the animal kingdom, and its relation to the higher powers in man*. New York: Putnam.

Craig, W. (1918). Appetites and aversions as constituents of instincts. *Biological Bulletin*, 34, 91–107.

Cravens, H. (1978). *The triumph of evolution: American scientists and the heredity–environment controversy 1900–1941*. Philadelphia: University of Pennsylvania Press.

Darwin, C. (1873). Inherited instinct. *Nature*, 7, 281–282.

Darwin, C. (1896). *The origin of species by means of natural selection* (6th ed.). New York: Appleton. (Original work published 1859)

Darwin, C. (1897). *The descent of man and selection in relation to sex* (2nd ed.). New York: Appleton. (Original work published 1871)

Darwin, C. (1897). *The expression of the emotions in man and animals*. New York: Appleton. (Original work published 1872)

Darwin, E. (1974). *Zoonomia*. New York: AMS Press. (Original work published 1796)

Davey, G. (1989). *Ecological learning theory*. London: Routledge.

Dawkins, R. (1976). Hierarchical organisation: A candidate principle for ethology. In P. P. G. Bateson & R. A. Hinde (Eds.), *Growing points in ethology* (pp. 7–54). Cambridge, England: Cambridge University Press.

Degler, C. N. (1991). *In search of human nature: The decline and revival of Darwinism in American social thought*. New York: Oxford University Press.

Dewey, J. (1917). The need for social psychology. *Psychological Review, 24*, 266–277.

Dewsbury, D. A. (1984). *Comparative psychology in the twentieth century*. Stroudsburg, PA: Hutchinson Ross.

Diamond, S. (1971). Gestation of the instinct concept. *Journal of the History of the Behavioral Sciences, 7*, 323–336.

Drever, J. (1917). *Instinct in man: A contribution to the psychology of education*. Cambridge, England: Cambridge University Press.

Dunlap, K. (1919). Are there any instincts? *Journal of Abnormal Psychology, 14*, 307–311.

Eibl-Eibesfeldt, I. (1989). *Human Ethology*. New York: Aldine.

Feinstein, H. M. (1984). *Becoming William James*. Ithaca, NY: Cornell University Press.

Gray, P. H. (1962). Douglas Alexander Spalding: The first experimental behaviorist. *Journal of General Psychology, 67*, 299–307.

Gray, P. H. (1967). Spalding and his influence on research in developmental behavior. *Journal of the History of the Behavioral Sciences, 3*, 168–179.

Harlow, H. F. (1969). William James and instinct theory. In R. B. MacLeod (Ed.), *William James: Unfinished business* (pp. 21–30). Washington, DC: American Psychological Association.

Herrnstein, R. J. (1972). Nature as nurture: Behaviorism and the instinct doctrine. *Behaviorism, 1*, 23–52.

Hill, D. J. (1888). *The elements of psychology: A text-book*. New York: Sheldon.

House, F. N. (1936). *The development of sociology*. New York: McGraw-Hill.

Huxley, T. H. (1874). On the hypothesis that animals are automata, and its history. *Nature, 10*, 362–366.

James, W. (1880). Mind in the lower animals. *The Nation, 30*, 270–271.

James, W. (1887a). What is an instinct? *Scribner's Magazine Illustrated, 1*, 355–365.

James, W. (1887b). Some human instincts. *Popular Science Monthly, 31*, 160–170, 666–681.

James, W. (1890). *The principles of psychology* (2 vols.). New York: Holt.

James, W. (1892). *Psychology: Briefer course*. New York: Holt.

James, W. (1895). Experimental psychology in America. *Science, 2*, 626.

James, W. (1899). *Talks to teachers on psychology: And to students on some of life's ideals*. New York: Holt.

Jaynes, J., & Woodward, W. (1974). In the shadow of the enlightenment I. Reimarus against the epicureans, and II. Reimarus and his theory of drives. *Journal of the History of the Behavioral Sciences, 10*, 3–15, 144–159.

Krantz, D. L., & Allen, D. (1967). The rise and fall of McDougall's instinct doctrine. *Journal of the History of the Behavioral Sciences, 3*, 326–338.

Lewes, G H. (1873). Instinct. *Nature, 7*, 437–438.

Lindsay, W. L. (1880). *Mind in the lower animals*. New York: Appleton.

Lindsley, O. R. (1969). The secret life of William James. In R. B. MacLeod (Ed.), *William James: Unfinished business* (pp. 35–43). Washington, DC: American Psychological Association.

Logue, A. W. (1978). Behaviorist John B. Watson and the continuity of the species. *Behaviorism, 6*, 71–79.

Lorenz, K. Z. (1950). The comparative method in studying innate behaviour patterns. In J. F. Danielli & R. Brown (Eds.), *Physiological mechanisms in animal behaviour* (pp. 221–268). New York: Academic Press.

McDougall, W. (1910). Instinct and intelligence. *British Journal of Psychology, 3*, 250–266.

McDougall, W. (1930). William McDougall. In C. Murchison (Ed.), *A history of psychology in autobiography* (Vol. I, pp. 191–223). Worcester, MA: Clark University Press.

McDougall, W. (1936). *An introduction to social psychology* (23rd ed.). London: Methuen.

Morgan, C. L. (1895). Some definitions of instinct. *Natural Science, 7*, 321–329.

Myers, G. E. (1986). *William James: His life and thought*. New Haven: Yale University Press.

Perry, R. B. (1935). *The thought and character of William James* (2 vols.). Boston: Little, Brown.

Richards, R. J. (1987). *Darwin and the emergence of evolutionary theories of mind and behavior*. Chicago: University of Chicago Press.

Romanes, G. J. (1882). *Animal intelligence*. London: Kegan, Paul, Trench.

Romanes, G. J. (1883). *Mental evolution in animals*. New York: Appleton.

Schneider, G. (1880). *Der thierische Wille*. Leipzig, Germany: Abel.

Scott, F. J. (1986). *William James: Selected unpublished correspondence, 1885–1910*. Columbus: Ohio State University Press.

Snow, C. P. (1959). *The two cultures and the scientific revolution*. New York: Cambridge University Press.

Spalding, D. A. (1872). On instinct. *Nature, 6*, 485–486.

Spalding, D. A. (1873a). Instinct. With original observations on young animals. *Macmillan's Magazine, 27*, 282–293.

Spalding, D. A. (1873b). Flight not an acquisition. *Nature, 8*, 289.

Spalding, D. A. (1873c). Herbert Spencer's psychology. *Nature, 7*, 298–300, 357–359.

Spalding, D. A. (1875). Instinct and acquisition. *Nature, 12*, 507–508.

Spencer, H. (1890). *The principles of psychology* (3rd. ed.). New York: Appleton. (Original work published 1880)

Sulloway, F. J. (1979). *Freud, biologist of the mind.* New York: Basic Books.

Thorndike, E. L. (1900). Instinct. *Biological Lectures From the Marine Biological Laboratory of Woods Holl 1899* (pp. 57–67). Lexington, MA: Ginn Press.

Thorndike, E. L. (1907). *The Elements of psychology.* New York: Seiler.

Thorndike, E. L. (1913). *Educational psychology. Volume I. The original nature of man.* New York: Teachers College, Columbia University.

Thorndike, E. L. (1949). Human instincts and doctrines about them. In E. L. Thorndike (Ed.), *Selected writings from a connectionist's psychology* (pp. 176–181). New York: Appleton-Century-Crofts.

Thorpe, W. H. (1953). Editorial. *British Journal of Animal Behaviour, 1*, 3–4.

Timberlake, W., & Lucas, G. A. (1989). Behavior systems and learning: From misbehavior to general principles. In S. B. Klein & R. R. Mowrer (Eds.), *Contemporary learning theories: Instrumental conditioning theory and the impact of biological constraints on learning* (pp. 237–275). Hillsdale, NJ: Erlbaum.

Tinbergen, N. (1951). *The study of instinct.* Oxford, England: Oxford University Press.

Titchener, E. B. (1904). *A primer of psychology* (rev. ed.). New York: Macmillan.

Trotter, W. (1915). *Instincts of the herd in peace and war.* New York: Macmillan.

Untitled note. (1887). *Science, 9*, 254.

Warren, H. C. (1919). *Human psychology.* Boston: Houghton Mifflin.

Watson, J. B. (1914). *Behavior: An Introduction to comparative psychology.* New York: Holt.

Watson, J. B. (1919). *Psychology from the standpoint of a behaviorist.* Philadelphia: Lippincott.

Watson, J. B. (1928). *The ways of behaviorism.* New York: Harper.

Watson, J. B. (1930). *Behaviorism* (2nd ed.). New York: Norton.

Weiss, P. (1941). Self-differentiation of the basic patterns of coordination. *Comparative Psychology Monographs, 17*, (88), 1–96.

Wilm, E. C. (1925). *The theories of instinct.* New Haven, CT: Yale University Press.

Woodworth, R. S. (1948). *Contemporary schools of psychology.* New York: Ronald.

Wundt, W. (1896). *Lectures on human and animal psychology* (2nd ed.). London: Swan Sonnenschein.

19

WILLIAM JAMES: CLOSET CLINICIAN

GEORGE S. HOWARD

William James was a genius—an absolute genius! James's genius lay in his ability to write lucidly and insightfully on almost any topic under the sun. My research on self-determination and free will led me to become acquainted with James's views on will from the *Principles of Psychology* (1890). But for this chapter, I will address the other parts of James's work that might be helpful to clinicians. After all, clinicians are interested in far more than issues of will and intentionality.

The array of topics concerning James that has been written about recently has been nothing short of staggering. It seemed to me that the pundits had analyzed James's views on virtually every topic that might be of interest to modern clinicians, for example, the self, emotions, spirituality, intentionality, the effects of experience, curiosity, fear, and creativity. And so my depression began to grow, for it seemed as though they had taken it all. Although there was still more of interest to clinicians in the *Principles*, it fell in domains in which I was incompetent to discuss.

When one is depressed, the world seems to conspire to drag the person even further into the abyss. And so it was that when an issue of the journal

Psychological Science arrived—wouldn't you know it—there I found "The William James Symposium," which was highlighted (at least for me) by a wonderful article by Hazel Markus (1990) on James's view of the self as the arbiter of all experience. I could feel the wind slipping out of the sails I had begun to unfurl around an idea of the self as the author, director, and leading actor in each of our own life stories—a contemporary, yet thoroughly Jamesian, idea. I was foiled again! No sooner had I groaned that the fates had dealt me every possible low blow, than I received a copy of Johnson and Henley's (1990) new book, entitled *Reflections on the Principles of Psychology: William James After a Century*. The chapters by Rand Evans, Amedeo Giorgi, David Leary, Howard Pollio, and James Deese were especially insightful, and so my despondency grew.

Psychologists have set before them a veritable smorgasbord of delights in reflection on James's *Principles*. What have I to offer to this already-overflowing agape? And so, in my anguish and despair, I cried out, "Oh, Father in heaven, help me! What am I to do? What can I write?"

And to my surprise, God didn't answer, but the founder of scientific psychology in America (Boring, 1929) did. "You know, George," William James began, "it's funny you should bring up that point. I've been told that psychology has done an admirable job in mining the golden nuggets of wisdom from my *Principles of Psychology* (James, 1890). But psychology has left my later work largely untouched. It's my more philosophical work, like *Pragmatism* (James, 1907/1946), *The Varieties of Religious Experience* (James, 1902/1929), *A Pluralistic Universe* (James, 1909/1977), *The Will to Believe* (James, 1897/1956), and *Talks to Teachers on Psychology* (James, 1899/1921), that still bear (largely unmined) treasures for psychology.

"Remember, George, when I delivered the *Principles* to Henry Holt, my publisher in 1889, I was only 47 years old. I still had another two decades of productive scholarship ahead of me. Furthermore, the types of psychologists best prepared to profit from these later, more philosophical observations will be those who struggled with problems of human life daily—those who are, so to speak, up to their rumps in the primordial ooze of the human condition—applied psychologists of every sort, such as clinical psychologists, counseling psychologists, school psychologists, consulting psychologists, and a host of others too numerous to mention. So, Georgie-boy, in your chapter, *don't* end the William James story in the middle by discussing only the insights found in the *Principles*. Try to use my later works to round out the picture of human nature that I eventually envisioned."

And then there was silence. Now for most people, to suddenly hear the voice of William James would be quite an unsettling experience. But for me, this sort of thing is old hat. On occasion, I've had fascinating conversations with Aristotle (Howard, 1990), George Kelly (Howard, 1988),

Don Bannister, and God (Howard, in press). So I just joined in the conversation and didn't think twice about it.

"Oh, goody," I chirped, "I've wanted to have a conversation with you ever since I read Jacques Barzun's (1983) wonderful book, *A Stroll With William James*. Not only do I find your ideas friendly, I find your writing style, your vivid images, and your humor irresistible. But what I see as your greatest strength, Barzun saw as something of a liability,

> The real handicap one notes in James as writer of philosophy is his irrepressible humor. He shares with Swift, Lamb, Samuel Butler, Shaw, Chesterton, and Mark Twain the disadvantage of having used yet one more rhetorical means which, though legitimate in itself and generally pleasing, somehow distracts all but the fittest readers. Most people seize on it as an opportunity to escape from the serious thought just preceding and thus miss the seriousness in the next, the humorous one. The great humorist always runs the risk of not being taken thoughtfully, while the normal men of ideas, faithful to solemnity, invariably are. (Barzun, 1983, p. 295)

Barzun's point reminds me of a quote, "I, too, have tried in my time to be a philosopher; but I don't know how, cheerfulness was always breaking in" (Edwards, 1791, p. 85). So, Professor James, I hope you won't be insulted if I joke with you about your ideas.

"Not at all," the old philosopher replied with an impish gleam in his eye. "I'll see your joke, and raise you a quip! So, what shall we discuss, my friend?"

"Well," I began, "your earlier point that applied psychologists would resonate to your later work more than academically oriented psychologists reminds me of a quote by Rom Harré:

> Two images of human psychology compete for our attention. Academic psychologists, particularly those who work in the experimental tradition, make the implicit assumption that men, women and children are high-grade automata, the patterns of whose behavior are thought to obey something very like natural laws. . . . It is assumed that there are programs which control action and the task of psychology is to discover the mechanisms by which they are implemented. Lay folk, clinical psychologists, lawyers, historians and all of those who have to deal in a practical way with human beings tend to think of people as agents struggling to maintain some sort of reasoned order in their lives against a background flux of emotions, inadequate information and the ever-present tides of social pressures.
>
> I shall try to show that the great differences that mark off these ways

of thinking about human psychology are not ultimately grounded in a reasoned weighing of the evidence available to any student of human affairs. They turn in the end on unexamined political and moral assumptions. . . . Although these profoundly different ways of interpreting and explaining human thought and action have their origin in preferred linguistic forms rather than any compelling facts of the matter, they do have profoundly different practical consequences. They carry with them very distinctive stances as to the moral, political and clinical problems with which modern people are beset. (Harré, 1974, p. 4)

It seems to me that Harré was playing a theme that you introduced long ago—the distinction between *tough-minded* and *tender-minded* thinking. Harré suggested that academically oriented psychologists tend to be tough-minded; whereas applied psychologists are of a more tender-minded stripe. How do you react to that? Is that a Jamesian view?"

"It's an early Jamesian view," my Bostonian friend shot back, "it reflects my thinking in the *Principles,* and that's the part of my work that psychologists know best. But I'm afraid it was something of a misstep to think of things so dichotomously—either your're thinking tough-mindedly or tender-mindedly. You see it was all too black and white. Eventually, I came to a more wholistic view of human thought. But I must say, in my own defense, that because of our shared Western intellectual heritage, I was as susceptible to the excesses of Cartesian dualism as the next person. I didn't invent the bugaboo of dichotomous thinking."

"Professor James," I interrupted, "would you mind if I played psychologist for a moment and offered a bit of psychohistory of your intellectual life?"

"Hey, buddy, you've got a union card. Give it your best shot," he replied.

"Buddy? Union care? Best shot?" I stammered incredulously.

"Oh, I know that doesn't sound like me," James opined, "but that's the wonderful thing about heaven. Your horizons expand; you see things more clearly; you escape the petty biases of time and culture; you become a citizen of the universe."

That sounded fine to me, so I just continued talking. "Okay, here's the point I want to float by you, Professor James. A number of people (and here I'm thinking of James Deese, 1990, and Amedeo Giorgi, 1990) have suggested that many of the paradoxes in Jamesian thought are rooted in your dichotomous thinking about the free-will–determinism problem. As long as we need to choose one or the other of these two stances on human action, then we will be forced into similar, unhappy, either–or choices, such as natural science or human science, consciousness or materialism, mind or brain, and rationalism or empiricism. The point is that there is a split personality that runs through every chapter of the *Principles,* and it almost becomes a theme of Jamesian psychology. Johnson and Henley (1990) said, "This theme concerns the tension between the role of experience (or phenomenological data) within a scientific psychology, and the viability of a materialistic (or biologically reductive) account of mental life" (p. 2). In the *Principles*, you seem to be constantly bouncing back and forth between James as a natural scientist–psycholosist and James as a humanistic philosopher of the common person. This divided character of your thought still plagues psychology to this day. That's the problem I'd like to hear you address. And the psychohistory part of my concern is that several commentators claim that this free will versus determinism aspect of your thinking is traceable to your father's interest in Swedenborgian theology."

"Well," James sighed, "you've thrown a lot of questions, and some accusations, at me. Let me try to reply to them calmly and with candor. First, my father was a great influence on my thinking, that much is correct. But your statement of that fact sounds more like an accusation than an insight. Therein lies a good bit of my problems with psychological explanations in general and psychohistorical analyses in particular. Any fool knows that our beliefs and ideas come from somewhere; none of us believe that our faiths, hopes, theories, philosophies, plans, and goals spring into our minds ex nihilo. We are all influenced—no, more than influenced—we are actually formed by the important people, places, and experiences in our lives. But psychological explanations all too often come out sounding demeaning. 'Oh, poor Willie James, he was probably hamstrung by his father's antiquated religious beliefs.' That's not an explanation; it's more like slander by innuendo. Academics tend to think of people's lives, beliefs, and actions from the third-person perspective. They do so in order to be more dispassionate; the hope being that this will somehow make their psychological explanations more objective. But this research strategy is misplaced; it loses the heart and soul of human intentionality. The most useful explanation of the influence that my father's religious beliefs had on my construal of the free-will–determinism issue would be the following: I learned a great deal from my father's wisdom; I am one acorn who would have considered it an absolute tragedy had I fallen very far from my family tree!"

I guess he told me a thing or two!

"See how differently that comes out," the Bostonian continued. "I freely chose to use my father's beliefs to help steer the course I navigated through the rocky shoals of the free-will–determinism debate. I think Rom Harré said it well when he suggested that applied psychologists typically conduct their ministrations from a totally different moral and epistemological standpoint than do more academically oriented, experimental psychologists. And because these two types of activities are situated within somewhat incommensurate language systems (as Wittgenstein, 1958, said), or different paradigms (as Kuhn, 1970, might have claimed), or alternative modes of thought (as Bruner, 1986, saw it), the insights from each perspective are largely incompatible with knowledge garnered from the other frames of reference. And, by the gods, more and more, I see the wisdom of the applied, first-person perspective. Try this on for size, George. If I came back to psychology in 1992, I think I'd choose to come back as a clinician!"

Now that was the William James that I heard and loved in his writings. He was speculative, provocative, and feisty. This was not the James who was the founder of scientific psychology in America and the author of the *Principles*. This was the James of the *Varieties of Religious Experience*, *Pragmatism*, *A Pluralistic Universe*, and *The Will to Believe*. But before I could question him further, he continued.

"And don't try to lay blame for the free-will–determinism problem on me or on my father's religious beliefs. That thorny philosophical conundrum antedates me by at least 2,500 years. Besides, by the time I published *Pragmatism* in 1907, my penchant for dichotomous thinking had declined dramatically. Although I still exhibited the contrast between tough-minded and tender-minded types, the text of *Pragmatism* made clear that I had a more integated view of the relationship between the poles of our existence. I referred to this relationship as a *pluralistic monism*. Although it might be gauche to quote oneself, let me quote from *Pragmatism*.

"Go ahead," I encouraged, "I do it all the time."

James began, "Now, as I have already insisted, few of us are tenderfoot Bostonians pure and simple, and few are typical Rocky Mountain toughs, when it come to philosophy. Most of us have a hankering for the good things on both sides of the line. Facts are good, of course—give us lots of facts. Principles are good—give us plenty of principles. The world is indubitably one if you look at it in one way, but just as indubitably is it many, if you look at it in another. It is both one and many, so let us adopt a sort of pluralistic monism. Everything, of course, is necessarily determined, and yet our wills are free; a sort of free-will–determinism is the true philosophy."

"Exactly!" I blurted out. "You are exactly correct! The free-will–determinism problem is based on a mistaken premise."

"What?" James asked.

"Psychology's made some progress in the 100 years since you converted to philosophy," I continued, "We've now demonstrated that one can (I dare say *should*) be both a free willist and a determinist."

"Now isn't that always the case," James mused sadly.

"Isn't what the case?" I asked.

"Make one little mistake, like not reading a single psychology journal for a 100 years, and you almost begin to feel a little bit behind the times."

Well, I was so into the free-will–determinism issue that I didn't laugh. So James asked, "What's the matter, kiddo? No sense of humor?"

And it occurred to me why I enjoy talking to people who were born in the first half of the nineteenth century—they make me feel *so* young.

"Now that we see the solution to the free-will–determinism problem," I continued, "it seems silly that it could have remained such an intractable problem for so long. But, come to think of it, until recently, we thought a person had to be either masculine or feminine; we didn't know that a person could be both."

"Come again?" James stammered. "A person can be both what?"

I'd forgotten that I was dealing with a nineteenth-century mind, and so I had to explain what's happened in sex-role research in the last 30 years. "Professor James," I began, "you think that free will and determinism represent polar opposite extremes of a single dimension, but I'd like to suggest, instead, that these two concepts are better understood as being located on two separate dimensions. A similar conceptual revision (Constantinople, 1973) sparked an enormous surge of research in the domain of sex-role orientation. If 20 years ago I had complimented you on your fine feminine characterists, you might well have been insulted by my compliment. Why?"

"Because you'd insulted my manhood," the Bostonian fired back.

"That's exactly how people viewed things," I replied. "Masculinity and femininity were thought to be polar opposites. So highlighting one's feminine characteristics meant denying that person's masculine aspects. This was not only an accepted conceptual position, it was also a computational fact of life with all of the then-existing sex-role orientation measures. But Constantinople's (1973) conceptual reorganization allowed for the possibility of two independent dimension: masculinity and femininity. From this new vantage point, one is not forced to deny one set of characteristics in order to assert possession of high levels of the other. Now people can be (both conceptually and computationally) high on both masculinity and femininity (androgynous), high on one and low on the other (stereotypically masculine or stereotypically feminine), or low on both dimensions (undifferentiated). Many claim that it was this simple, conceptual reformulation that touched off the revolution in sex-role research we now witness. Here W.J., let me sketch a picture of this reformulation of our understanding of the relationship between masculinity and femininity."

"Might a similar reformulation of the free-will–determinism problem stimulate new solutions to an antinomy that has perplexed thinkers for more than 25 centuries? Before sketching a reconceptualization of the free will versus determinism issue, note that it is a working scientist's specification of the issues, not a philosopher's reformulation of this seemingly everlasting controversy. That is, the definitions of terms (such as *free will*, *determinism*, and *nonagentic mechanism*) are empirically operationalizable and, thus (in this form), amenable to empirical scrutiny. However, in so defining these terms, it becomes unclear exactly what the implications of these conceptual

Single Bipolar Dimension

Masculine _____ Feminine

===

Independent Dimensions

Masculinity

High _____ Low

Femininity

High _____ Low

Figure 1: A reconceptualization of the masculinity–femininity dichotomy into two independent bipolar dimensions.

moves (and research findings) might be for philosophical debate on the issues of agency, mechanistic determinism, self-determination, and free will.

What, then, is the working scientist's definition of determinism? It is the belief that actions (or events) are produced by some prior events (or causes). For our purposes, reasons can also serve as causes. The opposite of determinism, then, would be acausality. That is, things occur randomly, spontaneously, and are sometimes uncaused. Remember that uncertainty (cf. Price & Chissick, 1977) is a distinctly different concept from the acausality that is being suggested as the polar opposite of determinism. From this perspective, one can readily see why Kimble (1984) found that virtually all psychologists are determinists, because acausality represents the enemy of scientific analysis.

"Now, one can specify a second, independent dimension that is anchored on one end by free will or complete self-determination; this is defined as an agent's ability to act in a domain completely independently of all nonagentic, mechanistic influences. The opposite of free will, then, would be complete mechanistic determination (whether by physiological factors, environmental influences, unconscious motivations, social influences, or genetic predispositions). At this latter extreme, human choice is seen as completely causally impotent, *or* human choice itself is seen as a completely mechanistically determined phenomenon and not the creation of a free agent." I drew a second figure that outlined the reconceptualization of the

Determinists	<======>	Nondeterminists
All actions result from some cause(s).		Things are uncaused; they just happen randomly and spontaneously.

==

Free Willists	<======>	Nonagentic Mechanists
Belief in self-determination and agency! People are largely the cause of their own actions.		Our actions are the result of mechanisms (e.g., environmental, physiological, genetic, and cultural) that are completely coercive.

Figure 2: A reconceptualization of the free-will–determinism dichotomy into two independent bipolar dimensions.

old free-will–determinism debate. Finally, I broke James's philosophical reverie by asking him what his reactions were.

"Your conceptual move is simplicity itself," the father of pragmatism replied, "but its implications are enormous."

"I think so," I replied excitedly. I know of no serious scholar who advocates complete acausality in the world; however, most scientists espouse strongly (if not completely) deterministic belief systems in their roles as professionals. Thus, few scientists would be far from the determinist pole of the first dimension. But what of the self-determination versus nonagentic mechanism dimension? Scientists in the natural sciences would seem to be severely skewed toward the nonagentic mechanism pole in their professional work. Although individuals in the biological sciences might not be as heavily skewed in this direction, they certainly would not approach belief in complete self-determination. But for researchers in the human sciences, compelling arguments can be offered for the role of *both* self-determination and mechanistic determination in human action. And although the mechanist has always been free to offer a deterministic vision of human action that is scientific, because of this reformulation, a proponent of some version of human self-determination (or free will) can now also be deterministic in his or her theory of human action.

"So, Professor James, your earlier claim that free-will–determinism is the true philosophy, suggests that you would position yourself close to the determinist pole of this two-dimension reconceptualization, which is where I am inclined to rest also. But what about this free will versus mechanism dimension? My research shows clearly that humans can self-determine their actions to some extent: however, they do not have the complete freedom to do anything they please. Similarly, there is a great deal of research that demonstrates the influence of nonagentic, mechanistic influences on human action, such as physiological factors, environmental influences, unconscious motivations, social forces, and genetic predispositions, precisely the phenomena you wrote about so brilliantly in the *Principles*. But there is no evidence that nonagentic causal influences are completely coercive in human actions. So, where are you on this free-will–mechanism dimension? I think you are somewhere in the middle, as I am. You see the power of self-determination acting within a world of nonagentic, causal influences."

"Hot dog!" James yelped, "Now that's the kind of experimental psychology with which I'd be *proud* to be associated.

"I suspected that you'd be pleased," I replied.

"You know," the old man continued, "I've always had my reservations about psychology as an experimental science. When I delivered the manuscript of the *Principles* to Henry Holt, I exclaimed that it testified that 'there is no such thing as a *science* of psychology and, second, that W.J. is an incapable.' "

I immediately fell to my knees and mocked him mercilessly, "Please God, strike me with just such an incapacity," I begged.

He smiled at my buffoonery, but it was clear that something was troubling him. "Although the notion of a science of free will is initially appealing," James mused, "the thought of a science and a psychology that arrive at conclusions on important philosophical and theological issues, like human freedom, is quite troubling. I've always kept my theology and philosophy at arms length from my psychology and science."

"Yes," I conceded, "you were always quite clear on that point. I remember an admonition in *Pragmatism* that we should let psychology be psychology and science be science, but that neither of them should touch religion. Or consider Gerald Myers's interesting analysis of your fundamental beliefs, Professor James:

> As a young man, he was interested in religion, morals, abnormal psychology, and psychical research; his life and thought were motivated by the need to find a place for religion in a Darwinian era, to view the world as being morally modifiable, to discover ways of making "sick" souls into healthy ones, to uncover the hidden powers of the human psyche. He was, accordingly, opposed from the beginning to positivistic and antireligious philosophies, to declarations that science will eventually answer philosophy's questions, and to claims that our philosophies must be determined by so-called objective factors alone. . . . James, at the outset of his career, was stating what he believed till the end, that *choice* and *subjectivity* play proper and indispensable roles in deciding whether to adopt a religous philosophy, whether to adhere to a pessimistic or optimistic world view, or whether to accept a materialistic, mechanistic philosophy of psychology. (Myers, 1981, p. xix)

I finished with the opinion that because philosophy, theology, and the human sciences (to a certain extent) all have the same explanandum, namely, human nature, I really didn't know if it is possible to wall them off from one another—to keep them, so to speak, at arm's length.

"George," James asked, "a phrase in Myers's quote, 'troubled souls,' raises a question for me: In 1992, how do psychologists deal with troubled minds and troubled souls?"

How could anyone answer a question like that in a few brief sentences? I opted for a lightening-fast historical overview. "Professor James, I know that you met Sigmund Freud at Clark University shortly before your death. Well, Freud eventually developed an array of therapy techniques that helped people who were dealing with a variety of problems in living. He put forth a theory of personality based on psychodynamics that buttressed his therapeutic techniques. Before long, behaviorists, gestaltists, transactional analysts, reality therapists, humanists, family therapists, and a swarm of others almost too numerous to count sprang up to offer different ways of ministering to people who experienced problems in living. Recent estimates find several hundred distinct schools of psychotherapy."

"Oh my God, no!" my old friend gasped in disbelief. "It soulds like a therapeutic tower of Babel."

"Well," I countered, "it's not as bad as it sounds. One of the most promising and exciting contemporary trends is the ground swell toward developing integrative models of therapeutic change. They even have a new society devoted to conceptual integration within psychotherapy. My colleagues and I have developed one such integrative model called *adaptive counseling and therapy* (Howard, Nance, & Myers, 1987). We advocate an eclectic use of therapeutic techniques that are all managed from an integrated, theoretical perspective."

"By the gods," James blurted out, "*pluralistic monism*. That kind of thinking could have come straight out of my works such as *Pragmatism* and *A Pluralistic Universe*."

"Well, I'm afraid it didn't," I replied, "but it sure could have. The similarities are unmistakable. We call it *systematic eclecticism* instead of your phrase, pluralistic monism. But ours is not the only such model. Similar metatheoretical positions have been offered by Beutler (1983), Mahoney (1990), Garfield (1980), and Brammer and Shostrom (1977). It's a welcome relief from the theoretical and technical fragmentation within the fields of counseling and psychotherapy that characterized the 1950s, 1960s, and 1970s."

"I can imagine," James replied. "So much about therapies for troubled minds, George, what do we now do for troubles souls? Or have I touched on a sore spot?"

My sheepish grin told him he had. "I don't have to tell you that psychology has always had a rather uneasy truce with religion," I began modestly, "and that characterization probably still reflects the state of the relationship. Of course, people experiencing what is principally a spiritual malaise would probably be well-advised to seek out the counsel of a spiritual advisor. But I take it that the point you are making, William, is that every spiritual crisis also represents a psychological crisis, and similarly, very few psychological problems do not have spiritual implications. However, I'm a bit uneasy in saying even that. You see, through the first 7 decades of the twentieth century, it became ever-more difficult to speak of religious or spiritual issues within psychology. However, of late, it *seems* that the trend has begun to reverse. And although there might have been some great breakthrough in research on psychology and religion, I'm unaware of it if there is one. So, I guess I'd hve to say that there's no news to report. In fact, I routinely hear people claim that your *Varieties of Religious Experience* still represents the best work on psychology and religion."

"Well, I'm sorry to hear that," James replied.

"But," I continued, "applied psychologists have always had to deal with religion in their work with clients' problems. Clinicians use clients' life stories as the basic data for their ministrations. For example, therapy usually begins with an invitation to the client to tell his or her story. Therapists have favored ways of phrasing their readiness to hear the client's tale, such as 'Can you tell me what brings you here?' or 'How can I be of help to you?' or 'What seems to be the problem?' Clients generally know that these invitations do not call for the telling of one's complete life story. Rather, clients understand that their task is to tell the part of their life story that appears most relevant to their presenting problem. Thus, therapists hear beginnings like, 'I've always been a bit shy and withdrawn, but since the breakup of my engagement last year, I have been completely unable to . . .' or 'I never worried too much about my weight, but since coming to college, I've put on . . .' or 'Drinking and and socializing were always a large part of my job in sales. Although I always drank a lot, I could always handle it. But lately . . .'

In the course of telling the story of his or her problem, the client provides the therapist with a rough idea of his or her orientation toward life, his or her plans, goals, ambitions, and some idea of the events and pressures surrounding the particular presenting problem. Over time, the therapist must decide whether or not this problem represents a minor deviation from an otherwise healthy life story. Is this a normal, developmentally appropriate adjustment issue? Or does the therapist detect signs of more thoroughgoing problems in the client's life story? Will therapy play a minor, supportive role to an individual experiencing a low point in his or her life course? If so, the orientation and major themes of the life will be largely unchanged in the therapy experience. However, if the trajectory of the life story is problematic in some fundamental way, then more serious, long-term story repair (or rebiographing) might be indicated. So, from this perspective, part of the work between client and therapist can be seen as life-story elaboration, adjustment, or repair (Howard, 1991)."

"George," he replied, "I like it! I really do. It's an approach that respects the dignity of the individual; it's teleological, goal oriented, and pragmatic; it's pluralistic because each client can see reality from his or her own perspective; and it calls the client to *action* in repairing his or her life story. It has all of the important elements in my later philosophical writings."

"Oh, don't I know about that, W.J.," I replied. "George Cotkin (1990) wrote a wonderful book, entitled *William James: Public philosopher* which came out 2 years ago. Here's his summary of the point you just made:

> Pragmatism and pluralism were James's preferred vehicles for initiating a strenuous attitude. They did this by presenting a universe in the making, one in which morality was added, rather than inert within the realm of experience. Indeed, the point our ideals "ought to aim at [is] the *transformation of reality*—no less!" Pluralism demanded emotional strength, rather than "fatty degeneration," from the individual. James claimed that the pluralist world "demands" a strenuous stance, "since it makes the world's salvation depend upon the energizing of its several parts, among which we are." The pragmatic individual, living in a universe of chance and change, plastic to his or her will, became, by definition, a reformer. The world stood "malleable, waiting to receive its final touches at our hands." This partly constituted what Gerald E. Myers has called James's "ethics of optimism," his strenuous refusal to accept passivity in psychology and the world, thus translating into "a philosophy of action." (Cotkin, 1990, pp. 169–170)

"By the gods," James stammered, "it's as if he read my mind."

"Not your mind, Willie—he read your books," I replied.

"Now here's where psychotherapy and religion come together," I continued. "A recent Harris Poll found that 94% of adult Americans believe in God. So, it turns out, clinicians are frequently engaged in modifying and repairing maladaptive parts of client stories that have a heavy religious or spiritual theme and flavor to them. And although I have no data to prove it, it's my sense that more and more clinicians themselves possess strongly religious beliefs. It is now becoming more prevalent for some therapists to advertise that their approach to therapy is respectful of clients' religious beliefs, or even to use therapeutic approaches that are appropriate for clients with fundamental religious beliefs. So, I think that psychology's closest and best interaction with religion might now be taking place in the clinic."

"You're making a second career as a psychotherapist sound better and better," James replied. "The sort of religious belief that I endorsed was an active, heroic sort. I summed up my vision of religion in the essay, "Is life worth living?" as follows: "Be not afraid of life. Believe that life *is* worth living, and your belief will help create the fact" (James, 1896/1943, p. 31). George, religion is, in my view, an important *pragmatic* way of making each of our lives better."

"And that fact, Professor James, represents religion's chief warrant for *asserting its own truth*," I replied. "But this pragmatic criterion of truth still sounds odd to many of my contemporaries, who think that religion would be true if there really is a God in heaven who wants us to believe as their religion dictates."

"Oh I love it when you talk pragmatically to me," James kidded, "but are you telling me that most psychologists still believe the mirror-image view of reality in 1992?" the Bostonian asked fearfully. He sighed sadly as I nodded my reply, and James returned to our previous topic. "But tell me, George, how far does this therapy-as-story-telling analogy go? I mean, when I talk to myself, am I telling myself a story? When a community of believers share a history and theological belief system, are they telling a group religious story? When we develop scientific theories, are they just scientific tales? Are scientific facts nothing but human constructions within a given scientific, theoretical fable? Is mathematics itself simply a story of procedures within a universe of rules that places a high demand on internal coherence?"

"Yep," I replied, "It's quite radical, but I now believe that all forms of human thinking represent instances of story telling (Howard, 1991). To use an evolutionary metaphor, the genus of thinking is *story telling*, but among the various species of thought are science, religion, mathematics, common sense, politics, literature, and art. I know that your initial reaction is to recoil from any claim that radical, but I think. . ."

"No! No! No!" James interrupted. "Not at all. I find your thinking-as-story-telling notion quite convivial with what I put forward in A *Pluralistic Universe* and *The Will to Believe*. No, George, I'm not a bit put off by it."

James seemed lost in thought for a moment, and when I caught a glimpse of the clock on my office wall, I noticed that time was passing.

"Look what time it is," I blurted out. "Hey, this is a publish-or-perish world, William, and I still don't have a clue as to what I'll write for the American Psychological Association (APA) volume on your thought. Let's get task oriented, fella."

"Okay," James said as he rolled up his sleeves. "First, you say the book will be based on papers presented at at APA convention. Where was the convention held?"

"Boston," I replied.

"Boston," he chirped as a beatific smile rolled across his face, "on the centennial of my *Principles*. How wonderful!"

I could see a time-consuming, nostalgia trip brewing, and I didn't like it one bit. But I'm afraid he was on a roll.

"And while you were in Boston, George, did you get a chance to visit Harvard?"

"Yes, I did," I grumbled.

"Harvard! Ah, Harvard! How has Harvard fared these past 80 years?"

"Pretty well, I guess," I allowed, "but they still have a crappy football team."

"What?" James asked, "but Harvard was never known for its soccer team."

Soccer! I'd had it with this guy, and I was about to tell him just that when he asked, "George, does your institution have a good football team?"

My voice was dripping with sarcasm as I replied, "Oh, yes, Notre Dame is world famous for its soccer team!"

And without missing a beat, James deadpanned, "Oh, that's nice. Every institution should have *something* at which it excels."

I could take it no more; I was reduced to begging. "Professor James," I pleaded, "I have to pick my kids up from school in 10 minutes Please, help me come up with a theme for this book chapter."

"Okay, George," he began, "as I see it, psychology has explored the research programs staked out in the *Principles* during the last 100 years, and a number of books, articles, and conference papers have fleshed out that picture. Am I right?"

I nodded my assent, and he continued, "But most of my more philosophical insights, in the works after the *Principles*, have remained largely untouched by psychology. Well, why don't you take a stab at laying out psychology's conceptual agenda for the next 100 years, based on the lines of inquiry found in my later, philosophical books?"

"Wait a minute," I began, "if we really do implement research strategies that appreciate your notion that free-will–determinism is *the* true philosophy, it might go a long way toward healing some of the wounds reflected in the scientist–practitioner schism within psychology. It might also lessen some of the problems associated with practitioners entertaining different models of humans than do experimental psychologistis, as suggested in Harré's quote earlier."

"There you go, Georgie," James joined in, "and you can find lots more on that topic in *Pragmatism*. Also, that movement toward integrated eclectisicm in psychotherapy is a wonderful, straightforward application of my notion of pluralistic monism in A *Pluralistic Universe*. And your notion that all forms of thought are variants on stories also fits well with my pluralistic monism. The self is the sole storyteller, and therein lies the unity. But each self can entertain an enormous array of story forms, and therein lies the plurality of perspectives. Each of us tells tales of science, religion, philosophy, common sense, family, country, and politics—often switching perspectives back and forth in rapid succession."

"Yes, that's right," I agreed, "and as we indicated earlier, psychology might now be better able to appreciate stories of religious beliefs. Certainly your *Varieties of Religious Experience* is an important touchstone for anyone who today wanted to seriously pursue psychology and religion. And *The Will to Believe* is another important source. You know, William, I once toyed with the idea of writing a book that was tentatively titled *The Varieties of Religious Experiences in Therapy: The Good, The Bad, and the Ugly*."

James didn't seem to catch my allusion, so I gave him a hint. "Think that will make a good script for a cowboy movie?" I asked. He stared at me blankly and asked. "What are you talking about?"

I gave up. "Forget it, William, It's *after* your time."

But he wouldn't give it up. "Oh my," James blurted out, "that religious experience in therapy idea is a project in which I'd love to be involved. It combines my interest in pluralism, pragmatism, and religion. Plus, it deals with important psychological phenomena like human character, the meaning of life, reality construction and elaboration, and, of course, human-change processes. I'd love to study the paths of religious belief in the clients that I saw in therapy."

"That reminds me," I blurted out, "I once read a letter you wrote to your wife where your said. . ."

"You read a letter that I wrote to my wife?" James interrupted with irritation.

"Why, yes," I replied, "your son William published a volume of them."

"Oh, wonderful," the Bostonian replied.

"In fact, other volumes of your personal correspondence were published by Ralph Barton Perry and your brother Henry, plus your diary was published, as well as . . ."

"Oh, that's just peachy" James bellowed. "I can see that the notion of personal privacy takes a beating in the twentieth century."

"I'm afraid it does," I agreed, "but getting back to that letter to Alice Gibbons, James, you wrote,

> I have often thought that the best way to define a man's character would be to seek out the particular mental or moral attitude in which, when it came upon him, he felt himself most deeply and intensely active and alive. At such moments there is a voice inside which speaks and says: "This is the real me!" (H. James, 1920, p. 73)

You felt psychologists should study a person in that moment and that attitude when he or she was most at one with (or in touch with) the true self. Now it seems to me that psychotherapists are told by clients that there is 'a real me' that they have lost and that they now seek to recover through therapy. Something is very wrong with them at present, and they are unable to find their true self on their own. William, I think that you would find the clinic to be a wonderful laboratory of the human spirit. It is your brand of empirical psychology at its best."

"Quite so!" James roared. "The honorific title of 'the father of scientific psychology in America' (Boring, 1929, p. 660) sat poorly with me in life —and even more so in death. I believe Rand Evans had it right when he said,

> As a transitional figure, James was among the first of the "new" psychologists and the last of the "old." He was an *empirical* psychologist, in the truest meaning of the word, in the same way that Darwin and Freud were. Whether the source of knowledge came through experimental manipulations or common observation in a natural setting, the goal was to gain understanding of the nature of mental life. James' disappointment with experimental psychology had less to do with the method than the paucity of understandings he saw coming from the laboratory. The merit of a psychologist, according to James, whether of experimental or of philosophical stripe, consisted—in the state of the discipline at the time—much less in the *definitiveness* of his conclusions than in his suggestiveness and fertility. (Evans, 1990, p. 23)

"You see, George," James continued, "by the end of my career (by the time I wrote *Pragmatism*), I had come to see knowledge as *activity*, not as contemplation. For the clinician (and for me), 'Theories become instruments, not answers to enigmas in which we can rest. We don't lie back upon them, we move forward, and on occasion make nature over again by their aid' (H. James, 1920, p. 380). The Harré quote emphasized earlier that clinicians use what I call *funded knowledge*, that is, knowledge whose chief claim to truth lies in the fact that it is useful and functional. *Funded* means it was based on both common sense and scientific inquiries. Clinicians are experts in the psychological phenomenon called *coping*, and coping blends elements of knowledge, action, and hope together. All of this is in *Pragmatism*. If there is a secret or truth about human nature, we won't come to know it solely through detached, dispassionate laboratory experiments. We'll gain insights into human nature by studying acts of self-creation—by accompanying clients as they struggle with the important tasks of devising ways of 'being good at being human. Now, if that describes what clinicians do in therapy, then their philosophy is pragmatism—whether or not they know it or acknowledge it."

"You're absolutely correct, Professor James," I said as I stood to leave in order to fetch my kids from preschool. "The *Principles* staked out a conceptual domain for an empirical, experimental psychology. As you once put it, 'I wished, by treating Psychology *like* a natural science, to help her become one' (James, 1890, p. 1237). Because most psychologists became familiar with the *Principles*, but not your later works, you became known as the founder of scientific psychology in America. But through your efforts (as well as those of Charles Sanders Peirce and John Dewey), pragmatism became the unofficial American approach to philosophy. Pragmatism also became the approach that clinicians took in creating and using knowledge in their applied activities. And, if that's so, then you might have become known as the father of clinical psychology if only psychologists had instead focused on your later writings. This is fascinating stuff! It's almost as if James, the clinician, has been lying dormant in your later works, waiting to be discovered, and waiting to come out of the closet. Think of it—William James: A closet clinician!"

As I moved toward the door to leave, James mused, "If I were to become a clincian, I wouldn't do it simply to help people. That is, my clinic would be my laboratory for the study of human nature. My intellectual goal of understanding human nature would be at least as important as the therapeutic benefits I'd hope to engineer. Is that an acceptable ambition for applied psychologists in the 1990s?"

"It sure is," I replied, "it's even got a name; it's called the scientist–practitioner model."

"Wonderful!" James bellowed. "So here's your title for the book chapter, George: *William James: Father of the Scientist–Practitioner Model*. I love it, George! Will you do it?"

I thought for a moment and said, "No, I think not. I don't believe you used the term *scientist–practitioner* once in your writings. So people would probably respond by saying, 'Come on George, you made all that stuff up.' And we wouldn't want them to say that, now would we?"

REFERENCES

Barzun, J. (1983). *A stroll with William James*. New York: Harper & Row.

Beutler, L. E. (1983). *Eclectic psychotherapy: A systematic approach*. New York: Pergamon Press.

Boring, E. (1929). *A history of experimental psychology*. New York: Century.

Brammer, L. M., & Shostrom, E. L. (1977). *Therapeutic psychology* (3rd ed.). Englewood Cliffs, NJ: Prentice-Hall.

Bruner, J. S. (1986). *Actual minds, possible worlds*. Cambridge, MA: Harvard University Press.

Constantinople, A. P. (1973). Masculinity–femininity: An exception to a famous dictum? *Psychological Bulletin, 80,* 389–407.

Cotkin, G. (1990). *William James, public philosopher.* Baltimore: The Johns Hopkins University Press.

Deese, J. (1990). James on the will. In. M. G. Johnson & T. B. Henley (Eds.), *Reflections on the principles of psychology: William James after a century* (pp. 295–309). Hillsdale, NJ: Erlbaum.

Edwards, O. (1791). *Life of Johnson.* London: Dent.

Evans, R. B. (1990). William James and his *Principles.* In M. G. Johnson & T. B. Henley (Eds.), *Reflections on the Principles of Psychology: William James after a century.* Hillsdale, NJ: Erlbaum.

Garfield, S. L. (1980). *Psychotherapy: An eclectic approach.* New York: Wiley.

Giorgi, A. (1990). The implications of James' plea for psychology as a natural science. In M. G. Johnson & T. B. Henely (Eds.), *Reflections on the Principles of Psychology: William James after a century* (pp. 63–75). Hillsdale, NJ: Earlbaum.

Harré, R. (1974). Blueprint for a new science. In A. Nigel (Ed.), *Reconstructing social psychology* (pp. 3–25). Baltimore: Penguin Books.

Howard, G. S. (1988). Kelly's thought at age thirty-three: Suggestions for conceptual and methodological refinements. *International Journal of Personal Construct Psychology, 1,* 263–277.

Howard, G. S. (1990). Aristotle, teleology and modern psychology. *Theoretical and Philosophical Psychology, 10,* 31–38.

Howard, G. S. (1991). Culture tales: A narrative approach to thinking, cross-cultural psychology, and psychotherapy. *American Psychologist, 46,* 188–197.

Howard, G. S. (in press). Steps toward a science of free will. *Counseling and Values.*

Howard, G. S., Nance, D. W., & Myers, P. (1987). *Adaptive counseling and psychotherapy: A systematic approach to selecting effective treatments.* San Francisco: Jossey-Bass.

James, H., Jr. (Ed.). (1920). *The letters of William James* (2 vols.). Boston: Atlantic Monthly Press.

James, W. (1890). *The principles of psychology* (2 vols.) New York: Holt.

James, W. (1921). *Talks to teachers on psychology: And to students on some of life's ideals.* New York: Holt. (Original work published 1899)

James, W. (1929). *The varieties of religious experience.* New York: Random House. (Original work published 1902)

James, W. (1943). *Essays on faith and morals.* New York: Times Mirror. (Original work published 1896)

James, W. (1946). *Pragmatism.* New York: Longmans, Green. (Original work published 1907)

James, W. (1956). *The will to believe*. New York: Dover Publications. (Original work published 1897)

James, W. (1977). *A pluralistic universe*. Cambridge, MA: Harvard University Press. (Original work published 1909)

Johnson, M. G., & Henley, T. B. (1990). *Reflections on the Principles of Psychology: William James after a century*. Hillsdale, NJ: Earlbaum.

Kimble, G. A. (1984). Psychology's two cultures. *American Psychologist, 39*, 833–839.

Kuhn, T. S. (1970). *The structure of scientific revolutions* (2nd ed.). Chicago: University of Chicago Press.

Mahoney, M. J. (1990). *Human change processes*. New York: Basic Books.

Markus, H. (1990). On splitting the universe. *Psychological Science, 1*, 181–185.

Myers, G. E. (1981). Introduction: The intellectual context. In W. James, *The principles of psychology* (Vol. I). Cambridge, MA: Harvard University Press.

Perry, R. B. (1935). *The thought and character of William James*. Boston: Little, Brown.

Price, W., & Chissick, S. (1977). *Uncertainty principle and the foundation of quantum mechanics: A fifty years survey*. New York: Wiley.

Wittgenstein, L. (1958). *The blue and brown books*. New York: Harper & Row.

20

WILLIAM JAMES ON THE MIND AND THE BODY

DANIEL N. ROBINSON

When I was asked to contribute some thoughts on William James and the mind–body problem to this volume, I hesitated. After all, the mind–body problem is not one that benefited in any enduring way from James's attention, nor is it the sort of problem likely to enjoy much by way of original solutions. The imaginable alternatives were well in place by the time Gassendi mounted his criticism of Descartes, and the two of them debated the issues in print. The sort of *epiphenomenalism* espoused by Huxley—of which I will say more—was newer in name than in substance and, in any case, was just another way of advancing the cause of naturalistic philosophy against the antievolutionists.

Yet, the narrow sense in which William James failed to be original in his comments on the mind–body problem is the same sense in which so much of his philosophy and psychology is unoriginal. They are, as it were, assiduously unoriginal. The absence of novelty in James's discourse is attributable not to any lack of intellectual power or agility, but to a disciplined—one should say stubborn—refusal to edit nature or rewrite her facts and principles. Moreover, as is abundantly clear from the scholarship displayed in *The Principles of Psychology*, (1890/1981), James was widely and deeply read in every branch of philosophy and biological science. He was a masterful student of the history of ideas long before he set out to contribute to it, and so he knew enough to recognize that most of the putatively original ideas of his own day had been articulated and developed time and again throughout the Long Debate. In light of this, it makes very good sense to examine James's understanding of and position on the mind–body problem, for such an examination serves to illustrate what might be called the Jamesian method of *organon*, which has very much to recommend it, particularly in an age that places a high premium on the new.

Students of James, considering his contributions to this specific if venerable problem, will quickly discern those telltale marks of James the realist, the pragmatist, the antimetaphysician, the pluralist, and the radical empiricist. James understood the world by the very doings of the world, and this is how James, too, must be understood. His psychology was just the totality of his mental exertions expended on behalf of the subject. His psychology, that is, was just the way he did psychology, and this included his exertions on behalf of the mind–body problem.

Although this assignment is sound, it is not at all easy. Of the truly consequential figures in psychology's long and varied history, James is among the most difficult to summarize or compress, for his entire system of thought is opposed to every species of reduction, simplification, and finality. The task of conveying his position on the mind–body problem is especially daunting because he dealt with it in quite different contexts and, therefore, in quite different ways. Of the traditional solutions to the problem, one might well find evidence for his tolerance for *all* of them at one time or another, in one passage or another. This very fact could suggest superficiality on James's part, but, as already noted, this tolerance in James is official and instructive. It is a central part of the more general lessons to be gleaned from the entire corpus of his work.

MIND–BODY ISSUE IN THE NINETEENTH CENTURY

Perhaps the most direct path to James's approach to the mind–body issue is by recalling the attitudes toward the issue prevalent in James's day. His earliest systematic discussion of the matter is to be found in the still unpublished notes he composed for the 1878 Lowell Lectures, given at Johns Hopkins University and then later in the same year at the Lowell Institute in Boston.[1] By 1878, the battle lines were fairly well drawn in psychology

---

[1] A most informing discussion of these notes is provided by Daniel W. Bjork (1988) in *William James: The Center of His Vision*.

between and among the British empiricists, the radical Darwinists, the Kantian and Hegelian transcendentalists, and the garden-variety materialists. John Stuart Mill had wisely elected to respect both the laws of the body and the laws of the mind, but his tentativeness here invited criticism even from so admiring a friend as Alexander Bain.[2] Moderation was to be more the exception than the rule. It was John Tyndall who insisted that, as the liver secretes bile, the brain secretes thought, and it was the ever formidable Thomas Henry Huxley who took the realm of the mental to be no more than an epiphenomenon of brain function. "The soul," wrote Huxley, "stands related to the body as the bell of a clock to the works, and consciousness answers to the sound which the bell gives out when it is struck" (1874, p. 576).

Across the channel, a less orderly metaphysics was being applied to the emerging scientific psychology. Recall that Kant had declared the impossibility of any such discipline. Science requires measurement, and measurement requires that the object of inquiry remains constant during the observational interval. The mind is notoriously inconstant and, Kant (1781/1965) argued, is altered by the very act of reflecting on its own operations. Nonetheless, through his famous transcendental analytic, Kant was able to reveal those pure categories of the understanding that necessarily stand at the foundation of all cognitive–noetic processes.[3] Thus, a critical philosophy is able to deduce what no science could possibly disclose. Herbart (1891, p. 4) conceded the main points on this, but pressed on toward something of a deductive science of psychology and, in the process, laid the foundations for Fechner's derivation of the psychophysical law from Weber's ratio law. All this was sufficient to encourage Wundt that an experimental psychology, far from being impossible, was very nearly in place, but nothing occurring in the Leipzig laboratory was regarded by the transcendentalists as even relevant to the issue.

This same critical philosophy of Kant's had set limits on the reach of reason itself and had come to authorize what might ambiguously be referred to as *intuitive* means by which to break through the barrier dividing the phenomenal world of appearances and the noumenal world of things as in themselves they really are. It was one of the promises of the Hegelian system that the *phenomenological science*—a science constructed out of the analysis of *Geist*—would transcend the limited and one-sided nature of the empirical sciences. For the mind—for the spirit—to be analyzed phenomenologically requires nothing less than an inquiry into the various manifestations of

---

[2]Mill's position is discussed in chapter 2 of Daniel N. Robinson's (1982) *Toward a Science of Human Nature: Essays on the Psychologies of Hegel, Mill, Wundt and James.*

[3]This is developed by Kant in his *Critique of Pure Reason* (1781/1965), in "Analytic Concepts" (pp. 104–119).

Geist, not merely into consciousness and self-consciousness, but, more important, into human history and culture. Compared with the Hegelian agenda, the project of experimental psychology seemed to many to be puny and jejune. Where the latter would busy itself with reaction time and memory drums, the Hegelian phenomenology was offered as a "Psychologie der Weltanschauungen."

As for the Darwinists, the mind–body problem was a problem that solved itself, once one adopted a purely naturalistic perspective and recognized that the psychological and material organization of animals has been shaped by the struggle for survival. The successful creature is one whose adaptive features have been favored, as it were, by an environment to which these features happen to be suited. Creatures lacking these attributes soon and simply leave the breeding pool. A scientific psychology, based on this construal, might profitably confine itself to modes of adaptive behavior and to studies of the manner in which the evolution of specific brain mechanisms makes such behavior possible.

By the time of the Lowell Lectures of 1878, then, the world of psychology was torn between reductionisms and transcendentalisms, each now so radicalized that debates were more or less confined to members of the same party and faction. "Each one of us," James said,

> probably is to some extent a partizan in the matter. . . The worst of it
> is that in this matter of the brain and the mind people are ready to
> become very eager partizans on a very slender basis of study. (Bjork,
> 1988, p. 113)

As James considered the matter, he was satisfied that extreme positions were simply untenable, for they were confuted by the facts of everyday life as these facts are recorded and integrated in experience. Radical materialism, even in the form of radical naturalism, explains everything except what actually matters to us and, for that matter, to all of the developed species. As James would write in *Pragmatism* (1907), "No, the true objection to materialism is not positive but negative. . . We make complaint of it . . . for what it is *not*—not a permanent warrant for our more ideal interests, not a fulfiller of our remotest hopes" (McDermott, 1977, p. 398). From the pragmatic perspective, it would matter not in the least were the entire history of life on earth the result of purely material processes or, instead, the consequence of nonmaterial influences. The facts of the world remain just what they are on either account and must be dealt with in a manner that accords with our "ideal interests" and our "remotest hopes," whatever theory we adopt to explain them.

What is salient about James's position is his learned impatience with psychological speculations that are *merely* speculative, that is, speculative but inconsequential. It is worth pausing here to reflect on the position James might take now, a century later, when we possess information regarding human brain function that would have seemed incredible to scholars a century ago. Clearly, his position on radical materialism would not be affected in the least, for it is a position that requires of psychological theories attention to our "ideal interests" and "remotest hopes," and these, it would seem, remain stable even over eons.

LIMITATIONS OF DARWINISM

Turning to these hopes and interests, one discovers what James always found incomplete and rather innocent in the Darwinian school of psychology as applied not only to human beings, but even to much of the animal kingdom at large. In the chapter, "The Automaton Theory," in the *Principles*, James came to grips with the purpose of consciousness in the animal kingdom and the implications arising from this in regard to Darwinian comparative psychology. It is in this chapter than James advanced a form of interactive dualism, but this, as mentioned earlier, is less notable than the manner in which he set out to understand the problem itself. In highly redacted form, this is the problem as James understood it: At the most general level, there are two theoretical alternatives which account for the adaptive behavior of the advanced species. There is the *automaton theory*, a vestige of Descartes's celebrated depreciation of infrahuman psychology, which is the strongest argument I can think of for requiring philosophers to keep pets. According to this theory, even the most complex modes of behavioral adaptation can be fully explained by considering no more than the sensory, integrative, and motor anatomies of the organism and the principles of their operation.

The alternative to this is a theory arising from the presumption of consciousness, at least in the advanced species, and the recognition that, if there is such, it must serve some fundamental purpose or interest of the organism. To argue for the automaton theory abstractly is something James rejected with vigor. As he put it, "To urge the automaton-theory upon us, as it is now urged, on purely *a priori* and *quasi*-metaphysical grounds, is an *unwarrantable impertinence in the present state of psychology*" (1890/1981, p. 141). Instead, psychologists must consider theories of this sort practically and scientifically. Does the alleged function of consciousness manifest itself in the actual life of the organism and permit adjustments otherwise less efficacious in its absence? This brought James to the nub of the matter. Complex nervous systems are inherently unstable and indeterminate in their performance. "Consciousness," said James, ". . . is at all times primarily *a selecting agency*" (1890/1981, p. 142) by which the operations of the system are brought to bear on some central interest of the organism. In animals in which consciousness seems most highly developed, there is apparently the greatest instability of the cortical systems, owing to their complexity. Consciousness, James argued, helps to overcome this defect and increases the efficiency of the brain "by loading its dice" (1890/1981, p. 143) and otherwise biasing its activity in the direction of those interests consciousness has selected.

But, of course, every interest is *someone's* interest. That is, there are no disembodied interests nor, alas, can mere bodies qua bodies have interests. Accordingly, the Darwinian account is insufficiently psychological to handle the apparent facts of the matter. James put it this way:

> Loading its dice would mean bringing a more or less constant pressure to bear in favor of *those* of its performances which make for the most permanent interests of the brain's owner; it would mean a constant inhibition of the tendencies to stray aside . . . And the interests in whose favor it seems to exert them are *its* interests and its alone, interests which it *creates*, and which, but for it, would have no status in the realm of being whatever. (1890/1981, p. 143)

Of course, the materialist might well reply that these alleged interests are no more than conditions of need or deprivation at the level of cells and organs and that it is the state of the body that impels the relevant drive-reducing behaviors. Indeed, the passage from James just cited is something of an invitation to the psychobiologist to advance a homeostatic theory or, worse, a Hullian one! But this would miss the main point of James's analysis, which is given special emphasis in the following lengthy quotation in which the distinction is drawn between mindless adaptation and the pursuit of real interests:

> We talk, it is true, when we are darwinizing, as if the mere *body* that owns the brain had interests; we speak about the utilities of its various organs and how they help or hinder the body's survival; and we treat the survival as if it were an absolute end, existing as such in the physical world, a sort of actual *should-be*, presiding over the animal and judging his reactions, quite apart from the presence of any commenting intelligence outside. We forget that in the absence of some such superadded commenting intelligence (whether it be that of the animal itself, or only ours or Mr. Darwin's), the reactions cannot be properly talked of as "useful" or "hurtful" at all. . . In a word, survival can enter into a purely physiological discussion only as an *hypothesis made by an onlooker* about the future. But the moment you bring a consciousness into the midst, survival ceases to be a mere hypothesis. No longer is it, "*if* survival is to occur" . . . It has now become an imperative decree:

"Survival *shall* occur. . ." *Real* ends appear for the first time now upon the world's stage. (James, 1890/1981, pp. 143–144)

These passages attempt to establish a core of propositions that illustrate with convenient efficiency and clarity James's overarching perspective on psychological issues. First is his famous impatience with a priori or deductive approaches to questions that call for actual data and scientific inference. Of all the ways the animal economy might have been brought about, it is surely not a logical requirement that the psychological dimensions of life be reducible to material organization; it is surely not necessary that animals be automata. Thus, whether or not this is the case is a matter to be settled by observation and inferences warranted by observation.

CONSCIOUSNESS

What everyone recognizes as a fact of one's own mental life is the principal function of consciousness, its *selecting* function. And what is finally selected is what bears on our interests—those that are immediate or those that are more remote. Consciousness, then, is the pragmatic function par excellence; it is the means by which "ideal interests" and "remotest hopes" might incline all of the systems of the body, but certainly the highest nerve centers, in such a way as to be ever more efficacious. The evidence that this may well be the case is that it must be the case with creatures such as ourselves whose brains are otherwise unstable and indeterminate and whose bodies qua bodies cannot have any interests at all. It becomes more clear how materialism and Darwinism fail the pragmatic test applied to psychological theories.

If materialism fails because it ignores our actual interests and remotest hopes, does the transcendental option thus recommend itself? For to read James's critique of materialism and our darwinized manner of speech is, after all, to expect him to affirm some idealistic or Hegelian alternative. But it must be recalled that this same William James titled one of his most famous and influential articles, "Does Consciousness Exist?" (James, 1904), and described consciousness and the transcendental ego as having evaporated into an "estate of pure diaphaneity" (McDermott, 1977, p. 69). James's impatience with what he called *hegelisms* was at least as developed as his irritation with materialists. What both shared, in James's view, was a preference for theory over honest labor, a delight in single-cause accounts of complex phenomena, and a tendency to foreclose debate and to confine perspective. James was no more inclined than Ryle to install ghosts in the machinery of the body, but he was entirely unwilling to surrender to metaphysicians the facts of his own mental life. In the very essay in which he asked whether consciousness exists, he made clear that he had no doubt at all about consciousness as a function. Moreover, James wrote, "Whoever blots out the notion of consciousness from his list of first principles must still provide in some way for that function's being carried on" (McDermott, 1977, p. 170).

Materialism and transcendentalism offer two different realities, but both of these realities must be wedged into that *block universe* that is the object of such lively criticism in James's *A Pluralistic Universe* (1909). There is a passage in that estimable work in which the spirit of James's radical empiricism is clearly revealed, this time in opposition to those philosophies of the absolute arising from the Hegelian system. James was considering the pantheistic beliefs that acknowledge the participation of ultimate forces or principles in the facts of the cosmos, and he made this observation:

> But we say that this pantheistic belief could be held in two forms, a monistic form which I call the philosophy of the absolute, and a pluralistic form which I call radical empiricism, the former conceiving that the divine exists authentically only when the world is experienced all at once in its absolute totality, whereas radical empiricism allows that the absolute sum-total of things may never be actually experienced or realized in that shape at all, and that a disseminated, distributed, or incompletely unified appearance is the only form that reality may yet have achieved. (James, 1909, p. 43)

The final fragment of this book-length sentence deserves closest attention. James was referring not to the limits of our knowledge as such, but to the actual level of completion reality itself has attained. There may indeed be some distant time in which the absolute ego has been liberated from the gross and troubled state of corporeal life or a time when the vaunted productions and pretensions of the mind are fully absorbed into the clutter and clatter of the body–machine. Whatever the long-range prospects, they are not deducible, and it is nothing less than an impertinence for ordinary mortals, even those in possession of doctoral degrees, to legislate human destiny or dictate the final act of the cosmic story. James respected the complexity *and* the limitations of the mind. He was fearful—with good reason—that those eager to give psychology scientific respectability would do so by depreciating or ignoring this complexity. Reductive approaches to the mind–body problem were illustrative of this tendency, which is just the old psychologist's fallacy in another of its manifestations. One begins with a simplistic theory and proceeds to conduct comparably simplistic research leaving no room for contradicting outcomes.

As on so many other topics, William James on the mind and the body is not likely to please those who consult either philosophy or psychology for ultimate answers. It has long been my own judgment that James and Aristotle remain the psycholgists most worth reading in the entire history of what James called this nasty little subject, but people look in vain for a Jamesian school or faction in psychology. This is not surprising. Schools, systems, and factions arise when there is general agreement that a problem has been solved, alternative perspectives have been vanquished, and remaining possibilities have become worthless or silly. It was in response to this very agreement, these prematurely settled positions, however, that James wrote and lectured for 40 years. Scientific psychology was attempting to overcome the complexity of its own subject matter by adopting one or another reductive scheme, chiefly of the materialistic stripe. Transcendental psychologies were attempting to salvage the spiritual side of human life by depreciating the ordinary facts of life, because these occur in life as it is actually lived and experienced.

In rejecting both programs, James could not please the votaries of either or their disciples in succeeding generations—including our own—who were seeking the comforts of intellectual fraternity. "There is no possible point of view," wrote James,

> from which the world can appear an absolutely single fact. Real possibilities, real indeterminations, real beginnings, real ends, real evil, real crises, catastrophes, and escapes, a real God, and a real moral life, just as common sense conceives these things, may remain in empiricism as conceptions which that philosophy gives up the attempt either to "overcome" or to reinterpret in monistic form. (James, 1897, pp. vii–x)

Progress of a sort has been made in working out some of the details connected with problem solving, cognition, information processing, and other events in the brain as these psychological functions take place. This progress has fortified many in the belief that psychology's enduring issues will soon be settled in the laboratory and primarily by the so-called *brain sciences*. In the present context, it may be useful to apply again the *pragmatic* standard that James found so serviceable. Suppose every significant aspect of life were the result of events in the brain. How would any one of these aspects differ in the actual lived life of that person? How would its significance be affected?

If we are to honor the memory of James, we might do so most faithfully by following his counsel, which, in the present circumstance, would urge us to concern ourselves primarily with those scientific or experimental details that make some intelligible contact with the actual lives lived by actual beings pursuing their "ideal interests" and "remotest hopes." His counsel would go further, of course, and oblige us to appreciate that, in the very act of entering the laboratory or consulting the brain sciences, we have limited our perspective; that, in order to see clearly, we may see everything but what made the inquiry vitally important in the first place.

REFERENCES

Bjork, D. W. (1988). *William James: The center of his vision*. New York: Columbia University Press.

Herbart, J. F. (1891). *A text-book in psychology. An attempt to found the science of psychology on experience, metaphysics, and mathematics* (Margaret K. Smith, Trans.). New York: Appleton.

Huxley, T. H. (1874). On the hypothesis that animals are automata and its history. *Fortnightly Review, 16*, 555–580.

James, W. (1897). *The will to believe and other essays in popular philosophy*. New York: Holt.

James, W. Does consciousness exist? *Journal of Philosophy, Psychology and Scientific Methods, 1*, 477–491.

James W. (1907). *Pragmatism: A new name for some old ways of thinking*. New York: Longmans, Green.

James W. (1909). *A pluralistic universe*. New York: Longmans, Green.

James W. (1981). *The principles of psychology* (3 vols.). Cambridge, MA: Harvard University Press. (Original work published 1890)

Kant, I. (1965). *Critique of pure reason* (Normal Kemp Smith, Trans.). New York: St. Martin's. (Original work published 1781)

McDermott, J. (1977). *The writings of William James*. Chicago: University of Chicago Press.

Robinson, D. N. (1982). *Toward a science of human nature: Essays on the psychologies of Hegel, Mill, Wundt and James*. New York: Columbia University Press.

21

WILLIAM JAMES AND THE CONCEPT OF FREE WILL

JOSEPH F. RYCHLAK

William James received his MD in the spring of 1869, and by the fall of that year, he had slumped into a depressed state of mind that was to last for the next 2 years (Perry, 1948). Apparently, there were both career and religious concerns troubling James. He struggled with the concept of predestination, as embraced in his beloved father's Calvinism, and as a countermeasure, he studied the French philosopher, Charles Bernard Renouvier. James's biographer, Ralph Barton Perry (1948), said that Renouvier "was the greatest individual influence on the development of James's thought" (p. 153). By April 30 of 1870, James had found some reassurance in his studies, for he recorded in his diary on that date the following:

> I think that yesterday was a crisis in my life. I finished the first part of Renouvier's second *Essais* and see no reason why his definition of free will [i.e.,] "the sustaining of a thought *because I choose to* when I might have other thoughts"—need be the definition of an illusion. At any rate, I will assume for the present . . . that it is no illusion. My first act of free will shall be to believe in free will. (H. James, 1920, p. 147)

Renouvier was a Kantian idealist who believed that only phenomena (and not noumena) have real existence and, then, only through a logical tie to other phenomena, as in the case of one phenomenal meaning predicating another. Yet James's formal approach to psychology seems more Lockean than Kantian, more in the vein of British empiricism than continental philosophy. In the early 1870s, James was a member of a small group of intellectuals who regularly discussed philosophy with what one of their members called a clearly "English accent" (Perry, 1948, p. 130). This point will be returned to later.

James clearly wanted to present human beings as intentional organisms. He may have been a bit more apparent and even successful in this regard when writing as a philosopher than when writing as a psychologist (Dooley, 1975). But in this chapter, the focus will be primarily on *The Principles of Psychology* (James, 1890/1952) as this book has been in print for just over 100 years. This chapter will begin with a consideration of what I call James's *second-event* argument, will carry this argument forward to his treatment of consciousness, and then will show its relevence to his understanding of free will. The chapter will then focus on some problems with his formulation before ending with the suggestion that there is an alternative Jamesian explanation of free will to be found in his writings, one that he seemed to have been cognizant of but rejected for specific reasons.

JAMES'S SECOND-EVENT ARGUMENT

As early as 1868, before he had completed medical school, James was planning to apply the findings on the physiology of the nervous system to the fledgling field of psychology (Perry, 1948). In 1878, he signed a contract with the publisher Henry Holt to complete a book on psychology within 2 years. But it wasn't until 12 years later, in 1890, that the book we now celebrate reached print. One can see an interesting theoretical maneuver being repeatedly applied by James in *The Principles of Psychology*.

I am referring here to James's second-event argument. He used this argument in the *Principles* to explain many things. One of the chief explanations was how biophysiological beginnings of actions result in learned behaviors. James argued that because behavior is based on physical action and because an action must happen before it is an action, the very first actions made by an organism must have been built into its biological and physiological structures as instinctive or reflexive movements.

Organisms can have no a priori idea of a movement because, as James said, "Before the idea [of movement] can be generated, the movement must have occurred in a blind, unexpected way, and left its idea behind" (1890/1952, p. 827). Memory changes the circumstances of a behavioral action. Once these actions have occurred, as a first event, it becomes possible for such actions to be known, recalled, adapted, and delayed as a second event in the subsequent actions of the organism concerned. James also explained the functioning of sensation in this second-event manner. Thus, he observed that a *"pure sensation can only be realized in the earliest days of life"* (1890/1952, p. 456). Following this initial, spontaneous experience, one's grasp of a sensation becomes colored by memories of these now past events, plus the associated contexts within which they had previously occurred.

This second-event form of theorizing is apparent in James's well-known interpretation of the emotions, although in this case, he did not focus on the changes that an organism with a memory can inflict on the spontaneous physical experience. The so-called *James–Lange theory* holds that bodily changes occur first, quite reflexively, and then, second, the feeling that an organism has of these changes is the emotion (James, 1890/1952). In this instance, James was focusing more on the purely physical changes as a second event than on the cognitive factors that trail such physical actions in memory. This theory means that we see the bear, run, and are afraid. But having done this a couple of times, the timorous hunter with a memory might be seeing yet another bear, running again, but this time feeling shame rather than fear. James did not discuss this possibility, but it is surely implied in all that he has to say about the reflexive versus the remembered physical action.

THE NATURE OF CONSCIOUSNESS

The first- and second-event style of theorizing appears in James's treatment of consciousness and thought. Renouvier's neo-Kantian philosophy would have described thought as a first event, one that actively conceptualized what was to be known in a priori fashion. The mind was phenomenally framed. But James, however, did not make thought out to be conceptualizing in this fashion. If thought begins in the physical processes of the brain, then something like a conceptualization would have to arise as a second event, after the first event of some reflexive brain action had taken place. It is therefore not surprising that James suggested that, rather than conceptualization, *"emphasis and selection* [italics added] seem to be the essence of the human mind"* (1890/1952, p. 670). Consciousness is primarily a *"selecting agency"* (1890/1952, p. 91). Certain mental contents are selected for attention. Attention, defined as the "taking possession by the mind" (1890/1952, p. 261), is the way in which emphasis is given to certain mental contents rather than to others.

Thought flows along in consciousness as a stream, and through the attention's emphasis, a portion of this stream can be arrested or blocked off from flowing for a time. Of course, we do not exactly bestow attention on the stream of objects flowing by in consciousness. Bestowal would make attention a first event. An object in consciousness has the initiative and then draws our attention to it secondarily. We see the door leading out of the room. It draws our attention. We can then attend to this object, giving it emphasis, and find our way out of the room intentionally. This form of second event is what is meant by *volition*. Cognition is therefore a stream of simultaneous possibilities, and "consciousness consists in the comparison of these [various possibilities] with each other, the selection of some, and the suppression of the rest by the reinforcing and inhibiting agency of attention" (James, 1890/1952, p. 187). This is how choice occurs.

This view of the mind as a second event carries over to James's philosophy of pragmatism. The pragmatic method involves taking an idea that has been framed as a first event and then "tracing its respective practical consequences" (James, 1907/1943, p. 42) as a second event. It is not the initiating side of thought that James fixed on as a pragmatist. He was not impressed by the a priori meanings of an initiating idea. We must look to the practical consequences or cash value of an idea if we are to determine whether it expresses something meaningful. Does the idea make a difference in what transpires following its utterance? If there is no such secondary outcome discernible, then, for all practical purposes, the idea lacks truth value (James, 1907/1943). It is difficult to see the influence of Renouvier in this style of explanation. The strong influence of a John Locke is much easier to discern here, which leads me to consider the Jamesian interpretation of free will.

JAMES'S EXPLANATION OF FREE WILL

James's explanation of free will in the *Principles* relied heavily on the second-event line of argument. The first event is the stream of consciousness. Ideas are associated, one to another, but this is not a mere chain-linking, mechanical process. As James (1890/1952) expressed it,

> Consciousness . . . does not appear to itself chopped up in bits. Such words as "chain" or "train" do not describe it fitly as it presents itself in the first instance. It is nothing jointed; it flows. A "river" or a "stream" is the metaphor by which it is most naturally described. (p. 155)

As I have already suggested, the second event in consciousness, from which a free-will action takes root, is attention. Attention fixes the various possibilities to be found, flowing along in consciousness, under their own weight. Attention selects from among these possibilities by lending emphasis to certain alternatives rather than to others. Continuing with his river metaphor, James suggested that attention causes logjams to occur at certain points as follows:

> The stream of our thought is like a river. On the whole easy simple flowing predominates in it, the drift of things is with one pull of gravity, and effortless attention is the rule. But at intervals an obstruction, a set-back, a log-jam occurs, stops the current, creates an eddy, and makes things temporarily move the other way. . . . Just so with our voluntary acts of attention. They are momentary arrests coupled with a peculiar feeling. (1890/1952, pp. 293–294)

The "peculiar feeling" referred to in this quote is that of effort. James held to the so-called *ideomotor action theory*, which states that the mere idea of an action can bring it about. However, James realized that sometimes an additional cognitive element "in the shape of a fiat, mandate, or express consent" (1890/1952, p. 790) must be added to the idea in order to get it enacted, and this is sensed as effort. It is the ego or the "I" as a pure sense of personal selfhood that levels the fiat. James (1899) once suggested that by willfully acting in a cheerful manner, an uncheerful person could sometimes induce a happier mood. This effort is a manifestation of will, which relies on attention—attending to the possibilities flowing by in the stream of conscious thoughts.

James, therefore, concluded that a freely willed action "could only be to hold some one ideal object, or part of an object, a little longer or a little more intensely before the mind" as the stream of thought flowed by (James, 1890/1952, p. 825). The free-will controversy, he suggested, "relates solely to the amount of effort of attention or consent which we can at any time put forth" (1890/1952, p. 822). But James went even further to equate will and belief. He actually paraphrased the quote from his diary concerning Renouvier as follows: "The free-will question arises as regards belief. If our wills are indeterminate, so must our beliefs be, etc. The first act of free-will, in short, would naturally be to believe in free-will, etc" (1890/1952, p. 661).

James argued that a freely willing person would act as if his or her beliefs were real, thereby literally bringing them about in overt behavior— much as the cheerful mood is willfully brought about. This is an early phrasing of what would come to be known as his pragmatic philosophy. Beliefs become overt truths thanks to their willful execution by the believer. One is little surprised, therefore, to read in James's Lowell Lectures that free will, pragmatically, means a belief that there are novelties in the world, with the attendant "right to expect that in its deepest elements as well as in its surface phenomena, the future may not identically repeat and imitate the past" (James, 1907/1943, p. 84). He went on to refer to free will as a cosmological theory of promise, "just like the Absolute, God, Spirit or Design" (1907/1943, p. 84). He even suggested that the free-will concept would be unnecessary if the world were "perfect from the start" (1907/1943, p. 84).

PROBLEMS WITH JAMES'S EXPLANATION OF FREE WILL

I have two major criticisms to make of James's treatment of free will. The first has to do with what I call a *confounding of process with content*. If one uses the phrase "free will" in the sense of a process, then one is talking about some way in which it may be said to work in the cognitions of people. The task here is akin to the biophysiologist's task of describing how the stomach contributes to the digestive process. How does the stomach work? But, here, the phrase free will is also used to describe a belief, which is more like a content being carried along by a process. Even if a psychologist could show that all people work according to a free-will process of cognition, this does not mean that everyone working this way would believe that they do indeed have free will. This belief is something different from a process; it is a content within a process. In like fashion, just because the biophysiologist has proved that all people can digest insects, this does not mean that all people actually eat insects. In fact, most people may not eat them. The process of digestion per se is different from and should not be confused with, the contents put through this process by the digesting organism.

James's statement about accepting Renouvier's definition of free will nicely summarizes the distinction that I am making: "My first act of free will shall be to believe in free will"(H. James, 1920, p. 147). James was both acting in a presumably freely willing manner (*process*), even as he affirmed his belief in free will per se (*content*). Because this commitment to the belief will be carried over pragmatically into his ongoing cognitions, James found it reasonable to equate the process of willfully accepting a belief with the belief itself. But I find this a questionable practice. James seemed to have tied the free-will concept to religion, which is ever pointed to improving a person's lot in this world. As a result, he found it implausible to think that people would use their free will in a self-defeating manner: " 'Freedom' in a world already perfect could only mean freedom to *be worse*, and who could be so insane as to wish that?" (James, 1907/1943, p. 85).

I would suggest that an accurate psychological explanation of free will as a process must include the possibility that people will use this process to worsen their lot, to intentionally do things to others and to themselves that are harmful and destructive. So, in a process explanation of free will, the end result need not be construed positively. It is only when free will is considered in the context of a religious belief system that the positive outcome is to be desired. At one point in the *Principles*, when James was contemplating free will more as a process than a belief, he seemed to give up on an explanation as follows:

> My own belief is that the question of free will is insoluble on strictly psychologic grounds. After a certain amount of effort of attention has been given to an idea, it is manifestly impossible to tell whether either more or less of it *might* have been given or not. To tell that, we should have to ascend to the antecedents of the effort, and defining them with mathematical exactitude, prove, by laws of which we have not at present even an inkling, that the only amount of sequent effort which could *possibly* comport with them was the precise amount which actually came. Measurements, whether of psychic or of neural quantities, and deductive reasonings such as this method of proof implies, will surely be forever beyond human reach. (James, 1890/1952, p. 822)

The second objection that I have to James's treatment of free will has been made previously in criticisms of John Locke's handling of this topic. Locke began his theorizing with the assumption that there are a number of uneasinesses (motives) that impel the person's will to choose some course in life, such as feeling hungry before bedtime. But as a mental action, the will does not have to be carried forward immediately. It can hang fire, so to speak, and suspend the execution of actions that might terminate the uneasinesses. One can delay his or her impulse to raid the refrigerator before retiring. During the suspended course of action, the human being can look over things from several angles and judge the benefit or harm, good or evil, of what it is that he or she is about to do. Eating before bedtime can result in a weight gain or an upset stomach, but it is sometimes easier to fall asleep when one is satiated, and it is pleasurable to snack at night in any case. Depending on how one analyzes the situation during the delay, he or she heads for the kitchen or the bedroom. Based on this line of theorizing, Locke (1690/1952) concluded, "This seems to me the source of all liberty; in this [suspension of action] seems to consist that which is (as I think improperly) called *free-will*" (p. 190).

Locke's treatment of free will is obviously not much different from James's position. As Rickaby (1906) said, the problem with such a "suspending action" (Locke) or "focusing attention" (James) explanation is that it fails to make clear how and why the mental process suspends or focuses in the first place. Why do people sometimes *not* focus or suspend, but carry behavior forward in an unexamined, spontaneous manner? Locke's understanding of the cognitive process was as a chain of ongoing ideas, either simple or complex in nature; although James preferred the stream to the chain metaphor, he too had ideas carried along associatively from their beginnings in reflex action of other first events that have been carried inward to the mind from life experience. Although they both sought to capture cognition as an active process, neither Locke nor James construed the essence of the mind to be a conceptualizing first event, as was true of Kant—and Renouvier!

Recall that James had mind playing primarily a selection and emphasis role in the flow of conscious experience (James, 1890/1952). To account for the choice made in selection and emphasis, James had to bring in an essentially unexplained identify process—the "I, me, myself," or pure ego as the agent to serve as the chooser (James, 1890/1952, p. 155). But this is tantamount to assigning an unexplained homunculus to do the choosing in a machine process. The homunculus becomes the telic agent, but the process by which it decides is not known in the first place. There is no way of picturing how the fiat is accomplished. One can see the river flowing along and imagine logjams occurring, but if these logjams are brought about by the pure ego purposively, what is the process by which this feat is achieved? James never really answered this satisfactorily.

IS THERE AN ALTERNATIVE JAMESIAN EXPLANATION OF FREE WILL?

Based on what has been seen thus far, I have difficulty accepting Perry's claim that James was so greatly influenced by Renouvier. As a neo-Kantian idealist, Renouvier's idea of the mind was much more conceptual, organizing a first-event frame of reference that brought meaning to bear at the outset rather than waiting around for something to happen so that it could be selected and emphasized in a second-event manner. Of course, it must not be forgotten that James was an eclectic thinker. There are intimations of an alternative treatment of free will in James's broader writings, a treatment that Renouvier probably would have endorsed. I will draw out this alternative theory of free will, because I think it is more on the mark than the theory that James actually settled on.

First of all, I will distinguish between what I have termed a *mediational* and a *predicational* model of behavior (Rychlak, 1990). By a mediation model, I mean a form of explanation in which something formed outside a process is taken in and comes to play a role in that process that is not intrinsic to it. In cognition, for example, the meanings under conveyance by a mediational process are always taken in as a completed given, formed by some source exterior to the mediational process. Mediational processing per se never articulates or forms this meaning. Mediational processes are, therefore, second events by definition.

Traditional stimulus–response (S–R) theory (e.g., Hull, 1952) is a prime example of mediational modeling, in which the Jamesian second-event argument fits very nicely. In explaining the learning of language, the S–R theorist might suggest that, initially (first event), the child makes some sounds such as "ma ma." These responses occur reflexively and are then shaped externally by the (second event) reinforcements of the doting mother. They are stored in the form shaped by the reinforcement and used later as mediators to facilitate even further learning. All learning occurs this way, with events shaped by external experience brought inward to influence the form and course of cognitive processing. The process itself is more the shaped than the shaper of behavior, acting like a conveyor belt in moving ongoing (second) events along. Modern cognitive theories relying on the computer analogue have not significantly altered this style of explanation, for they too are mediational models.

The problem with the mediational model is that it is hard pressed to account for agency or free will. What James called the selection and emphasis role of attention is explained by pointing to the reinforcement history of the mediating mechanism. Those mediators that were reinforced in the past would be selected and emphasized today. James would certainly not have preferred this mechanistic (nontelic) style of explanation. He apparently tried to avoid it by using his stream of consciousness metaphor, but the second-event argument seems to have pulled him back into this mediational style of explanation again and again. What would have saved James from this predicament? He would need to have some way of thinking about the mind as a first event, a conceptualizer rather than a selector and emphasizer. James was committed to the second-event argument because it adapted so well to his physiological emphasis in the *Principles*. But in his broader, philosophical writings, James also used concepts that are better suited to a first-event argument, based on a predication model of the mind.

By a predication model, I mean a logical process involving the act of affirming, denying, or qualifying broader patterns of meaning in relation to narrower or targeted patterns of meaning. The course of predication is always from the wider to the narrower range of meaning under consideration. For example, when one makes a statement, such as "William James was eclectic," one is taking a wider range of meaning (*eclecticism*) within which one places and thereby lends meaning to a narrow range of meaning (*William James*). One could readily diagram the logical relationship here through the use of Euler circles—with the larger circle labeled "eclecticism" or "eclectic theorists" and the smaller circle placed within it labeled "William James." Predications also establish contexts, as in the major premise of a syllogism, which provides the realm of meaning within which the minor premise and conclusion are situated, each in succession focusing this meaning to a greater extent (e.g., All human beings are mortal. This is a human being. This human being is mortal).

Note that the essential process in predicational modeling is a first-event patterning of meaning, rather than a conveying of meanings that have been patterned elsewhere and then brought into the process secondarily. Selection and emphasis occur in the initiating source of meaning creation, as the thinker frames what will be known. The initiative is with the thinker, not with the objects being thought about. Choice occurs at the initiating conceptualization, for there is no meaning to select until it has been brought to bear (related or patterned) predicationally. But how can this predicational, form-lending, meaning-creating process be described?

To picture this logical process, one must return to the large Euler circle, the one that was labeled "eclecticism." In drawing this circle, the line made delineating its circumference separated the meaning symbolized inside of the circle from the meaning symbolized outside of the circle. Thus, necessarily, one must consider the meaning of *noneclecticism*—the non-circle—even as one considers *eclecticism*. If one were to process the smaller circle labeled "William James" by locating it outside this large circle, the meaning logically and instantly generated would be that he is *not* eclectical in outlook. It is therefore clear that oppositionality is fundamental to the predicational model, whereas it is totally absent from the mediational model. In mediation, an opposite is a separate and distinct input to whatever it opposes. Thus, in a predicational model, the meaning of *left* is intrinsically tied to, and actually delimits, the meaning of *right*. The two meanings cannot be separated, as the inside of the circle cannot be separated from its outside. But in a mediational model, each of these meanings would be considered as existing separately. Meaning is unipolar in the mediational model, whereas it is bipolar in the predicational model.

This oppositionality has great relevance to a theory of free will. The intellect that confronts experience based on opposite-meaning possibilities must continually be taking a position on what eventuates. This occurs because every meaningful possibility can be seen to have its negation, its contradiction, or contrariety immediately as it is being framed in thought. The child who reflexively says, "ma ma," and is then encouraged to continue this vocal sound in relation to the mother should not be described as being shaped from without, but as taking a position from within. The mother's visage in the child's mind is literally predicated in the "ma ma" sound. The child is not shaped unidirectionally into making this predication. The child does so intentionally, to lend logical order to experience.

This is a different conception of the mind altogether, one that meshes nicely with the axiologist's dictum to the effect that "an act is free if and only if the agent [i.e., person] could have done otherwise, *all circumstances remaining the same*" (O'Connor, 1971, p. 82). This dictum is encompassed in James's quotation of Renouvier (earlier in the chapter), who noted that the thinker might have other thoughts even as certain thoughts are underway. How are these other thoughts brought about? What James failed to take from Renouvier is the Kantian dialectic, the capacity that intellect has to frame meanings in opposition to any now being processed without further input!

There is an intrinsic duality of meaning suggested by the Kantian, predicational model that is lacking in the mediational stream metaphor. If a person is selecting and emphasizing thoughts flowing past in the mind, there is little ground for saying that the person might do otherwise, all circumstances remaining the same. The ideas in the stream are like fish to be caught individually, held for a time, and then thrown back. Opposite ideas are akin to different fish, each entering the stream as a separate unity. Once such an individual idea is devoured, it is brought into overt behavior unidirectionally, thanks to ideomotor action, or, it might be pondered for a time in relation to other ideas pulled from the stream. Some of these other ideas are opposites and some are not. Indeed, if a fish defining an opposite idea is not caught, then the person never will succeed in framing a negation or contradiction. The person qua thinker is not free to generate a meaning contradicting each and every idea pulled from the stream. The person can merely select and emphasize those that are already there.

But in a predicating mind, there is always a bipolarity presaging the meaning to be affirmed and carried forward. The person is pictured as responsible for what will eventuate, because he or she must affirm which of the opposite possibilities will be taken on as a framing predication and overtly enacted. All things remaining the same, either this or that (nonthis) can be affirmed in the predicational process. Once an affirmation has been made and the predication has been framed, the course of subsequent events is determined. Based on this formulation, free will becomes the selection of grounding assumptions from within congeries of opposite possibilities for the sake of which behavior is then determined. The person's affirmed predication is both a choice and a determination of what will follow, but this choice is a first-event formulation that takes the initiative to lend meaning to experience, rather than selecting and emphasizing meanings after they have been framed by experience and brought to the person's attention.

This theorizing is obviously in the continental rather than the British philosophical tradition. As I read James, I have the sense that he had—especially in his philosophical writings—recognized a certain cogency in this view of the mind. Yet he was distrustful of it. He, quite consciously, avoided what he took to be rationalistic (as opposed to empiricistic) arguments. His criticisms of Hegel are precisely on this point (James, 1909/1967). He was suspicious of dialecticians, who wanted to see opposites dividing and uniting in what he took to be a mysterious fashion. Invariably, he brought in religious themes, which he felt were overextended on the side of a priori universals. Such first-event claims were made ex cathedra in an absolutistic sense that he could not abide. He felt that such monistic zealots were continually trying to press their favored universals as first-event certainties onto others (James, 1912/1967). He favored a *radical empiricism*, which is related to pragmatism, for it will neither "admit into its constructions any element that is not directly experienced, nor exclude from them any element that is directly experienced" (James, 1912/1967, p. 42). James seemed to have consciously fought against what he took to be the intellectual tyranny so typical of continental philosophers like Kant and Hegel, who framed the mind from above, putting forth concepts that were not empirically discernible, but that supposedly had the capacity to create and influence the reality of overt events.

Despite this clear evidence that James did not follow the more Kantian lines of Renouvier, I am fascinated by the fact that one can find James sketching in, as a counterpoint to his formal position, precisely the kind of predicational theory for which he was temperamentally suited. I apologize in advance if I am about to stretch to distortion James's informal comments on oppositionality and predication. I will present some quotes that capture the Renouvierian side of his theorizing.

First of all, I am struck by James's recognition that there seems to be a fundamental logical relationship in the mind that is not shaped by experience, as when he wrote,

> There is . . . no denying the fact that *the mind is filled with necessary and eternal relations which it finds between certain of its ideal conceptions, and which form a determinate system, independent of the order of frequency in which experience may have associated the conception's originals in time and space.* (James, 1890/1952, p. 879)

This observation by James suggests a Heraclitian Logos, a realm of patterned meanings that are not reducible to the external, associated inputs of experience. Such an intrinsic tie of "necessary and eternal relations" could include oppositionality, of course. What if human cognition has the capacity to frame not only what external experience is like, but immediately and without further input, to frame the direct opposite—what external experience is not like.

This view of cognition was common in the Logos formulations of ancient Greece. James actually said that in the stream of thought, there are "many ideas simultaneously present to the mind and acting upon each other . . . some in an antagonistic way" (1890/1952, p. 794). Antagonistic ideas are frequently oppositional ideas. You get a sense of oppositionality in his discussion of phenomenal experiences like thunder, as when he observed, "Into the awareness of the thunder itself the awareness of the previous silence creeps and continues; for what we hear when the thunder crashes is not thunder *pure*, but thunder-breaking-upon-silence-and-contrasting-with-it" (1890/1952, p. 156).

I believe it is possible to suggest that James looked at oppositional (or dialectical) reasoning as another second event. Thus, he even seemed to modify the ideomotor theory, as in the following:

> We may then lay it down for certain that *every representation of a movement awakens in some degree the actual movement which is its object; and awakens it in a maximum degree whenever it is not kept from so doing by an antagonistic representation present simultaneously to the mind.* (1890/1952, p. 792)

James even presented the opportunity to bring predication into play when he defined this concept as follows: "Predication [is] . . . a theoretic function which, though it always leads eventually to some kind of action, yet tends as often as not to inhibit the immediate motor response" (1890/1952, p. 666). He was referring to the will's capacity to inhibit for a time the ongoing flow of consciousness. Even so, he brought in predication as a way of describing this process. This is not a formal theoretical statement, of course.

If the person is construed as intrinsically capable of reasoning oppositionally, to create thereby antagonistic representations of experience, then it follows that there would be grounds for speaking of a freely willed movement. For example, infants who are capable of walking refrain from walking until they somehow gain the confidence to do so (Kagan, 1984). They seem to sense that they can walk, but also that maybe they cannot do so. James would apparently consider this doubt, this negation of the idea that walking is possible, as a second event, pulled from the stream of consciousness. But one might also embrace an oppositional thesis here and consider such doubt as a first event, based on the fact that the person always sees a this and that (i.e., this and not this) way to construe things. If he had not been so opposed to the Hegelians, maybe James would have found room in his image of the person for such duality, which is made possible by a dialectical formulation.

When James discussed the self, he frequently fell into oppositional phraseology. His basic concept was underwritten by a distinction between me and not me or mine and not mine (James, 1890/1952). He noted that self-complacency and self-dissatisfaction were "two opposite classes of affection [that] seem to be direct and elementary endowments of our nature"

(1890/1952, p. 197). He was but a step away from framing a predicational model, for as he noted concerning self-identity, "The sense of personal identity . . . is the sense of a sameness perceived *by* thought and predicated of things *thought-about*" (1890/1952, p. 214). Sameness is the broader circle, lending meaning to things *thought about*. But outside this *sameness* circle, nonsameness or difference would occur by definition. One can also see intimations of oppostionality in James's recognition that human beings have a self-reflexive intelligence, that they can indeed turn back on their outlooks and bring them into question. This is readily understood through oppositional mentation, in which simultaneous believing and not believing, knowing and doubting, would be routine phenomenal experiences. But such intrinsic contradiction is impossible to describe in unipolar terms.

James's very definition of life is based on such oppositional phraseology. He said "Life is one long struggle between conclusions based on abstract ways of conceiving cases, and opposite conclusions prompted by our instinctive perception of them as individual facts" (James, 1890/1952, p. 887). This them is expressed more fully in a paper he wrote in 1896, entitled "The Will to Believe," where he noted that for every idea there is a countering idea, such as the belief in purpose versus the belief in no purpose in life:

> There is this,—there is that; there is indeed nothing which some one has not thought absolutely true, while his neighbor deemed it absolutely false; and not an absolutist among them seems ever to have considered that the trouble may all the time be essential, and that the intellect, even with truth directly in its grasp, may have no infallible signal for knowing whether it be truth or no." (James, 1896/1967, pp. 132–133)

Despite these clear suggestions of oppositionality and predication in James's writings, I am unable to suggest that William James secretly favored the predicational image of human mentation that I prefer. There are too many clear indications of second-event, mediational modeling in his writings for this claim. For example, James (1890/1952) denied that we can arrive at new associations or acts of attentions endogenously. Reasoning to the opposite of ideas would be such an endogenous act. At one point in the *Principles*, James quoted from the writings of John Locke that "the mind can frame unto itself no[t] one new simple idea" (1890/1952, p. 480). Simple ideas are those that arise reflexively or are put into the mind from an external source. If humans reasoned oppositionally, then they would indeed be capable of framing entirely new simple ideas—at the initial point of experiencing the reflexive action or the input from the environment. This would occur through intrinsic or endogenous reasoning to the opposite of what had been activated or input. Finally, in discussing disbelief, James said this:

We never disbelieve anything except for the reason that we believe something else which contradicts the first thing. Disbelief is thus an incidental complication to belief, and need not be considered by itself. . . . *The true opposites of belief*, psychologically considered, *are doubt and inquiry, not disbelief.* (p. 636)

To the dialectician, doubt arises through an intrinsic oppositionality, and "outside the Euler circle" that can indeed be termed *disbelief.*

So, as I said before I began this little excursion through the back eddies of James's mind, there are no grounds for saying that he secretly harbored a desire to fulfill Renouvier's neo-Kantian aspirations. In his free-will speculations, James focused on the sustaining of thought following a person's choice to think of some object flowing by in the stream. He did not focus on the Renouvierian point concerning the possibility of dialectically thinking otherwise, all things remaining the same. Was it that his attention was simply drawn mediationally to the former rather than the latter theoretical account? Or did he predicate circumstances in a way that was consistent with his physiological approach to the description of behavior, even though this view can be immediately brought into doubt by its opposite implication? I much prefer the latter way of accounting for James's cognitions and only wish that he had taken this same theoretical stance in his formal position. But he did not.

REFERENCES

Dooley, P. K. (1976). *Pragmatism as humanism: The philosophy of William James.* Totowa, NJ: Littlefield, Adams & Co.

Hull, C. L. (1952). *A behavior system.* New Haven, CT: Yale University Press.

James H., Jr. (Ed.). (1920). *The letters of William James* (2 vols.). Boston: Atlantic Monthly Press.

James, W. (1899). The gospel of relaxation. *Scribner's Magazine, 25,* 499–507.

James, W. (1943). *Pragmatism.* New York: The World Publishing Company. (Original work published 1907)

James, W. (1952). *The principles of psychology.* In R. M. Hutchins (Ed.), *Great books of the western world* (Vol. 53). Chicago: Encyclopedia Britannica. (Original work published 1890)

James, W. (1967). *A pluralistic universe.* Gloucester, MA: Peter Smith. (Original work published 1909)

James, W. (1967). *Essays in radical empiricism.* Gloucester, MA: Peter Smith. (Original work published 1912)

James, W. (1967). *The will to believe.* In A. J. Beck (Ed.), *Introduction to William*

James: An essay and selected texts (pp. 3–147). Bloomington, IN: Indiana University Press. (Original work published 1896)

Kagan, J. (1984). *The nature of the child.* New York: Basic Books.

Locke, J. (1952). *An essay concerning human understanding.* In R. M. Hutchins (Ed.), *Great books of the western world* (Vol. 35, pp. 85–395). Chicago: Encyclopedia Britannica. (Original work published 1690)

O'Connor, D. J. (1971). *Free will.* Garden City, NY: Doubleday & Co.

Perry, R. B. (1948). *The thought and character of William James.* Cambridge, MA: Harvard University Press.

Rickaby, J. (1906). *Free will and four English philosophers.* London: Burns and Oates.

Rychlak, J. F. (1990). George Kelly and the concept of construction. *International Journal of Personal Construct Psychology, 3,* 7–19.

22

WILLIAM JAMES: PIONEERING ANCESTOR OF MODERN PARAPSYCHOLOGY

GERTRUDE R. SCHMEIDLER

William James wrote extensively on psychical research, but he did more than that; he worked actively in it. He wrote a long report on research of his own (James, 1909) in addition to some shorter reports; he cooperated in others' projects; he was the president of the (English) Society for Psychical Research for 2 years; and he helped found the American Society for Psychical Research.

The depth of his interest may not be clear from *The Principles of Psychology* (1890/1904), where references to psychical research are sparse and usually are glancing. James made casual mention, for example, of "the phenomena of thought transference . . . alleged nowadays on better authority than ever before" (1890/1904, p. 350), but he did not trouble to explain why nowadays the evidence looks better. In describing hypnotic phenomena, he cited an apparent instance of ESP and implied it was one of many, but said he would not describe others because "such cases . . . seem rather to belong to 'psychical research' than to the present category" (1890/1904, p. 609).

OVERLAP BETWEEN PSYCHOLOGY AND PSYCHICAL RESEARCH

Does this mean that James thought psychical research and psychology were unrelated? No, juxtaposing his definitions of the two fields makes it clear that he thought they overlapped or even were too closely related to separate from each other. One of the definitions was stated when (largely on James's initiative) the American Society for Psychical Research was founded, with a single purpose, defining psychical research, written into its constitution. The purpose was "the systematic study of the laws of mental action" (American Society for Psychical Research Executive Committee, 1886, p. 55). Compare this to the definition of psychology with which James opened the *Principles*: "Psychology is the Science of Mental Life, both of its phenomena and of their conditions" (1890/1904, p. 1). The one rephrases the other; they convey the same meaning. For James, both psychical research and psychology were the studies of mental activity.

Why, then, did James not write of them together? I suggest two reasons. One is that a major thrust of the *Principles* was its integration of experimentation with other kinds of psychological study, but the psychical research of his period, unlike the parapsychology of today, was not an experimental science. His other reason may have been public relations, a desire not to antagonize his readers. A hint along this line comes from another passage in the *Principles*:

> I am myself persuaded by abundant acquaintance with the trances of one medium that the (personality she assumes in trance) may be altogether different from any *possible* waking self of the person. In the case I have in mind it professes to be a certain departed French doctor; and is, I am convinced, acquainted with facts about the circumstances, and the living and dead relatives and acquaintances, of numberless sitters whom the medium never met before, and of whom she has never heard the names. I record my opinion here unsupported by the evidence, not, of course, to convert anyone to my view, but because I am persuaded that a serious study of these trance-phenomena is one of the greatest needs of psychology, and think that my personal confession may possibly draw a reader or two into a field which the *soi-disant* "scientist" usually refuses to explore. (1890/1904, p. 396).

I will turn next to James's writings on psychical research. What did he affirm or deny? Where did he withhold judgment? What recommendations did he give? How do all of these answers stack up against parapsychology in 1990? I will start with his advice on methods of inquiry.

METHODS OF INQUIRY INTO PSYCHICAL RESEARCH

James's three-pronged advice for psychical research was the same as his advice on methods for psychology. First came a demand for rigor and careful controls. An early publication deplored the loose conditions as well as the ambiguity of messages from the planchette; it called for work that was "*minutely* controlled" (James, 1869/1960, p. 21). This was a consistent theme. Forty years later, the first words of a major article praised the founders of the Society for Psychical Research for their insistence that material be "treated rigorously" (James, 1909/1960, p. 309).

A second part of James's advice was that theory should be based on facts. Facts should never be denied. Where they conflict with theory, theory must yield. Theories are permissible when facts are sparse, but it is better to have no theory than to form one prematurely. The article cited earlier gave a charming brief statement of this advice (and of James's faith in the empirical method). His words were "Your genuine inquirer . . . lets the data collect, and bides his time" (James, 1909/1960, p. 318). This article echoed the *Principles* where James wrote, "Facts are facts, and if we only get enough of them they are sure to combine . . . and theoretic results will grow" (1890/1904, p. 193).

The third prong of James's advice on method, often and vehemently repeated, is that claims of phenomena should be examined. They should be studied rigorously and critically, but they should never be brushed aside, even when they conflict with theory or when they seem bizarre.

One instance of this unpopular advice deals with the provocative topic of faith or psychic healing. Then, as now, the attempt to heal a physical ailment by mental action alone was often followed by what seemed to be a miraculous cure. Then, as now, it was unclear how many of those cures were only the result of suggestion or only the statistical accident of a concurrent spontaneous recovery or remission. James visited one mental healer without benefit, so his personal experience was unfavorable. But when a bill, supported by his medical colleagues, would have required a medical degree for mental healing, James wrote to oppose the bill, "I assuredly hold no brief for any of these healers . . . But their *facts* are patent and startling; and anything that interferes with the multiplication of such facts, and with our freest opportunity of observing and studying them, will, I believe, be a public calamity" (1894/1960, p. 10). Those are strong words!

How well do modern parapsychologists follow these three trails that James marked out for them? I'd give mixed grades to the bulk of parapsychological work (including my own)—perhaps as high as an A or A– on rigor (and surely an A for effort). We try our best, and so do the referees of parapsychological journals. They want prestated hypotheses, well-calibrated instruments, random assignment, carefully controlled conditions with double blinds, and conservative statistical treatment; or else, they demand that conclusions be so qualified that they are little more than a call for further research. And where controls are inadequate, those in psychical research have always been critical; we all police each other.

On theory, modern parapsychologists deserve a B+. We try to be properly tentative in generalizing unless the facts seem full and clear, but sometimes the urge to state a theory firmly is irresistible.

For the third part of James's advice, to study all claims of phenomena no matter how bizarre, our grade is at best a C–. Modern parapsychology excludes the study of UFOs, astrology, and almost anything labeled *occult*. In addition, the investigation of any claim of strong psychic ability will typically start with a presumption of fraud or self-delusion. Perhaps the effort to be rigorous in experimentation and careful in theory has led to a spread of inhibition. It is rare to find someone like James, who could balance openness with caution.

JAMES'S CONVICTIONS ABOUT PSYCHICAL RESEARCH

But James was not always cautious. "I wish to go on record," he wrote, for three strong convictions. The first was the commonness of rubbish in psychics' statements due to the "will to make-believe," not only in mediumistic utterances, but in "every sort of person." The last was his cosmic faith, which will be quoted later. The second is relevant to this chapter. It is *"the presence, in the midst of all the humbug, of really supernormal knowledge"* (1909b/1960, p. 322). His wording was careful. Supernormal knowledge can include telepathy, but is a broader term; it is equivalent to ESP.

Has the controlled research of modern parapsychology supported James's conviction? Yes, by now the evidence for ESP seems to be unequivocal and comes from each of two research designs. The first is simple; it compares ESP scores with chance expectation. Often, some gifted subject has, under rigorously controlled conditions, made scores so high that the odds against chance are astronomical, and fairly often, if unselected subjects are tested for many trials, they too have cumulative scores that are significantly higher than expected by chance.

The second research design gives more information. It compares ESP scores from differing groups of subjects or from different conditions, and repeatedly, it has found the difference in scores that was predicted. This line of evidence, of course, is consistent with James's thesis that psychical research, like psychology, is a study of "the laws of mental action."

One example of this is the *experimenter effect*. Years before Rosenthal

(1966) named it, Pratt and Price (1938) stumbled over it, then studied it formally. Pratt was a reserved man, and Price was an outgoing and friendly young woman. They tested boys and girls for ESP, using same-sex experimenters. Midway, Price asked Pratt what was wrong with his subjects. Pratt said nothing was wrong; they followed instructions. He then asked what she meant. She said that his boys did not open up; they did not talk to him. When their data showed that Price's girls made ESP scores above chance, but Pratt's boys did not, they began a new study. In this study, each tested about equal numbers of both sexes, and each acted as the other's research assistant to check that their formal procedures were the same. This time, they found no sex difference, but just as before, subjects in the warm experimental climate that Price created made ESP scores that were significantly higher than the scores of subjects in the cold experimental climate created by Pratt.

Probably because there are few parapsychologists, and each of us has our own exciting problems to tackle, only two other experiments have been formally designed to compare warm with cold experimental conditions. One of these experiments tested subjects individually, assigning alternate subjects to the warm condition (a friendly preliminary chat and encouraging remarks in the rest periods) or to the cold one (no preliminary chat and discouraging remarks in the rest periods). Formal test conditions were identical. ESP scores were significantly higher than chance expectation in the warm condition; in the cold condition, ESP scores were significantly lower than chance expectation (Honorton, Ramsey, & Cabibbo, 1975). (Significantly low scores in unfavorable conditions imply either deliberate or unconscious avoidance of the targets and are found so often that they have been given a name—*psi-missing*.)

The third experiment was a group test, a continuation of Crandall's research on certain ESP displacement effects. Crandall (1985) used two similar groups of subjects. He tested one group in his usual way, with an introduction that was sympathetic to studying ESP. The young man who tested the other group implied a lack of sympathy by saying that he was just filling in for someone else and didn't know much about "this stuff," and he was brusque in responding to questions. Test procedures were identical, but the displacement effect that Crandall had found in earlier work (and that he and others have often replicated since) appeared only in the warm atmosphere.

Seven experiments have also tested a second part of the experimenter effect: the experimenter's positive versus negative expectations. There were 11 separate series, and I will not review them individually. The bottom line is that 8 of the 11 series gave significant results in the predicted direction: ESP scores were higher when there were favorable rather than unfavorable expectations. Overall findings on the experimenter effect, thus, do more than give evidence that ESP occurs. They imply in addition that, as James had expected, parapsychology was studying the same processes as psychology.

If an experimenter's expectations influence ESP success, a subject's expectations should influence it too. This was the hypothesis that I formulated for my first ESP research. The cutoff for expectations was the negative extreme; thus, the prediction to be tested was that subjects who were certain that ESP could not possibly occur in the conditions of the experiment would have lower ESP scores than all other subjects (even if the others thought ESP very improbable). I myself, thought ESP very improbable at the time, and it astonished me to see the data support the hypothesis—although after each of two replications with individual testing also gave significant results, I came to accept it. My later series with classroom testing were less consistent, but they too were significantly supportive when pooled (Schmeidler & McConnell, 1958). A review of 15 later tests of the hypothesis gave results similar to mine (Palmer, 1971). The hypothesis stands up, on average, rather well.

Given that ESP occurs, the finding seems reasonable. When one thinks a task is impossible, one does not do it well. James anticipated my results. He made the point succinctly when he wrote, "When one knows that he has no power . . . the sense of impotence inhibits the volition" (1890/1904, p. 560).

At this point, data on another topic fall neatly into place. The topic is hypnosis, and with regard to hypnosis, James also anticipated what later experiments have shown. "The hypnotic trance is not *in itself* clairvoyant," he wrote, but it "is *more favorable* to the cause of clairvoyance or thought transference than the waking state" (1896/1960, p. 69). A review of ESP and hypnosis (Schechter, 1984) found 20 experiments that compared subjects' ESP scores after hypnotic induction with their scores under normal conditions. The findings supported James's moderate statement. In 16 of the 20 reports, ESP scores were higher after hypnotic induction than in the control condition, and they were significantly higher for 7 of the 16, but significantly lower for none.

This can perhaps be considered a special confirmatory set of data on the experimenter effect. The expectations of all experimenters seem to have been that hypnotic induction would be conducive to ESP success, and presumably, the hypnotic conditions were warmer as well.

More data, most of them from psychometric measures, mesh well with these. A sizable body of research compares ESP scores of open subjects with those of defensive subjects, and the open ones have the higher scores. Anxiety or neurotic tendencies tend to have a negative relation to ESP success. Especially on tests that they find congenial, extraverts tend to have higher ESP scores than introverts. (See Schmeidler, 1988, for summaries.) And surely openness, freedom from anxiety, and spontaneous, extraverted behavior are all more likely to be associated with a warm atmosphere than with a cold one.

Several other ESP findings relate to these. An example is autonomic activity (reviewed by Braud, 1981). As would be anticipated from the negative relation of anxiety and ESP success, there is a negative relation between autonomic activity and ESP scoring. But ESP is only one of the three areas in modern parapsychology (the other two are PK and the mind–body problem). Instead of citing other supportive data, I will mention only two subtopics, each provocative, where as yet the results of ESP research are null.

One of these subtopics is cognition. Attempts to have subjects learn to achieve higher ESP scores have used many different methods, some with initial success, but none have stood up to replication. Cognitive development shows no clear relation to ESP success; children with their spontaneity and enthusiasm often score high, but so do enthusiastic or spontaneous adults. Results vary with regard to IQ. It seemed at first to have a positive relation to ESP score, but this may be because the ESP test was administered as an intellectually oriented test of theory. And there is counterevidence: retarded children scored high when tested by a lovable teacher (Bond, 1937). As for creativity, it is true that measures of creativity usually show a positive relation to ESP scores, but this is not necessarily due to a cognitive link. Noncognitive variables such as openness may be the common factor. ESP data on perceptual discrimination seem to imply that ESP can make only the most primitive discriminations. I infer that ESP is a precognitive process and that its occasional apparent tie-in with cognition means only that both are modulated by personality or social variables.

The other ESP subtopic with null results is the study of physical variables. No relation has yet been found between ESP and distance, time, or shielding from electromagnetic waves, nor does ESP relate such variables as the target's size or complexity. Some quantum physicists are not fazed by this because quantum phenomena show a similar independence of space and time. They and others, for example, in holography, have integrated parapsychology into physical theory (see, e.g., Bohm, 1986; Jahn & Dunne, 1987; Schmidt, 1989; Walker, 1984). But to me, a psychologist who has only superficial acquaintance with either quantum theory or holography, it is troubling that ESP should be so independent of the usual physical constraints of distance and time, when, in other ways, ESP seems so orderly psychologically.

JAMES'S TENTATIVE ACCEPTANCE OF PSYCHOKINESIS

The second major division of modern parapsychology is psychokinesis (PK), popularly called *mind over matter*. In James's time, most, but not quite all, research on physical phenomena involved darkened séance rooms. It was so hard to rule out fraud that many of James's most respected colleagues in psychical research brushed aside all claims. James, as was typical, continued to examine the evidence that a physical change could be mentally produced. He found the evidence increasingly impressive, and his final evaluation was the following: "It may be a genuine class of natural phenomena" (1909b/1960, p. 312).

PK is for many even more mind-boggling than ESP, and yet experimental research has justified James's judgment. PK seems to be one of those uncomfortable facts that conflict with theory or common sense, which James warned must stand and the theory yield. I will sketch out four of the lines of PK research.

The first line of PK research began after J. B. Rhine heard a professional gambler claim that he could sometimes influence the fall of dice. Rhine studied dice casting and soon instituted two types of control. One type was for muscular skill (dice bounced many times or were cast by machine). The other type was for imperfect dice (subjects hoped for one die face on 24 trials, then had 24 trials on each of the other five faces). Subjects were unselected; results varied, but with many trials they averaged significantly better than chance. A recent meta-analysis of 69 studies showed that the effect cannot be attributed to selective reporting (Radin & Ferrari, 1992).

An interesting secondary effect showed up during this tedious procedure of 24 successive calls for each die face. Successes clustered at the beginning of the sets of 24, then fell off, so that the difference between first and last quarters was highly significant. It can be inferred that as subjects grew more and more bored by repetition, their motivation for PK success diminished or vanished.

Today, research with dice has almost vanished too. PK is most often studied by a sophisticated device called the *random event generator* (RNG), introduced by Schmidt (1969). It uses a truly random source (radioactive emissions or electronic noise) to generate the targets for PK or ESP. The subject tries to influence the RNG's output for PK or to guess its output for ESP. (Physicists say there is no normal way to succeed at either, short of tinkering with the machine). A button push signals the beginning of a trial; the RNG records trials and successes. The experimenter is relieved of the burden of recording. The subject remains interested because feedback with flashing lights and numerical displays makes the trials fun, like an electronic game. It is no wonder that the RNG supplanted dice for PK research.

What is a wonder is that mere wishing has shown a relation to the output of these well-calibrated machines. It should not seem especially odd that most subjects do not know what change in the RNG produces the desired score, for our ignorance of the means by which we achieve a goal has long been familiar to psychologists. Few of us have any notion of which muscles we flex or relax when we walk. James's comment on this issue was "What interests us are the ends which the movement is to attain" (1890/1904, p. 519). PK, like normal activities, appears to be goal directed.

RNG research in many laboratories has found that the goals can be achieved. Repeated trials from the same subjects show consistent individual differences (Jahn & Dunne, 1987). Overall scores average higher than chance expectation. This is no artifact. Instruments are carefully calibrated. Well-controlled research has the subject aim for slow rates of radioactive emission as often as for fast, and for low electronic noise as often as for high. Meta-analysis of the 73 RNG reports from 1969 to 1984 shows that the results are not due to the file drawer effect or to any identifiable procedural error, nor are they associated with only a few of the investigators (Radin, May, & Thomson, 1986). I see no way of faulting this body of research.

A third line of PK research, called *placement*, asks subjects to influence where objects fall. It too has a long history of successful outcomes, but only one careful series from the school of engineering at Princeton University will be described (Nelson, Dunne, & Jahn, 1983, 1988).

This study may be shocking because it tampers with a modern icon, the normal probability curve. Nelson and his colleagues built a *mechanical cascade*, a device expected to produce a normal curve. It is big with a glass front 10 ft. by 6 ft. At the top, 9,000 plastic balls are released. They drop through a matrix of 330 pins, bouncing and colliding, and then fall into 19 bins. A machine records the number in each bin. The subject sits some distance from the device, but can hear the racket and see the activity. One run takes about 12 min, and each session has three runs: one to hope the distribution will be skewed to the left, one to hope it will be skewed to the right, and one for baseline.

Scores were evaluated by analysis of variance for left versus right versus baseline, and they showed a highly significant difference. Further analysis found the difference to be due to a large shift to the left when the subjects had hoped for a left shift; left versus right and left versus baseline differences were highly significant; right versus baseline differences were not. The effect was so marked and so consistent across varied subsets of the data that it seems to be a clear demonstration of PK. In addition, subjects' scores tended to be self-consistent; the individual differences were reliable.

One post hoc finding in PK is interesting because of its psychological relevance. It is an anomaly in baseline scores and is especially clear in RNG data. When subjects pushed the RNG button hoping not for high scores but for a normal control score, the mean of such baseline runs was, as expected, close to the theoretical mean, but the shape of the curve was too narrow for a normal distribution. There were too few extreme scores; the variance was significantly low. The results resemble what naive students think a chance distribution ought to be. They expect scores to cluster closely around the theoretical mean.

A similar effect shows up in ESP. Often, if subjects are asked to make control runs, the data differ from theory and show psi-missing. Their direction is opposite to what the subjects hope to see in experimental runs (see, e.g., Jackson, Franzoi, & Schmeidler, 1977). The control data make the experimental data look better. This resembles the way hypnotic subjects who are asked to use their normal strength or normal ability to recall will often do less than their best; their low scores in the control condition make their hypnotic scores look better.

The only other line of PK research that will be mentioned in this chapter may also be shocking. This method uses living animals or plants as PK targets. Half a dozen experiments on one-celled organisms, with well-controlled, double blind methods, have each shown significant effects of wishing on the organisms' rate of growth. In many but not all of the well-controlled studies on facilitating plant growth, experimenters reported some significant results. Well-controlled work with humans or other animals has been scant, but a long series by Braud and his coworkers is worth noting.

Braud and Schlitz (1983) used volunteers for research to find out if psychic healing could reduce anxiety. In both of the two sessions, subjects were asked to remain in as ordinary a condition as possible while listening to randomly generated sounds and watching random lights, and their electrodermal activity was measured. Data from the first session were used to select two groups: 16 subjects with higher autonomic activity (who presumably had greater need for anxiety reduction) and 16 with lower. It was predicted that, in the second session, when there were attempts at psychic healing, the group with more spontaneous activity would have less autonomic activity than the other group.

In the second session, subjects were told that, at some times, the experimenter would try psychically to calm them. They were not told (and at that time the experimenter did not know) what the times would be. The experimenter then went to a room about 20 m away and found (randomly determined) directions for timing. In ten 30-s periods, the experimenter was to try to exert a calming influence. Interspersed among these were ten 30-s periods when the experimenter was to make no attempt to influence the subject.

The data strikingly confirmed the prediction. For the 16 subjects in the higher spontaneous activity group, whose need for healing was presumably greater, electrodermal activity was significantly less when the experimenter tried to calm them than when the experimenter was inattentive, and their electrodermal activity during those calming periods was significantly lower than the activity of the other 16 subjects. For the 16 subjects whose need was presumably less, there was a negligible difference between calming and inattentive periods. Braud and Schlitz examined many possible interpretations of the findings and concluded that the most reasonable is that response to an attempted psychic influence depends on the subject's need. The conclusion is reminiscent of Gardner Murphy's frequent reminders that motivation is the key factor in psychic events (e.g., Murphy, 1943, 1970).

JAMES'S CERTAINTY ABOUT INTERRELATED CONSCIOUSNESS

Although ESP and PK are its chief topics, modern parapsychology includes other scattered studies that bear on mind–body relations or on issues like survival after death. It investigates claims of ghosts and poltergeists, out-of-body travel, and reincarnation. Sometimes the claims can be attributed to attempts at deception, to the overinterpretation of scant evidence, to normal sources of information, or to natural causes (as when the ticking of a beetle sounds like a haunt, or a change in water level produces unexpected movement of the objects in a house). Sometimes a meticulously careful investigation gives strong evidence that the events were paranormal. When this happens, most modern parapsychologists try to interpret the case as a special example of unusually strong PK or ESP. Spiritistic explanations are out of fashion. A few dissent, but the consensus seems to be that hypotheses about spirits are both untestable and unparsimonious and that even a new postulate about what PK or ESP can do is preferable.

James would surely have found this disappointing. He spent many research hours and much thought on the survival issue. He felt frustrated that after all his effort he could neither accept nor deny the spiritistic hypothesis, but he thought the problem so important that it deserved further study. Parapsychology has not followed him on this path.

The year before his death, he described his uncertainty, but also put on record his three convictions. Two have already been described. Here is the third:

> Out of my experience, such as it is (and it is limited enough), one fixed conclusion dogmatically emerges, and that is this, that we with our lives are like islands in the sea, or like trees in the forest. The maple and the pine may whisper to each other with their leaves, and Conanicut and Newport hear each other's foghorns. But the trees also

commingle their roots in the darkness underground, and the islands also hang together through the ocean's bottom. Just so there is a continuum of cosmic consciousness, against which our individuality builds but accidental fences, and into which our several minds plunge as into a mother-sea or reservoir. Our "normal" consciousness is circumscribed for adaptation to our external earthly environment, but the fence is weak in spots, and fitful influences from beyond leak in, showing the otherwise unverifiable common connection. (1909b/1960, p. 324)

This is like poetry, and it goes far beyond the prosaic caution of modern parapsychology.

REFERENCES

American Society for Psychical Research Executive Committee. (1886). *Proceedings of the American Society for Psychical Research, 1* (2), 55–57.

Bohm, D. J. (1986). A new theory of the relationship of mind and matter. *Journal of the American Society for Psychical Research, 80,* 113–135.

Bond, E. M. (1937). General extrasensory perception with a group of fourth and fifth grade retarded children. *Journal of Parapsychology, 1,* 114–122.

Braud, W. G. (1981). Psi performance and autonomic nervous system activity. *Journal of the American Society for Psychical Research, 75,* 1–35.

Braud, W. G., & Schlitz, M. (1983). Psychokinetic influence on electrodermal activity. *Journal of Parapsychology, 47,* 95–119.

Crandall, J. E. (1985). Effects of favorable and unfavorable conditions on the psi-missing displacement effect. *Journal of the American Society for Psychical Research, 79,* 27–38.

Honorton, C., Ramsey, M., & Cabibbo, C. (1975). Experimenter effects in extrasensory perception. *Journal of the American Society for Psychical Research, 69,* 135–149.

Jackson, M., Franzoi, S., & Schmeidler, G. R. (1977). Effects of feedback on ESP: A curious partial replication. *Journal of the American Society for Psychical Research, 71,* 147–155.

Jahn, R. G., & Dunne, B. J. (1987). *Margins of reality.* New York: Harcourt Brace Jovanovich.

James, W. (1904). *The Principles of psychology* (2nd ed.). New York: Henry Holt. (Original work published 1890)

James, W. (1909). Report on Mrs. Piper's Hodgson control. *Proceedings of the American Society for Psychical Research, 3,* 470–590.

James, W. (1960). Lecture before the Lowell Institute. In G. Murphy & R. O.

Ballou (Eds.), *William James on psychical research* (pp. 68–69). New York: Viking. (Original work published 1896)

James, W. (1960). Letter to the Boston Transcript. In G. Murphy & R. O. Ballou (Eds.). *William James on psychical research* (pp. 68–69). New York: Viking. (Original work published 1894)

James, W. (1960). Review of "Planchette." In G. Murphy & R. O. Ballou (Eds.), *William James on psychical research* (pp. 19–23) New York: Viking. (Original work published 1869)

James, W. (1960). The final impressions of a psychical researcher. In G. Murphy & R. O. Ballou (Eds.), *William James on psychical research* (pp. 309–325). New York: Viking. (Original work published in 1909)

Murphy, G. (1943). Psychical phenomena and human needs. *Journal of the American Society for Psychical Research, 37,* 163–191.

Murphy, G. (1970). Are there any solid facts in psychical research? *Journal of the American Society for Psychical Research, 64,* 3–17.

Nelson, R. D., Dunne, B. J., & Jahn, R. G. (1983). *A psychokinesis experiment with a random mechanical cascade.* Princeton, NJ: Princeton University School of Engineering/Applied Science.

Nelson, R. D., Dunne, B. J., & Jahn, R. G. (1988). *Operator related anomalies in a random mechanical cascade experiment.* Princeton, NJ: Princeton University School of Engineering/Applied Science.

Palmer, J. (1971). Scoring in ESP tests as a function of belief in ESP: Part I. The sheep-goat effect. *Journal of the American Society for Psychical Research, 65,* 373–408.

Pratt, J. G., & Price, M. M. (1938). The experimenter-subject relationship in tests for ESP. *Journal of Parapsychology, 2,* 84–94.

Radin, D. I., & Ferrari, D. C. (1992). Effects of consciousness on the fall of dice. In L. Henkel & G. R. Schmeidler (Eds.), Research in parapsychology 1990 (pp. 39–44). Metuchen, NJ: Scarecrow Press.

Radin, D. I., May, E. C., & Thomson, M. J. (1986). Psi experiments with random number generators. In D. H. Weiner & D. I. Radin (Eds.), *Research in parapsychology 1985* (pp. 14–17). Metuchen, NJ: Scarecrow Press.

Rosenthal, R. (1966). *Experimenter effects in behavioral research.* New York: Appleton-Century-Crofts.

Schechter, E. I. (1984). Hypnotic induction vs. control conditions: Illustrating an approach to the evaluation of replicability in parapsychological data. *Journal of the American Society for Psychical Research, 78,* 1–27.

Schmeidler, G. R. (1988). *Parapsychology and psychology: Matches and mismatches.* Jefferson, NC: McFarland.

Schmeidler, G. R., & McConnell, R. A. (1958). *ESP and personality patterns.* New Haven, CT: Yale University Press.

Schmidt, H. (1969). Precognition of a quantum process. *Journal of Parapsychology,* *33,* 99–108.

Schmidt, H. (1989). The strange properties of psychokinesis. *Journal of the Society for Scientific Exploration, 1,* 103–118.

Walker, E. H. (1984). A review of criticisms of the quantum mechanical theory of psi phenomena. *Journal of Parapsychology, 48,* 277–332.

EPILOGUE

23

A CENTENNIAL NOTE: WHAT WOULD WILLIAM JAMES SAY ABOUT THE AMERICAN PSYCHOLOGICAL ASSOCIATION TODAY?

RAYMOND D. FOWLER

Nineteen hundred and ninety-two: The centennial of the founding of the American Psychological Association (APA) represents not only the passing of the first 100 years of psychology as an organized and recognized discipline in North America, but also an embarkation into the second 100 years and into the twenty-first century. If history is, at least partly, the history of individual figures, then William James looms large both as a seminal and as an ongoing presence in the course that APA is charting as an organization. As an ardent admirer of James, I have sometimes mused about what he would have made of the discipline that he helped introduce in the United States and, more particularly, of the Association that he helped to found and that he twice served as president.

What follows are indeed musings—they are speculations about what William James might have thought and about how he might have participated in the APA as it is today.

James would have been astounded by the rate of growth within the APA and by the sheer number of professionals who make up its membership. Although, within his own lifetime, the Association's membership grew from

31 to 228 (a 700% increase in 18 years). But would he have anticipated the current membership of some 114,000 professionals, or that the Association would represent one of the largest professional organizations in the United States? Or would James, the influential and highly popular educator, have possibly foreseen that psychology would become one of the most popular elective courses in American higher education and, indeed, one of the most popular undergraduate majors?

It is just possible that he would have foreseen this expansion, for William James was nothing if not highly enthusiastic and optimistic about the potential of psychology as a useful discipline with many practical applications. Rather, it is more likely the ways in which the Association evolved and the complex and broad range of activities that it supports that would surprise him.

James was one of a small group that met in the office of G. Stanley Hall in the summer of 1892 to found the APA, and he served as its president in 1894 and 1904. Because of his personal mastery of four major disciplines—medicine, physiology, psychology, and philosophy—he was able to bridge and integrate those disciplines as no one had before or has since. And because of his fluency in German and French and his friendship with most of the American and European psychologists of his time, he was able to bring together both people and ideas that otherwise might have remained separate.

Over the past 100 years, the APA has evolved into a complex, large-scale structure. Aside from the executive and the financial and administrative offices, the core organizational units of the Association are the four directorates—Science, Education, Public Interest, and Practice—and the Office of Publications and Communications. To a greater or lesser extent, James would probably have had his hand in all of these areas.

For instance, it is relatively simple to predict James's interest in the Science and Education Directorates; these were the areas of activity that occupied him throughout his adult life. James's primary identification was as an educator. In his years at Harvard, he influenced thousands of undergraduate and graduate students, many of whom had substantial impact on the evolving discipline in the United States. *The Principles of Psychology* (James, 1890) was for many years a standard text in psychology and has served as the inspiration for many subsequent texts. Many testimonials to his talent and skill as a teacher exist. Some students, like the brilliant George Santayana, were critical but, nevertheless, showed grudging respect; others, among whom was Gertrude Stein, were generous in their praise. At a time when professors were unquestioned authorities in the university lecture hall, James invited students to discuss and argue his classroom observations. His care in preparing for lectures was legendary. For example, the preparation of a series of lectures for teachers that he delivered in

Cambridge, Massachusetts, occupied him for months. Published later as *Talks to Teachers on Psychology* (1899), this influential series added to his growing national reputation and resulted in invitations to lecture all over the country. James would almost certainly have been a member of the APA's Divisions of the Teaching of Psychology and of Educational Psychology, and it is not difficult to imagine him as a probable recipient of the Association's Distinguished Teaching Award.

Regarding James's support for the Science Directorate, although never very enthusiastic about doing laboratory work himself, he was a strong supporter and a firm believer in the vital importance of laboratory work in the education and training of psychologists. In fact, he established what is frequently referred to as the first psychology laboratory in the United States. James located Hugo Munsterberg, a former student of Wilhelm Wundt, and brought him to Harvard to take over direction of this laboratory. Although James's deep and abiding interests would eventually take him away from laboratory work and on to philosophy, his role in affirming the importance of the scientific tradition of inquiry in psychology cannot be underestimated.

Speculations about James's affinity for the Public Interest Directorate seem less certain, but there is ample evidence that he was enthusiastic about the application of psychology for the benefit of society. For instance, he was an outspoken opponent of war and sought every opportunity to use his influence on behalf of peace. In 1898, during the mounting tensions that gripped the United States after the sinking of the battleship Maine in Havana harbor, he joined the Anti-Imperialist League and spent considerable energy and time composing letters of protest and appearing publicly to counter growing war sentiment. Another example of his interest in the public welfare was his 1910 address "The Moral Equivalent of War," in which he proposed that all American youth spend 3 years in public service. James's ideas of social responsibility take their place in a line of thinking that would eventually lead to such public service programs as Franklin Roosevelt's Civilian Conservation Corps and, later, John Kennedy's Peace Corps.

James was perhaps the first American psychologist to try to influence legislation. He was far ahead of the Association in so doing, for public policy advocacy was an activity that was not firmly established on an ongoing basis in the APA until the 1960s. Now, of course, legislative advocacy is an important component of all four directorates. In 1884, James appeared before the legislature of the commonwealth of Massachusetts in support of psychotherapy. (He apparently did this on his own behalf, although he was the APA president at the time.) The medical profession was the impetus behind the introduction of a bill in the legislature that would limit the practice of mental therapy to licensed physicians. James, who was a physician by training, was often dubious of the claims made by therapists, but his own personal experience had convinced him that the therapeutic approach had great potential and should continue to be explored. He argued accordingly before the legislature and in the press. His efforts were successful, and the bill was killed.

With respect to the Practice Directorate, the branch of the Association particularly charged with representing the interests of professional psychology, I cannot venture to say what James would have made of the enormous number of practicing therapists or of the almost bewildering number of different schools of psychotherapy. It is clear that he found the prospect of applying psychology to both everyday and extraordinary human problems to be challenging and intriguing, and he was in practice. He had come early to the belief of the contribution of certain psychological factors to mental and physical illness and, in 1899, he began to see patients at his home, including some depressed persons and some with multiple personality disorder. He himself sought psychological treatment for severe spells of depression to which he was periodically prone.

Aside from the four directorates, James would certainly have approved of the activities of the Office of Publications and Communications, with its goal being to disseminate knowledge about psychological theory, research, and practice. In fact, James had a direct connection with the early stages of the Association's journal-publishing activities. Soon after the APA was organized, he began to correspond with Hugo Munsterberg and other about the founding of a new journal to be sponsored by the Association. After some organizational, policy-making, and political contretemps, a new journal was launched in 1884, *Psychological Review*. James had made it known that he would decline to serve as editor if asked and so avoided being the founding editor.

James's participation in and approval of the current APA would have extended beyond its in-house activities to involvement in the governance structure. It is easy to envisage him serving on one of the many boards or committees, such as the Committee for International Relations in Psychology, the Board of Scientific Affairs, the Board of Educational Affairs, or the Board for the Advancement of Psychology in the Public Interest. As for membership in the Association's 47 divisions, there are a few obvious areas of interest. James would certainly have been a member of Division 2, Teaching of Psychology; Division 3, Experimental Psychology, and Division 15, Educational Psychology. There are, moreover, several other divisions that would probably have enticed James to participate.

Division 1, General Psychology, is one obvious choice, for James was, in the best sense of the word, a generalist interested in all of the parts and in the whole of psychology. He never imagined that active involvement in one area would preclude active interest and participation in another. Division 6, Physiological and Comparative Psychology, would also have been a natural choice, because the focus of James's career moved from physiology to psychology and, finally, to philosophy. His early medical training and teaching (he continued to teach anatomy and physiology until 1878) gave him a solid ground for his deep interest in neurology and the functions of the brain and the nervous system.

Even before he became interested in science, James seriously considered becoming an artist. He studied drawing and painting in his early years and achieved a certain degree of skill and talent, but his father, who distrusted painting as a profession, was convinced that William's talents were predominantly scientific and urged him in that direction. James continued to draw and to illustrate his diaries and letters with sketches throughout his life. He most certainly would have found Division 10, Psychology and the Arts, a congenial arena for the exchange of ideas about the relationship between art and the human mind and personality.

Division 12, Clinical Psychology, and Division 29, Psychotherapy, all would have been of interest to James. Although primarily known for his contributions to other areas, the study of mental disorders and their treatment were a source of abiding interest throughout his adult life. In addition to his defense of psychotherapy noted earlier, James taught a course on mental pathology at Harvard for 3 years, and, in 1896, he delivered eight lectures at the Lowell Institute on "Abnormal Mental States," which covered such topics as dreams, hypnosis, hysteria, multiple personality, and genius.

By the middle of James's career, Division 24, Theoretical and Philosophical Psychology, would have captured his attention, as he focused less on psychological science and became deeply involved in theory, eventually coming to view himself primarily as a philosopher. (When he received his honorary doctorate from Harvard, James took great satisfaction in the fact that it was awarded for his achievements in philosophy.) Similarly, Division 30, Psychological Hypnosis, clearly would have claimed his attention and participation. Sometime after 1885, once he had started his own psychological laboratory, James began to experiment on a large scale with hypnotism, using students as subjects. He urged his stoic and skeptical sister, Alice, to try hypnotism to relieve her of the insomnia and pain from which she suffered, recommending to her Charles Lloyd Tuckney, a pioneer in hypnotherapy. (Alice found no particular relief from the pain, but did experience a great calming effect that permitted her to fall asleep without terror and to sleep uninterruptedly for 5 or 6 consecutive hours for the first time in years.)

Division 36, Psychologists Interested in Religious Issues, is another obvious choice. James wrote extensively on the topic, and his famous book, *The Varieties of Religious Experience* (1902), enjoys widespread success and admiration. Likewise, his enthusiasm for Division 48, Peace Psychology, is almost certain given his active and prominent role as a peace advocate during the Spanish-American War. Division 8, Personality and Social Psychology, and Division 9, the Society for the Psychological Study of Social Issues, would have undoubtedly been attractive to James.

I am no more capable than anyone else to speculate about how William James would have responded to the discipline and the Association as they have evolved over the past 100 years. I wish we had his advice and counsel today. He was broad, expansive, and inclusive in his view of psychology. He had a lively and inquiring mind. William James believed that psychology had something important to offer humanity.

REFERENCES

James, W. (1890). *The principles of psychology* (2 vols.). New York: Holt.

James, W. (1899). *Talks to teachers on psychology: And to students on some of life's ideals*. New York: Holt.

James, W. (1902). *The varieties of religious experience*. New York: Longmans, Green.

INDEX

Ecological systems, 149–150

Edie, J., 154

Education, of psychologists, 129

Effect theory, 162

Ego. *See* Self

Einstein, A., 95, 115

Elective affinity, 253–261

Elements of Psychophysics (Fechner), 254

Embretson, S., 39

Ememory, 51

Emerson, R. W., 11

Emotions, 50, 51, 61, 102, 114, 115
    ambiguity of, 231–232
    anesthesia and, 244
    bodily changes and, 221–224
    cognitive theory of, 212, 324–235
    correlated responses, 213
    empiricism and, 243–250
    instincts and, 274
    James on, 10, 221–229, 231–239
    primary, 214
    radical empiricism, 243–250
    self, 227
    theory of, 211–219
    See also Affective factors

Empiricism, 132, 155–157, 191, 221
    emotion and, 243–250
    fact and, 79
    introspection and, 346
    method and, 31, 101–117
    self and, 176
    See also Radical empiricism

Environment, 35, 128

Epiphenomenalism, 313

Epistemology, 153–166. *See also* Truth

Equilibation, 158

ESP studies, 339–352

Essays in Radical Empiricism (James), 58, 80,
    92, 101–117, 244

Estes, W. K., 51

Ethics, 86

Ethology, 270, 286–287

Evans, R., 309

Everyday life, 77–81, 88

Evil, 96

Evolution, 149
    instincts and, 267–268, 280
    interactive view, 143
    limitations of, 317–319
    pragmatism and, 196–197, 319
    reception of, 156
    selection and, 139–153
    See also Darwin, C.

Experience, 85, 191
    metaphysical basis, 102
    nature of, 77–89
    process theory, 247–248
    reality and, 102, 105
    See also Empiricism; Reality

Experimental–behavioral relations, 135

Experimental method, 23, 97, 158, 341

Experimenter effect, 342

Expression, 133–135

Facial feedback, 225

Faculty psychology, 272

Fallibilism, 155–156

Fechner, G., 149, 253–261, 315

Feedback, 161, 217, 222

"Feeling of Effort, The" (James), 161, 162

Feelings, 50, 56, 57, 232
    central role of, 115
    cognition and, 113–114, 135
    See also Emotions

Femininity, 299

Feyerabend, P. K., 97

Field theory, 112

First Principles (Spencer), 158

Flournoy, T., 11

Foundationalism, 98

Frankl, V., 115

Free will, 293, 323–338
    Huxley on, 162
    James on, 96, 297–298
    Renouvier on, 141

Freud, S.
    consistency in, 184
    on drives, 214
    James and, 303